Contemporary Philosophy of Religion

Contemporary Philosophy

Each volume in this series provides a clear, comprehensive and up-to-date introduction to the main philosophical topics of contemporary debate. Written by leading philosophers, the volumes provide an ideal basis for university students and others who want an engaging and accessible account of the subject. While acting as an introduction, each volume offers and defends a distinct position in its own right.

Published Works

Contemporary Philosophy of Social Science
Brian Fay

Contemporary Philosophy of Mind
Georges Rey

Contemporary Metaphysics
Michael Jubien

Contemporary Philosophy of Religion
Charles Taliaferro

Forthcoming

Contemporary Philosophy of Thought
Michael Luntley

Contemporary Philosophy of Law
Dennis Patterson

Contemporary Philosophy of Physics
Simon Saunders

Contemporary Philosophy of Language
Kent Bach

Pluralism and Contemporary Political Philosophy
Daniel Weinstock

Contemporary Philosophy of Religion

Charles Taliaferro

Department of Philosophy
St. Olaf College

First published 1998

2 4 6 8 10 9 7 5 3 1

Blackwell Publishers Inc.
350 Main Street
Malden, Massachusetts 02148
USA

Blackwell Publishers Ltd
108 Cowley Road
Oxford OX4 1JF
UK

Library of Congress Cataloging-in-Publication Data

Taliaferro, Charles.
Contemporary philosophy of religion: an introduction / Charles Taliaferro.
p. cm. – (Contemporary philosophy)
Includes bibliographical references and index.
ISBN 1–55786–448–9 (hardback : alk. paper). – ISBN 1–55786–449–7
(pbk. : alk. paper)
1. Religion–Philosophy. I. Title. II. Series: Contemporary
philosophy (Cambridge, Mass.)
BL51.T35 1997
210–dc21

97–5458
CIP

British Library Cataloguing in Publication Data

A CIP catalogue record for this book is available from the British Library.

Typeset in $10^1/_2$ on $12^1/_2$ pt Garamond 3
by Best-set Typesetter Ltd., Hong Kong
Printed and bound in Great Britain by MPG Books Ltd, Bodmin, Cornwall

This book is printed on acid-free paper

"Taliaferro's work is a major contribution. It shows mastery of the field, the capacity to think creatively within it, and an unusual ability to write clear and engaging prose. It can be read with pleasure and intellectual profit by those who know little or nothing about philosophy of religion and those who have worked in the field their whole lives. Taliaferro manages both to summarize current wisdom and to advance it, perhaps most strikingly in his effort throughout to show how philosophically important it is to treat arguments for (or against) particular religious claims as parts of comprehensive views of the world. This book will quickly become an indispensable teaching tool." *Paul J. Griffiths, University of Chicago.*

"Professor Taliaferro's book combines a staggering breadth of research with a careful attention to organization and development. The result is an extremely helpful map of the conceptual landscape in contemporary philosophy of religion. The author displays an unusual sensitivity to the complexity and range of religious traditions; his work will be of interest not simply to technicians in the field, but to anyone with a thoughtful interest in religion. This is an ambitious book, not only in the ground it covers, but in the tone it adopts. It accurately reflects contemporary discussion in the philosophy of religion while at the same time opening up new horizons of discussion by virtue of its inclusivity and nondogmatic style." *Patricia Sayre, Saint Mary's College*

"Taliaferro has written a lively, engaging introduction to contemporary philosophy of religion. It combines current 'front-burner' issues with a solid background of traditional themes, and incorporates welcome attention to non-Western religious traditions." *William Hasker, Huntington College*

"A highly readable and well-informed survey of the main issues being discussed in contemporary philosophy of religion. Taliaferro provides an open-minded and stimulating introduction which will encourage readers to form their own views about some of the deepest issues confronting human beings." *Roger Trigg, University of Warwick*

"Charles Taliaferro's book is at once an accessible analysis of many exciting and difficult topics in contemporary philosophy of religion, a creative comparative survey of the world's great religions, and an unexpectedly effective introduction to philosophical method and fundamental problems in metaphysics, epistemology, and moral philosophy. No other book on philosophical theology so successfully illustrates the intersection of topics across the range of philosophy. Students and teachers will find the carefully crafted exercises concluding each chapter to be pedagogically sound and intellectually engaging." *R. Douglas Geivett, Biola University*

"This is an important work for anyone interested in contemporary philosophy of religion for several reasons. One, while it places at the center of the book the philosophical articulation of theism and theistic themes, author Taliaferro develops these themes in conversation with four other living world religions, Judaism, Islam, Hinduism, and Buddhism, and with various atheistic or agnostic challenges to them. His treatment of the alternatives to theism is philosophically sophisticated and fairminded. He avoids simple caricatures. Two, attention to theism prompts philosophical discussion of a number of other issues and perplexities which are interesting to English-speaking philosophers in their own right. Three, discussion questions at the end of each chapter promise provocative exercises for individual reflections and classroom discussions. Four, while providing insight into the work of some leading contemporary philosophers of religion, often Charles Taliaferro exhibits philosophical dexterity and originality in his treatment of the topic at hand. Finally, [as the book is] written with admirable precision, both the beginning student and the professional philosopher will profit from Taliaferro's clear exposition of difficult issues such as eliminative materialism and the nature of time. This is a first-rate book and will be useful in the classroom." *Michael Beaty, Baylor University*

"Professor Taliaferro's *Contemporary Philosophy of Religion* is an example of how a first-rate philosopher can assist all of us in understanding the philosophical issues which permeate religious belief. The book is wide-ranging in scope and the clarity of the author's presentation of the various issues is commendable. The inclusion of suggested questions and topics at the end of each chapter helps make this an excellent book for an introductory course in the philosophy of religion." *Stewart Goetz, Ursinus College*

"This remarkably comprehensive review of contemporary philosophy of religion mamages to provide a balanced treatment of controversial issues without being in the least dull. It should capture the interest of beginners and broaden the perspective of more experienced readers." *Basil Mitchell, University of Oxford*

"I can think of no better way of introducing students to contemporary philosophy of religion than by working with them through this book. The main focus is, of course, theistic; but each topic is contextualized broadly on a world-wide comparative basis, and the challenges from both naturalism and anti-realism are fairly presented and scrutinised. Full space is given to the ethical dimension of religious and secular world views. A particularly attractive feature of the book is the way in which each chapter concludes with an extensive section setting out suggested questions and topics for essays and discussion, and also a substantial note on further reading and considerations." *Brian Hebblethwaite, University of Cambridge*

Contents

Contents

Acknowledgments

I thank the scholars who have provided helpful comments and suggestions on either part or all of this text through its many revisions. I am especially grateful to Jordan Curnutt, Joseph D'Allelio, Brian Davies OP, Douglas Geivett, Stewart Goetz, Paul Griffiths, William Hasker, Derek Jeffreys, Michael Martin, Charles Mathews, Elizabeth Olson, D. Z. Phillips, Bruce Reichenbach, Patrick Richmond, Steve Smith, Mel Stewart, B. R. Tilghman, Roger Trigg, David Vessey, and James White. I am grateful to an anonymous reviewer for Basil Blackwell and to Kelly Clark and Stephen Evans for helpful advice and encouragement at the outset of this project. I thank my colleagues, especially Piotr Boltuc, Edward Langerak, Doug Schurman, Ken Casey, John Poling, Gordon Marino, and Mark Linville, for their review of the manuscript. I also thank Tony Grahame and Douglas Mac Lean for their editorial work. I am also especially grateful to the many students with whom I have worked both on this manuscript as well as in the many classes from which much of this material has been forged. It is not possible to list all to whom I am indebted, but I note my gratitude specifically to Lisa Bautch, Suzanne Debuhr, Katie Freeborn, Garrett Gentry, Christian Gossett, Jennifer Larson, Scott Miller, Erik Norsted, Christa Olson, Andrew Pfieffer, James Powell, Kimberly Ronning, Carol Scholz, Mari Tollefson, and Andrew Urch. I am *eternally* grateful to Dorothy Bolton for her assistance in preparing the manuscript and to Michel LeGall for his friendship, wit, and high standards in scholarship and teaching. I dedicate this book with respect and affection to my students. It is also for my parents, and for Phyllis, Jim, Robin, James, and Barclay, with love, my first teachers. And for Jil with all love.

Introduction

This book is an introduction to the themes and projects in contemporary philosophy of religion. The breadth of topics that are now addressed in philosophy of religion is wider than at any earlier time and there has been a steady increase of contributions to the field by some of the most brilliant philosophers working today.

Reflection on religious beliefs and concerns is evident in the earliest recorded cases of philosophy. In the ancient Greco-Roman world and in ancient India, beliefs about the gods, God, or the sacred, played an important role in the philosophical quest to understand human life and the cosmos. Throughout the subsequent history of ideas the interplay between philosophical and religious reflection on the nature and significance of birth, life, and death has been substantial. At times philosophy and religion have been in profound tension, but there have also been extended periods of mutual support and fruitful exchange. Consider briefly just two areas where some contemporary scholars claim that religious beliefs inform philosophical thinking: moral theory and the theory of truth.

Some scholars argue that a prevailing concept of moral duty is historically rooted in the belief that there is an omnipresent, all-powerful law-giver. On this view, a philosophy of moral rules according to which each of us has strict duties to do good and avoid evil was forged in the context of a belief in an absolute divine ruler who commands us to act in certain ways. Such a connection between morality and religious belief may explain why many in the nineteenth and twentieth centuries linked doubts about the existence of God with doubts about the existence of objective moral duties. In *The Brothers Karamazov*, the Russian novelist Fyodor Dostoyevsky (1821–81) has the character Ivan Karamazov advance the dictum that without God, everything is

1

permitted. More recently, Albert Camus (1913–60) contended that "If God exists, all depends on him and we can do nothing against his will. If he does not exist, everything depends on us" (Camus 1955, p. 58). To test such claims involves undertaking a central task in philosophy of religion: investigating the relationship between religious conceptions of ultimate reality and our under-standing of good and evil.

Belief in God has often been linked with what may be called a strict, realist understanding of truth. Roughly, a realist view of truth is that truth is absolutely determinate, independent of culture and historical context. Accord-ing to realism, it makes no sense to claim that something – the number of planets in our solar system for example – is true for one person but not true for another. This sort of relativism is not countenanced in realism. If one posits an all-knowing, rational, omnipresent God, then one introduces the notion that there is an all-encompassing God's eye point of view, an ultimate perspective which constitutes a comprehensive picture of *the way things actually are.* Belief in an omnipresent, good God who knows all truths, enlists a concept of objective truth. Hilary Putnam argues: "The whole content of realism lies in the claim that it makes sense to talk of a God's eye point of view" (Putnam 1990, p. 23; see also Dummett 1992 and Jay 1993). Some scholars contend that belief in a God's eye view of truth and belief in God's creating us to discover truths about ourselves and the world, lie at the foundation of mod-ern science in the West. A. N. Whitehead famously attributed the origin of Western modern science to the belief in "the rationality of God" (Whitehead 1931, p. 18). Isaac Newton (1642–1727) described his task as a scientist in terms of trying to think God's thoughts, a position Albert Einstein (1879–1955) echoed when he spoke of the scientific quest to trace the intelligence of God. An examination of such claims exhibits the way philosophy of religion plays a role in investigating the theory of truth as well as related issues in the history and philosophy of science.

Philosophy of religion has a central location in the history of philosophy and continues to have an enduring place in the West and East as part of a philosophy curriculum and general education. The philosophy of religion has a prominent role for many religious traditions as well. A range of studies on the roots of Christian faith, for example, display the many ways in which a religious tradition has been enriched by philosophical reflection. H. M. Kuitert takes note of the influence of philosophy on Christianity: "There is much in our religion we have philosophy to thank for" (Kuitert 1981, p. 237). Whether gratitude or ingratitude is in order, philosophy of religion is a vital arena in which to explore the roots and character of religious traditions.

2

By the mid-twentieth century the arena of philosophy of religion in the English-speaking world became driven by a fascinating, heated debate on a scientifically oriented critique of religion. Are religious ideas merely the heritage of a superstitious era and based on conceptual confusion? "God" or "Brahman" seemed to many philosophers to be precariously remote from the more evident objects and processes described and explained in the natural sciences. For reasons to be explored later in this book, some philosophers went so far as to compare traditional concepts of God to obvious absurdities like the concept of a square triangle. In such an intellectual climate, those sympathetic to religious belief focused much of their energy either on defending the intelligibility of basic religious claims or on revising religious beliefs to accommodate the pervasive, skeptical temperament.

Skepticism about religious concepts like "God," "spirit," and "Brahman" remains very much in force. Sophisticated skeptical arguments are advanced in much of the best contemporary philosophy of religion. But at present philosophy of religion is not as dominated by assessing the challenge of full-scale skepticism as it was in the 1950s and early 1960s. Since then many philosophers have conceded that concepts of God and other components of different religions cannot be ruled out as obvious nonsense or clear cases of superstition. Important work has gone into building a case for the intelligibility of the concept of God. There is also important criticism of such work, but the debate on these matters is now more open-ended without being less rigorous. Ronald Hepburn summarizes a widely held conviction: "There can be no short-cut in the philosophy of religion past the painstaking examination and re-examination of problems in the entire field . . . No single, decisive verification-test, no solemn Declaration of Meaninglessness, can relieve us of the labor" (Hepburn 1963, p. 50).

Recent developments in the natural sciences themselves have had some role in unsettling the skepticism that became entrenched after the Second World War. Many scientists have become increasingly bold in their speculation about the origin of the cosmos, the nature of time, energy, the sub-atomic world and so on. There is even debate about whether certain scientific theories such as big bang cosmology offer evidence to support a religious conception of the cosmos. As a result, it now appears to many philosophers to be less easy to dismiss religious descriptions and accounts of the cosmos as clearly incompatible with science. Bas van Fraassen suggests that religious concepts may even be less bewildering than concepts in current scientific theories: "Do the concepts of the Trinity [and] the soul . . . baffle you? They pale beside the unimaginable otherness of closed space–times, event–horizons, EPR correlations, and bootstrap models" (van Fraassen, in Churchland [ed.] 1985, p. 258).

With comprehensive, religious skepticism in recession since the 1960s, the floodgates in philosophy of religion have opened. Projects in the field are up and running on such topics as God's nature, comparative reports of religious experience, religious ethics, diverse theories about the origin of evil, and religious teachings about divine incarnations. We are now in an era that is more friendly to philosophical experimentation and conjecture on such matters. Earlier a principal goal of a respectable project in philosophy of religion would be to assess whether religious beliefs made any sense at all. Now a proper philosophical project may be focused on a far more specific question such as: Is divine foreknowledge compatible with free will? Putting the question more directly: Given that God knows the future, can one, in the future, perform any free actions?

In a sense, the field of philosophy of religion today is both novel and historical. It is historical insofar as questions that propelled earlier inquiry are now seen as fitting topics for cutting-edge philosophy. It is novel not just because fresh arguments are advanced that bear on historically important topics, but also because there are new issues. Philosophers view religious concerns in light of new treatments of political life, the environment, technology, medicine, history, gender, the emotions, art, and so on.

Here are only some of the questions that animate the field today:

Are religious views of God, human life and the cosmos true or false?

How can one responsibly and fairly assess different conceptions of God or of God's will?

According to traditional Judaism, Christianity, and Islam, God is all-powerful, all-knowing, all-good, present everywhere, and the creator of the cosmos. How are these descriptions of God to be understood and integrated, if at all?

Is it possible to assess religious beliefs impartially? If so, is this desirable?

Do religious convictions *require* evidence, so that it would be intellectually irresponsible to have those convictions in the absence of evidence?

What reasons are there for and against the belief that God exists?

Is it possible that the world of particular objects in space and time could be a manifestation of some overriding spirit or transcendent, divine reality?

Are religious and scientific views of the cosmos compatible?

Can God be perceived?

Could God exist eternally or outside of time?

Can there be credible faith in an all-good, all-powerful God in light of the magnitude of evil?

What are the ethical consequences of different religious conceptions of God and the cosmos? Is religious belief necessary in order to justify morality? How do concepts of God affect the general concept of the good as well as particular views of justice, class, gender, race? How are beliefs about God and the environment interrelated, if at all?

In what respects are the ideals of democracy which give pride of place to individual rights and liberties compatible with the ideals of religions which give center-stage to obeying God's will?

Do the major world religions share, at base, a common view of ultimate reality?

If they do not share a similar *picture* of ultimate reality, could these religions still constitute equally legitimate, alternative *paths* or *ways of living* that lead to some ultimate religious good, union with God or Brahman for example?

Is there an afterlife? Is it even possible for persons to survive death?

Is reincarnation possible? What understandings of the person, mind, and soul, are compatible with different pictures of an afterlife?

What philosophical sense can be made of the Christian claim that God became incarnate as Christ or the Hindu claim that Krishna was a manifestation of Vishnu?

This book takes up these and many other questions with the aim of providing an overview of philosophy of religion.

This book is designed as a workbook. My aim is to offer an introduction to the issues that command the field both through the main text as well as through suggested questions and topics outlined at the end of each chapter. These are not constructed to check whether one has read the chapter; they are, rather, intended to be questions and topics to address in order to further one's own exploration of philosophy of religion. They are integral to the book, rather than a series of appendices. The questions and topics vary in difficulty and conventionality – some are downright unconventional – and are designed to engage and stimulate work that goes beyond what can be included in the main body of an introductory text.

The Presentation and Order of Topics

Chapter 1 begins with an overview of some of the salient features of world religions. In a world of diverse religions, a comprehensive philosophy of religion needs to address more than one religious tradition. This chapter also highlights the importance of imagination in the course of philosophically exploring religious and secular ways of conceiving the world.

Chapter 2 considers the nature of religious beliefs themselves. It can no longer be safely assumed that there is a universal understanding of religious beliefs. Philosophers of religion therefore need to attend to a fundamental question: What is religious belief?

Chapters 3 through 5 chart a central religious conviction found in Jewish, Christian, and Islamic traditions: the cosmos is the creation of an all-powerful, all-knowing, immaterial reality. Before we can raise the question of whether such a belief is true, we need to consider its meaning. In these chapters arguments are considered for and against the very intelligibility of the concept of God. What are power, knowledge, and creativity, and are any of these attributable even in principle to a being that transcends the physical cosmos? These chapters set up a key contrast between those who adhere to versions of naturalism, according to which the cosmos is all that exists, and those who believe that reality extends beyond the cosmos. The ethical and social implications of belief in an all-powerful God are also considered.

Chapter 6 addresses a fundamental challenge to philosophy of religion in both the West and East. Is it arrogant even to attempt to philosophize about the divine? This chapter considers whether God may be so radically distinct from our spatio-temporal world that all our language about God is profoundly at fault. This chapter also brings into focus transcendent, nonWestern concepts of the divine. A Hindu understanding of Brahman is articulated and defended.

Chapter 7 introduces some central ethical issues in contemporary philosophy of religion. Religious conceptions of ethical justification are important to examine at close range. It is increasingly clear that world religions are not bygone institutions and that political negotiation across national boundaries and even within single nations must take religion and religious values seriously. Insofar as an increased understanding of different faiths and the ideals of secular society is essential for humane, intelligent political resolutions of regional and global conflict, there are good political and ethical reasons for philosophically investigating religious values and the ideals of a secular society. Recent work in history, political science, sociology, and theology on current religious conflict raises concerns that are ripe for philosophical analysis. This has been borne out in philosophical studies of tolerance, respect, rights, and ideas of human welfare that are informed by religious beliefs.

Philosophical inquiry into such issues is urgent not only in light of the harm that can be caused by conflict between religious and secular forces, but also because of the possible benefits of collaboration.

Chapters 8 through 10 concentrate on the evidential case for and against religious conceptions of life. These chapters consider the concept of evidence, the nature of religious experience, and the case for and against the belief that there is a God. For some readers this may seem like the whole point of the enterprise of philosophy of religion, but I submit that even if that is correct, it is crucial to cover the subject matter of the earlier chapters first. For example, the question "Is there a God?" presupposes many things about the concept of God and about the task of thinking of God and our ability to answer the question. Like the so-called *Lawyer's fallacy* of asking a question that carries many assumptions ("At what time did you rob the bank?"), we need to be clear about the assumptions before we are ready for questions about God's existence. Even the concept of "evidence" needs to be addressed.

The term "evidence" is derived from the Latin *ex videre* meaning "from seeing" and, according to some philosophers today, it is less than obvious what should be assumed to be seen or evident. For example, should a religiously neutral or secular way of seeing reality receive any prior authority over an explicitly religious view of reality? Alternatively, why should we think evidence is important in religious matters in the first place? What for one person counts as "evidence" may seem utterly inconsequential to another. Some contemporary Christian philosophers endorse practicing philosophy on the basis of their faith, in which such faith enjoys an authority and importance in advance of any sort of detached critical reflection on the evidence that this faith is true. In a nutshell, it is not as clear as it once seemed to be when someone may be rightly accused of dogmatism. Yesterday's "dogmatist" may now be described as operating from within a perfectly respectable framework that differs from the one you hold. The entry for "Dogmatism" in the book *A Companion to Epistemology* is a case in point: " 'Dogmatism' is an indexical term; whether you properly apply it to a given doctrine or belief depends upon where you yourself stand" (1992, p. 109). These and other claims are taken up in the last chapters of this book.

As an introduction to *contemporary* philosophy of religion this book gives prominence to the field from the 1950s to the present. But the book is by no means restricted to the current scene as contemporary philosophy of religion addresses religious traditions that encompass thousands of years of history. Many historically important figures are addressed, for they have largely defined many of the issues now under discussion and their work is a rich resource for contemporary reflection. *Contemporary Philosophy of Religion* is in a series of introductions that generally emphasize philosophical work in the English-speaking world. While I follow this practice, I also draw upon other work and provide references for further, wider investigations. The aim of this text is to provide access to the field and a general map for additional exploration.

In this Blackwell series of introductions, authors are invited to offer an overview of the central movements and arguments in their field while also exercising the freedom to offer arguments of their own. I believe this policy has merit, allowing authors to provide more than a dry catalogue with a string of "Perhaps this is promising . . . or perhaps that is..." To use Ezra Pound's phrase, books can be "too damned perhapsy." But while I commend some projects I find especially exciting, I intentionally leave open-ended all the topics under discussion. My principal aim is to challenge readers to develop their own views of the issues. Proficiency in philosophy of religion involves developing skills in reflecting carefully on religious and philosophical issues for oneself and with others. To encourage participation in the field, I list at the end of this Introduction an array of societies in the English-speaking world that are dedicated to philosophy of religion. Any of these may be contacted for information on relevant conferences, recent publications, and membership. I also list other resources that can aid research into different topics. Philip L. Quinn and I have co-edited *A Companion to Philosophy of Religion* (1997), a collection of 78 essays by different scholars on the main topics in the field. At the end of each chapter, sections of the *Companion* are identified that can amplify discussion of the topics at hand.

Let me offer two further observations about the state of the field and this book.

First, there is a growing trend in philosophy of religion to see arguments as part of comprehensive positions. That is, rather than viewing arguments as completely independent, solitary lines of reasoning, it is now often thought that several distinct arguments can be mutually supportive and part of a "big picture" of what is at stake. The nature of comprehensive and cumulative arguments will be discussed in the text, but I refer to it now because the conviction that arguments can be intertwined and mutually supportive has an important role in this book. At different points I note how two or more arguments together serve to support a given conclusion. Also, as part of the effort to take seriously comprehensive philosophical outlooks, topics of general philosophical significance are sometimes addressed. Philosophers of religion frequently draw out the religious repercussions of positions and arguments in other areas of philosophy. In order to do justice to this breadth, this book sometimes features work in the philosophy of human nature, ethics, the theory of knowledge, and other areas. Philosophy of religion often takes place at the crossroads of different areas of philosophy and, indeed, at the intersection of philosophy and other fields such as the natural and social sciences.

Secondly, philosophy of religion, and philosophy in general, can often be laid out in a debate format with two or more sides represented with *pro* and *contra* arguments. I find this format useful as it can untangle complex, sometimes densely-packed arguments and highlight the different points where philosophers disagree. It can also help one identify points of agreement and set the stage for articulating a philosophy mid-way between opposite positions. But this format can also be misleading. A debate format may suggest that the parties in a philosophical conversation are competitive adversaries, each trying to win points against the other. In the study *Metaphors We Live By*, George Lakoff and Mark Johnson bring to the surface the ways in which argumentative language suggests not just a contest of outwitting opponents, but a belligerent, warlike confrontation. Lakoff and Johnson collect common argumentative phrases such as: Your claims are *indefensible*; He *attacked every weak point* in my argument; Her criticisms were *right on target*; I *demolished* his argument; I've never *won* an argument with her; You disagree? Okay, *shoot!*; If you use this strategy, he'll *wipe you out*; He *shot down all* of my arguments, and so on (Lakoff and Johnson 1980, p. 4). In this context, a hearty philosophical exchange looks like intellectual assault and battery. I see no reason, however, why we should carry out philosophical debate in this combative fashion.

Philosophical argument and debate, even when it is quite intense and sustained, can be part of a joint undertaking in which different parties work collaboratively to understand one another, to explore each other's points of view, and to undertake this task in a good-hearted context of respect, camaraderie and affection. In such a setting, one may well think of arguments in terms of very different, nonhostile metaphors. Arguments may well be construed as different ways of sculpting, casting and re-casting beliefs (the word "argument" comes from the Latin term for "refashioning'), as a comparison of different maps (locating beliefs, as it were), different excavations (digging for reasons) or expeditions. In line with this last suggestion, one could employ the English philosopher Thomas Hobbes' (1588–1679) description of thoughts: "Thoughts are to the Desires, as Scouts . . . to range abroad, and find the way to the Things Desired" (*Leviathan*, trans. 1950, p. 41). I mention these nonmilitant alternative ways of thinking about philosophical debate, because religious matters can involve profoundly intimate beliefs, desires, and feelings. Insofar as it addresses such substantial concerns, the conduct of philosophy of religion can benefit greatly from sensitivity and patience. My point is not that we should avoid referring to philosophical arguments and positions as "defensible," "indefensible," and the like, but that it is desirable that the overall context of such talk and reflection be one of good will.

Notes and Further Reading

Quotations are referenced by the author–date system with the bibliographical information noted at the end of the book.

Resources

Philosophy of religion is represented in virtually all the main philosophy journals, but it is the specific focus of *The International Journal for Philosophy of Religion*; *Religious Studies*; *Faith and Philosophy*; *Philosophy and Theology*; *Sophia*; *American Catholic Philosophical Quarterly* (formerly *New Scholasticism*); *American Journal of Theology and Philosophy*; and *The Thomist*. Theology journals also carry considerable philosophy of religion, especially *The Journal of the American Academy of Religion*; *The Journal of Religion*; *Theological Studies; The Journal of Religious Ethics*; *Heythrop Journal*; *The Annual of the Society of Christian Ethics*; *Theology Today*; *New Blackfriars*; *Modern Theology*; *Harvard Theological Review*; the *Scottish Journal of Religious Studies*; and the *Scottish Journal of Theology*. Philosophy of religion can also be found in some cross-disciplinary journals like *Law and Religion*; *The Journal of Law and Religion*; *Literature and Theology*; *The Journal of Humanism and Ethical Religions*; and *Christian Scholar's Review*.

Several scholarly presses produce series of books in philosophy of religion. Cornell University Press publishes *Cornell Studies in the Philosophy of Religion*; Indiana University Press publishes *The Indiana Series in the Philosophy of Religion*; Kluwer Academic Publishers publishes *Studies in Philosophy and Religion*; and the State University Press of New York publishes *Toward a Comparative Philosophy of Religions*. University presses such as Oxford, Cambridge, Notre Dame, Pennsylvania State, and Temple regularly publish work in philosophy of religion. Prometheus Books produces a substantial number of works in philosophy of religion, most of them highly critical of theism.

Topics in the philosophy of religion are indexed in the *Philosophers' Index*, published by the Philosophy Documentation Center, Bowling Green State University. Entries are listed under such titles as "God," "Religious Experience," and "Buddhism." This is a highly valued tool for writing papers, whether these be for a class or for making a contribution to the field. The *Philosophers' Index* offers brief abstracts summarizing the main tenets of books and articles. It is available on CD-ROM covering works published from 1940 to the present through DIALOG Information Services. Philosophy of religion is also indexed in yearly publications of the *Religion Index* (in two volumes). These are produced by the American Theological Association, Evanston, Illinois, USA, and are also available on CD-ROM. Books in philosophy of religion are also regularly reviewed in the journal *Philosophical Books*.

There are regular sessions involving philosophy of religion on the programs of the annual meetings of the three divisions of the American Philosophical Association, as well as on the program of the annual meeting of the American Academy of Religion. Societies and institutions focusing on the philosophy of religion include: the British Society for the Philosophy of Religion; the Society for Philosophy of Religion; the Society of Christian Philosophers; the Philosophy of Religion Society; the American Catholic Philosophical Association; Boston University Institute for Philosophy of Religion; the American Humanist Association; the American Maritain Association; the Fellowship of Religious Humanists; the Jesuit Philosophical Association; the Society for Medieval and Renaissance Philosophy; and the Society for Philosophy and Theology. Addresses for most of these organizations are listed in the *Directory of American Philosophers*, a publication of the Philosophy Documentation Center, Bowling Green State University.

There is a Center for Philosophy of Religion at the University of Notre Dame which offers fellowships to undertake research in the field. Information about the center is noted in the journal *Faith and Philosophy*. St Olaf College is the site of the Kierkegaard Library, a Publication and Study Center dedicated to the Danish philosopher Søren Kierkegaard (1813–55) who made an enormous contribution to philosophy of religion. Fellowships to study at the Center are available.

References

The emergence of the societies listed above as well as the founding of such journals of high quality and the number of regular conferences in philosophy of religion, are evidence of the growth of the field. Also worthy of note is the inclusion of philosophy of religion not just in standard contemporary introductions to philosophy, but in newer developments, such as the literature in environmental ethics and on the meaning of life. All the anthologies I am acquainted with on environmental ethics and the meaning of life contain sections on the philosophy of God. For some of the ways in which the philosophy of religion ties in with the search for meaning in life, see *God and the Philosophers* edited by T. V. Morris and *Philosophers who Believe* edited by Kelly Clark. Richard Swinburne offers a moral argument for investigating the philosophy of God in *Faith and Reason*.

An important, additional force behind the growth of philosophy of religion in the English-speaking world is due to the growing interest in "Continental thought," roughly referring to nineteenth and twentieth-century philosophical and literary work on the European continent. Many who are considered "Continental thinkers," such as Søren Kierkegaard, Friedrich Nietzsche (1844–1900), Martin Heidegger (1889–1976), Jean-Paul Sartre (1905–80), Simone de Beauvoir (1908–86), Albert Camus, Karl Jaspers (1883–1969), Gabriel Marcel (1889–1973), Emmanuel Levinas (1906–95), as well as contemporaries H. G. Gadamer, and Paul Ricoeur address religious themes. As a result, work on these philosophers has compelled some commentators and critics to address issues in the philosophy of religion. For an overview of some of this recent work, see David Brown's *Continental Philosophy and Modern Theology*.

Further references on the interaction between the history of philosophy and religious tradition are offered later in the text. For important work on the connection between belief in God and the concept of moral duties, readers may find the work of Arthur Schopenhauer (1788–1860) and Friedrich Nietzsche (1844–1900) of special interest. See especially chapter 7 for material on the relationship between moral theory and a philosophy of God. I note here several additional references that complement the material in the introduction. For interesting arguments on the role of the belief in God on the development of modern science with its realist treatment of the world, see work by Alfred North Whitehead, M. B. Foster, and Eric Mascall. Don Cupitt is aligned with Putnam in linking realism and theism. "The stronghold of . . . realism is no doubt the doctrine of Creation and the postulation of an objective metaphysical God as world-ground" (Cupitt 1984, p. 159). Alisdair MacIntyre, Charles Taylor, Richard Rorty and others, have done important work on analyzing our contemporary intellectual climate and documenting the respects in which the ebb and flow of religious ideas has had cultural and philosophical repercus-

12

sions. In "Christianity," in *A Companion to Philosophy of Religion,* William Wainwright points out how many of the philosophical projects in Western philosophy (e.g. debate over free will, necessity and contingency) have religious roots. The complex ways in which philosophy and religion are interwoven is also borne out in recent studies of women philosophers from ancient times to the present. Contemporary work aimed at expanding the canon of philosophy brings this to light. See the important, four-volume work, *A History of Women Philosophers* edited by M. E. Waithe. Important work in philosophy of religion and the history of philosophy has been especially evident in the renewed attention given to medieval philosophy. In a comparison between Eastern and Western philosophy one may see how the different prevailing religions have brought to the fore different philosophical problems. See the entry "Chinese Confucianism and Taoism" for some observations and documentation of this in *A Companion to Philosophy of Religion.* Indian philosophy and religion has, at times, been so intermixed that Wilfred Cantwell Smith once remarked that there was no difference between the two (cited by Avrind Sharma 1990, p. ix).

On the appreciation for tracking down the religious implications of one's philosophical views, see the introduction to *Consciousness and the Mind of God.* Another book in the Blackwell series of introductions, *An Introduction to Contemporary Epistemology* by J. Dancy, underscores the importance of investigating background assumptions in posing philosophical questions about knowledge.

Thomas Chance and I discuss various uses of the adversary method in philosophy in "Philosophers, Red Tooth and Claw," *Teaching Philosophy* (1991). Chance has published a superb study of philosophical method in *Plato's Euthydemus; Analyses of What Is and Is Not Philosophy.* The history of philosophy is packed with different imagery in the description of argument and debate. Compare Hobbes' depiction of thought, cited in the Introduction, with Thomas Reid's (1710–96) description of a philosophical analysis: "A philosophical analysis of the objects of taste is like applying the anatomical knife to a fine face. The design of the philosopher, as well as the anatomist, is not to gratify taste, but to improve knowledge" (Reid 1991, p. 721).

For an excellent essay that distinguishes constructive from pointless debates, I highly recommend Harry Frankfurt's essay "On Bullshit" (1988). Frankfurt distinguishes between BS and conversation that is mindful and built on a concern for truth. For an illuminating analysis of sensitivity see Larry May's "Insensitivity and Moral Responsibility," especially pp. 8–13 (1992).

1

Religious Beliefs

This chapter surveys the main features of world religions that attract the most attention in contemporary philosophy of religion. I introduce some fundamental philosophical terminology and outline some of the focal points of this text. The chapter concludes with observations about the use of imagination in undertaking philosophy of religion.

Five World Religions

In living religious traditions there are many different strands, sometimes profoundly at odds with one another. Any general description of these traditions will therefore have to be in very broad terms, with the understanding that matters are far more complex than these terms and categories can capture. But however generalized, it is good to begin with an overview of such traditions in order to secure a stable set of shared references at the outset and to have before us a sketch of religious diversity. Philosophers of religion need to take seriously the great variety of religious traditions and practices. Beginning with a survey of these religions may also help underscore that philosophy of religion is not principally driven by reflection on merely academic matters, but first and foremost by philosophical inquiry into extant, living traditions.

In the English-speaking world the better known religions are still Judaism, Christianity, and Islam, and so they are a reasonable starting point for this book.

In the main, Judaism, Christianity, and Islam are *monotheistic*. Monotheists believe one and only one God exists and is to be worshipped. *Polytheists* believe in many gods and *henotheists* align themselves with one God without denying the existence of other deities. Judaism, Christianity, and Islam each depict God as omnipotent (all-powerful), omniscient (all-knowing), and completely good. God both created the cosmos and conserves it in existence. Without God's conserving power, the cosmos would cease to be. God is imperishable, incorruptible, without beginning, and worthy of obedience. In their traditional forms, Judaism, Christianity, and Islam represent God, not just as creating and conserving the cosmos but also as acting in human history to reveal His nature.

The term *theism* is customarily used to name those monotheistic religions in which God is distinct from the world and yet causally active in it, while *deism* names monotheistic religions, according to which, God is the creator of the cosmos, but not active in the world. Deists, then, deny that God authors any revelation, providentially guides human history, causes miracles or becomes incarnate. An *atheist* is someone who maintains that theism is false (from the Greek *atheos* meaning "without God"). While being an *agnostic* (from the Greek *agnosis* meaning "without knowledge") simply means being unsure whether some belief is true, the term is commonly used with respect to theistic belief. Generally speaking, an agnostic claims not to know whether theism is true. A more radical agnostic claim would be that the truth or falsehood of theism *cannot* be known by any human beings.

Judaism, with its roots going back at least to the second millennium BCE (BCE = "Before the common era"), portrays God as calling the people of Israel to be a just and merciful community, dedicated to worshipping and serving God. Its most important early figures are Abraham (*circa* eighteenth century BCE) and Moses (*circa* fifteenth and fourteenth centuries BCE). In the annual ceremony of Passover there is a ritualized recounting of God's liberation of the people of Israel under Moses' prophetic leadership after a prolonged enslavement in Egypt. In Judaism enormous value is placed on community life, a life which is displayed in the Hebrew Bible as a covenant between God and the people of Israel. The Torah refers to the first five books of the Hebrew Bible, while the Talmud is an extensive commentary on the Torah and religious life in general, outlining religious faith, ethics and ritual observance. Modern Judaism has different strands, including the Orthodox, Conservative, and Reformed. The more traditional representatives of Judaism, especially the Orthodox, adopt a stringent reading of what they take to be the historic meaning of Hebrew scripture as secured in the early stages of its formation. Other groups within Jewish tradition treat scripture as authoritative but do not depend on a specific, historically defined interpretation of that scripture. In line with this open-ended approach to religious identity, Jacob Neusner, a contemporary Judaic scholar, offers a very broad depiction of Judaism: "When a religious system appeals as an important part of its authoritative literature or canon to the Hebrew Scriptures of ancient Israel, or Old Testament, we have a Judaism" (Neusner 1991, p. 59). Taken alone, this definition might appear to some to be too broad, for Christianity would then count as a form of Judaism. This result is not clearly undesirable, for it underscores that Christianity is rooted historically in Judaism and this is why certain cultures as well as the Christian religion itself are sometimes referred to as "Judeo-Christian."

Christianity emerged from Judaism in the first century and looks to Jesus Christ, a Jew, as its founder. The Christian Bible ("Bible" comes from the Greek *biblia* meaning "the books") consists of two parts: the Old Testament with its record and literature of the religion of the people of Israel (the Hebrew Bible) and the New Testament with its representation of Jesus and his followers. Generally speaking, the New Testament has been interpreted by Christians as depicting Jesus Christ as the incarnation of God, a great healer, a teacher of mercy and justice, who was crucified and later raised from the dead, appearing to his followers after his death, and establishing a community of faith. Salvation is attained through fellowship with and trust in Jesus, following his teaching and example, and finding, in him, God's forgiveness and mercy. The term "Christ" comes from the Greek term for "anointed" and is sometimes used to highlight the role of the person, Jesus, in bringing about salvation. Subsequent developments within Christianity gave rise to formal treatments of salvation, the incarnation, and the Godhead, according to which monotheism is preserved alongside belief in a diversity within God of three persons, Father, Son, and Holy Spirit. Jesus is identified as the incarnation of the Son, the second member of the Trinity. Some unity of Christian belief and practice was gradually achieved in the course of developing various creeds that defined Christian faith in formal terms (from the Latin *credo*, "I believe"). What unity Christianity achieved was broken, however, in the eleventh century with the split between the Western, Catholic Church and Eastern, Byzantine Christianity (now the Christian Orthodox Churches), and broken again in the sixteenth century with the Reformation and the split between Roman Catholicism and Protestantism. As the Reformation unfolded, many denominations emerged, including the Anglican, Baptist, Lutheran, Methodist, and Presbyterian Churches. And more recently, additional Christian movements and denominations have been formed. In this century, strides have been made to achieve a greater unity between Christian communities throughout the world. One sign of this ecumenism is the establishment of the World Council of Churches in the late 1940s.

Islam traces its roots back to Judaism and Christianity, acknowledging a common past at various points. All three religions are sometimes called "Abrahamic" because each acknowledges the importance of Abraham as the early progenitor of the life of faith. Islamic teaching was forged by the Prophet Mohammed (570–632) who proclaimed a radical monotheism that explicitly repudiated the polytheism of his time and the Christian understanding of the Trinity. The Qur'an (from *Qu'ra* for *to recite* or *to read*), its holy book, was composed by Mohammed who dictated this revelation of Allah (Arabic for "God") which, according to tradition, was given to him by the Archangel Gabriel. The Qur'an has a high place in the tradition and is taken to be God's very speech. Central to Islam is the sovereignty of Allah or God, God's providential control of the cosmos, and the importance of living justly and compassionately following a practice of prayer, worship, and pilgrimage. A follower of Islam is called a Muslim, an Arabic term for "one who submits," for a Muslim submits to God. The Five Pillars of Islam include the requirements of reciting the Islamic creed, praying five times a day while facing Mecca, alms-giving, fasting during Ramadan (the ninth month of the Muslim calendar), and making a pilgrimage to Mecca. The two greatest branches of Islam are the Sunnis and Shi'ites, which developed early in the history of Islam over a disagreement about who would succeed Mohammed. Sunnis comprise the vast majority of Muslims. Shi'ites put greater stress on the continuing revelation of God beyond the Qur'an as revealed in the authoritative teachings of the *iman* (holy successors who inherit Mohammed's "spiritual abilities"), the *mujtahidun* ("doctors of the law"), and other agents.

Common among most adherents of these three religions is belief in an afterlife, God's wisdom, and a final consummation of human history in divine judgment and its consequences. In general, then, Judaism, Christianity, and Islam are theistic, but there are members of each tradition who would more accurately be described as *panentheists* (from the Greek meaning "all is within God") who hold that God and the world are in a close, virtually co-dependent relationship. The evident diversity of such positions drives home the point that for some adherents of these religions, something like the descriptions offered here would count as characterizations of a religious heritage that may be subjected to considerable reinterpretation. Jacob Neusner underscores how the Jewish and Christian traditions can encompass new developments and interpretations of their past:

> While the world at large treats Judaism as "the religion of the Old Testament," the fact is otherwise. Judaism inherits and makes the Hebrew Scriptures its

own, just as does Christianity. But just as Christianity rereads the entire heritage of ancient Israel in light of "the resurrection of Jesus Christ," so Judaism understands the Hebrew Scriptures as only one part, the written one, of the "one whole Torah of Moses, our rabbi." . . . In both cases, religious circles within Israel of later antiquity reread the entire past in light of their own conscience and convictions. (Neusner 1986, p. xi)

Some theologians have gone so far as to reread their heritage in such a way that they claim to be Christian atheists. From a traditional point of view, "Christian atheism" is an outrageous contradiction in terms. I will not try to settle such disputes of classification and, instead, simply register here the importance of recognizing that, for some, the above categories are neither clear cut nor forever fixed. In Christianity two classic treatments of the need to constantly reinterpret and reappraise one's religious heritage are Augustine's (354–430) *Christian Doctrine* and John Henry Newman's (1801–90) *Development of Christian Doctrine*.

While Judaism, Christianity and Islam originated in the Near East, Hinduism and Buddhism originated in Asia. Hinduism allows for so much diversity that it is difficult even to use the term "Hinduism" as an umbrella category to designate a host of interconnected ideas and traditions. "Hindu" is Persian for "Indian" and names the various traditions that have flourished in the Indian subcontinent, going back before the second millennium BCE. The most common feature of what is considered Hinduism is reverence for the Vedic scriptures, a rich collection of work, some of it highly philosophical especially the *Upanishads* (between 800 and 500 BCE). Unlike Judaism, Christianity, and Islam, Hinduism does not look back to a singular historical figure such as Abraham for its root inspiration.

One strand within Hinduism that has received a great deal of attention, especially from Western philosophers in this century, is Advaita Vedanta, according to which this world of space and time is ultimately illusory; it is *Maya* (literally "illusion"). Behind the diverse objects and forms we observe in what may be called the phenomenal or apparent world there is the formless Brahman. The principal aim of this Advaita school of thought is the rejection of all duality ("Advaita" comes from the Sanskrit term for "non-duality"). The appearance of diverse objects is ultimately due to our ignorance. Note this passage from Shankara's *Crest Jewel of Discrimination*: "In dream, the mind creates by its own power a complete universe of subject and object. The waking state [too] is only a prolonged dream. The phenomenal universe exists in the mind" (p. 71). Brahman alone is ultimately real. This position is often

18

called *monism* (from the Greek *monus* or "single") or *pantheism* ("God is every-thing"). Shankara (also spelled Sankara, Samkara, Sankaracharya, 788–820) was one of the greatest teachers of this monist, nondualist tradition within Hinduism. Shankara held that "Brahman alone is real. There is none but He. When He is known as the supreme reality there is no other existence but Brahman" (p. 82).

Advaita Vedanta is not the only form of Hinduism. While Brahman is treated as being beyond form in Advaita Vedanta, and thus an impersonal reality, theistic strands may also be found within Hinduism which construe the Divine as personal, all-good, powerful, knowing, creative, loving, and so on. Theistic elements may be seen at places in the *Bhagavad Gita* (sixth century BCE) and its teaching about the love of God. Madhva is one of the better known theistic representatives of Hinduism (thirteenth and fourteenth centuries). There are also lively polytheistic elements within Hinduism. Popular Hindu practice includes a rich polytheism, and for this reason it has been called the religion of 330 million gods. The recognition and honor paid to these gods are sometimes absorbed into Brahman worship as the gods are understood to be so many manifestations of the one true reality. As Simon Blackburn observes: "It is not easy to count gods, and so not always obvious whether an apparently polytheistic religion, such as Hinduism, is really so, or whether the different apparent objects of worship are to be thought of as manifestations of the one God" (Blackburn 1994, p. 292).

Whether in its monist or theistic form, it is widely believed among Hindus that a cardinal, supreme manifestation of Brahman is a trinity of Brahma, Vishnu and Shiva. Brahma is the creator of the world, Vishnu is its sustainer and manifested in the world as Krishna and Rama, incarnations or avatars (from the Sanskrit for "one who descends") who instruct and enlighten, and Shiva is the destroyer.

Most Hindus believe in reincarnation. The soul migrates through different lives, according to principles of *karma*. Karma (Sanskrit for "deed" or "action") is the name for the moral consequences of action. The final consummation or enlightenment for the Hindu is *moksha* or release from *samsara*, the material cycle of birth and rebirth. In its monist forms, liberation comes from overcoming the apparent dualism of Brahman and *atman* (literally "breath"), which refers to the individual self or soul, and sometimes a transcendental self with which all other selves are identical.

Hinduism is often associated with (and believed to be a chief justification for) a social caste system that groups persons into strict orders of social classification. Not all Hindus support such a system, and some Hindu reformers argue for its abolition. One of the well-known movements opposed to traditional understandings of caste is the Arya Samaj, which was founded by the Hindu reformer Swami Dananda Saraswati (1824–83). The Arya Samaj movement continues to exist within India, especially in the Punjab, and among many Hindu immigrants in the West. As part of its openness to other faiths, Hinduism has a legacy of inclusive spirituality by which it understands other religious practices as different ways in which one may ultimately converge on enlightened unity with Brahman. Hinduism has thereby absorbed and, to some extent, integrated some of the teaching and narratives of Buddhism. Christian elements have also been assimilated historically into Hinduism, especially since British colonialism, with Jesus being seen as the tenth avatar of Vishnu. Many Hindu texts extol the multifaceted paths to the Divine. The following passage from the *Bhagavad Gita* represents Krishna making an inclusive declaration.

> If any worshipper do reverence with
>   faith to any god whatever,
> I make his faith firm,
>   and in that faith he reverences his
>   god,
> and gains his desires,
>   for it is I who bestow them.
>
> (vii. 21–2)

Although historically Hinduism and Islam have sometimes been in painful conflict, there are cases of tolerance and collaboration. One of the aims of Sikhism, a sixteenth century reform movement within Hinduism, was to bring together Hindus and Muslims.

Buddhism emerged from Hinduism, tracing its origin to Gautama Sakyamuni (sometime between the sixth and fourth centuries BCE) who lived in northern India and came to be known as the Buddha ("Enlightened One"). The teaching of the Buddha centers on The Four Noble Truths. These are that: (1) Life is full of suffering, pain, misery (*dukka*); (2) The origin of suffering is in desire (*tanha*); (3) The extinction of suffering can be brought about by the extinction of desire; (4) The way to extinguish desire is by following the Noble Eightfold Path. The Eightfold Path consists of right understanding; right aspirations or attitudes; right speech; right conduct; right livelihood; right effort; mindfulness; contemplation or composure. In its earliest forms, Buddhism was not associated with a developed metaphysics (that is, a theory of the structure of reality, the nature of space, time and so on), but there was belief in reincarnation, skepticism about the substantial nature of persons existing over time, and a denial (or treating as inconsequential) of the existence of Brahman. Early Buddhist teaching tended to be nontheistic and nondeistic, underscoring instead the absence of the self or *anatta* and the impermanence of life. The goal of the religious life is *Nirvana*, a transformation of human consciousness that involves the shedding of the illusion of selfhood. Theravada Buddhism is the oldest and strictest in terms of promoting the importance of monastic life. Mahayana emerged later. It displays less resistance to Hindu themes and does not place as stringent an emphasis on monastic vocation. Other versions of Buddhism include Pure Land Buddhism and Zen.

Other religions will be addressed in the book. At this point, let us consider the underlying question of what should and should not count as a religion. What is the definition and scope of the term "religion"?

Definitions of Religion

It is not easy to achieve a precise, universally acceptable definition of religion. This is largely due to the vast differences between the traditions that are commonly categorized as religions. Many philosophers of religion today regard this difficulty of definition and diversity of religions in a positive light. Rather than advance a narrow definition from the beginning of what must make up a religion, there are advantages to demarcating "religion" simply by appealing to the examples that most people recognize as religions. This strategy secures a substantial terrain to investigate and ensures that philosophy of religion will be relevant to extant traditions that are widely regarded as religion as opposed to being relevant only to academic circles. Thus, a common delineation of religion is as follows: *Religions include Judaism, Christianity, Islam, Hinduism, and Buddhism, and those traditions that resemble one or more of them.* By this definition, Confucianism, Taoism, Baha'ism, Sikhism, Zoroastrianism, aboriginal spirituality, and many other traditions are easily seen to be religious. This characterization of religion may be termed a *definition by example,* though more technically it may be referred to as a *paradigm case definition* (in which a case is identified where a term applies and other applications are designated in virtue of their resemblance to it).

This definition by example of religion carries no implication that the five world religions are more credible or satisfying than others. The five world religions encompass such diverse practices and beliefs, that employing them as

21

an initial reference point ensures flexibility and breadth in identifying other religions. The definition can, of course, be expanded by explicitly noting other cases of paradigm religions, e.g. Religions include Judaism, Christianity, Islam, Hinduism, Buddhism, Confucianism, Taoism, Baha'ism, Sikhism, Zoroastrianism, aboriginal spirituality, and those traditions that resemble one or more of them.

The earlier definition by example is used in this text, but it is good to be wary of its limitations. In the present context it succeeds (if it succeeds at all) only as a rough demarcation of the ground that needs to be covered in subsequent philosophical inquiry. For this definition by example does not dig into the details of what makes these traditions religions. The same problem would arise if one were to define "religion" in terms of its Latin root. The term *religio* means "to bind" and highlighting this may be useful to bring to the fore the notion that religion draws people together or delimits a person's identity. But it provides no more help than that. Presumably not *everything* that draws people together or defines a person's identity is religious. More needs to be done to investigate the binding character of religious traditions, and the aim of this book is to carry out such further investigation. But before proceeding to this task, consider some of the difficulties that face other demarcations of what constitutes a religion. Here are three proposals for defining religion and some of their difficulties.

"Religion" may be defined in terms of the belief and worship of God or gods. But this has the undesirable consequence of classifying atheist versions of Buddhism as nonreligious.

Alternatively, "religion" may be defined in terms of reverence and awe such that to have reverence and awe toward something believed to be sacred is to be religious. But this would prohibit from being considered religious those members of the world religions who treat their relation with the sacred as one of self-interest, rather than of awe and reverence. Some early religions are described as lacking in the awe and reverence that typically characterize "worship," and so these might also be excluded by such a definition of religion. It would also require us to classify as religious those groups that treat nature, their nation, or even their egos as sacred and deserving awe and reverence.

In one of the better texts, *Reason and Religious Belief: An Introduction to the Philosophy of Religion*, the following is proposed as a working definition:

> Religion is constituted by a set of beliefs, actions, and emotions, both personal and corporate, organized around the concept of an Ultimate Reality. (Peterson et al. 1991, p. 4)

This appears to be satisfied by traditional forms of the five world religions outlined above, but if it is advanced as a sufficient condition of what is to be classified as a "religion" it is hazardous. For example, it may be argued that the mainstream scientific community is constituted by a set of beliefs, actions, and emotions as well – whether these be the love of discovery, truth and inquiry, the desire to make certain predictions, and the like – centered around the concept of an ultimate reality (the cosmos). But for all that, it would be a stretch to consider the scientific community a religion. One might try to avoid classifying the scientific community as a religion by adjusting the concept of "Ultimate Reality" so that it would have to refer to something beyond the physical world. Scientists focus on the physical world whereas religious believers focus on the nonphysical. This, however, would have the undesirable consequence of excluding many versions of polytheism, Mormonism (the popular name for a nineteenth century Christian movement, the "Church of Jesus Christ of Latter Day Saints") and other religions which construe the divine in physical terms. The authors of *Reason and Religious Belief* do not make this move, for they leave the description of "Ultimate Reality" quite broad: "This Reality may be understood as a unity or a plurality, personal or nonpersonal, divine or not, and so forth" (Peterson *et al.* 1991, p. 4). It is easy to sympathize with this resistance to a more precise definition.

I encourage readers to consider nine other definitions of religion that I list at the end of this chapter among the suggested questions and topics. Readers may also wish to survey and debate the many proposed definitions of "religion" in J. H. Leuba's *A Psychological Study of Religion* (especially chapter 2 and the appendix).

The problem facing the project of precisely defining religion is that when we move beyond the definition by example offered at the outset we seem to be without a clear-cut, principled way to delimit what does and does not count as a religion. How can one settle disputes over whether Marxism, atheistic humanism, New Age movements, fervent forms of nationalism and so on, should be considered religions? The definition by example does not provide an *automatic* answer, but it challenges us to undertake a comparative study of the cases at hand. Questions about religious identity are addressed by investigating the resemblance of these movements and traditions to Judaism, Christianity, Islam, Hinduism, and Buddhism. For example, a question about whether atheistic humanism should be considered a religion can be phrased in terms of asking about whether it resembles those cases of religion that are already widely recognized. If it can be argued plausibly that there are significant similarities between atheistic humanism and any of the five world religions, then these would count as good reasons for treating atheistic humanism on the same footing as Judaism, Christianity, Islam, Hinduism, and Buddhism. This reasoning by resemblance or analogy has had a role in many United States court cases in which judges have struggled with the definition of what counts as a religion. In the case of *United States* v. *Seeger*, for example, the Supreme Court characterized religious belief as "belief that is sincere and meaningful and occupies a place in the life of its possessor parallel to that filled by the orthodox belief in God." (For other legal references, see suggested question two at the end of this chapter.)

The stance adopted here of accepting a definition by example does not supplant other definitions of religion. For example, insofar as the five world religions really do fit any of the more specific definitions, these may be used in identifying other religions in virtue of their also satisfying such definitions.

By avoiding narrow definitions, contemporary philosophy of religion remains open to exploring new religious concerns. The arena of what many in the English-speaking world count as religion seems to be profoundly fluid at present, which is why so many definitions of religion wind up facing what Galileo's critics faced. When persecuted for his view that the earth moves, Galileo is reputed to have said: *eppur si muove* (Italian for "and yet it [the earth] moves"). One may well have a definition of religion that maps significant, but still bounded terrain, and then the terrain itself seems to move. Philosophy of religion is, at the end of the day, philosophical reflection on *religion*, and any generalization about religion needs to take into account both ancient and emerging traditions that comprise its subject matter. The same is true in philosophy of science, art, history, and so on.

The Focus of Philosophy of Religion

Having stressed the open character of philosophy of religion, we need to find a point of entry into more detailed inquiry. The survey of the five world religions is at too high an altitude for the grounded approach needed for precise philosophical reflection.

Some work in philosophy of religion today focuses on only a single religion, and there are certainly advantages in doing so. With such a concentration there is less danger of oversimplifying religious traditions and more of an opportunity to reflect philosophically on the way different philosophical ideas are interconnected within a specific religious way of seeing the world. Notwithstanding these merits, a broader approach is required here because of the

24

religiously diverse society many of us live in and also because an exclusive focus on any one religion can have little hope of being completely successful. Each world religion has been influenced in its development by at least one other religion and so the focus on a single religion is hard to sustain if one wants to bring to light its historical development.

Still, *some* selectivity is in order lest one's philosophical investigation become altogether too generalized. It is also warranted here in order to do justice to the current state of the field. In the English-speaking world, the majority of contemporary philosophy of religion is concentrated on theism, and I estimate that more than half of the current non-English-speaking philosophy of religion literature addresses theism or theistic themes. This book explores nontheistic religious topics, but the philosophical articulation and assessment of theism and theistic themes will be a centerpiece. This does not amount to favoring theism by suggesting we begin with the assumption that it has greater credibility than its alternatives. Atheists and agnostics may find the focus on theism desirable insofar as they are committed to establishing that theism is either false or not known to be either true or false. One may even stress the philosophical investigation of theism in order to establish the off-the-wall, rogue second definition of "Theism" in the *Oxford English Dictionary*: "A morbid condition characterized by headaches, sleeplessness, and palpitations of the heart, caused by excessive tea-drinking"! Be that as it may, serious attention is given in this book to nontheistic religions as we shall consider Advaita Vedanta Hindu conceptions of Brahman, Buddhist theories of the self, and the similarities and differences between theistic and nontheistic religious experiences.

In addition to the widespread representation of theism in contemporary philosophy of religion, there are two other advantages to highlighting theism in the present work.

First, there is some reason to believe that because theism has such a large role in religion world-wide, it may well be the most widely held of religious positions today. Reliable statistics are, of course, difficult to secure, but *The World Almanac* (1997) has some credibility. Its figures provide a reason for thinking theism is at least relevant to a majority of religious people. The *Almanac* estimates there are 1,927,953,000 Christians, 1,099,634,000 Muslims, and 14,117,000 Jews. Insofar as Christianity, Islam, and Judaism are theistic, then theistic religions seem to include the greatest numbers in the world population. Sikhism has a strong theistic component (19,161,000) and there are theistic strands in Confucianism (5,254,000) and among Baha'is (6,104,000). It is estimated that there are 780,547,000 Hindus and

323,894,000 Buddhists, but these are not exclusively atheistic, and for those who are atheists, theism will still be an important topic. Historically a great deal of Buddhist philosophy is devoted to the critique of Hindu forms of theism. Those practicing what are termed "tribal religions" or "ethnic religions" are 111,777,000 (sometimes called "primal," "primary" or "aboriginal" religions) and while many of these are polytheistic, they also have monotheistic or henotheistic elements. Thus, many African societies recognize a multiplicity of gods and spirits and yet acknowledge a supreme being. Kwasi Wiredu observes that,

> African world views usually, though not invariably, feature a supreme being who is regarded as responsible for the world order. Generally, that being is explicitly conceived to be omnipotent, omnibenevolent and . . . omnipotent. A sense of dependency, trust, and unconditional reverence is almost everywhere evident in African attitudes to the supreme being. (Wiredu 1997, p. 35)

Similarly, some native North Americans religions acknowledge a "Great Spirit" (on "Creaton").

Of course these statistics should not be treated in a simplistic manner. The United States today has a population of roughly 265 million people, and although it is a democracy, it would be false to conclude that each of its 265 million citizens believes in democracy. Still, democracy, both as a form of government and as a topic, is relevant to a majority of such a large population, and that is all I am claiming about theism.

Second, giving more attention to theism will place at center-stage theories about persons and human nature and thus, presumably, locate the investigation of religion in a context of great interest to many philosophers and students of philosophy alike. In theism, God is said to know the world and to act, and some theists speak of God having intentions, desires, and feelings. All these are terms that find their ready use in describing ourselves. Indeed, one of the marked objections to theism is that such language of intentions and so on is *too* indebted to human categories. The charge that religious conceptions of the divine tend to mirror images from human life is a familiar complaint. In the fifth century BCE Xenophanes is recorded as lamenting over the temptation to import limited, mundane categories into our understanding of the divine:

> If cattle and horses or lions had hands, or were able to draw with their hands and do the works that men can do, horses would draw their gods like horses, and

cattle like cattle, and they would make their bodies such as they each had. (From *The Pre-Socratic Philosophers* (1984), by G. S. Kirk et al., entry 168)

Is it philosophically legitimate to employ our conceptions of self, action, desire, power, knowledge, emotion, and so on in describing, however metaphorically, a supremely perfect divine reality? Are there good reasons for rejecting this as naïvely anthropomorphic, or rather, can these terms be developed in religious contexts to describe God with philosophical credibility? Focusing on theism has the advantage of confronting us immediately with the task of elucidating our conception of ourselves and testing the limits of philosophical inquiry.

As noted earlier, investigating theism in what follows will certainly not be exclusive and it by no means amounts to supposing that theism has any initial advantage over its secular and religious alternatives.

In turning to the task of assessing religious beliefs and perspectives, several observations are in order on the importance of a tool that is regularly employed in philosophy of religion as well as other areas of inquiry.

Thought Experiments in Philosophy of Religion

R. G. Collingwood (1899–1943) proposed that in the course of composing history, it is pivotal for the historian imaginatively to project him or herself into the events under study. On this view, a study of some other epoch requires that one try to imagine oneself in that setting. One should seek to understand historical matters from within, imaginatively re-enacting past experience, as if one were truly a person of that time with its presuppositions and outlook.

Collingwood's account of history has been challenged by some historians (see suggested question eight at the end of this chapter), but his promotion of imaginative projection has a strong claim in the philosophical investigation of different religions. In assessing a religion there is merit in imagining what it would be like (or what it *is* like) to hold the religious beliefs and to adopt the religious life that is being studied. This kind of projection may be severely limited and not required for reaching some justified conclusions, though for one who is committed to exploring a religion in depth it is useful to try to see matters from the inside. Perhaps one must also see a religion from the outside, viewing it from the standpoint of different religions or of a secular view of the world. But the point Collingwood highlights is the importance of an *engaged imaginative identification*. One risks developing a philosophy of religion that is estranged from its topic, namely *religion*, without some appreciation for how religious life seems to its participants. This use of imagination is not a substitute for first-hand experience, but it can be vital in enhancing one's own experience and appreciating the experience and points of view of others.

The cultivation of an appreciation for different religions requires the use of what some philosophers call *thought experiments*. Philosophers sometimes refer to descriptions of the way things might be as thought experiments. As the term is used here, to engage in a thought experiment is to develop a conception of a state of affairs which may or may not be the case or, putting it differently, may or may not occur or obtain. The term "state of affairs" is not meant to be overly technical and can refer to *the way things might be*. The description of states of affairs may be at any level of generality. The following may all be considered states of affairs: *There being a cosmos*; *There being elephants*; *There being unicorns*; and so on. The first two states of affairs occur or obtain, while the third (probably) does not. To employ a thought experiment in philosophy of religion is, in a sense, simply to use one's imagination in an experimental fashion, to envisage the way things might be. Some of these thought experiments may involve the kind of personal projection commended by Collingwood, while others may not. The descriptions of world religions in this chapter may be read as laying the groundwork for thought experiments which need to be enriched by greater details and enlivened by an imaginative engagement with the teachings and practices of each religion.

The role of thought experiments in philosophy as well as in ordinary life is difficult to overstate. Roy Sorensen notes the widespread appeal to thought experiments in the course of ethical reflection. This involves both imagining different states of affairs as well as the imaginative identification commended by Collingwood.

> Thought experiment is universal to all cultures. This is evident from the persuasiveness of the golden rule: "Do unto others as you would have them do unto you." The role reversal that constitutes the application of this moral test is a form of thought experiment. The agent need not recognize his role reversal as such. Indeed, he may lack the concept of thought experiment. Just as one does not need the concept of sublimation to sublimate one does not need the concept of thought experiment to thought-experiment. (Sorensen 1992, p. 67)

Thought experiments in such ethical reflection may bring to light our own biases, and force us to clarify points left obscure otherwise. Would one still have the same views on famine relief if the roles were reversed and those who are well fed were victims of malnutrition? In imagining that the roles are reversed in such matters, one may well be imagining a state of affairs that is profoundly unlikely. It is unlikely that Mr X will ever have a gender or ethnic change, but can he imagine, even marginally, what it might be like to be a female or to have a different ethnic identity? The testing ground for answering such questions involves the use of the imagination, the appeal to what we are acquainted with, and the prospects of considering ourselves in profoundly altered states. So, someone who is imagining that reincarnation occurs may well seek to fill out a description of re-embodiment across gender, ethnicity, time, and species. A critic who thinks reincarnation is impossible will try to expose the errors involved with such imaginative descriptions. All this involves a process that is commonplace in the appreciation and criticism of literature. As C. S. Lewis observes in *An Experiment in Criticism*: "We want to see with other eyes, to imagine with other imaginations, to feel with other hearts, as well as with our own" (Lewis 1961, p. 137). Philosophical as well as literary criticism is very often taken up with such imaginative testing.

Novelists, ethicists, philosophers and historians are not the only ones who pay explicit attention to thought experiments. Thought experiments have a rich role in the history of mathematics, economics, and science. Galileo's famous proposal about the rate of falling bodies was at first a thought experiment, and one can readily see thought experiments in Newton's reflections on absolute space, and Einstein's work on the speed of light. The fact that a scientific thesis may be tested by empirical experimentation does not rule out the important role of thought experiments both in the construction of the empirical investigation and in considering its implications (see "Thought Experiments in Einstein's Work" and other entries in *Thought Experiments in Science and Philosophy* edited by Horowitz and Massey).

In philosophy of religion the thought experiments and their analysis can be highly complex. The task of developing and comparing thought experiments, one that is theistic and one that is monistic or deistic for example, will take considerable time, ingenuity and scrutiny. Can one very easily imagine that there is an all-powerful God? The effort to go as far as Collingwood commended in the imaginative projection of oneself into different religious settings may be more difficult still. The best way to come to terms with thought experiments is to see them in action, which we will do in further chapters.

Suggested Questions and Topics

(1) Consider the following characterizations of religion. Do you find any of these successful as either definitions or descriptions of religion? Even if unsuccessful as definitions, in what respects do you find any of these to be philosophically illuminating or helpful in thinking about the nature of religion?

The following are cited by John Hick in his *Philosophy of Religion*:

(A) "The feelings, acts, and experiences of individual men in their solitude, so far as they apprehend themselves to stand in relation to whatever they may consider the divine." William James

(B) "A set of beliefs, practices, and institutions which men have evolved in various societies." T. Parsons

(C) "A body of scruples which impede the free exercise of our faculties." Salomon Reinach

(D) "Ethics heightened, enkindled, lit up by feeling." Matthew Arnold

(E) "Religion is the recognition that all things are manifestations of a power which transcends our knowledge." Herbert Spencer (Hick 1989, p. 2)

The following are cited in *Reason and Religious Belief: An Introduction to Philosophy of Religion*:

(F) "Religion is, in truth, that pure and reverential disposition or frame of mind which we call piety." C. P. Tiele

(G) "Religion is rather the attempt to express the complete reality of goodness through every aspect of our being." F. H. Bradley

(H) "Religion is the belief in an ever living God, that is, in a Divine Mind and Will ruling the Universe and holding moral relations with mankind." James Marineau (Peterson et al. 1991, pp. 3–4)

Consider Swinburne's proposal:

(I) "I propose to understand by a religion a system which offers what I shall term salvation. . . . I shall understand that a religion offers it if and only if it offers much of the following: a deep understanding of the nature of the world and man's place in it; guidance on the most worthwhile way to live, and an opportunity so to live; forgiveness from God and reconciliation to him for having done what we believed morally wrong; and a continuation and deepening of this well-being in a happy afterlife." (Swinburne 1981, p. 128)

30

(2)   Analyze the way in which "religion" has been defined in Supreme Court cases from the 1940s on. See, for example, the *Congressional Quarterly's Guide to the Supreme Court*, 2nd edition. In an important case in 1943, Justice Frankfurter cited the following passage from federal judge Augustus Hand. You may wish to assess this in light of subsequent court cases:

> It is unnecessary to attempt a definition of religion; the content of the term is found in the history of the human race and is incapable of compression into a few words. Religious belief arises from a sense of the inadequacy of reason as a means of relating the individual to his fellow men and to his universe. . . . [I]t may justly be regarded as a response of the individual to an inward mentor, call it conscience or God, that is for many persons at the present time the equivalent of what has always been thought a religious impulse. (*United States* v. *Kauten*)

(3)   In this chapter it was assumed the scientific community is not by its very nature religious. But some scientific projects have been described in religious terms. Consider Douglas Hofstadter's construal of his pursuit of a reductionist theory of life:

> [People] have an instinctive horror of any "explaining away" of the soul. I don't know why certain people have this horror while others, like me, find in reductionism the ultimate religion. Perhaps my lifelong training in physics and science in general has given me a deep awe at seeing how the most substantial and familiar of objects or experiences fades away, as one approaches the infinitesimal scale, into an eerily insubstantial ether, a myriad of ephemeral swirling vortices of nearly incomprehensible mathematical activity. This in me evokes a cosmic awe. To me, reductionism doesn't "explain away"; rather, it adds mystery. (Hofstadter 1980, p. 434)

(4)   If there are difficulties defining "religion," there are difficulties defining philosophy of religion. Are there problems in defining other areas of philosophy that are similar to the problems of defining philosophy of religion? Consider some of the following areas: the philosophy of art, history, science, law, language, economics, knowledge, action, education, logic, and mind. An interesting project would be to explore the ways in which competing definitions of some other area, art for example, can be used to construct parallel definitions of "religion." An advanced project, for example, may examine the strengths and weaknesses of a definition of religion built on Arthur Danto's definition of art. See *A Companion to Aesthetics* for detailed references.

(5)   This chapter takes note of the number of people currently estimated

as belonging to different religions. Do such figures carry any weight in your assessment of the credibility or truth of any religion? At one time it was popular to advance a common consent argument for the existence of God. This argument is criticized in the 1967 *Encyclopedia of Philosophy*, volume one, pages 147–55. You may wish to speculate as to how such an argument may be defended against this criticism and then assess the overall strength and weakness of the revised argument. It would also be useful to compare an argument from common consent with the literature in the philosophy of art on the test of time. Some hold that if a work of art is judged to be good over time, one has some reason to believe the work is indeed a good work of art. See, for example, Anthony Savile's *The Test of Time*. Savile offers a modest defense of appealing to the test of time in assessing art work. He proposes the following criterion:

> A well-chosen autographic or allographic work of art securely survives the test of time if over a sufficiently long period it survives in our attention under an appropriate interpretation in a sufficiently embedded way. This condition will only be satisfied if the attention that the work is given is of a kind that generates experience relevant to its critical appreciation and attracts the attention that is given to it in its own right. (Savile 1982, pp. 11–12)

Savile outlines the conditions for appropriate interpretation in his text. How much of his analysis may be applied to religions? You may also wish to consider the extent that his analysis of beauty and depth may be applied to religious traditions and practices.

(6)   Can one truly know a religion without at some time having believed and practiced it? Putting the matter differently, can a skeptic truly understand what it is like to be a religious believer? In *The Concept of Mind*, Gilbert Ryle distinguished two forms of knowing, what he called *knowledge how* and *knowledge that*. Apparently, one may well know how to do certain things like tell a joke but without knowing that jokes are to be told in such and such a way. An interesting project would be to employ Ryle's categories in an analysis of what may be involved in knowing a religion (e.g. compare knowing how to be religious with knowing that a religion involves certain beliefs and practices).

(7)   There is a considerable literature on subjects reporting "out-of-the-body experiences," in which traumatized persons appear to leave their bodies for a time. This sometimes occurs in clinical settings during a period when a patient's heart stops. Chapter 4 in this book cites some of the literature and some of the ways these cases have been critically assessed. Compare the credibility of reported "out-of-the-body experiences" with what may be called

"out of tradition experiences," the experience someone may have in leaving their religious tradition and either adopting an alternative religion or remaining without a religion. A useful review of the nature of out-of-the-body experiences and the ways they have been critically assessed is the entry "Out-Of-The-Body-Experience" in *The Oxford Companion to the Mind*.

(8) Critically assess Collingwood's approach to history and philosophy. Here is a key passage from "History as Re-enactment of Past Experience".

> Suppose, for example, he [a student of history] is reading the Theodosian Code, and has before him a certain edict of an emperor. Merely reading the words and being able to translate them does not amount to knowing their historical significance. In order to do that he must envisage the situation with which the emperor was trying to deal, and he must envisage it as that emperor envisaged it. Then he must see for himself, just as if the emperor's situation were his own, how such a situation might be dealt with; he must see the possible alternatives, and the reasons for choosing one rather than another; and thus he must go through the process which the emperor went through in deciding on this particular course. Thus he is re-enacting in his own mind the experience of the emperor; and only in so far as he does this has he any historical knowledge, as distinct from a merely philological knowledge, of the meaning of the edict.
>
> Or again, suppose he is reading a passage of an ancient philosopher. Once more, he must know the language in a philological sense and be able to construe; but by doing that he has not yet understood the passage as an historian of philosophy must understand it. In order to do that, he must see what the philosophical problem was, of which his author is here stating his solution. He must think that problem out for himself, see what possible solutions of it might be offered, and see why this particular philosopher chose that solution instead of another. This means re-thinking for himself the thought of his author, and nothing short of that will make him the historian of that author's philosophy. (Collingwood 1946, p. 238)

Collingwood's account of history has been criticized on a number of grounds. It has been objected that his view of history only works for certain histories (biography not economics). It has also been objected that it is impossible to recreate the thought-world of earlier periods and that the explanation for some historical events involve natural causes that are contingent upon neither psychology nor society. Assess whether such objections expose any weaknesses in Collingwood's account of history. Do these or other objections apply against using Collingwood's methods in the course of a philosophical examination of religion? For an introductory critical overview of Collingwood's work see W. H. Walsh's *Philosophy of History*, chapter 3.

33

(9)   Does the reliance upon thought experiments in philosophical inquiry about religion or about other areas of philosophy require a fully developed theory of their precise nature? In developing a theory, some of the following questions are relevant: When one conceives of a state of affairs must this involve forming images? If so, where are they? Can we conceive (in the sense that this does not essentially involve images) of more than we can imagine (or picture)? What is the status of the possible ways the world might be that are described in thought experiments? How can one individuate thought experiments? Contrast, for example, a thought experiment in which one imagines a very powerful being, able to do almost anything whatever, with imagining a being that has no limits to its power. A study of the power and limitations of thought experiments may benefit from an analysis of a particular case. Assess Richard Swinburne's theistic thought experiment in *The Coherence of Theism* (1977, p. 105). Peter van Inwagen reproduces Swinburne's work and criticizes it in *God, Knowledge, and Mystery* (1995, pp. 19–21). How might Swinburne's view be defended, if at all?

(10)   Some highly critical observers treat religious traditions on a par with ruins. This analogy may be worthy of an essay in which one links aesthetics and intellectual history. In the philosophy of architecture there is a considerable literature on ruins. Donald Crawford distinguishes the classical and romantic account of ruins as follows:

> On the classical theory, the ruin embodies the past by presenting a fragment of a missing whole, which we then imaginatively reconstruct. The aesthetic enjoyment is said to be in the imaginative apprehension of the past aesthetic unity . . . On the romantic conception, the ruin stirs the perceiver's sense of the past and awakens associations of mystery. We are thrilled as we "glimpse the unknown" and as we imaginatively live for a moment in the irretrievable past while simultaneously aware of the power of time to negate the present. (Crawford 1992, p. 604)

Assuming, if only for the sake of argument, that the great world religions are indeed the equivalent of intellectual ruins, you may wish to explore the respects in which they might still serve an important role, aesthetic and intellectual. (See Crawford's essay for further reference on ruins and the role of time in the life of an art work.)

A different essay may be of interest that draws on architecture. One may examine the ways in which different religions have promoted alternative philosophies of architecture (the form and function of buildings).

Further Reading and Considerations

From *A Companion to Philosophy of Religion*, the following entries are relevant to material in this chapter and contain valuable bibliographies: "Hinduism," "Buddhism," "Confucianism and Taoism," "African Religions," "Judaism," "Christianity," and "Islam." For a general survey of world religions, see *Our Religions* edited by Arvind Sharma. For single-authored books on world religions discussed here, the following are especially useful: *A Survey of Hinduism* by Klaus Klostermaier; *The Vision of Buddhism: The Space Under the Tree* by Roger Corless; *God in Search of Man: A Philosophy of Judaism* by Abraham Heschel; *Judaism in Modern Times* by Jacob Neusner; *Christian Theology* by Alister McGrath; *Jesus Through the Centuries: His Place in the History of Culture* by Jaroslav Pelikan; *The Islamic Tradition* by V. Danner; *The Islamic Middle East* by Charles Lindholm; *Shi'ite Islam* by Yann Richard; and *Concepts of God in Africa* by John Mbiti. As a general resource, it is difficult to surpass the magisterial *Encyclopedia of Religion* edited by Mircea Eliade (New York, 1987). Additional texts on world religions are suggested in other chapters.

For a defense of thought experiments, see Sorensen's *Thought Experiments*. For criticism see Wilkes' *Real People: Personal Identity Without Thought Experiments*. An artful, interesting use of thought experiments is developed by Søren Kierkegaard in *Philosophical Fragments* (see especially the first chapter, "Thought-Project"). I defend the legitimacy of appealing to thought experiments in *Consciousness and the Mind of God*. The imagination and the use of thought experiments has a checkered history in philosophy and theology. At times the imagination is credited with being the root of error and at other times a vital faculty whereby we may come to know of God and the world. The imagination may well serve either purpose depending on its use. For a superb treatment of the history of the concept and use of the imagination in philosophy see Eva Brann's *The World of the Imagination*. Richard Kearney's *The Wake of Imagination: Toward A Postmodern Culture* is also recommended. An interesting theological analysis of the imagination is *The Analogical Imagination* by David Tracy. There is some reason to think that our cognitive development is essentially dependent upon the use of imagination and thought experiments. A good textbook introduction on the use of imagination in cognitive development is *Understanding Children* (1990) by K. Hansen and P. D. Forsyth; see especially chapter 6.

2

Religious Practices and Pictures of Reality

The first chapter surveyed different religions and highlighted the role of imagination in philosophy of religion. Collingwood advised historians to exercise their imaginations in re-creating the thoughts and conditions of other eras and this advice was used as a cue to commend a similar use in the philosophical exploration of religion. What Collingwood recommended for the study of the past is an asset in the study of alternative, contemporary religions and philosophies. But in the course of using thought experiments to imaginatively engage one or more religions, we are confronted by a fundamental question: Should we think of religions principally in terms of various beliefs that are true or false? This chapter considers the proposal that religions are not principally made up of beliefs that function as different *pictures of reality* that may or may not correlate with *the way things are*. Instead, religions are what some philosophers refer to as different forms of life. A form of life may be satisfactory or unsatisfactory without itself being true or false. On this view, to think of the belief in God as a straightforward case of truth or falsehood (the belief that God exists is true if and only if God exists) is to misinterpret the grounded, practical meaning of religious life.

One inspiration for this alternative reading of religion comes from the work of Ludwig Wittgenstein (1889–1951). According to many of those who align themselves with Wittgenstein, to assimilate religious convictions to beliefs that are objectively determined as true or false in the sciences is to be saddled with a wrongheaded intellectualist theory about the very structure of religious life. On their view, to think of religion in terms of true and false belief in abstraction involves a mistake much like the one Hans Christian Andersen pokes fun of in *The Shadow*. In the story, the main character's shadow comes to life and menaces him. Obviously shadows cannot do this because they are

36

merely the absence of light caused by shadowed objects and not substantial things. In a sense, some philosophers contend that to think of religion in terms of true and false beliefs is to attend merely to the shadows cast by religion and not its very substance. If these philosophers are right, then thought experiments and the imaginative projection that Collingwood commended are useful in the investigation of different ways of living, but not in determining the truth and falsehood of competing religious accounts of the nature and origin of the cosmos.

Forms of Life

Wittgenstein launched a radical critique of traditional philosophy. By his lights, much classical and modern philosophy is built on what he termed "the picture theory" of reference, according to which statements are true or false depending upon whether the pictures they present are in accord with the way the world is. Initially this picture theory seems like good common sense, and indeed Wittgenstein did not deny that something like it has a role in nonphilosophical, social practice. He had no quarrel with the commonplace understanding that the proposition "Snow is white" is true if and only if snow is white. The mistake, Wittgenstein claimed, is to use this model of correlating beliefs or propositions and the world as an account of the meaning of thought and language. Such a model of correlation suggests we are subjects who can achieve an objective, ideal observation of both our own beliefs and the way the world is. According to Wittgenstein, we are primarily active, involved participants in the world, not spectators. Rather than promoting intellectual detachment and seeking a "God's eye point of view" from which to survey world religions or world history, we should take more seriously our implanted, grounded practices in the world. Language about God is something that is caught up in the general structure of *the way people live*. Concepts like *God, prayer, the afterlife*, and so on, make sense as part of a religious practice, but have no business being placed in the same category as the concepts of physics in descriptions and explanations of what exists. Wittgenstein employed the term "language game" to distinguish certain domains of meaningful use. In this view the language game of religion is profoundly different from the language game of physics.

Wittgenstein insisted on the complex variability of forms of life and language games. Language is like "an ancient city: a maze of little streets and squares, of old and new houses with additions from various periods" (1953,

37

entry 18). While Wittgenstein never said, "'God exists' may be true for those who believe it, and false for those who do not," he allowed that statements about God may make sense, that is they might have a proper use, in some forms of life, and yet might not in others. Paul Feyerabend embraced a view of philosophy much like Wittgenstein's at this point, though he took it much further and allowed for a profound relativity of truth.

> Not everybody lives in the same world. The events that surround a forest ranger differ from the events that surround a city dweller lost in a wood . . . The Greek gods were a living presence; 'they were there.' Today they are nowhere to be found. (Feyerabend 1987, p. 104)

According to Feyerabend, if Greek gods are no longer to be found in modern Western cultures it is because the forms of life in which gods play a role are no longer in evidence. Insofar as talk of the divine still finds a place in a living tradition, then, and only in such a context, would it make sense to invoke the presence of God or gods, to pray to them, and so on. David Bloor makes a similar point:

> Suppose the tribe on this side of the river worship one god, and the tribe on the other side of the river worship another god. If the worship of the gods is a stable feature of tribal practice, if they are spoken of routinely, if courses of action are justified by reference to them, then I would say both beliefs are objective. (Bloor 1984, p. 236)

This socially-based interpretation of "objectivity" displaces a more bounded, defined framework according to which either there is a God or there is not. On the contrary, Feyerabend, Bloor, and others allow that we may very well be said to live in different worlds (Goodman 1978).

Contemporary philosophers differ radically on the concept of truth and the role it should play in understanding language and social contexts. Two positions have taken shape in this debate: realism and nonrealism. I offer a general overview of these comprehensive positions and then focus on their place in philosophy of religion.

Realism is the thesis that propositional claims are either true or false, independent of human conceptual frameworks or whether any human being knows or believes whether they are true. The truth of the claim that "There are planets" does not depend on the existence of any human beings or language. Realists differ on the finer points as to how to define "truth," but they agree that truth is not relative to human language in general or specific language games, conceptual frameworks, or historic eras. For example, there would still be truth in a cosmos where there were no human beings; in such a world it would be true that there were no humans. A realist about theism contends that if there is a God then it is true that God exists regardless of whether any human beings think God exists or practice forms of life in which God is recognized.

Nonrealism refers to the view that all propositional claims about the world are neither objectively true nor false, where "objective" means independent of all language, social forms of life, and conceptual frameworks. If nonrealism is adopted, it makes no sense to claim "God exists" in the abstract as a claim about *how things are* without this being understood in terms of the context in which such a claim is made. There are different forms of nonrealism. The most radical appear to leave no place at all for a world that exists independently of human language and culture. More qualified versions simply maintain that our view of truth needs to be anchored first and foremost in a study of social context; the meaning of terms is principally to be found in their use.

In a final section to this chapter we will consider whether there is a way to bridge these two camps or somehow to build an alternative position that draws on the strengths of each. But first let us consider the prospects of a nonrealist interpretation of religious belief. Richard Bell spells out a nonrealist treatment of religious categories:

> The concepts . . . like "God," and its correlates "love," "suffering," "poverty," and "hope" do not derive their meaning from objects antecedent to their being conceptually formed in the language. They are not like phenomena in need of penetration. Rather, the depth these concepts have is related to the person, or group of persons, who uses them. (Bell 1975, p. 311)

On this view, in a search for the meaning of religious discourse we should not look for objects that are somehow *behind* or *beyond* religious terms the way one seeks to discover the contents of a room behind a door. One should instead seek the meaning of religious terms as they are used in religious lives.

In the next section I outline three major reasons for adopting a nonrealist philosophy of religion. Each is articulated before considering a realist response. Here, as in many areas of philosophy, the case for and against a position is best seen as part of an accumulation of different arguments. Rarely in philosophy are comprehensive theories advanced on the basis of a single, narrow line of reasoning. As John Wisdom once commented, a substantial philosophical position is often supported by more than one argument and thus like a chair that is supported by more than one leg. Because such positions are usually not supported by a single line of reasoning, they are not like a chain that is only as strong as its weakest link (Wisdom 1944–5, p. 195).

Three Reasons for Religious Nonrealism

(A)   An important argument for nonrealism and against realism is based on the appeal to religious practice. D. Z. Phillips and Don Cupitt both valorize the practical dimension of religion and contend that realist philosophy of religion rests on a fundamental error by construing religion as chiefly a matter of pictures of reality that may or may not be true.

Phillips has closely investigated theistic religious practices such as prayer, the rituals employed when facing death, and the religious use of sacred texts. According to Phillips, the religious belief in an afterlife is best not seen as a "prediction that certain things are going to happen" (Phillips 1970, p. 71). Instead:

> To ask someone whether he thinks these beliefs are true is not to ask him to produce evidence for them, but rather to ask him whether he can live by them, whether he can digest them, whether they constitute food for him. If the answer is in the affirmative then no doubt there will be factual consequences for him. If a man does believe that death has no dominion over the unity of the family, that the family are one in heaven, he will make decisions and react in ways very unlike the man who holds ideas such as that everyone has his own life to live, that the old have had their chance and should make way for the young, that no one should stand in anyone else's way, and so on. In this way, belief may not simply determine one's reactions to events that befall one, but actually determine what one takes the alternatives facing one to be. If a man asks, "I wonder whether it's all true?" that question, if not confused, is not a request for a proof, but an expression of his doubt regarding whether there is anything in all this. (Phillips 1970, p. 71)

On Phillips' account, then, to believe in an afterlife in a properly religious context is not to traffic in evidence that at death a person goes to some other place, as when one moves from one country to another. Rather, to believe in an afterlife is to live humbly in this life with a spirit of self-renunciation and generosity to others. Similarly, the prayer for a child's recovery from illness is best not understood as an attempt to influence God to act on the child's behalf:

40

If one thinks in terms of causing God to save the child, one is nearer the example of non-religious parents who pray "O God save our child." Here the thought behind the prayer is that God could save the child if He wanted to. The prayer is an attempt at influencing the divine will. In short one is back in the realm of superstition. (Phillips 1981a, p. 120)

The deeper, religious meaning of prayer is instead to be found in the role it plays in helping one form a resolution to be steadfast and loving, to resist despair and bitterness. In this light, prayers that petition God for aid are not built on superstition. Such prayers may instead reflect a resolution to live with dignity despite a sharp understanding of human vulnerability, and to honor and express one's care for others.

Don Cupitt preserves prayer to God and other religious practices notwithstanding his conviction that "objective theism" is false.

I continue . . . to pray to God. God is the mythical embodiment of all one is concerned with in the spiritual life. He is the religious demand and ideal . . . the enshriner of values. He is indeed – but as a myth. (Cupitt 1981, p. 167)

Cupitt casts traditional religious claims such as "God created the heavens and earth" as expressions of a resolve to live according to high values.

In confessing God as creator I testify to my experience of rebirth and renewal insofar as the religious concern and religious values really have come to take first place in my life. Faith in divine providence expresses my conviction that if I am unflinchingly loyal to this concern and these values they will not fail me. (Cupitt 1981, p. 55)

Cupitt seeks to retain a religious spirituality without religious realism.

Phillips maintains that biblical literature does not appear to invite anything like a realist quest for evidence. A realist philosophy of religion places biblical writers in an unflattering and ultimately false light:

It seems as if all these [biblical] writers were shirking their essential task: failing to attempt to prove God's existence or to seek evidence for his existence. The question of God's existence, as something for which evidence must be sought, simply does not find a place in the traffic of their discourse. They agree or disagree over whether someone or something is of God, or from God, but not over whether there is a god at all. (Phillips 1988, p. 10)

41

In Phillips' view, to treat biblical literature as a set of propositions to be tested for truth and falsehood does not do justice to the living, practical side of scripture and religious life in general.

Some nonrealists grant that religious believers talk *as though God exists and there is a heaven* and *as though they are trying to change God's mind about something.* But, so it is argued, this does not require a realist interpretation about what religious believers actually think exists:

> To say of someone "He'd sell his soul for money" is a natural remark. It in no way entails any philosophical theory about a duality in human nature. The remark is a moral observation about a person, one which expresses the degraded state that person is in. A man's soul, in this context, refers to his integrity, to the complex set of practices and beliefs which acting with integrity would cover for that person. (Phillips 1970, p. 43)

One need not believe there is some kind of *thing*, a soul, in order to use the term "soul" meaningfully. Arguably, talk of the soul would not have developed at all without *some* notion that there are such things as "souls," but (so it is argued) that is no reason to think that the use of the term or the use of terms like "God" are primarily realist nor that we should only treat the term along realist lines today.

Common to Phillips and Cupitt is the conviction that the meaning of religion is to be found *within* religion and not in comparing the religious view of reality to something "out there." Realism is grounded on the mistaken assumption that an external assessment of religion is feasible. As Phillips puts it, "the criteria of meaningfulness cannot be found outside religion, since they are given by religious discourse itself" (Phillips 1971, p. 4). To try to understand or to assess the adequacy of religious discourse from a neutral, removed vantage point is not possible. "Religion forbids that there should be any extra-religious reality of God," writes Cupitt (1981, p. 96). To evaluate critically a whole way of life from outside requires the feasibility of setting up an alternative framework from which to assess it. Consider the following analogy. When evaluating different rule-governed activities like chess, for example, it makes sense to judge it from within the game in terms of correcting errors. But once one criticizes the game of chess with all its rules and components one needs another framework from which to form the criticism, as when someone might charge that chess is an overrated practice, a waste of human ingenuity in a world plagued by so many ills. The basis of the criticism is a broader understanding of life. But when assessing a religion it appears that one is assessing something that by its very nature is so comprehensive and encompassing that an external critique of it becomes impossible. Another analogy may be of use. Questions about measuring time make sense chiefly because they occur within a framework in which one makes comparisons following an agreed upon set of rules. The comparison of seconds, minutes, hours, years, centuries, and millennia can all be managed in a formal fashion, but consider a question about the time of time. We may answer a question like "How long is an hour?" by referring to 3,600 seconds or $\frac{1}{24}$ of a day or some other temporal unit, but what if the question is put more generally still: "How much time does time take?" Arguably, such a question is unanswerable. In a similar vein, some nonrealists contend that to step back from all linguistic and social religious practice and to ask questions of its justification over against a reality somehow "out there" makes no sense.

To summarize (A): A nonrealist philosophy of religious belief has been advanced on the basis of an appeal to religious practices. These practices include the role of prayer, belief in an afterlife, and the use of sacred scriptures. Moreover, nonrealists appeal to the comprehensive, encompassing character of religious life and practice.

(B)   In the estimation of some philosophers, a second, religious reason for adopting nonrealism is that the realist, philosophical project is a dead end. If one is convinced that there are no good reasons to believe any religion is true, one may be bound to suspend religious belief and practice. If, however, one embraces nonrealism one can opt out of having to "play the game" of intellectually justifying religious beliefs in light of the evidence.

In *An Introduction to Philosophy of Religion*, B. R. Tilghman concludes that although none of the philosophical arguments work in justifying the belief that there is a God, this should not be considered a catastrophe for religious believers. It was a mistake from the outset to think such justification was necessary or important for religious practice:

> Some of the reasons we listed [in earlier chapters of his book] for why people say they believe God exists were that the Bible says so, the existence and complexity of the world, the fact of miracles, how belief changed a life, that one has been taught to believe. When we tried to make these reasons into premises of deductive arguments or as evidence toward inductive conclusions, the results, we saw, were hopeless . . . If we put aside the question of whether God exists as somehow a mistaken or at least irrelevant question for the believer, then we can better understand the other "reasons" that people can give as reasons for "believing that God exists." Religious statements are not like the propositions of mathematics or logic which can be established by deduction. Nor are they like

those of science to be shown true by gathering evidence. "What evidence is there for the existence of God?" is not a proper question. The concept of God and the concept of evidence don't go together. (Tilghman 1993, p. 225)

Tilghman thereby treats arguments that may be advanced to support religious belief as built on a misunderstanding of what it is to be religious. The complexity and order of the world are not to be seen as clues to God's existence, but, rather, as occasions for one both to see and to act in the world in religious ways. Tilghman claims this is exemplified in the biblical portrait of the awareness of God:

Psalm 19 says, "The heavens declare the glory of God, The sky proclaims his handiwork." Note that the psalmist did not say that the heavens are evidence for the existence of God. A person can be impressed with the world and with its workings. This can take the form of seeing the starry heavens, for example, as the handiwork of God or even seeing God in all of that. One does not have to think of God and His glory as something that lies behind the starry heavens and for which the heavens are only evidence any more than one has to think of the smile on the face of a child on Christmas morning as evidence of her delight. The delight is not something lurking behind the smile, it is declared right in the smile! (Tilghman 1993, p. 211)

If Tilghman is right, then a religious reading of the Hebrew and Christian Bibles and of the natural world is not held hostage to the realist preoccupation with evidence.

If the (supposed) poverty of positive reasons for adopting a particular religion provides some motivation for adopting nonrealism, it is all the clearer that nonrealism increases in attractiveness for religious believers in light of any forceful reasons for thinking one's religion is false. There are, as shall be noted later, important objections to each of the world religions, if construed along realist lines. Can one plausibly believe in an all-good God despite all the evil that exists? Can one adopt with credibility the Advaita Vedanta teaching of Brahman, according to which all diversity of objects is illusory, in light of the common perception of a world of distinct individuals? If nonrealism is adopted, then a major presupposition behind these questions is undermined. The questions are not, in Tilghman's phrase, proper questions.

In summary, nonrealists have argued that religious belief seems to require a level of confidence that simply cannot be backed up by independent philosophical argumentation. "Do Christians speak of their beliefs about God as hypotheses which may or may not be true?" asks Phillips. "It seems pretty

44

clear that they do not. Their beliefs are absolute for them" (Phillips 1971, p. 193). God does not "probably exist" (Phillips 1988).

(C)   Another reason to adopt a nonrealist philosophy of religious belief is that doing so removes an important cause of religious intolerance. Historically, intolerance toward others has often been motivated by thinking that the religious beliefs of various groups are false. "Only the truth has rights" is a slogan once used to ban publication of beliefs that were thought to be false. If one abandons the quest for objective religious truth, an important source of intolerance has been removed. Tilghman emphasizes this benefit of nonrealism:

> Religious believers can realize that they don't have to convert heathens or refute atheists with arguments and evidence, arguments that are invariably bad and evidence that is more than suspicious, but can get on with serving God, teaching the children, tending the sick, and being an example for those they seek to influence. And atheists, in their turn, can give up belittling believers for their intellectual naïveté and be content with the realization that they do not see the world that way nor live that kind of life. (Tilghman 1993, p. 225)

According to Tilghman, abandoning the traditional project of arguing for the truth or falsity of religious belief does not land one in the intellectual equivalent of an isolated ghetto. Rather, one may come to see one's religion as part of a practical ethical way of living.

Replies to Arguments for Religious Nonrealism

Realists have responded vigorously to the cumulative case for nonrealism. This section outlines how the above arguments have been addressed.

REPLY TO (A): Realists argue that much religious practice (or forms of life) requires realist beliefs about the way things are.

Can prayer, worship, religious pilgrimage, works of charity that are carried out with explicit religious devotion, and so on, have the meaning and importance that they are taken to have if none of them are based on factual beliefs about God or the sacred? John Hick resists nonrealism at this point. "If . . . the entire range of religious beliefs were regarded as nonfactual, none of them could possess the kind of significance which depends upon a connection with objective reality" (Hick 1973, p. 24). This reply has force insofar as it appears that nonrealists' interpretations of prayer, the use of sacred writings, and other religious practices have undermined the intelligibility and integrity of these activities. Why cry out for divine help if you do not think it makes sense to believe that it is objectively true that there may be a divine reality that can help? One may pray to God without *knowing* God exists. Perhaps the prayer is fueled only by a desperate hope that God exists and may respond. But Hick contends that the intelligibility of such prayer still requires a realist view of God. To assess the merits of realism and nonrealism, consider the following nonrealist account of one of Tolstoy's stories and a realist reply.

In the course of advancing nonrealism, Tilghman focuses on Tolstoy's "Father Sergius" (originally published in 1898). In the story a Christian monk undergoes various temptations, succumbs to some, wrestles with his spiritual pride, ultimately abandons his religious vocation and tends the sick, teaches children, and serves others. Along the way Tolstoy records Sergius' thoughts: "There is no God for the Christian man who lives, as I did, for human praise. I will now seek Him!" Tilghman uses this to illustrate his view that the religious claim "God exists" is not to be interpreted as a realist claim that is dependent upon evidence:

> Father Sergius' "There is no God" is not offered as a *proposition* whose truth value is on the table for discussion; it is rather, a cry of despair. He has at last realized that his pride and ambition were always stronger than his religious faith. When he said that "There is no God for a Christian man who lives, as I did, for human praise" we do not have to understand him to be denying a proposition that others have affirmed. We can understand his expression, instead, as making the conceptual point that to live for human praise is not to live a truly religious life. There can also be a certain amount of amusement in the picture of the philosophers confronting Sergius after the resolution of his spiritual crisis and his exile to Siberia. They explain to him their arguments and then ask him whether, as a truly religious man, he does not agree with them. We can imagine him replying, "That's all very interesting and when I was a young student it surely would have intrigued me, but there are things to be done now. So, won't you come with me to help teach the children and tend the sick?" (Tilghman 1993, p. 222)

Granted that Father Sergius' reply is wholly appropriate in such a context, how far does this count in promoting nonrealism? Tilghman's position has force to the extent that the very appeal to propositions here represents an altogether different order of discourse, something that rests on a mistaken view of the religious form of life at stake. On the other hand, the strength of

46

a realist reply rests on the extent to which religious propositions represent a crucial aspect of such religious life. The following may be among the more plausible cases of (apparent) propositional truth-claims that have a role in the way of life that Father Sergius chooses: "To feed the hungry and tend the sick is to do what God loves," "God hates injustice," "Cruelty to the poor causes God sorrow." Realists hold that such statements may both be subject to philosophical inquiry as well as forming the backbone of a dramatic, bold commitment to social justice.

Realists like Roger Trigg contend that in the religious practice of prayer, serving the oppressed, worship, and so on, there is an ineluctable commitment to the existence of the object of prayer, service, and worship. Trigg holds that it is precisely because religious believers like theists hold that God exists that the religious believer is so moved to prayer, service, and worship. Granted, certain frameworks or forms of life may not allow one to recognize this religious reality. So if, due to some crazed reason, one's language and outlook were restricted only to abstract mathematical formulas, one might not be able to articulate anything about God. Cupitt's and Phillips' observation that the meaning of religion is to be found *within* religious discourse may be partly right in that certain religious contexts may be best suited for persons to encounter the divine or to begin to form an idea of what such an encounter might amount to. But granting this would not entail that the being (God or some other divine reality) that one thereby encounters in a religious context has no independent reality.

To put this rejoinder in terms of imagination and thought experiments, realists contend that to imagine the form of life that comprises Judaism, Christianity, Islam, Hinduism, Buddhism, and other religions is not just to imagine practical ways of living, but a commitment to the truth of the relevant beliefs such as "God loves the world," "Mohammed is God's Prophet" and so on. Religious conceptions of the cosmos are, as it were, so big that they cannot be restricted to particular forms of human life. John Wisdom comments on the significance of the question as to whether God exists: "And to this question every incident in the history of the world is relevant – whether it is the fall of a sparrow, the coming of the harvest or the fading of a smile" (Wisdom 1970, p. 21). Arvind Sharma makes a related, realist point about Advaita Vedanta Hinduism. In a very restricted sense, Advaita Vedanta may seem allied with nonrealism insofar as it treats the world of diverse objects as ultimately insubstantial and something like a language game: "The universe itself, according to Advaitic metaphysics, is a language-game, but it is a self-transcending language-game which intends to take the player to the reality

47

underlying the game" (Sharma 1995, p. 139). So while this form of Hinduism treats a large tract of a so-called commonsense view of the observable world as though it were a language game, it is nonetheless committed to searching for a deeper reality. Peter Forrest grants that Cupitt's notion of a nonrealist religious spirituality has value, but he claims that it does not do justice to important aspects of religious experience:

> Like Cupitt, I respect . . . nontheistic spirituality, but what it lacks is *bhakti*, as Hindus call it – the love of devotees for their God. In this case the problem of myth is that if God is really just a myth, the love of God is illusory. (Forrest 1996, p. 24)

If there are good grounds for thinking there is no God, then perhaps Cupitt has brought to light a radical way in which a nontheistic religious "spirituality" may be bolstered using theistic language. But if Forrest is right, this operation is in danger of courting illusions.

A critic of both Christianity and Hinduism, Bertrand Russell, charged that philosophers face serious difficulties when they seek to salvage the benefits of such religions without having to justify them in a realist framework. "There are philosophers . . . who keep a *shadow* of religion, too little for comfort, but quite enough to ruin their systems intellectually" (Russell 1969, p. 250). As an atheist, Russell could grant that if God exists then certain questions about God such as "How long has God existed?" would make as little sense as asking "How much time does time take?" But he nonetheless thought it made sense to ask whether there were good reasons to think there is a God at all.

Is Phillips right about the absence of realist arguments in sacred scriptures like the Christian Bible? It is not clear that all such sacred texts are shorn of arguments (albeit these may not be intellectual in some academic sense) for the objective truth of their fundamental claims. In the Hebrew Bible there are many narratives in which it appears that the reality and intentions of God are described as being made apparent through signs (I Kings, Elijah disputing the followers of Baal, for example), and the Christian New Testament has its various references to miracles, resurrection appearances, and general claims about God being manifest in creation (Romans 1, for example). These narratives and teachings may all be interpreted by contemporary readers as highly metaphorical, but they may also be construed as providing (in principle) something that can serve as evidence for religious belief. The debate here involves competing conceptions of religious experience, miracles, and so on (all these topics arise in later chapters, see especially chapters 8 and 10; see also question seven at the end of this chapter). Nonrealism is bolstered to the extent that the appeal to miracles constitutes something both intellectually embarrassing and foreign to the religious forms of life. Realism is served to the extent that such appeals to miracles and experience are best read in a realist framework of providing signs of Divine activity.

Would the alleged absence of arguments in sacred scriptures for realist conclusions, lend weight to nonrealism? One realist response is that any such arguments might have been deemed out of place because of the prevalent confidence in the objective reality of the sacred. Such confidence might be due to superstition or, alternatively, due to the prevalence of widespread religious experience. Maybe people were so aware (or thought they were aware) of God's reality, that argumentation would have been beside the point. As John Hick has argued, to some devout religious believers it may well seem as peculiar to muster evidence for the existence of the divine as it would be for two intimate friends who live together to muster evidence for each other's existence (Hick 1966).

REPLY TO (B): If one has religious beliefs, and is convinced that these beliefs are not supported by evidence, does one have a religious reason for abandoning realism? At least three options may be entertained by realists.

First, there are different conceptions of evidence and its role in grounding beliefs. It may be argued that religious faith does not require evidence in order to be acceptable. This is an option explored in chapter 8. Here I simply note that there is testimony by some religious believers that faith in God can be held in the midst of very serious doubts about God's existence. Søren Kierkegaard (1813–55) had no enthusiasm for the philosophical project of establishing that God's existence is highly probable nor did he think of religion as a bare objective matter, if that means something cut off from one's passion and personal identity. Nonetheless, Kierkegaard construes religious faith as something that is not just compatible with radical uncertainty; faith requires uncertainty:

> Without risk there is no faith. Faith is precisely the contradiction between the infinite passion of the individual's inwardness and the objective uncertainty. If I am capable of grasping God objectively, I do not believe, but precisely because I cannot do this, I must believe. If I wish to preserve myself in faith I must constantly be intent upon holding fast to the objective uncertainty, so as to remain out upon the deep, over seventy thousand fathoms of water, still preserving my faith. (Kierkegaard 1974, p. 182)

49

If this outlook makes sense, religious belief can exist alongside the conviction that the intellectual backing for such belief is tenuous.

Second, it may be feasible to build a pragmatic or ethical case for religious belief even in the face of strong contrary evidence. There are practical reasons that can be articulated for religious beliefs, reasons that will be considered in chapters 7 and 10. A modest analogy is that a person may have good practical reasons for believing that she will recover from an illness (the positive attitude will enhance her prospects of regaining health), even if the evidence available to her is on the other side. Religious nonrealists give center-stage to practical reasons for accepting a religious form of life, but there is no reason in principle why realists cannot make a similar case for assuming certain religious beliefs are true. Realism, as defined here, is a view about truth and to adopt it does not amount to committing oneself to the thesis that determining what to believe religiously is "a purely intellectual matter," set apart from practical and ethical concerns.

Third, someone who has religious beliefs and is convinced that these are not supported by evidence may well suspend their religious beliefs, at least temporarily. At the heart of many of the world religions is the injunction that one should be honest and truthful. These injunctions may be understood as commending certain ways of living faithfully and with integrity in accord with specific forms of life. But these injunctions may also include a duty of conscience not to profess to believe in what one honestly takes to be unjustified or even false. According to some accounts of religious growth, some skepticism of religious convictions is healthy and to be expected (see, for example, the reflections of Charles Williams on this point as outlined by Shideler 1962). Philosophers who advance constructive religious accounts of God and the world sometimes acknowledge the way in which religious skepticism plays an important role in one's philosophical and religious formation. Francis Bacon (1561–1626) notes this from a theistic vantage point: "It is true, that a little philosophy inclines a mind to atheism; but depth in philosophy, brings men's minds to religion" (*Essays*, p. 51). As the Jewish monist philosopher Benedict Spinoza (1632–77) remarked in a reply to Bacon, one may not come back to the same religion, but the point to note here is that in various quarters of different religious communities skepticism is recognized either as an important period in the life of faith or even as an honorable alternative to faith. One of the most well-known texts arguing for both the religious and ethical requirement of free inquiry (including inquiry leading to skepticism) is John Stuart Mill's (1806–73) *On Liberty*. Mill argued that if religious believers do not subject themselves to a critical investigation into the credibility of their faith then they risk losing a grip on both the meaning and vibrancy of their faith. John Barbour has recently advanced an important study of the religious function of skepticism (in *Versions of Deconversion*, 1994), as has Merold Westphal (in *Suspicion and Faith: The Religious Uses of Modern Atheism*, 1993).

So, realists have contended that religious faith by its very nature creates some breathing space for philosophical debate over its truth. They have argued further that there is no incompatibility between faith and rigorous philosophical inquiry. Some of the positive reasons for adopting religious faith are considered in future chapters.

REPLY TO (C): Is it the case that realist accounts of religious claims are likely to promote intolerance? At least some versions of realism seem especially important for an ethical and social policy of tolerance. Realism appears to be an essential presupposition in making the claim that there are objective human rights, for example. Arguably, realism enables one to recognize that human rights are viable across cultures, whereas a nonrealist would have to articulate a theory of rights in terms of different societies or forms of life and otherwise without objective credence. But granting that realism may provide an important background for political tolerance in general, what about religious nonrealism? Realists about religious belief may advance at least three reasons to show that they have resources by which to justify tolerance and secure it rather than threaten it.

First, realism seems well placed to allow that one's beliefs can be mistaken. If you hold that the truth of your religious beliefs depends upon what lies independent of one's beliefs and form of life ("God exists," "There is an afterlife"), then one has some grounds for humility. A reason to tolerate other positions on such matters is that one's own views may be wrong and the views of others may be right. A nonrealist interpretation of forms of life with only internal criteria of assessment, seems to rule out external challenge. Some realists worry that the repudiation of objective, external ways of evaluating forms of life can lead to insularity and wind up justifying communities and traditions that, at least by our lights, seem ethically appalling. Atheists like Michael Martin and Kai Nielsen as well as theists like Richard Swinburne and Roger Trigg are concerned that the appeal to religious forms of life with only internal checks might lead to justifying all sorts of horrifying, cultic nightmares, secular and religious. What of a community that intends to slaughter the weak, enslave other people, and so on?

51

Second, as noted earlier in reply to (B), being a realist implies nothing by itself about one's theory of evidence. One may be a realist, adopt a religious belief assumed to be the best grounded for oneself, and yet believe that those who adopt other religions have (or may have) equally good grounds for their beliefs. On this view, toleration may be owed to others due to a respect for their exercising their own reason in choosing a religious or a secular view of life.

Third, it might be the case that on realist, religious grounds one believes that all religions represent some good, even if they cannot all be true on all points. So, imagine theism is false and a monist version of Hinduism is true. One might still very much value theism as providing something close to the truth. Theists may be wrong philosophically and yet on the right road to enlightenment insofar as they repudiate egotism and seek religious satisfaction in a higher power. As noted in chapter 1, in Hindu tradition there is a widespread belief that all religions offer different paths to the one religious end of *moksha* or liberation. Alternatively, if theism is true and one has reason to accept it, one might also believe that monism has great value in opposing narrow self-interest, promoting an openness to a "higher reality," and so on.

A sustained examination of the more general debate between realists and nonrealists would take us well beyond what may be packed into an introduction to philosophy of religion, but I refer to some of the relevant arguments at the end of this chapter under suggested questions and topics, number six. For further reflection on toleration see chapter 7.

Is there a position mid-way between realism and nonrealism?

Common Ground?

Some of the force of the nonrealist critique of realism is based on the conviction that realism commits one to believing that religious beliefs must be assessed in an arid, intellectual fashion or on the basis of a stringent theory of evidence that is unable to take into account different cultural and individual circumstances. Realists may acknowledge that this is indeed a serious problem and recast their form of realism.

One may be a realist and also maintain that the justification of religious beliefs is highly contextualized and subject to a wide array of conditions. As noted earlier, there is nothing about realism *per se* that denigrates appealing to religious experience or any number of routes to ground religious belief. A realist appropriation of nonrealist insight here may come to light in examining a proposal made by Norman Malcolm.

Norman Malcolm sought to curtail the realist project of using religious discourse isolated from its religious context. According to Malcolm, whereas *belief in God* is intelligible when seen as part of a religious form of life with its practices, desires, and emotions, it is less clear whether it makes sense to believe *that God exists* when this is shorn of such a life:

> For myself I have great difficulty with the notion of belief in *the existence of God*, whereas the idea of belief *in* God is to me intelligible. If a man did not ever pray for help or forgiveness, or have any inclination toward it; nor ever felt that it is "a good and joyful thing" to thank God for the blessings of this life; nor was ever concerned about his failure to comply with divine commandments – then, it seems clear to me, he could not be said to believe in God. Belief in God is not an all or none thing; it can be more or less; it can wax and wane. But belief in God in any degree does require, as I understand the words, some religious action, some commitment, or if not, at least a bad conscience. (Malcolm 1960, p. 155)

Realists may be able to make *some* progress in accommodating Norman Malcolm's reflections about *believing in God* and *believing that God exists*. On the realist side, it can be argued that without *believing that God exists*, it makes no sense *to believe in God* (see, for example, Trigg 1973). Having advanced this point, however, realists may then at least partly take on Malcolm's thesis. Once the concept of God that is at work in traditional religious claims is sufficiently filled out, realists seem to have reasons for holding that it is unlikely (if not conceptually absurd) for someone to believe that a theistic God exists without this having some affective consequences. One may believe in deism without much affect, because a deistic God is construed as quite removed from human affairs. The God of deism has been called *deus otiosus*, meaning "God without work" or "God at leisure." However, if one believes God is the all-present God of supreme power, knowledge, and goodness of Judaism, Christianity or Islam, who calls one to justice and compassion, it may well be incredible to think someone can actually believe this and yet such a belief has no bearing on their emotions, desires, and actions.

Religious language did not begin in abstract academic contexts and I believe that nonrealists have been right to remind other philosophers of this fact. The vast majority of religious discourse is embedded in practical contexts with considerable histories and therefore to treat them in isolation from these contexts places one at risk philosophically. A philosophical inquiry into the belief that God is all-powerful might be acceptable as far as self-consistency and intellectual clarity are concerned, but if it consists of the analysis of a concept that has *no* religious bearing then the result may fail to be important for the philosophy *of religion*. Moreover, as C. S. Peirce (1839–1914) notes:

> It is absurd to say that religion is a mere belief. You might as well call society a belief, or politics a belief or civilization a belief. Religion is a life and can be identified with a belief only provided that belief be a living belief. (Peirce 1931–68, 6.439)

Realists can acknowledge the lived, practical side of religion without abandoning their understanding of truth and falsehood.

Another area where realists can gain from nonrealist work concerns the nature of objectivity. Even if realism is true, it does not follow that our *forms of life* or *conceptual schemes* are independent of us or not fashioned by humans. As Willard Quine points out, "Even the notion of a cat, let alone a class or number, is a human artifact, rooted in human disposition and cultural tradition" (Quine 1992, p. 6). This is an observation that advocates of realism can appreciate without adopting a full-scale nonrealism.

As we struggle to locate some common ground between realism and nonrealism it is important to consider how versions of each need not be "full scale" – that is, radically opposed. D. Z. Phillips opposes realism as defined in this chapter in that he does not think propositional claims can be analyzed and properly understood independently of human conceptual frameworks. He further opposes what self-described realists obten do, namely, focus on assessing the probability of the truth of these claims. But Phillips' work, unlike Don Cupitt's, may be read as leaving open-ended and intelligible the assertion that there is a God. Just because our propositional claims about the world, and beyond, must be understood in terms of the form of life that gives them meaning, does not mean that such claims cannot play a role in referring to reality. In other words, one can emphasize the *use* of terms in a theory of sense and then look at their viability for reference. If Phillips is right, then standard realist projects may be mistaken insofar as they rely upon a detached point of view and treat religious claims as if they were quasi-scientific. But even if that is right, Phillips can still allow either that there is or is not a God. At this point in time, Phillips appears to hold that the project of determining which position to embrace goes beyond the power of philosophy.

"Philosophy is neither for nor against religious belief. After it has sought to clarify the grammar of such beliefs its work is over" (Phillips 1993, p. 77). But that does not mean that asserting either that there is or is not a God is nonsense.

So, while one can juxtapose radical versions of realism and nonrealism, one can also see how each stance can be modified and thus edged closer. Alternatively, one can devise a position that draws on both, retaining the referential meaning of religious language ("God exists" if and only if God exists) while heavily emphasizing the embedded, social meaning of such discourse.

At present, the majority of philosophy of religion in the English-speaking world is realist. Can a radical (nonmodified) nonrealist find this work valuable?

There is a minimal sense in which nonrealists have an interest in realist work. As noted earlier, one of the reasons for adopting nonrealism has been the conviction that realism is ultimately unsuccessful. But this interest hardly amounts to a positive appreciation. Alternatively, a nonrealist may well appreciate how a realist exploration of religious belief involves investigating concepts that are embedded in forms of life. Thus, while radical nonrealists about God or Brahman will not interpret debate about the existence of God or Brahman as debate about whether to enlarge or shrink one's conception of what exists objectively, they still have a stake in the moral implications of such conceptions of ultimate reality. What are the consequences, say, of believing that there is a God who is all-good or that there is an ultimate, divine reality, Brahman? What form of life do these beliefs reflect or promote? Nonrealism does not require its adherents to believe that a realist philosophy of religion is altogether unfruitful. Even if realism is judged to be mistaken, it may serve as a natural complement to nonrealism. After all, to use the analogy of Hans Christian Andersen's *The Shadow* again, shadows may not be things in themselves, but their shape, location and movement may tell us a great deal about the object shadowed and the light. Similarly, realist descriptions of divine power and liberation may shed light on important religious practices and forms of life.

The next chapter considers a key characteristic that defines much religion, a conception of divine power. Religions may often be distinguished in terms of the ways in which they conceive of power. Is the physical cosmos all that exists or might it be the case that the whole cosmos is the result of an all-powerful divine power? This question may be phrased in accord with realism, but nonrealists can focus on imagining the form of life that makes such questions possible.

Suggested Questions and Topics

(1)   Adress Wittgenstein's claim about Christianity:

> Queer as it sounds: The historical accounts in the Gospels might, historically speaking, be demonstrably false and yet belief would lose nothing by this . . . because historical proof (the historical proof-game) is irrelevant to belief. This message (the Gospels) is seized on by men believing (i.e. lovingly). That is the certainty characterizing the particular acceptance-as-true, not something else. A believer's relation to these narratives is neither the relation to historical truth (probability), nor yet that to a theory consisting of "truths of reason." (1967, 32e)

(2)   In what respects might nonrealism or realism have a bearing upon the ethics and the likelihood of toleration between religions? (Additional material on toleration is considered in chapter 7.)

(3)   In the debate on the nature of truth in religion, nonrealists appeal to the meaning of terms as used in religious discourse. Thus, some non-realists defend their stance on the basis of what religious believers say and do. Is the case for religious nonrealism stronger if cast as providing reasons as to why one ought to embrace nonrealism as a reconstruction or reinterpretation of older beliefs which, if interpreted along realist lines, are false or unjustified?

(4)   In the course of reviewing the case for nonrealism in this chapter, Tolstoy's story "Father Sergius" was discussed. You may wish to consider further Tilghman's use of the story or consider nonrealist versus realist readings of some of Tolstoy's other short stories and novels. See, for example, the collection *Great Short Works of Leo Tolstoy* (1967). For another use of Tolstoy's "Father Sergius" story quite apart from the debate on realism, see Caroline Simon's "Evil, Tragedy and Hope: Reflections on Tolstoy's 'Father Sergius'" (Simon 1995). To what extent, if any, do you think that literature should be an important resource in philosophy of religion? Do you hold the same view of the contribution of literature to ethics or to other areas of philosophy?

(5)   How might theists employ what may be termed a supernatural version of nonrealism? Nonrealists claim that truth is a matter of relativity to conceptual framework and context. If theism could be developed in a satisfactory fashion such that it made sense to speak of God's conceptual framework or context, could this provide a platform for an overarching notion of truth anchored in God? On this model, would the difference between realism and nonrealism collapse? You may wish to consider Plantinga's work on this

(1982). Alternatively, consider the following claim by Peter Geach: "God does not contemplate truth from outside, as if in principle the correctness of his thoughts were judgeable for their conformity to a standard ('judgeable by whom?' one might well ask); rather, he constitutes all truth" (Geach 1977, p. 90). Do these claims make sense? If so, what are their implications?

(6)　Consider some general arguments for and against realism:

(A)　On the most general level, it has been objected that a radical nonrealism across all categories would render nonsense a host of commonsense beliefs (Alston 1979; Plantinga 1982; Harris 1992; Trigg 1993; van Inwagen 1993). For example, does it not seem quite sensible to believe that there were truths about the world before humans evolved and when there were neither languages nor conceptual schemes? When no human beings existed and dinosaurs roamed the planet, was it neither true nor false that dinosaurs roamed the planet?

(B)　Assess one nonrealist strategy in reply to (A). Some nonrealists interpret statements about prehuman life as presupposing for their intelligibility a human social, contextual life. Is not the term "dinosaur" a human category? And is not the meaning of "dinosaurs existed" analyzed in terms of what we would have experienced if we had been there? Michael Dummett writes that "To describe what would make a statement true is to describe what it would be to recognize it as true, even if the means of recognition are not available to us" (Dummett 1973, p. 465). Assess the strength of this strategy.

(C)　Do the natural sciences rest upon realist foundations? Consider the merits of the following nonrealist approach to science. Bas van Fraassen and other nonrealists have proposed that the sciences are best thought of as institutions that promote standards of empirical adequacy. If these nonrealists are correct, then scientific progress is principally defined in terms of meeting these standards; good science is science that is useful, not science that is true in the realist sense. Van Fraassen describes the procedures of science in a fashion that is thoroughly pragmatic and, at least in principle, not committed to realist truth claims:

> In so far as they [scientists] go beyond consistency, empirical adequacy, and empirical strength, they do not concern the relation between the theory and the world, but rather the use and usefulness of the theory; they provide reasons to prefer the theory independently of questions of truth. (van Fraassen 1980, p. 88)

Realists propose that the search for consistency in scientific theories and the search for empirical adequacy to support them is made intelligible chiefly because of the prospects that such theories are objectively true or false, while nonrealists have responded, in the words of van Fraassen, that "the theory of science can be developed without the realists' metaphysical baggage!" (in Churchland [ed.] 1985, p. 289).

(D)   Roger Trigg and some other realists have argued that nonrealism is self-contradictory. Assess the following argument:

> If all reasoning only takes place within particular social practices, what is the status of any reasoning *about* social practices as such? Is it merely the product of another social practice? If it is, it must be of little interest, since whatever form it may seem to have comes from its being understood to be making a claim about what is the case. The fragmentation of reason . . . mean[s] that wide claims about reason, even about its fragmentation, cannot be made. (Trigg 1993, p. 7 [emphasis Trigg]; see also Siegel 1987)

(E)   Trigg characterizes the traditional framework for doing philosophy as realist. "A traditional metaphysical view is one of the self reasoning about truth in a manner that can be detached from place and time" (Trigg 1993, p. 27). How might a nonrealist reply?

(7)   Offer realist and nonrealist interpretations of the narrative of Elijah's triumph over the priests of Baal (1 Kings 18, Hebrew Bible, Christian Old Testament).

(8)   At the close of this chapter it was suggested that there may be some ways in which the realist and nonrealist projects may be complementary. You may wish either to criticize the proposal or to suggest further ways in which it may be developed.

(9)   A question for those acquainted with contemporary political theory: There is today a lively dispute between political liberalism and so-called communitarian theories. Those often classified as communitarian include Alasdair MacIntyre, Charles Taylor, Joseph Raz, Michael Sandel, and Michael Walzer, among others. Roughly, these critics claim that liberalism excessively promotes the role of rights over conceptions of the good. Our identity instead is constituted by traditions and communities in a way that liberalism is not able to accommodate. (Communitarianism is discussed in chapter 7.) What are the parallels, if any, between the nonrealist case against realism and the communitarian case against liberalism?

(10)   An off-the-beaten-track question for those who have read the Pre-Socratics: One of the religious reasons reviewed in this chapter for adopting nonrealism, was the (apparent) failure of realist philosophical projects to secure the justification of religious belief. Consider some of the recorded beliefs of the

Pre-Socratic philosophers, e.g. Thales on water, Anaximander on the boundless, and Anaximenes on air. If their beliefs are false if read along realist lines, how would these beliefs fare if read in a nonrealist framework? Alternatively, what if their philosophies were read as highly metaphorical descriptions of the world? If Thales' view of water is false literally, could contexts arise in which it were true metaphorically or it had a role in a worthy form of life? You may also wish to consider this with respect to scientific theories and hypotheses now believed to be false (the earth is flat, the speed of light is instantaneous, and so on).

Further Reading and Considerations

From *A Companion to Philosophy of Religion* see the entries "Wittgensteinianism" and "Theological realism and antirealism." For a sustained development of a Wittgensteinian theology, see Fergus Kerr's *Theology After Wittgenstein*. For a succinct review of Phillips' recent work, see Jay Wood's review of *Faith After Foundationalism* (Wood 1994). Kuitert argues that Phillips is inconsistent in "Is Belief a Condition for Understanding?" (Kuitert 1981). Phillips offers a fascinating treatment of the meaning of religious beliefs in literature in *From Fantasy to Faith*. For an alternative reading of Kierkegaard than the one used in this chapter, see Phillips, *Religion Without Explanation*. For a realist reading of Kierkegaard that is juxtaposed to Phillips, see work by Stephen Evans. Wittgenstein's view is sometimes called "fideism," a view that will be discussed in chapter 8. Fideism – or "faith-ism" – names several different views of faith, united in rejecting the thesis that religious faith requires strong, evidential reasons to be justified. The proximity of Malcolm's views to Wittgenstein's is brought out in Malcolm's *Ludwig Wittgenstein*. Some of Wittgenstein's early work may be read along realist lines. The ending of his *Tractatus Logico-Philosophicus* has sometimes been interpreted as vindicating a mystical, religious approach to the world. Nonrealism is a dimension of American pragmatism, especially in work by John Dewey and Charles Peirce. It may also be seen in earlier work by William James, though I believe James is far less radical than Dewey. The view described in this chapter as nonrealism has also been called noncognitivism and irrealism. A variety of positions are now under debate that seek some middle ground between extreme realist and nonrealist views, such as "quasi-realism," "nonfactualism," and "internal realism." The issues are highly complex. There

59

is a useful delineation of the central positions in the entry "Realism" in the Blackwell publication *A Companion to Epistemology*. Some contemporary thinkers endeavor either to call the whole division between realism and nonrealism into question, or to accommodate both in different respects. The work of Paul Ricoeur is an important representative.

W. C. Smith is skeptical about assessing religious beliefs of extant traditions like Christianity within a realist framework: "It is a surprisingly modern aberration for anyone to think that Christianity is true or that Islam is – since the Enlightenment, basically, when Europe began to postulate religions as intellectualist systems, patterns of doctrines, so that they could for the first time be labeled 'Christianity' and 'Buddhism,' and could be called true or false" (cited by Sharma 1990, p. 159; see Smith 1963). Smith is right to draw attention to the "intellectualist" development of the study of religion in the Enlightenment, but it is not obvious that realist notions of truth only come into play with the European Enlightenment. The existence or nonexistence of God and gods at least appears to have been a lively issue in Ancient Greek Philosophy and these debates are both difficult to read along nonrealist lines, and difficult to separate from debates about the status of religious belief. For what appears to be a straightforward realist notion of truth about religious convictions note Aristotle (384–322 BCE) in *The Metaphysics*: "To say of what is that it is not, or of what is not that it is, is false, while to say of what is that it is, and of what is not that it is not, is true" (1011). For an overview of the historical development of the field of philosophy of religion, see the entries from Part II in *A Companion to Philosophy of Religion*: "Ancient Philosophical Theology"; "The Christian Contribution to Medieval Philosophical Theology"; "The Islamic Contribution to Medieval Philosophical Theology"; "The Jewish Contribution to Medieval Philosophical Theology"; "Early Modern Philosophical Theology"; and "The Emergence of Modern Philosophy of Religion." For some of the important distinctively theological work on realism, see especially George Lindbeck's *The Nature of Doctrine* and Schubert Ogden's *The Reality of God*. Gordon Kaufman, Stanley Hauerwas, and Hans Frei have also made important contributions to this debate.

3

Divine Power

In philosophy of religion enormous energy is concentrated on the concept of power. This is a natural focal point given the history of religion. The great historian of religion Mircea Eliade, the editor of the sixteen-volume *Encyclopedia of Religion*, has argued forcefully that at the center of religious experience is the appearance of sacred power:

> The man of the archaic societies tends to live as much as possible *in* the sacred or in close proximity to consecrated objects. The tendency is perfectly understandable, because, for primitives as for the man of all pre-modern societies, the *sacred* is equivalent to a *power* and, in the last analysis, to *reality*. The sacred is saturated with *being*. Sacred power means reality and at the same time enduringness and efficacity . . . Thus it is easy to understand that religious man deeply desires *to be,* to participate *in reality*, to be saturated with power. (Eliade 1959, p. 12)

Eliade suggests that a concept of sacred power is not merely accidental to religious experience but is at its heart. Very early accounts of both Eastern and Western religious experience speak of encounters with powerful gods, God or some sacred reality. At times this encounter is described in stark terms in which the divine is depicted as a dangerous force that is not disposed either to consistency or to mercy. Important stages in the history of many religions are marked by periods when the divine is portrayed in terms of sheer force or in terms of power as well as goodness or perfection.

The concept of divine power is pivotal for Judaism, Christianity, and Islam. In these traditions, appeal to God's power is important not just in articulating substantial claims about the origin and cause of the cosmos, but in making sense of beliefs about God's providential acts in history, God's ability to answer prayers and to bring about miracles, God's freedom, love, trustworthiness and, for some, God's being worthy of worship and obedience. Sacred texts in Hinduism also feature a high view of God's power: "I behold Thee without beginning, middle or end, of infinite power" (*Bhagavad Gita*, chapter 11). Reliance upon God's power is also vital in the theistic confrontation with evil. Without the belief that God is all-powerful as well as all-good, the religious faith that good will somehow triumph over evil would very likely give way to despair.

In contemporary philosophy of religion, a concern with power is at the heart of a major debate between theists who locate the sustaining cause of the cosmos in a divine power outside of the cosmos and those who claim that the cosmos is neither created nor in any way derived from an external power. Critics of theism have charged that the very idea of supreme power is obscure and the result of conceptual confusion.

This chapter addresses the concept of supreme power or omnipotence. The mainstream philosophical literature on omnipotence and other divine attributes is among the most analytical in philosophy of religion. It is therefore important to canvass some of the techniques of analytical philosophy before considering the central arguments to be addressed in this chapter.

An Analytical Prelude

Much analytical philosophy (from the Greek *analytikos* meaning "to resolve into elements") in general, and philosophy of religion in particular, consists of proposing different analyses of a concept, and then articulating examples, some of which involve sophisticated thought experiments, to illustrate and clarify them, while objectors appeal to other cases and thought experiments in an effort to expose weaknesses in the various analyses. Ideally, an analysis of the concept of a property like *being omnipotent* (from the Latin *omnis* for "all" and *potens* for "powerful") sets forth the necessary and sufficient conditions for having the property. An analysis enables one to identify individuals that exemplify the property and to conclude that there cannot be any individual that meets these conditions that would not exemplify the property. An analysis of omnipotence, then, lays out the necessary and sufficient conditions for being omnipotent.

We can subject an analysis to many objections. It may be self-contradictory or built upon a mistaken conception of the world and so on, but analyses are most often critically evaluated with special emphasis on two factors: *scope* and *clarity*. Scope: An analysis of a concept X is too broad if it classifies some individual as having X that does not have it. It is too narrow when it fails to classify as having X an individual that does have it. Clarity: An analysis is clear when it does not admit of borderline cases where it is undetermined whether a given concept applies. In other words, an analysis is clear to the extent that it avoids vagueness. Vagueness is not always capable of elimination. Can one have a nonvague conception of "baldness" or "middle age" or "heap"? Perhaps not. Indeed, the proposal, in chapter 1, that we treat the concept of "religion" and thus "philosophy of religion" in an open-ended fashion is tantamount to proposing that we recognize that these terms do not have precise, fixed meanings and that they are, therefore, vague. But while some vagueness in an analysis may have to be tolerated (Frederick Waismann has argued that vagueness haunts virtually all our language; see Waismann 1952), analyses can be faulted when they are exceedingly vague or fail to illuminate the concept under investigation. An analysis is empty when it is circular and uses in the analysis the very term(s) it was designed to shed light on. Two definitions together may also be circular. An example of circular and thus uninformative definitions would be an analysis of "knowledge" as "the opposite of ignorance" and an analysis of "ignorance" as "the opposite of knowledge." This chapter explores four analyses of omnipotence and charts the main moves in the current debate on divine power.

Maximal Power

If some ethicists are right, then the literature on omnipotence should come with a warning label. Because this literature chiefly focuses on power alone without explicitly invoking the concepts of goodness or value, philosophical work on maximal power is thought to be dangerous. Why should sheer boundless power by itself (power, considered without ethical restraint) be thought of as valuable from a religious point of view, let alone as a key to unlock the concept "God"? As Rush Rhees once warned, "If you think that the difference of God from his creatures is one of power, you will not naturally speak of compassion" (Rhees 1969, p. 110). This concern will be taken up as the chapter proceeds. It is useful, however, to begin simply with the concept "power" if for no other reason than this will compel us to consider whether there is indeed some cause for suspecting the adequacy of a concept of God which gives center-stage to power.

In most of the philosophy-of-God literature, omnipotence is considered a defining characteristic of God, so that to ask the questions "How powerful is

God?" and "How powerful can an individual be?" is to seek the same answer. Standard theistic references to *the power of God* are references to the power of *an individual* or *a being* that is capable of acting deliberately. (In what follows, the terms "an individual" and "a being" are used interchangeably.) On such a reading, talk of the power of God is on a continuum with our talk of the power of persons. You have more power than me with respect to lifting weights, if you can lift more than I can.

Consider now the first of four analyses of omnipotence. The following analysis is fairly common.

Analysis 1

Being, B, is omnipotent if and only if B is able to do anything.

Given this analysis, if any being is omnipotent, it is able to do anything and if any being has this ability then it is omnipotent. At the outset this seems acceptable. Arguably, the ability of an omnipotent being would involve unimpeded maximal abilities. By construing power in terms of *ability* the definition does not collapse the distinction between *having power* and *exercising power*. Perhaps a being could be very powerful, maybe even omnipotent, and never exercise this power. "Ability" in the analysis should be interpreted so that one fails to have an ability to do something if circumstances prevent one from doing so. For example, I lose the ability to run when my legs are broken. On Analysis 1, an omnipotent being's abilities would be unimpeded and unbounded.

Is Analysis 1 in any way illuminating or is it empty of content? The analysis articulates the notion of omnipotence in terms of doing things. Insofar as we are acquainted with what it is like to act – what it is to be an agent – in our own case, then this analysis may be understood as building upon what is apparent in our own experience. Richard Swinburne explicitly relies upon this acquaintance with our own agency in the course of forming the concept of omnipotence. The "notion of pure limitless intentional power, is a very simple one, the maximum degree of a kind of causality known intimately to ourselves when we perform intentional actions" (Swinburne 1994, p. 227). Even if this statement needs qualification (for example, we only *seem to be acquainted with this kind of causality* as opposed to Swinburne's more confident claim about intimate knowledge), this depiction of omnipotence seems to open up the concept for review rather than provide us with something completely empty.

Despite this promising beginning, two forceful kinds of difficulty emerge that have received sustained attention in the philosophy of religion; these may be referred to as general and specific difficulties. General difficulties would hinder any being whatsoever from being omnipotent. If these problems are binding, then there can no more be an omnipotent being than there can be a greatest possible number. Specific problems cause difficulties for Judaism, Christianity, and Islam. Each tradition views God as omnipotent; but if some of these specific difficulties are insurmountable, then there is reason to conclude that if the God of these traditions exists, God is not omnipotent. This conclusion seems either untenable or highly paradoxical from a traditional theistic point of view. Let us work with the general difficulties first.

A general difficulty may be characterized in exclusively logical terms or it may be cast along broader metaphysical lines as well. There are problems with supposing any individual can do what is logically impossible. Can God make a square circle or make $2 + 2 = 6$? It would appear to be nonsense to suppose these tasks could be done by any being whatsoever. The problem has an additional edge if one assumes there are certain necessities, such as "time is one directional" (no one can reverse time), "red is a color," or "wisdom is a virtue" that are indeed necessary but not due to bare logical relationships (the denial of these propositions does not involve a logical contradiction). If it is granted that there are necessary metaphysical truths, then it seems that nothing can be omnipotent, because no individual can alter such metaphysically necessary truths. The most powerful being imaginable could not make something red and not colored or make time run in reverse where the past is future or make wisdom a vice.

These problems are often treated in one dramatic move by insisting that omnipotence should be analyzed as follows:

Analysis 2

Being, B, is omnipotent if and only if B is able to do anything that is logically or metaphysically possible.

This approach implies that the tasks cited above of making $2 + 2 = 6$ are idle pseudo-tasks, because they are absolute impossibilities. Conceding God cannot make $2 + 2 = 6$ is no worse than "conceding" that an omnipotent being cannot make the concept of justice jump around the number 7 while eating happiness. Both are impossible. It should be noted, though, that both are impossible not because they are syntactically meaningless as in the phrase "Up the or over Paris Run." Such a string of words fails to make grammatical sense. The other tasks of making square circles and so on can be described without grammatical errors (one can line up subject, verb, and direct object, following proper syntactic rules), but the descriptions are all conceptually nonsensical and not descriptions of what is truly possible. In his *Introduction to Logical Theory* Peter Strawson offers an analogy of the absurdity of supposing that a contradictory statement like "There is a shapeless triangle" can be true. He likens uttering a contradiction to a pointless walk:

> Suppose a man sets out to walk to a certain place; but, when he gets half-way there, turns round and comes back again. This may not be pointless. He may, after all, have wanted only exercise. But, from the point of view of a change of position, it is as if he had never set out. And so a man who contradicts himself may have succeeded in exercising his vocal chords. But from the point of view of imparting information, of communicating facts (or falsehoods) it is as if he had never opened his mouth. He utters words, but does not say anything. (Strawson 1952, p. 2)

Similarly, it may be argued that to suppose God can bring about contradictory states of affairs is akin to supposing God can bring it about that there is a world and there is not at the same time.

This approach to the general problem of defining omnipotence has antecedents in medieval philosophy of religion. Thomas Aquinas (1225–74) held that "the phrase 'God can do all things' is rightly understood to mean that God can do all things that are possible" (Aquinas, trans. 1947, 25.3 1a).

This analysis of omnipotence may be useful in addressing a paradox about freedom and omnipotence. Consider the question whether God can make something God cannot control. Many theists are committed to believing not just that God can do this, but that God has done so in that God has created human beings (and perhaps other creatures as well) that are free. Given a fairly standard characterization of freedom – a being is free only if that being is not completely under the control of another – if God creates a free creature then God must make a being that is not completely under God's control. This concession seems as straightforward as the claim that if God creates a triangle God must create something that has shape and is three-sided (or, even more obviously, if God creates something, call it Q, then God must create Q). Imagine God has created a free creature. Has God thereby ceased to be omnipotent because now there is a creature God cannot control? Presumably these sorts of "limits" on Divine freedom can be analyzed in terms of God's being limited by the limits God introduces. Arguably, it is no limitation of an individual's power, should it be the case that an individual's claim to power be intelligible; to expect an omnipotent being to be able to make a creature both free and not free at the same time would be akin to expecting an omnipotent being to make something that is square and yet lacks four right angles. Advocates of this use of Analysis 2 underscore that they are not limiting their view of God's power only to what we humans can conceive. They are, rather, insisting that the concept of omnipotence should not traffic in outright absurdity. (For more material on God and freedom see chapters 5 and 9.)

Is there some way in which a maximally powerful being can be envisaged that is the creator of the laws of logic and metaphysically necessary truths? Perhaps there is leeway to develop such a scenario if one adopts a conventionalist treatment of logic and metaphysics. According to conventionalism, apparently necessary logical and metaphysical laws are merely the codification of human language: they are human inventions. If one believes that the "truths" of logic and metaphysics were *invented* rather than *discovered* by humans, then one may well think of them as having been invented by God prior to human artifice. In a conventionalist theory, for 3 + 3 to equal 6, means that there is a formal relation of human concepts and rules, according to which this relation holds. If so, why not accept the possibility of a Divine conventionalism, according to which God decrees that there should be such truths and relations?

Historically, the best known representative of the view that God is responsible for all the necessary truths such as those in mathematics is René Descartes (1596–1650). Descartes reproaches those who think there are truths independent of God's power:

> The mathematical truths which you call eternal have been laid down by God and depend on Him entirely no less than the rest of His creatures. Indeed, to say that these truths are independent of God is to talk of Him as if He were Jupiter or Saturn and to subject Him to the Styx and the Fates. (Descartes 1970, p. 11)

Descartes' radical stance has not been widely accepted by theists on the grounds that crediting God with such powers would undermine the necessity of logical and mathematical truths. It at least appears as though such things as the law of identity (everything is itself or, to abbreviate it, "A is A") and the law of noncontradiction (it is impossible that something be A and not A at the same time in the same respect) cannot be otherwise. How could something not be itself? Or how could it be true that, say, an object was square and not square at the same time? Descartes seems to allow that God could have done otherwise, and the fact that many of us cannot imagine God's doing so is in virtue of God's firmly implanting in our minds the decisions that God has made. "It was free and indifferent for God to make it not be true that the three angles of a triangle were equal to two right angles, or in general that contradictories could not be true together . . ." (Descartes 1970, pp. 150–1). While Descartes' view of God's absolute power has not had a receptive press, a proposal has been recently introduced that is very similar to Descartes'.

Alvin Plantinga, Thomas Morris, Christopher Menzel, and others, propose preserving the necessity of logical and metaphysical truths while yet insisting that all these are true in virtue of God's all-encompassing creative will, a creative will that could not be otherwise. The necessity of "A is A" and other such truths is thereby affirmed and accounted for by a deeper Divine necessity. This revival of Descartes' position may be articulated with the use of a possible world terminology, now popular in metaphysics. A "possible world" is a complete, filled out state of affairs, a way things could be *tout court* or taken altogether. Earlier, the term "state of affairs" was used to refer to any state of affairs that might exist. As such, states of affairs may be described at any level of generality. Examples of states of affairs can be somewhat restrictive however, e.g. the state of affairs of *there being two blue birds in a forest*. The term "possible world" is typically used in the technical philosophical literature to refer to a complete, definite state of affairs which would delimit an entire the-way-things-might-be. Insofar as there are many ways reality might be, there are many possible worlds. There is the possible world that is substantially like ours except that there is one less planet, for example, and so on. Using this terminology, the revived (and revised) position of Descartes may be put as the claim that in all possible worlds, God wills that $1 = 1$, and so on for all necessary truths. As Plantinga writes: "God is a necessary being who has essentially the property of thinking just the thoughts he does think; these thoughts, then, are conceived or thought by God in every possible world and hence exist necessarily" (Plantinga 1982, p. 70).

This new move in the philosophy of God represents a shift from Descartes who seemed committed to preserving God's freedom to do otherwise in his creation. "Even if God has willed that some truths should be necessary, this does not mean that he willed them necessarily; for it is one thing to will that they be necessary, and quite another to will them necessarily or to be necessitated to will them" (Descartes 1970, pp. 150–1). Using contemporary philosophical terminology, Descartes appears to be committed to holding that God did not make "A is A" in some possible world, even though God did so in this one. While these contemporary defenders of Cartesianism ("Cartesian" describes views that are in the spirit of Descartes) are not willing to allow for such possibilities, they preserve Descartes' appeal to the sweeping, radical efficacy of God's power. They appeal to God's agency across all metaphysical categories to explain the origin of the cosmos as well as the existence of logical and other necessary truths. Descartes makes the point that in creation, it is the same power at work in all God's action. "You ask me by what kind of causality God established the eternal truths. I reply: by the same kind of causality as he created all things, that is to say, as their efficient and total cause" (Descartes 1970, p. 14). The new Cartesian project conceives of God's comprehensive, radical creation of necessary truths like $1 = 1$ as necessary (God could not have created otherwise or failed to create), and no less God's creativity because of this necessity. "The necessity of his [God's] creating is not imposed on him from without, but rather is a feature and result of the nature of his own activity itself, which is a function of what he is" (Morris and Menzel 1986, p. 357). This revised version of Descartes' stance has been commended on the grounds that it preserves the desired necessities, it offers *some* account of the truths at issue as opposed to leaving the necessities dangling as it were in some eerie philosophical stratosphere, and that its explanation is ultimately more simple than alternative accounts.

This new move is well worth developing further, both for the sake of speculating on the upper limits of power as well as for charting the boundaries of creation from a theistic point of view. Some theists resist the extension proposed by this Cartesian revival and their reasons are briefly noted.

It is objected that this exaltation of divine creativity cannot be achieved because any exercise of divine creativity must presuppose the necessary truths of logic (and perhaps metaphysics as well). How is it that God could make it the case that the law of identity (everything is itself) is necessarily true, unless the law of identity were already necessarily true? The point is not that the new Cartesians posit a problematic period of time before God creates the law of identity; they avoid this difficulty by assuming God has always existed, as has the law of identity and the other necessary truths. They yet posit a priority or primacy to God's will; God's willing that there be such laws is what accounts for the existence of the laws themselves. But the problem with this is that it is difficult to see how such a will, however powerful, could be deeper or prior or in some way causally anterior to the laws as the exercise of God's will would require.

Many theists who do not take the new Cartesian route counter that conceding the uncreated status of necessary laws does not at all mean compromising theism. Necessary truths of identity and so on are not things like planets or mountains. Technically, the truths and laws of logic are not "things" at all in the sense of concrete individual objects, nor are they like physical laws such as the law of gravity. Given a realist view of the issue, the laws of logic are, rather, the prerequisite of any thing whatsoever. God is not prey to them, but they are not somehow contained by God either. For these theists, God's being such that God did not create the laws of logic is no limitation. It is no worse a compromise of God's sovereignty than conceding that God is subject to God.

Consider one other way in which some contemporary philosophers of religion have speculated about the scope of omnipotence. Could a being be so powerful as to have created itself? The idea that any being could create itself (*causa sui*: cause of itself or self-caused) has been dismissed by many in the history of philosophy on the grounds that in order to create itself a being would have to exist before it existed, a rank and file absurdity, but it has recently been suggested that if a being was without origin or beginning and thus did not have to have a first moment of existing, the prospect for *causa sui* improves.

A proposal to establish the coherence of self-causation has been advanced by Thomas Morris and Christopher Menzel with the aid of the following thought experiment:

> We submit that God does create his own nature, and there is no absurdity or unacceptable circularity about this when properly understood. Consider the following thought experiment as a rough analogy. Suppose there exists a materialization machine, a machine about the size of a normal clock-radio, adorned with various dials. To demonstrate its remarkable ability to create matter *ex nihilo* [from nothing] in ordered arrangements, its inventor holds it waist-high, sets its dial, and materializes a table under it, on which it continues to sit as he releases it from his grip . . . Consider an extension of the story. The knobs of the materialization machine begin to wear out as their inventor experiments with producing all sorts of ordinary, and extraordinary, objects. Just as they are about to become unusable, they are set to produce, in a matter of seconds, new knobs qualitatively indistinguishable from the original knobs when they were first mounted on the machine. The old ones are pulled off, and presto, the new ones appear, as the machine continues to operate . . . Our inventor now proceeds systematically to replace each of its parts serially with parts materialized by the operation of the machine. The end state of this process is the materialization machine, sitting on a table, continually producing all of its own parts, batteries included . . . If the end-state of the replacement story is conceivable, if it is conceivable that the materialization machine be in this state at any time, it seems also conceivable that such an activity takes place at every time, or eternally. And that is what we have in the case of God. (Morris and Menzel 1986, pp. 359–60)

The crucial step in avoiding the traditional objection to *causa sui* is to appeal to the thesis that God, like the machine, had no first moment of existence. It is here that Morris and Menzel hope to block the objection that self-creation is absurd, because it would involve God existing before God exists.

The above proposal has not (or at least not yet) been widely accepted as a successful thought experiment, nor as an apt analogy for God's self-constituting powers. One may object to it on several fronts. Is the analogy between God and the machine suitable? If theism is true, God is no machine nor is God any other kind of thing with replaceable parts. Alternatively, one may object to the way Morris and Menzel construe the machine's status. Even if there could be such a machine, would it be a case of a thing creating itself? Arguably, the machine today is not the same as the self-creating machine which operated a year ago or 100 years ago, nor was that machine the same as the self-creating machine which operated 1,000 years ago, and so on. A machine that replaces all its parts no longer exists once all its parts are interchanged. Replace all the parts of a machine and you have replaced the machine.

The standard move for theists today is to think instead that, if there is a God, the state of affairs *God's being God* is not something God could have brought about or altered. Perhaps God did not make God omnipotent, but that would not mean God is held hostage by something external to God. As before, the issue is open for debate. Perhaps a better analogy can be devised or the Morris–Menzel case can be successfully defended (after all, we typically allow that complex physical objects can remain the same when at least some of their parts are replaced; one might well claim to own the same car despite the fact that all its original parts are replaced every so many years).

Until now, the property of omnipotence has been analyzed in terms of being able to do anything that is logically and metaphysically possible. Consider now some *specific* obstacles to analyzing omnipotence, especially as these challenge monotheistic traditions. Specific obstacles are those that stand in the path of identifying the God of Judaism, Christianity, and Islam, as omnipotent. Judaism, Christianity, and Islam each portray God as a nonphysical reality. But if God is nonphysical, then (so it is argued) God cannot do certain actions that require a material body such as swim, walk, jump, and so on. God is also portrayed in Judaism, Chistianity, and Islam as imperishable. God cannot cease to exist. If so, it appears that God cannot be omnipotent because God cannot cease to be. On this view, human beings may have an ability or power God lacks. We are capable of committing suicide whereas God is not.

These paradoxes have been addressed by theists in several ways. It has been proposed that God *can do the things as specified*. Perhaps God can assume a physical body and swim, walk, jump, and so on. Traditional Christianity

71

pictures God incarnate as a human being capable of such acts. Maybe God does not necessarily exist and God is thus capable of ceasing to be. On this schema, God exists everlastingly, without beginning and without end, but not necessarily so. God would be able to cease to exist – able to commit suicide as it were – even if God never will do so.

All these maneuvers involve adjusting the concept of God to fit the concept of omnipotence. The direction of influence may be represented as:

Concept of Omnipotence → Concept of God

Some difficulties still face this route. For example, belief in God's essential, necessary existence is deeply rooted in the traditional ways of conceiving of God. Arguably, to think that God is capable of ceasing to be and thus contingent, amounts to collapsing a key theistic distinction between the creation and creator. According to a central position in traditional theism, if God exists, God's existence cannot have been accidental or in any way preventable. At the very core of a great deal of monotheistic religion is the affirmation that God's existence is in some way absolute and noncontingent. (For further material on the belief in God's necessary existence, see chapters 4, 7, and 10.)

If one concedes that God cannot do certain things (e.g. commit suicide, only think about strawberries, make mistakes in addition), it may yet be possible to adjust the definition of omnipotence in such a way that it still allows that God is omnipotent. If only for the sake of argument, grant that God cannot do every possible task. The following definition of omnipotence does not require that an omnipotent being is able to do anything whatsoever. According to this definition, being omnipotent means being the most powerful being possible, not the possessor of every possible kind of power. Consider, then, this third analysis:

Analysis 3

Being, B, is omnipotent if and only if there is no other being that can have a greater scope of power.

Here the "scope of power" may be delimited in terms of the power to bring about certain states of affairs. This analysis emphasizes what an omnipotent being can do, not the way an omnipotent being does it. For variations of definitions of omnipotence in terms of maximal power in bringing about states of affairs see Hoffman and Rosenkrantz 1988; Flint and Fredoso 1983; and Wierenga 1989.

72

While specifying omnipotence in terms of the scope of power seems promising and, on some fronts, it appears to elude some of the difficulties cited earlier (i.e., God may not be able to do something a nondivine agent does but God can do indefinitely more), the definition may still cause problems for Jewish, Christian, and Islamic philosophers. If God is *essentially good*, presumably God cannot bring about any evil states of affairs for the sake of evil ends. An all-good God cannot create enormous suffering for the sake of entertainment, for example. Would the scope of power of an essentially good God be equal to or less than a being, call it Ahriman, who could do all that God is believed to be able to do but, because Ahriman was not essentially good, Ahriman could bring about evil states of affairs as well as good? For those theists willing to think God can do evil (even if God never does) there will not be a problem here. But for those who are committed to God's essential goodness this generates a disturbing consequence. It may mean that there could be a being more powerful than God. For religious believers who think God is unsurpasable, this outcome is unacceptable.

Addressing this problem has led some theists to take a new look at the task of conceiving of the divine attributes in general, and divine power in particular. Let us return to the warning label at the beginning of this section: some philosophers have protested against what they see as the exultation of sheer power. Consider Rush Rhees' observation:

> Suppose you had to explain to someone who had no idea at all of religion or of what belief in God was. Could you do it in this way? By proving to him that there must be a first cause – a something – and that this something is more powerful (whatever this means) than anything else: so that you would not have been conceived or born at all but for the operation of Something, and Something might wipe out the existence of everything at any time? Would this give him any sense of the wonder and glory of God? Would he not be justified if he answered, "What a horrible idea! Like a Frankenstein without limits, so that you cannot escape it. The most ghastly nightmare!" (Rhees 1969, p. 112)

While until now we have considered philosophical projects that use the concept of power to measure and test the concept of God, what about enlisting the concept of God to measure and shape a concept of power? Rather than cast an analysis of God and omnipotence as shown in the Concept of Omnipotence display (p. 72), some philosophers and theologians are exploring ways in which both concepts are intertwined. The result may be pictured as follows:

73

The concept of power ↔ The concept of God

The next section considers philosophies of God that work with this model.

Perfect Power

As stated above, in an effort to redress the power–value relation in the analysis of omnipotence, some philosophers urge that we reconsider the motivation for ascribing any excellences or great-making qualities to God. George Schlesinger and Thomas Morris, among others, contend that the rationale behind ascribing great-making qualities to God is to make explicit the emphatic, central belief that God is perfect or maximally excellent. In their view, the religious and philosophical allure of the idea of God is, in part, that it is the idea of a being that has all of the greatest properties or attributes. The expression that is sometimes used to express this essential feature of the Divine is that God has *the greatest compossible set of properties*. On this schema, two properties are compossible if they can both be instantiated simultaneously by the same being. If God's being perfectly good in any way limits God's being all-powerful, it does so only in a fashion that, overall, contributes to the excellence of God. According to Morris and Shlesinger, God would be less great, less worthy of worship if God could commit evil. Schlesinger writes:

> The remarkable predicate "absolutely perfect" has the unique feature that it contains, and thus by itself implies, all the other predicates traditionally ascribed to God. In proclaiming the existence of an absolutely perfect, or the greatest possible being, the theist offers a complete description of the deity thus postulated. The theist's brief statement, that his object of worship exemplifies a maximally consistent set of great-making properties, enables us in principle to determine for any property P, whether this Deity does or does not possess P . . . Suppose there is a P such that it is advantageous to have it up to, but not beyond, a certain degree. Obviously then, a perfect being will have P but not to higher than the desired degree. It would surely be a mistake to regard a being as inferior, simply because it possessed P less than to its full measure. For, on the contrary, it is a mark of perfection to have P just to the degree it is excellence-enhancing and no more. (Schlesinger 1987, p. 539)

The result of this emphasis on divine excellence leads to an analysis of omnipotence that is part of an overall philosophy of God. The following two-stage analysis reflects Schlesinger's and Morris's outlook.

74

Analysis 4

(i) *Being, B, is omnipotent if and only if it possesses perfect or supremely excellent power.*

(ii) *Being, B, possesses perfect or supremely excellent power if and only if there is no other being that could have a greater scope of power and possess a greater compossible set of excellent properties.*

By focusing on excellence and perfection, Morris and Schlesinger have brought to light a feature of religious concepts of God that has been obscured by some academic writers who conceive of maximal power shorn of an ethical context. While there have been periods of religious development in which God is thought of in terms of sheer power, there is also a lively important tradition in which divine power is thought of in terms of sheer goodness, supreme excellence and greatness.

Morris and Schlesinger describe their position as a revival of the religious philosophy of St. Anselm of Canterbury (1033–1109) for whom God's unsurpassable excellence was the chief point of reference. Commenting on Anselm's depiction of God as "that than which no greater can be conceived," Morris highlights the centrality of this conviction in elucidating the concept God:

> This core conception of deity is both very general and at the same time highly focused. It does not explicitly give us many specifics concerning God, hence its generality. But it provides a single focus for all our reflections about divinity, one point of light to guide all our thinking about the nature of God. The idea of God as the greatest possible being is not itself a full-blown conception of deity; rather, it is more like the main element in a recipe for cooking up our idea of God in detail. (Morris 1991, p. 35)

"Cooking up" concepts of God here may suggest this is an easy formula to follow; merely by invoking values and greatness one has not thereby conjured up a rigorous way to assess values. The point here, though, is that by taking on board a concern with values and goodness at the outset the analysis of power is then relocated away from the analysis of just the sheer ability to do things. On this view, not *every* ability to do something should be considered worthy of divine power.

This Anselmian shift of attention away from bare power has been heralded by some feminist and social critics of monotheism as a healthy departure from what has been described as a lurid male-based celebration of a power that only too quickly promotes oppressive, suffocating pictures of the Divine. Contrast the following point by Dorothee Soelle with a sample of analytical philosophy on omnipotence. Soelle questions the desirability of building a notion of God on the basis of a concept of power:

> As a woman I have to ask why it is that human beings honor a God whose most important attribute is power, whose prime need is to subjugate, whose greatest fear is equality. . . . Why should we honor and love a being that does not transcend but only reaffirms the moral level of our present male dominated culture? Why should we honor and love this being . . . if this being is in fact no more than an outsized man? (Soelle 1984, p. 97)

Consider the following philosophical criticism of a definition of omnipotence. The author criticizes an analysis of omnipotence because it would identify a being as omnipotent even if it lacked certain powers. Such a being not only does not but *cannot* do many things (murder, rape) that ordinary humans can do! Such a being has no claim at all to being judged omnipotent (Carter 1985, p. 54 [emphasis Carter]). Some philosophers may well concede the point and then bid good riddance to any claims about omnipotence, or God, that would make God defective if God failed to be able to rape, or made omnipotence desirable if murder and rape had to fall within its scope.

The Anselmian strategy receives support from a theory of agency once popular in ancient and medieval philosophy that still has defenders today. Although they differed in their development of the theory, Socrates, Plato, and Aristotle all held that when an agent does something intentionally, the agent must be motivated to bring about something that the agent him or herself conceives of as good or, putting the point more modestly, the agent does not conceive of as purely evil. The wicked murderer must somehow convince him or herself that the killing is not completely unjustified, e.g. the murderer may employ a profoundly disfigured concept of justice. In so many evil atrocities in history one can detect a host of rationalizations designed to justify the action. It may well be that human nature and moral laws are such that we cannot completely disguise from ourselves a certain level of moral knowledge and thus we cannot avoid self-conscious guilt feelings, but that does not always prevent us from at least trying to concoct some account to explain and excuse our evil acts while we shield our gaze from their evil character. Mary Midgley's account of motivation and agency backs up this position:

> Suppose, for example, that someone admits that he has murdered a total stranger, and when asked for his motive says, "I just thought he would look

better without his head." If he says no more, it is a motiveless crime, which does not mean that anybody doubts his word. He has named a precipitating cause, but not a motive. Even if he convinces us that he really did have that feeling, that it was very strong, and in fact determined his action, that he has had it before, and has always killed, or tried to kill, in consequence, these may be interesting and important facts about him, but they do not explain his act. At best they give quite incomplete causal explanations, by linking an isolated act with an isolated feeling, as people ignorant of electricity may link lightning with thunder. But they do not give the special sort of explanation which a motive gives. (Midgley 1984, p. 142)

On this view, for a reason to be recognized as truly motivating an action it must be possible to describe it intelligibly as, in some way, worth pursuing, however twisted or wicked the action might be.

If this value-based view of motivation is accepted it would provide a further reason to articulate a value-based understanding of divine power. But even if it is granted that persons may pursue what they know to be evil, this does not mean that one should recognize these capacities as divine powers. The point of this revival of Anselmianism is to reverse the trend of overhauling and critiquing the concept of God to fit some boundless notion of power and to insist instead that the only power that deserves to be considered divine or perfect is a power to do good. Anselm treated talk of the power to do evil acts such as "the power to lie" or "the power to be subject to corruption" as not genuine powers at all. The power to do evil

is not power, but impotence. For, he who is capable of these things is capable of what is not for his own good, and of what he ought not to do; and the more capable of them he is, the more power have adversity and perversity against him; and the less has he himself against these. (Anselm, trans. 1962, pp. 12–13)

Aquinas adopted a similar approach:

To sin is to fall short of a perfect action; hence to be able to sin is to be able to fall short in action, which is repugnant to omnipotence. Therefore it is that God cannot sin, because of his omnipotence. (Aquinas, trans. 1947, *Summa Theologica*: I, 25, 3; referred to hereafter as *ST*).

Such a philosophy of God explicitly builds a concept of goodness into the concept of "perfect action" and "omnipotence." If it is accepted, then claims that there can be a being more powerful than the God of Judaism, Christianity, and Islam (namely one that can do boundless good as well as boundless evil), can be placed to one side as entangled in defective, corrupt notions of power.

An analogy from the philosophy of law may be useful. Some (but not all) jurists in what is called the natural law tradition contend that the very concept of law is linked with the concept of justice so that, strictly speaking, there cannot be unjust laws. In order for a rule to be worthy of being considered a law it must be worthy of being considered just. On this view, a rule backed by sanctions (threats of punishment for disobedience) that required some profound injustice, such as racial segregation, would not be deemed worthy of being called a law. A racist "law" would be a law in name only; racist rules may be institutionalized and conventionally (and conveniently) referred to as laws but they fail to be proper laws. Martin Luther King, Jr held this position. In his famous *Letter from the Birmingham City Jail* he justified his active nonviolent, civil disobedience on the grounds that the segregation "laws" he was protesting against and breaking were not proper laws. In a sense, Anselmians have sought to do for the concept of divine power what King and others have sought to do for the concept of state power and jurisdiction (see question 13 at the end of this chapter).

The Anselmian philosophy of God – and all the alternatives that accord different powers to God – are all designed to provide an articulate framework for the religious belief that our cosmos is a creation. In Judaism, Christianity, and Islam, the cosmos is radically dependent upon God's creative power. While the Anselmian view of divine power may (or may not) bypass some of the conceptual and ethical problems of other analyses reviewed in this chapter, all extant theistic efforts to understand God's power still face what some philosophers believe is a devastating problem. It is objected that the very concept of divine power and character rests on a fundamental flaw: the concept of God as a nonphysical being is itself either empty of content or an outright absurdity.

Consider the final passage of the entry "God and the Philosophers" in *The Oxford Companion to Philosophy*:

> There is . . . the problem of how a purely spiritual being could be contacted, and how he (or she or it) could interfere in the universe. Suppose I suffer from an inoperable brain tumor and pray to God for a cure. If God is physical he might hear my prayer and send healing rays, unavailable to earthly physicians, that would break up the tumor. But how could a disembodied mind hear me in the first place, and, if he could, how could he, not being physical, apply the force that would send the rays into my brain? More basically, how could a pure mind create the physical universe, or for that matter how could he create anything at all?

We may well add: Is it even possible for there to be a nonphysical reality, divine or not? The next chapter addresses these difficulties.

(1) In considering candidates for maximal power, is it more reasonable to think that such a candidate would be an intentional agent rather than not? You may wish to assess the following proposal for thinking that the supreme power of an individual agent is a more promising model for analyzing the concept of omnipotence than one that does not. All descriptions of what may be produced by a power that does not involve intentions can be described as the possible effects of deliberate intentional power, but it is not clear whether the reverse is true. Take any list of powerful, and yet impersonal, nonintentional forces or events. This might include cosmic big bangs, indefinitely many micro-particle movements, and so on. What would be more powerful? *A being that is able deliberately to choose to make any of these as well as indefinitely other things at will.* We might well conceive of force fields, big bangs, and so on capable of producing a cosmos like our own or any number of different cosmic systems, but we would then face the question of whether the force field (or whatever) could do so by deliberate choice. If it is not able to choose which states of affairs to bring about, then presumably its power would be a function of chance and/or necessity. This seems less powerful than a being that can be credited with selecting when and how something comes about, a being that is able to choose when to create and when not to create, and a being that knows when to act in a way that allows for chance and when not to.

(2) Critically assess the following argument by J. L. Mackie:

> Can an omnipotent being make things which he cannot control? It is clear that this is a paradox; the question cannot be answered satisfactorily either in the affirmative or in the negative. If we answer "Yes" it follows that if God actually makes things which he cannot control, he is not omnipotent once he has made them: there are then things which he cannot do. But if we answer "No" we are immediately asserting that there are things which he cannot do, that is to say that he is already not omnipotent. (Mackie 1955, p. 210)

(3) Analyze the following: If God is all-powerful, God can create a stone that none can lift. If God is all-powerful, God can lift any stone. But then it

follows that God is not all-powerful, for either God cannot create a stone that none can lift (because God can lift any stone), or God cannot lift any stone (because God could make a stone that none, including God, can lift).

(4)   Could God be self-created? Consider the following argument by Gilbert Fulmer that no God or god can be responsible for the laws of nature:

> For if the god can impose his will on the world, it is a natural law that whatever he wills, occurs. That is, it is a fact of the universe that if god wills X, then X is the case; for example, if he wills that $e = mc^2$, it is so. And this fact cannot itself be the product of the god's will; for if it were not a fact, his will could produce no effects whatever – and to make his will effective would be to produce an effect. The fact that events occur as he wills them cannot be the result of his will. Thus this fact is logically more fundamental than the god's choices: his acts presuppose this fact, but not the converse . . . It is logically impossible that any agent could stand above and control the whole of nature, because his very power to act would be a fact which was not the result of personal agency, and hence natural. Therefore the being himself would be a part of nature: he would be subject, as are we all, to natural law. Thus the animistic belief that nature could be the work of a supernatural creator cannot be correct; the concept of such a being is incoherent. (Fulmer 1977, pp. 114–16)

(5)   Could an omnipotent being alter the past once it has occurred? Can there be a being so powerful that it has created the laws of logic? Would a God that could make itself cease-to-be be more powerful than a God that cannot?

(6)   Is it conceptually absurd to think there could be a being more powerful than God, as traditionally conceived? What difference does the answer to such a question make philosophically or religiously? How would you philosophically analyze this claim from the Christian New Testament: "For with God nothing will be impossible." (Luke 1:37, RSV)

(7)   Michael Martin has advanced a series of difficulties for the analysis of omnipotence. Can God bring about a state of affairs as follows: "Hidden Valley's being flooded is brought about directly or indirectly by a being that has never been omniscient" (Martin 1990, p. 309). Assuming that God has been omniscient at some time, how could God bring about the state of affairs Martin describes? God could not directly bring it about by a sheer act of creation, nor could God indirectly bring it about through creating indefinitely many intermediaries. How might a theist reply? Consider one possible strategy. Martin's puzzle is artificially generated by describing, not so much *an action*, but *an actor*. In reference to Martin's description, the state of affairs that should be considered relevant when assessing a being's scope of power is

whether or not she or he can flood a valley, not whether this can be done by someone with, say, knowledge of a nineteenth-century artist or in possession of only one ear or three eyes. If the focus is on the act, the puzzle disolves. God *can* flood the valley. Unless one somehow distinguishes between actor and act, then counter-examples to the claim that God is omnipotent can be generated with the greatest of ease. One can simply concoct the following state of affairs: *an event that is not created directly or indirectly by God.* If, in order to be omnipotent, God must be able to create such an event, then God cannot be omnipotent.

(8)   Can there be more than one omnipotent being? You may wish to consider this question in light of the different analyses of omnipotence that are developed in this chapter. For example, does Analysis 3 allow that there could be two omnipotent beings that have matching power?

(9)   Can a free action of yours be truly your act as well as an event that God chose to come about? Why or why not?

(10)   If God is omnipotent, must God be omniscient?

(11)   If God is omnipotent, could God know this? How could a being know that it can do anything whatever?

(12)   Do you think the power to do evil should be treated as a distinctive power separable from the power to do good? You may wish to analyze this in terms of literary representations of evil. Consider, for example, Shakespeare's Richard III or Iago or Milton's Satan in *Paradise Lost*. Richard, Iago, and Satan seem like powerful agents. Do they possess a power that an essentially (that is, necessarily) good God does not?

(13)   In this chapter the Anselmian view of divine power was compared with a theory of law to the effect that the concepts of law and justice are intertwined. An interesting paper could be written on the concept of omnipotence and the concept of law, drawing on the debate between those who embrace natural law (some of whom hold that an unjust law is not a law) and legal positivism (an account of law that resists the conceptual link between law and justice). See, for example, work by H. L. A. Hart, Lon Fuller, Ronald Dworkin, Joseph Raz, and John Finnis.

(14)   How important is it from a religious point of view to achieve a correct philosophical analysis of the divine attributes? Imagine that two members of the same religion agree that God is omnipotent, but they adopt different philosophical analyses of this divine attribute. What is the religious significance of this, if any? You may wish to consider this question in relation to the analyses of omnipotence discussed in this chapter.

(15)   When do doubts about discovering an adequate analysis of Divine

attributes amount to doubts that there is a divine being possessing these attributes? Consider the following statement by Kai Nielsen: "I am in doubt about the proper analysis of 'physical object' but in no doubt whatsoever about whether there are sticks and stones; however, in the religious case I am in doubt both about the proper analysis of 'God' and about whether there actually is or even could be such a reality" (Nielsen 1973, p. 29). Could a religious believer find him or herself in a similar position – in no doubt that there is a God but in doubt about the proper analysis of "God"?

(15)   In the religious literature of Judaism, Christianity or Islam, do you think the word "God" functions more like a descriptive title (e.g. "Creator") or a proper name? What are the implications of this, if any, for developing a philosophy of God?

Further Reading and Considerations

From *A Companion to Philosophy of Religion*, the following entries are relevant: "Omnipotence," "Personalism," "Divine Action," "Creation and Conservation," "Perfect Goodness." For further reading on omnipotence, see especially "The Definition of Omnipotence" by A. Kenny and "Maximal Power" by T. Flint and A. J. Freddoso, both reprinted in *The Concept of God* edited by Morris.

For further reflection on the goodness of God, Scott MacDonald's anthology, *Being and Goodness*, is highly recommended. Richard Swinburne defends the position that God's being rational, free, omnipotent, and omniscient, entails God's being a good moral agent, in *The Coherence of Theism*. Spinoza and Leibniz also thought the rationality of God prohibited God from doing evil. In this chapter I include Aristotle among those (Plato, Socrates) who think one cannot intentionally do that which one judges to be a thoroughly evil act. On this view, some kind of self-justification (and perhaps self-deception) enters the wrongdoer's view of the matter. This construal of Aristotle's position is based on a common reading of Aristotle but he is also often taken as holding that one can in fact perform what one explicitly and fully conceives to be an evil action. For a useful anthology on this topic see *Weakness of Will* edited by G. Mortimore. Further readings on God and values are suggested at the end of chapter 7. For a biting description of self-creation, see Friedrich Nietzsche's *Beyond Good and Evil*, part one, section 21.

4

Materialism, Positivism, and God

Naturalism refers to an account of the cosmos according to which there is no God, no powerful, immaterial divine force responsible for the existence of the universe. Most naturalists therefore judge religious beliefs about a spiritual world of higher power and intelligence as sheer human projections. Kai Nielsen characterizes naturalism in terms that explicitly rule out traditional theism:

> Naturalism denies that there are any spiritual or supernatural realities. There are, that is, no purely mental substances and there are no supernatural realities transcendent to the world or at least we have no good ground for believing that there are such realities or perhaps even for believing that there could be such realities. It is the view that anything that exists is ultimately composed of physical components. (Nielsen 1997, p. 402; see also Nielsen 1996)

Humans may posit powerful, invisible realities out of ignorance, fear, compassion or any number of other motivations. But, if naturalists are right, all such conjectures are ultimately unjustified.

The debate between naturalism and its alternatives will be considered at various places in this book. This chapter focuses on a specific, substantive naturalist claim that religious beliefs about a nonphysical, transcendent reality are either contradictory or empty of content. This charge is based on two, closely related positions that make up a robust form of naturalism widely represented since the Second World War: materialism and positivism. Materialism is a theory of what exists and positivism a theory of what can be known.

In brief, some materialists charge that there cannot in principle be anything

83

nonmaterial. Because God (and other transcendent realities such as Brahman) is supposed to be nonmaterial, God does not exist. In this chapter we shall consider in some detail two forms of materialism that fuel this argument: eliminative materialism and essential materialism.

Positivism follows naturally from certain assumptions about the nature of the material world and our powers of knowledge. According to a strong version of positivism, claims that are supposed to be factual should, in principle, be empirically confirmable or falsifiable. Any claims about the world or God that cannot be verified or falsified by empirical data, at least in principle, are empty of meaningful content and therefore to be dismissed as nonsense. Positivists allow for the intelligibility of abstract, logical propositions like "Triangles are three sided" and the statements of mathematics, but because religious assertions such as "God is everywhere," "God is nonphysical," "There is no God but Allah," "Krishna is an avatar of Vishnu," and so on, are neither abstract, logical claims nor (according to positivists) statements capable of being confirmed by empirical evidence, they are meaningless. What experience could possibly vindicate that God is nonphysical? Positivists judge traditional religious beliefs about God to be on the same footing as "Time is unreal," and "Invisible, intangible spirits roam the earth caring for gardens." We may verify the existence of straightforward physical objects and processes, but when it comes to mapping and verifying a nonphysical realm, we appear to be in far worse shape. A. J. Ayer compares the meaning of religious assertions with the following case of apparent nonsense:

> Suppose I suggest "There is a 'drogulus' over there," and you say "What?" and I say "Drogulus," and you say "What's a drogulus?" Well I say "I can't describe what a drogulus is, because it's not the sort of thing you can see or touch, it has no physical effects of any kind, but it's a disembodied being." And you say, "Well how am I to tell if it's there or not?" and I say "There's no way of telling. Everything's just the same if it's there or it's not there. But the fact is it's there. There's a drogulus there standing behind you, spiritually behind you." Does that make sense? (Ayer and Copleston 1965, p. 747)

Ayer thinks it does not. The general positivist strategy is to propose that traditional religious hypotheses fail to make sense because, unlike our language about the material world, they are impervious to evidence.

In addressing this naturalist critique, let us first consider the problems facing theism that stem principally from materialism, and then take into account its closely related theory of knowledge and meaning, positivism. As noted earlier, the two materialist positions that challenge religious belief in a

84

nonphysical, transcendent reality are eliminative materialism and essential materialism. Let us consider eliminativism first.

Eliminative Materialism and God

According to eliminative materialism, there are only material objects, properties, and processes, and there are no mental realities whatsoever. On this view, what many of us describe as mental states (thoughts, feelings, and sensations) are highly useful ascriptions for everyday activity and discourse but, in reality, they do not refer to anything that actually exists. Such so-called mental entities can be eliminated from a comprehensive, exhaustive account of ourselves and the world. What we call "pain," for example, is really certain neural activity. For an early statement of eliminativism, note Richard Rorty's claim:

> The absurdity of saying "Nobody has ever felt a pain" is no greater than that of saying "Nobody has ever seen a demon," if we have a suitable answer to the question "What was I reporting when I said I felt a pain?" To this question, the science of the future may reply "You were reporting the occurrence of a certain brain process, and it would make life simpler for us if you would, in the future, say "My C-fibres are firing," instead of saying "I'm in pain." (Rorty 1965, p. 30)

If eliminative materialism is accepted, "old-fashioned" talk of pain may be retained for practical purposes, but it is difficult to sustain meaningful reference to such entities in our theories of reality. Eliminative materialism creates a radical break between our ordinary, practical conception of life and our theories of existence. It also seems to leave the theistic notion of God out in the cold. As William Alston observes about the traditional notion of God as an agent: "Some significant carry-over from concepts of human action to concepts of divine action is required for us to make full-blooded attributions of particular actions to God" (Alston 1994, p. 43). If eliminativists are right, then there is nothing at the base of our descriptions of human life to carry over to the task of thinking about God.

A fully-fledged, systematic exploration of eliminative materialism would require a separate book and therefore cannot be managed here. It will have to suffice to consider the issues in only very general terms with the aim of stimulating further reflection.

Some of the reasons for adopting eliminative materialism are impressive. Its strongest suit lies in the advantage of bolstering a unified theory of science. Science faces a crucial obstacle in linking the mental and the physical. How do

85

we put on a single scale the appeal to *desires* and straightforward material processes like *molecules in motion* in the course of explaining events? It appears that desires do enter into explanations of why things occur; indeed, much of the study of history that appeals to desires and beliefs would have no explanatory role if eliminativism were true. But wanting to have them in the picture is one thing, and having a unified conceptual framework in which to formulate a comprehensive account of the events in the world is another. If one can get on without positing disparate mental phenomena, then there are surely some advantages to doing so, at least from the standpoint of scientific theory.

The history of science also provides some reason to take eliminative materialism seriously. Stephen Stich underscores the advance of the sciences in dismantling our ordinary notions of reality and in clearing the way for more respectable scientific notions. Just as a great deal of embedded "common sense" has given way to scientific advance, we should be prepared to jettison or eliminate our prevailing notions of the mental, what Stich calls "folk psychology."

> Folk astronomy was false astronomy and not just in detail. The general conception of the cosmos embedded in the folk wisdom of the West was utterly and thoroughly mistaken. Much the same could be said for folk biology, folk chemistry, and folk physics. However wonderful and imaginative folk theorizing and speculation has been, it has turned out to be screamingly false in every domain where we now have a reasonably sophisticated science. Nor is there any reason to think that ancient camel drivers would have greater insight or better luck when the subject at hand was the structure of their own minds rather than the structure of matter or of the cosmos. (Stich 1983, pp. 229–30)

Stich and other eliminativists see themselves as clearing the ground for future advances in the sciences, for eliminativists seek to prepare the way for scientific theories that are not held hostage to conventional "common sense."

Fortunately for theists and other proponents of a religious ultimate nonphysical reality, the case for eliminativism has not, or has not yet, been developed in a way that, in the estimation of most philosophers, is either necessarily true, or true at all. Most defenders of eliminativism concede that the burden of proof is on them. It at least *appears* as though we possess a mental life with beliefs, desires, pain and pleasure, and if so then it seems reasonable to assume that substantial reasons need to be brought forward to overturn the presumption in favor of recognizing mental life. In the absence of such reasons, some *non*eliminativist theory appears to be preferable. I cite two difficulties that critics raise against eliminativism along with references to the literature for further study.

Eliminativism is at radical odds with evident common experience (Searle 1992; G. Strawson 1995). This position is advanced by many opponents of eliminativism, who think of it as decisive. Colin McGinn is a staunch defender of materialism but he is convinced that any account of human nature must not eliminate the fact of consciousness and its apparent dissimilarity from physical things and processes:

> The property of consciousness itself (or specific conscious states) is not an observable or perceptible property of the brain. You can stare into a living conscious brain, your own or someone else's, and see there a wide variety of instantiated properties – its shape, colour, texture, etc. – but you will not thereby see what the subject is experiencing, the conscious state itself. (McGinn 1990, pp. 10–11)

McGinn insists that eliminativism is in radical tension with what is demonstrably clear in experience. Eliminativism would have us avoid these questions that McGinn thinks we must face, however hard: "How is it possible for conscious states to depend upon brain states? . . . How could the aggregation of millions of individually insentient neurons generate subjective awareness?" (McGinn 1990, p. 1).

Eliminativists like Patricia Churchland challenge us to consider whether persons are, in the ordinary sense of the words, ever aware of anything. "It is possible that the folk theory that gives 'awareness' its meaning might turn out to be displaced by a superior theory. Accordingly, just as it turned out that there was no such thing as impetus, there may be no such thing as awareness" (Patricia Churchland 1986, p. 309). But, so the objection from common experience goes, is not the apparent fact that we are aware of things so evident that giving it up would require enormously powerful arguments and empirical data? In the eyes of many of its critics, the prospects of accumulating such support is either inconceivable or profoundly unlikely.

Eliminativism cannot be coherently stated. To state the position requires the use of mental terms. To claim that one believes there are no beliefs or feels there are no feelings is untenable. If there are no beliefs one cannot believe there are no beliefs (Danto 1983 and Baker 1987). Some eliminativists reply that such an objection may be inevitable but it merely signals the fact that, eventually, we have to abandon talk of belief and other folk talk altogether in our scientific theories. We may not at present have the proper vocabulary to describe ourselves and the world; the proper reductive vocabulary is still taking shape (Paul Churchland 1981, p. 89).

In all, what troubles philosophical critics is the vast distance between what appears to be the intelligibility of our belief-desire, mental vocabulary and the starkness of eliminativism. Hilary Putnam summarizes a widely-held response to the prospects of an eliminativist program that successfully dispenses with the mental: "I would only say that until this program is more than a gleam in the eyes of some scientific realists, I do not myself expect it to succeed" (Putnam 1988, pp. 70–1).

Unfortunately, space does not permit a further review of the fascinating moves and counter-moves in this debate. For a defense of different versions of eliminativism, consider work by Paul Churchland (1981), Stich (1983, though note his second thoughts in 1996) and sections of Dennett (1978, 1987, 1991a). At the present stage in the philosophy of mind, eliminativism can be recognized as an important challenge to theistic and other nonphysical notions of God, but one that has yet to be supported sufficiently to command a great following. The challenge of *essential materialism* has been more widely endorsed.

Essential Materialism and God

Essential materialism, as the term is used here, is the view that there are mental realities (thoughts, feelings, desires, and the like), but they are physical and there *cannot be anything nonphysical*. Thoughts, feelings, desires and the like exist but they are either identical with or composed of material objects and processes (the brain or the physical body and its processes as a whole). Using the possible world terminology introduced in the last chapter, according to this theory there is no possible world in which there are immaterial things whether these be God, gods, angels or disembodied thoughts and feelings.

If essential materialism is true, then the description of a nonphysical agent, be it omnipotent or possessing any power at all, is incoherent, no matter how embellished. H. D. Lewis compared the problem facing theists with the following plight. Imagine that the notion of there being a nonphysical agentive reality is in the same category as other clear contradictions like "there being a square circle":

Suppose I were to tell a story about a square circle. There clearly can be no such entity, but I might go on to say who invented this curious object, what his early struggles were like and so forth, I might say how the square circle was lost at one time and what crusades and pilgrimages were undertaken to recover it, what battles were lost and won, what fortunes made and forfeited. This story might be told with more liveliness by some than by others, some would give it more colour and romance, some would tell it with much more intelligence and consistency than others and with a profounder understanding of human nature. But at the heart of it all there would be utter nonsense, for we cannot even conceive of anything being square and round in the same respect. (H. D. Lewis 1965, p. 71)

If essential materialism is plausible, then this places tremendous pressure on those who uphold traditional theism.

Paul Edwards presents a version of essential materialism in the following analysis of theism. By his lights, theism rests on a radical mistake in construing God as bodiless:

I have no doubt that when most people think about God and his alleged activities, here or in the hereafter, they vaguely think of him as possessing some kind of rather large body. Now if we are told that there is a God who is, say, just and good and kind and loving and powerful and wise and if, (a) it is made clear that these words are used in one of their ordinary senses, and (b) God is not asserted to be a disembodied mind; then it seems plain to me that *to that extent* a series of meaningful assertions has been made. And this is so whether we are told that God's justice, mercy, etc., are "limitless" or merely that God is superior to all human beings in these respects. However, it seems to me that all these words lose their meaning if we are told that God does not possess a body. Anyone who thinks otherwise without realizing this I think is supplying a body in the background of his images. For what would it be like to be, say, just without a body? To be just, a person has to *act* justly – he has to behave in certain ways. This is not reductive materialism. It is a simple empirical truth about what we mean by "just". But how is it possible to perform these acts, to behave in the required ways without a body? Similar remarks apply to the other divine attributes. (Edwards 1961, pp. 242–3)

Edwards is not, then, an eliminativist but he contends that the very nature of action, justice and so on, must ultimately be understood in bodily, material terms. A nonphysical, just agent is not a meaningful description.

Martin provides a forceful statement of the problem facing theists, echoing some of Edwards' criticism:

If one interprets God as a nonspatial, nontemporal being without a body, what sense can one make of God's performing a speech act? . . . The existence of a voice issuing commands seems to presume some physical vocal apparatus; golden letters written in the sky would seem to presuppose some physical writing appendage. However, this understanding of God assumes anthropomorphism rejected by sophisticated theologians today. (Martin 1990, p. 11)

Martin argues that this problem is not merely a contingent one, but necessary. We simply cannot bridge the physical–nonphysical gap in the way that theists need to:

Statements about experientially transcendent entities cannot be constructed from an observational language in terms of the experience of humans and other embodied beings, nor can they be confirmed relative to such a language. (Martin 1990, p. 64)

The broader worry is that theists and others will wind up with descriptions that turn out to be pseudo-descriptions, descriptions initially thought to make sense, but that we later observe are without content. Religious believers sometimes claim that God speaks, but if speech requires the possession of a body then these believers must also claim that God possesses a body. If that is intolerable, then they may withdraw either the claim that God speaks or the claim that there is a God.

Positivism and the Divine Activity

As noted earlier, the challenge of positivism is often linked to the case for materialism. In a material universe it appears that the world is open to public inspection. By comparison, a nonphysical reality seems to be not just unobservable but possibly of no intelligible substance whatsoever. Recall A. J. Ayer's description of the drogulus cited at the outset of this chapter. Lacking a body, its supposed location and activity begins to look suspect. Kai Nielsen takes aim at religious claims such as "God governs the world":

If "God governs the world" did have . . . significance, it would have to have a different empirical content than does "It's not the case that God governs the world" or "God does not govern the world" and the like. Note that the nonbeliever might very well accept the believer's claim about human love, a sense of the numinous, a concern for social justice and the incidence of commitment to human solidarity, and still not see how this gives us grounds for believing in God. (Nielsen 1971, p. 63)

If God were a physical reality then it would be possible in principle to identify God's activities; there would be grounds for articulating the empirical content of "God governs the world." But the concept of God as a nonphysical being places religious belief beyond our reach.

Antony Flew raises a similar problem, focusing on the theistic claim that God is loving:

> Now it often seems to people who are not religious as if there was no conceivable event or series of events the occurrence of which would be admitted by sophisticated religious people to be a sufficient reason for conceding "There wasn't a God after all" or "God does not really love us then." Someone tells us that God loves us as a father loves his children. We are reassured. But then we see a child dying of inoperable cancer of the throat. His earthly father is driven frantic in his efforts to help, but his Heavenly Father reveals no obvious sign of concern. Some qualification is made – God's love is "not a merely human love" or it is "an inscrutable love," perhaps – and we realize that such sufferings are quite compatible with the truth of the assertion that "God loves us as a father (but, of course . . .)." We are reassured again. But then perhaps we ask: what is this assurance of God's (appropriately qualified) love worth, what is this apparent guarantee really a guarantee against? Just what would have to happen not merely (morally and wrongly) to tempt but also (logically and rightly) to entitle us to say "God does not love us" or even "God does not exist'? I therefore put . . . the simply central questions, "What would have to occur or to have occurred to constitute for you a disproof of the love of, or of the existence of, God?" (Flew, in Flew and MacIntyre [eds] 1955, pp. 98–9)

Some religious believers treat faith as a virtue because of its resilience. But if Flew is right, religious faith may be so sturdy because it cannot in principle be shown up as false. And if it cannot be shown up as false, this may be because, at base, it is meaningless.

William Rowe provides the following summation of the naturalist case, combining a concern for the implications of believing God is nonphysical and for the prospects of verifying descriptions of God:

> One major difficulty with the view that terms which seem to designate mental activities (forgiving or loving) can be applied to God in their primary or literal sense is that the ways in which we tell whether an individual is forgiving or just do include bodily behavior – what she or he says and how she or he behaves.

How then does one determine that a purely immaterial being has performed an act of forgiveness? (Rowe 1993, p. 100)

Consider together the various properties that Edwards, Martin, Nielsen, Flew, and Rowe think are problematic for theists. The following traits and activities are singled out by these philosophers as requiring either being a physical body or having a physical body. In the absence of any bodily life, it appears that one is left with something that is either conceptually absurd or empty of any meaningful content:

Just	Performing a speech act
Merciful	Issuing commands
Good	Operating in space and time
Wise	Governing the world
Powerful	Being the object of human love
Kind	Forgiving
Loving	

How do theists respond to this materialist–verificationist challenge?

Theistic Replies to Essential Materialism

Theists have developed a series of replies to essential materialism and positivism. First consider a direct challenge to the claim that essential materialism is true. The more ambitious theistic response has been to take issue with essential materialism directly. Essential materialists maintain that our ordinary mental terms require reference to bodily life to be meaningful. Just as jumping or swimming require having a body, so do being just, merciful, and so on. Some philosophers, both theists and nontheists, have argued that even in our own case it is not clear whether either our identity or nature is exclusively bodily or whether our physical constitution is even necessary for us to carry out certain mental activities (Robinson 1982; Swinburne 1986; Hart 1988; Foster 1991). On this view, not only does it make sense to think God is immaterial, but it is also perfectly sensible to think *we* are immaterial (as a soul or as conscious beings) albeit we are thoroughly embodied. This view of human persons is called *substantive dualism*. If substantive dualism is right, then there is a fundamental distinction between the mind (person or self) and the physical world.

One way to fill out the substantive dualist picture would be to imagine for oneself the possibility of disembodiment or re-embodiment. This project will be further tested in chapter 7 when discussing different portraits of the afterlife. For now, a brief sketch of what is at stake will have to suffice. W. H. Hudson enjoins us to imagine a person, Smith, independent of his present, physical embodiment. Can you imagine yourself "stepping back" in the way Hudson describes?

> There is always a logical gap between an agent as such and what may be called his situation. Suppose Smith's situation is that he is bankrupt. It makes sense to ask Smith, "What are you going to do about your bankruptcy?" The idea of Smith, the agent, "stepping back" so to speak from his situation and forming some intention as to how he will deal with it makes perfectly good sense. Now, the point to take is that exactly the same will be true if Smith's situation is that he has a broken leg or is suffering from kleptomania, for example. That is to say, Smith's body and indeed Smith's psyche can be conceived as part of Smith's situation from which as agent he is logically distinct. He, as agent, is not to be identified with his broken leg or his compulsive psychological mechanism any more than with his bankruptcy . . . Mind and body cannot (logically) be reduced either to other or both to some unifying concept. If an agent is logically distinct from his body and if the latter can be regarded as part of his situation, then why not a like parallelism between certain intentional acts of God and certain spatio-temporal events in the world? (Hudson 1974, p. 174)

This "stepping back" may well strike one as absurd, but the thought experiment that one can survive the death of one's body and either become re-embodied, be reincarnated or exist disembodied, is widely believed in many cultures to be not just intelligible in the abstract but truly what will occur to each of us (P. and L. Badham [eds] 1987).

It may prove useful to consider a description of disembodiment, a radical "stepping back" from one's material body. What follows is not a report of an actual occurrence, but a philosopher's thought experiment involving disembodiment. W. D. Hart offers the following account that trades on the phenomenon of phantom limbs. A "phantom limb" refers to the sensed presence of a leg or arm after it has been amputated. One can have an arm removed and yet feel that it is still intact, sensing the "arm" stretched out in space and so on:

> Imagine first that when you awake your arm (only) is missing, but it feels (in your phantom arm) just as if your arm were there and against the bedclothes.

Your phantom arm drifts through the mattress; but then it feels to you there (in your phantom arm) just as if your arm were there among the bits of stuffing in the mattress. Indeed, when your phantom hand drifts (drift because we have not got as far as action yet) to the surface of your phantom shoulder, there is in each a feeling as if each were there touching the other. Now generalize; instead of a phantom arm, imagine you have a phantom body. The region at least over the surface of which you are sensitive is the relevant region. So the sense of touch could survive in a disembodied person. (Hart 1988, p. 141; see also Descartes' seventeenth-century *Meditations*)

Does this account contain any evident absurdities? Many substance dualists think it does not, and their position may be supported in part by the fact that such tales of disembodiment have been widely believed across virtually all cultures (see H. D. Lewis 1973; Hick 1976; Beloff 1989; and Huby 1991). On this front, it is interesting to note that A. J. Ayer himself reported having an out-of-the-body experience (see his "What I Saw When I Was Dead," anthologized in Edwards 1992). The bare fact that something is widely believed does not give one good reason to conclude it is true, but it may be argued that the fact that so many believe something is *some* evidence that what is believed is intelligible.

Some theists who are unwilling to put all their emphasis on the truth of substance dualism argue for a more modest, open picture of human nature. According to functionalism, our mental concepts are not essentially physical. Because functionalism does not necessarily pin down the mental to the physical, theists like William Alston have used it in their defense of the coherence of believing in an immaterial God.

According to functionalism, mental terms can be characterized in terms of causal roles without making any commitment as to the kind of thing occupying the role. Functionalists will thus analyze "pain," for example, as a state that is typically brought about by certain factors such as skin laceration and gives rise to certain effects such as pain avoidance. This construction of mental states places them in a network of causal relations without requiring us to make a decision whether, say, pain is the very same thing as a certain neurological state or a nonphysical mental state brought about by physical causes. Some theists adopt a materialist view of human persons, but also defend the legitimacy of functionalism and use it to advance a case for the meaningfulness of theistic language. Thus, while they believe that talk of human intentions and feelings ultimately should be cashed out in physical, observable categories, human life could have been otherwise. On this view, we can imagine intentions and feelings that are not thoroughly physical. Alston argues as follows:

Our ordinary psychological terms carry no implications as to the intrinsic nature of the structure, its neurophysiological or soul-stuff character. No such information is embedded in our common sense psychological conceptual scheme. (Alston 1987, p. 25)

The ordinary ways of describing our mental life are thereby seen as neutral, open notions. We are free, if Alston is right, to use them in our own case and then extend them in describing the action of God or some other nonphysical agency:

Can an immaterial spiritual being perform (some of) the same psychological functions as an embodied being? Are functional psychological concepts neutral as between different sorts of physical realizations? It would seem so. If a functional concept really is noncommittal as to what kind of mechanism, structure or agency carries out the function, then it would be noncommittal as to whether this is any kind of physical agency, as well as to what kind of physical agency it is if physical. (Alston 1987, p. 30)

John Locke (1632–1704) unsettled some theologians of his day by suggesting that while substantive dualism is true and the mind is immaterial, God could make exclusively material things into thinking minds. Alston's proposal may be seen as making the opposite point. Given (if only for the sake of argument) that we are actually material beings, that alone is not enough reason for concluding that mental states and activities are so inextricably bound up with the physical that it is incoherent to posit a nonphysical being. (See suggested question 6 at the end of the chapter for Locke's claim.)

Theists contend that essential materialists need to provide a demonstration not just that it is likely that everything is physical, but that *it is impossible that there could be nonphysical beings*, and, more specifically, impossible that there could be a nonphysical God. If there is no indication at all from our own case that our mental life is *essentially* physical, then (so it is argued) theism has not been placed in serious jeopardy. Alston replies to essential materialists this way:

If God has no body to move, how can he do anything, in the sense in which an embodied human being does things? But this is not an insuperable difficulty. The core concept of human action is not movement of one's body, but rather bringing about a change in the world – directly or indirectly – by an act of will, decision, or intention. That concept can be intelligibly applied to a purely spiritual deity. It is just that we will have to think of God as bringing about

95

changes in the "external" world directly by an act of will – not indirectly moving his body, as in our case. (Alston 1987, p. 31)

Granted *our* actions involve all sorts of complex physical phenomena, is it absurd to imagine that things could have been otherwise? In the absence of reasons for thinking that material embodiment is essential for all agents imaginable, it appears that theism is not refuted by the essential materialist challenge. As Robert Oakes remarks in a defense of the thesis that God may have feelings even if God does not have any neurophysiology: "While there appears to be an *empirically invariant association* between the possession of affective capacity and the possession of a neurophysiology – experience seems to record no case of the former minus the latter – this clearly fails to entail that possessing a neurophysiology is *conceptually necessary* for possessing affective capacity" (Oakes 1990, p. 134).

Essential materialists may charge that positing a nonphysical intentional being is as incoherent as supposing there could be a smile without a face, but it is not clear whether their position can be advanced on the basis of convictions that are very widely shared. William Wainwright notes the problem that Nielsen and other critics face:

> Nielsen has failed to provide anything remotely resembling a demonstration or proof. He is, in spite of his intentions, appealing to our intuitions. This is unsatisfactory because, given the fact that most people find talk of disembodied agents intelligible, the burden of proof would appear to be upon those who maintain that it is nonsense. (Wainwright 1978, pp. 16, 17)

Consider the concept "speech." If "speech" is defined in terms of speaking with the use of a mouth, larynx, and so on, then it follows that one cannot speak without a mouth, in the same way that one cannot run without having legs. But if by "speech" one means: making sounds or causing auditions, then, some philosophers argue and many nonphilosophers would seem to agree, it is not at all clear that this requires a body. Does the sentence: *Mary heard a sound* entail that *Mary heard some material being*? Those defending a theistic view according to which God does speak to human beings would want to allow that the first statement is not incompatible with the thesis that *A nonphysical being caused Mary to hear a sound* (see Wolterstorff 1995). To rule out the latter as absolutely impossible, essential materialists will need to establish more than merely that it is difficult to conceive of an immaterial agent causing Mary to hear things.

96

Theistic Replies to Positivism

Later chapters address the debate over the evidence for and against the existence of God. Does religious experience provide evidence that God does exist
(chapter 8)? Does evil provide reasons for thinking a loving God does not
govern the universe (chapter 9)? Does the order and structure of the cosmos
provide reasons for believing there is a God (chapter 10)? But here let us
consider a more fundamental challenge to positivism. Some philosophers
contend that positivism even fails to account for the meaningfulness of our
ordinary beliefs about one another. If these philosophers are right, positivism
faces problems straight away, and not just in the context of religious
discourse.

Return again to the list of properties picked out by some positivists, such
as forgiving and loving, on p. 92. Given a standard reading of these terms,
they each appear to involve some psychological dimensions of personal life.
Thus, to forgive someone seems to involve not harboring resentment toward
them and loving another person appears to involve a readiness to take pleasure
in the good of the one loved and to be saddened by his or her ills. Surely there
are customary ways in which we seem to be able to observe the love and
forgiveness of others. But are these observations infallible? Is it possible
(however bizarre and unlikely) for all the standard evidence to be to the effect
that someone loves and forgives another person when they have done neither?
Alternatively, could someone have forgiven or loved another person even if no
evidence whatsoever is publicly observable to that effect? Granted, some cases
clearly confirm the relevant psychological properties (it would be absurd to
suppose Gandhi hated other people), but some cases seem intelligible in which
the relevant psychological attributions are not reducible to, nor clearly corre-
lated with, physical attributions, and this suggests that the physical and
psychological attributions are different in an important way.

The following case described by Thomas Nagel is designed to bring to light
the elusiveness of our mental life, over against the specifications of physical
activities and states. His particular example involves sensations, but other
cases could involve more complex emotions like love:

> How much do you really know about what goes on in anyone else's
> mind? . . . How do you know, when you and a friend are eating chocolate ice
> cream, whether it tastes the same to him as it tastes to you? You can try a taste
> of his ice cream, but if it tastes the same as yours, that only means it tastes the
> same to you: you haven't experienced the way it tastes to him. There seems to

be no way to compare the two flavors directly . . . Well, you might say that you're both human beings, and you can both distinguish among flavors of ice cream – for example you can both tell the difference between chocolate and vanilla with your eyes closed – it's likely that your flavor experiences are similar. But how do we know that? The only connection you've ever observed between a type of ice cream and a flavor is in your own case; so what reason do you have to think that similar correlations hold for other human beings? Why isn't it just as consistent with all the evidence that chocolate tastes to him the way vanilla tastes to you, and vice versa? (Nagel 1987, pp. 79, 80)

Similarly, we may well ask whether cases can arise in which we are genuinely unsure about whether another person is truly loving and forgiving. In a passage cited earlier, Rowe asks: "How then does one determine that a purely immaterial being has performed an act of forgiveness?" Might it not be the case that a demand for such evident determination is too stringent even in our own case? Imagine that Smith goes out of his way to profess that he has forgiven John Doe. Doe has wronged Smith and yet Smith does not press legal charges against Doe, and, instead, gives him a gift, and appears to invite a renewed friendship. Can we not still imagine Smith secretly harbors resentment against Doe and refuses truly to forgive him? Perhaps our material observations of one another will always fail to secure an absolutely certain, exhaustive knowledge of each other's mental states.

The nature of this quandary is much debated in the current philosophy-of-mind literature. The point to be observed here is that if cases such as Nagel's strike you as possible and his skeptical questions well formulated, then you have *some* reason to resist a thorough-going positivist philosophy which requires that *all* factual claims be publicly confirmable. On this view, an individual's awareness of herself and the world may be intact and coherently describable even though it would not pass the positivist test for meaningfulness.

So, some theists argue, if we allow that psychological feelings and states do exist and that their presence does not necessarily admit of public confirmation, why complain similarly against the theist on this point? Could it be that our ordinary mental experiences are closer to "drogulus" than A. J. Ayer thought (as cited on p. 84)? Or, recalling a comment of Martin's (cited on p. 90), could it be that even in our own case, there is something that is "transcendent," and beyond material observation?

Another major difficulty widely thought to hamper the positivist program has been the problem of elucidating the character of empirical evidence that positivism is willing to countenance. Is there a pure, clearly delineated bedrock of experience that *all parties* can agree is to serve as the final court of appeal in confirming or disconfirming factual propositions? A. J. Ayer himself allows, in principle, for the admissibility of mystical experiences. Ayer writes:

> Nor do I wish to restrict experience to sense experience. I shouldn't at all mind counting what might be called introspectable experiences or feelings; mystical experiences, if you like. (Ayer and Copleston 1965, p. 743)

Because of such concessions and the difficulty of securing a sufficiently restricted account of the limits of experience, the positivist challenge is often considered today not to be decisive even by its current proponents. Despite his forceful objection against theism cited earlier, Michael Martin considers the positivist challenge a *prima facie* objection to theism and concedes that a full case against theism needs to be built on other grounds as well (see Martin's entry, "The Verificationist Challenge," in *A Companion to Philosophy of Religion*).

The general case against positivism outside of the philosophy of religion has been substantial. A chief objection has been that if empirical confirmability was required for meaningful discourse, this would rule out much of contemporary science. How can one strictly confirm hypotheses about the origin of the cosmos or the deepest substrata of the physical cosmos (which may, if there is a deepest final level, be unobservable)? If the demand for confirmability is loosened to insisting, rather, that there be simply *some* empirical evidence, in principle, for the truth or falsehood of propositions (as opposed to evidential definitive confirmation or disconfirmation), then there seems little, in principle, to rule out more substantial metaphysical and religious positions. I cite two other objections to positivism briefly.

(A)   It is argued that the very statement of the positivist's position (that meaningful discourse about the world must admit of empirical evidence) would not satisfy the positivist's own criterion for meaningfulness. How can one have evidence that such evidence is so required? It is difficult to make out how one might verify the positivist proposal of verificationism.

In response, positivists have sometimes treated their demand for evidence as a recommendation. As Ayer puts it: "What I do is to give a definition of certain related terms: understanding, meaning, and so on. I can't force you to accept them, but I can perhaps make you unhappy about the consequences of not accepting them" (Ayer and Copleston 1965, p. 745).

(B)   Like the cases cited above concerning the elusiveness of detecting the mental states of others, it is objected that if positivism were accepted then our beliefs about the external world might all be undermined. Is it at least possible – however bizarre – that what we take to be our world of objects and persons is a huge, systematic illusion? In the theory of knowledge literature there are flamboyant stories designed to dislodge our confidence that we could not be prey to a massive illusion. Peter Unger and others have argued that we cannot rule out as absolutely impossible the idea that while we think we are awake and talking with others, we are actually the subject of a cruel experiment and electrochemically stimulated to think the world is the way it appears (see Unger 1975). If these tales are coherent, then there is reason to think that states of affairs may be described in which many of their features are undetectable by the person being deceived. Indeed some skeptical scenarios are described in which no one at all could find out whether they were deceived or not.

It is important to bear in mind that all the above objections are open for considerable debate, and none are held by all philosophers to have *demonstrated* the inadequacy of positivism. Positivism has been an important force in the twentieth century and it may have a lively role in the next. The challenge of positivism has been appreciated by many theistic and other religious believers for its challenging them to elucidate their concepts of reality and to compare these with nonreligious concepts that apply to the material world.

At the close of this chapter, it needs to be noted that eliminative and essential materialism and positivism, are three important forms of naturalism, but not the only forms of naturalism. Naturalism is not limited to these, as we shall see later. Naturalism need not entail that *all* of nature is in principle subject to human cognition, nor that it is *impossible* that God exists. Also, there is no obvious reason why naturalism need be thought of as anti-religious. While the version of naturalism reviewed here would rule out any religion that posits a nonphysical realm, one may make a case that naturalism can provide grounds for a natural piety or love for nature that is fundamentally religious. The *Humanist Manifestos* of 1973 and 1993 both construe naturalism as a religion (reprinted 1973).

Suggested Questions and Topics

(1)   Is eliminativism possible to state coherently? Is it at odds with common sense? If eliminativism were accepted, could any of the world religions be interpreted as true or meaningful? Why or why not?

(2)   Is it impossible for there to be anything nonphysical? Take note of the difference between *not to be able to imagine or conceive of something nonphysical* and *to be able to see that something's being nonphysical is impossible.* Is the concept of God something that is merely difficult to conceive of, or may we see that the concept of God involves a contradiction or an incoherence?

(3)   Kai Nielsen thinks that the nonphysical, immaterial status of "God" renders theism incapable of verification. Theism faces the following problem of reference and conceptual accessibility. How might a theist reply?

> It is *logically* impossible to specify what "God" refers to such that we can ascertain what must be the case so that we can distinguish between it being the case that God exists and it being not the case that God exists. To understand the syntax of "God" (in nonanthropomorphic employments) is to understand that we cannot specify what "God" refers to in empirical terms. To speak of specifying his effects when we are logically debarred from specifying his effects makes no sense at all. . . . "God" is supposed to be some kind of referring expression standing for an infinite, non-spatio-temporal, non-indicable individual, utterly transcendent to the cosmos. When we reflect on the meanings of these terms, we recognize that it would be logically impossible to verify that such an alleged individual exists. Anything that we could apprehend or could be acquainted with would *eo ipso* not be such a reality. (Nielsen 1982, pp. 169–70)

(4)   You may wish to develop an analysis of Anthony Kenny's observation about the difficulty of making sense of there being a nonbodily intelligence:

> If there is a God, who has thoughts, what makes the thoughts *his* thoughts? If God has no body, then there is no divine bodily behavior to serve as the basis of attribution to him of thoughts and knowledge. (Kenny 1979, p. 124)

In your view, is it conceptually or metaphysically necessary that an individual that has thoughts either be physical or possess a physical body?

(5)   Consider the following exchange between Peter Geach and Anthony Kenny. Geach proposes the following thought experiment by which there would be evidence of a disembodied being:

> Let us imagine that over a period of time a roulette wheel gives only the numbers 1 to 26, and that this sequence of numbers spells out English sentences according to the obvious code (A = 1, B = 2, etc.). Let us further imagine that this goes on although the most elaborate precautions are taken against physical tampering with the wheel. All of this is clearly possible and raises no conceptual difficulties. I submit that we could then have conclusive evidence that the thoughts normally

expressible by the English sentences in question were being originated, and strong evidence that they were originated by no living organism. . . . This and the like examples can show the possibility of disembodied thought; thought unconnected with any living organism. (Geach 1969, p. 39)

Kenny does not think the thought experiment is successful for "there seems no clear way of answering the question *how many* minds are at work; the example suggests no criterion for the identification for and individuation of disembodied minds" (Kenny 1979, p. 125). Kenny goes on to raise the following questions:

Why, faced with such a situation, should one say that we have here a disembodied mind at all? No doubt we would be right to reject the idea that here we have a roulette wheel which, unlike other roulette wheels, has the power to think. But why should we not say that this roulette wheel is being worked upon by another embodied mind through some unknown force? It seems that there can be no reason for rejecting in advance non-material modes of agency which is not at least as good a reason for rejecting non-material substances or minds. (Kenny 1979, p. 125)

Can Geach's thought experiment be adjusted to meet Kenny's objections?

(6) William Alston's endorsement of functionalism may be viewed as the opposite of John Locke's. Locke held that although it appeared (to him) that God made us as nonphysical and yet embodied, God could have made thoroughly physical beings that are capable of thought and so on. You may wish to assess Locke's stance and compare it with Alston's. Here is one of the famous passages from *An Essay Concerning Human Understanding*:

For I see no contradiction in it, that the first eternal thinking Being should, if he pleased, give to certain Systems of created senseless matter, put together as he thinks fit, some degree of sense, perception and thought. (Locke 1979, p. 541)

(7) Assess William Abraham on the awareness of God as a nonphysical reality.

God by definition does not have a body; there is nothing equivalent therefore to our bodily actions by means of which we can begin to guess at what He is doing or what He intends. In His case we are even more dependent on His speaking to us than we are in the case of human agents. Incorporeal agents who do not speak are like invisible men who are dumb. (Abraham 1982, p. 15)

(8)   What would be gained or lost if God was believed to be identical with the cosmos? Is it coherent to suppose that the cosmos could, in some sense, be God's body? On this view, God would still be thought of as knowing, powerful, loving and so on, but materially composed. Could such a position have greater resources to meet the problem of verification than traditional theism? See Grace Jantzen's *God's World, God's Body* for an exploration of such an embodied theism. One interesting related project, that would link the philosophy of God and of mind, would be to outline parallel treatments of each. Thus, you might examine a functionalist philosophy of God and human persons, and so on for all the standard theories. An introductory text in philosophy of mind would provide enough information to launch the project.

(9)   Antony Flew uses the following parable (taken from John Wisdom's paper "Gods") to present a positivist challenge to religious belief. Assess Flew's stance. In what respects, if any, are theists in the same boat as those who posit the invisible gardener described in this story?

> Once upon a time two explorers came upon a clearing in the jungle. In the clearing were growing many flowers and many weeds. One explorer says, "Some gardener must tend this plot." The other disagrees, "There is no gardener." So they pitch their tents and set a watch. No gardener is ever seen. "But perhaps he is an invisible gardener." So they set up a barbed-wire fence. They electrify it. They patrol it with bloodhounds. (For they remember how H. G. Wells's *The Invisible Man* could be both smelt and touched though he could not be seen.) But no shrieks ever suggested that some intruder has received a shock. No movements of the wire ever betray an invisible climber. The bloodhounds never give cry. Yet still the Believer is not convinced. "But there is a gardener, invisible, intangible, insensible to electric shocks, a gardener who has no scent and makes no sound, a gardener who comes secretly to look after the garden which he loves." At last the Sceptic despairs, "But what remains of your original assertion? Just how does what you call an invisible, intangible, eternally elusive gardener differ from an imaginary gardener or even from no gardener at all?" (Flew, in Flew and MacIntyre [eds] 1955, p. 96)

(10)   John Hick defends the meaningfulness of religious discourse by appealing to the prospects of verification not in this world but in the afterlife. Assess what you take to be the strengths or weaknesses of the following description of meaningful disagreement:

> Two men are traveling together along a road. One of them believes that it leads to a Celestial City, the other that it leads nowhere; but since this is the only road there is, both men must travel it. Neither has been this way before, and therefore

103

neither is able to say what they will find around each next corner. During the journey they meet both with moments of refreshment and delight, and with moments of hardship and danger. All the time one of them thinks of his journey as a pilgrimage to the Celestial City and interprets the pleasant parts as encouragements and the obstacles as trials of his purpose and lessons in endurance, prepared by the king of that city and designed to make of him a worthy citizen of the place when at last he arrives there. The other, however, believes none of this and sees their journey – only the road itself and the luck of the road in good weather and in bad.

During the course of the journey the issue between them is not an experimental one. They do not entertain different expectations about the coming details of the road, but only about its ultimate destination. And yet when they do turn the last corner it will be apparent that one of them has been right all the time and the other wrong. Thus, although the issue between them has not been experimental, it has nevertheless from the start been a real issue. They have not merely felt differently about the road; for one was feeling appropriately and the other inappropriately in relation to the actual state of affairs. Their opposed interpretations of the road constituted genuinely rival assertions, though assertions whose status has the peculiar characteristic of being guaranteed retrospectively by a future crux. (Hick 1966, pp. 177–8)

Further Reading and Considerations

From *A Companion to Philosophy of Religion*, see "The Verificationist Challenge"; "Theism and the Scientific Understanding of the Mind"; "Theism and Evolutionary Biology"; "Incorporeality"; "Divine Action"; and "Creation and Conservation." For arguments favorable to eliminativism, see Paul Churchland's *Matter and Consciousness* and Stich's *From Folk Psychology to Cognitive Science*. An accessible noneliminative materialist is D. M. Armstrong, in his *A Materialist Theory of Mind*. For arguments on the effect of using mental terms to describe an immaterial being, see Gilbert Ryle's *The Concept of Mind*. Among those who defend views of the person that are not materialist, consider Foster's *The Immaterial Self*, Swinburne's *The Evolution of the Soul*, and Taliaferro's *Consciousness and the Mind of God*. Dualism is frequently characterized by its friends and foes alike as common sense, the philosophy of the "person on the street"; Michael Levin, a materialist, puts the point baldly: "Mankind's official view of itself is dualistic" (Levin 1979, p. 64). For a useful review of current philosophy of mind in light of philosophy of religion see the journal *Faith and Philosophy* 12:4, 1995. Eleonone Stump's contribution to the journal offers an interesting nonreductive picture of persons who avoid a radical dualism, Her work and others signal a Revival of Aquinas's view of persons. See also David Braine's *The Human Person*.

Michael Martin defends the verification principle in *Atheism*; Foster objects to it in his book *Ayer*. See also Graham Oppy's compact but lucid treatment of positivism in *Ontological Arguments and Belief in God* (1995; pp. 39–45). As for considering the prospects of positivism and the difficulty of knowing other minds and the external world, see Plantinga's *God and Other Minds*. The problem of establishing our knowledge of "external realities" is, of course, a substantial topic. See William Alston's *The Reliability of Sense Perception* for a good overview of issues. You may also wish to consult *A Companion to Epistemology* edited by Dancy and Sosa, and Dancy's *An Introduction to Contemporary Epistemology*. Members of the Vienna Circle that launched positivism included M. Schlick (1882–1936), R. Carnap (1891–1970), O. Neurath (1882–1945), and F. Waismann (1896–1959). The drive for empirical testing is not new to twentieth-century positivism. David Hume (1711–76) is perhaps the chief forerunner of the positivist movement. A. J. Ayer once characterized his positivist manifesto, *Language, Truth, and Logic*, as "no more than Hume in modern dress" (Ayer 1987, p. 24. See also his admission, p. 33).

5

Divine Intelligence and the Structure of the Cosmos

Judaism, Christianity, and Islam each hold that God is all-knowing or omniscient (from the Latin *omnis* meaning "all" and *scire* meaning "to know"). God's omniscience plays a key role in the theistic understanding of God's creative, intelligent power and the origin and structure of the cosmos. If theism is true, the cosmos is not the result of a mindless, impersonal power but the work of a being that was and is aware of all aspects of its constitution. In a theistic philosophy, God's power and knowledge comprise the axis around which everything else is ultimately defined. Omniscience is central to the religious belief in God's trustworthiness, wisdom, love, greatness, and providence. The supreme knowledge of God is commonly understood by theists to be an excellence or perfection of God and a reason why God should be worshipped. If knowledge is good in human life, then its perfection in God as the supreme knower of all that exists marks a high order of supreme excellence. The appeal to God's knowledge plays a pivotal role in reports of mystical experience. Nicholas of Cusa's (1401–64) prayer to God is representative: "Thy look is Thy being . . . I am, because Thou dost look at me . . . if Thou didst turn Thy glance from me, I should cease to be" (Nicholas of Cusa, p. xiii). Hindu scripture also enshrines a high view of God's knowledge:

> Thou dost pervade the universe,
> Thou art consciousness itself,
> Thou art creator of time,
> All-knowing art thou.
> (*Upanishads*, trans. 1957, p. 126)

106

Buddhists similarly have characterized the Buddha as a supreme, omniscient reality. The Buddha has *sarvajna* or "awareness of everything." "Buddha is aware of all possible objects of awareness, and is aware of them without error or distortion of any kind" (Griffiths 1994, p. 72).

Naturalists contend that the appeal to an all-knowing being is deeply problematic. If these philosophers are correct, then theists have not only a burden of explaining how we may come to know God, but they must also explain how God may come to know us and the cosmos. For many naturalists, the theistic concept of divine intelligence is not a philosophical breakthrough, but an intellectual breakdown. How may God know of the cosmos – what it looks like, for example – if God lacks eyes and other sense organs? Parts of the physical world have been described metaphorically as God's sensory organs but obviously a description of the moon and sun as God's eyes is not to be read literally (*Bhagavad Gita*, chapter xi). But how can we make sense of a description of supreme knowledge without using such metaphors? Reference to God's knowledge is also part of a central objection to theism, an objection to be considered at length in chapter 9. Those who reject theism on the basis of the problem of evil rely on the supposition that if there is a God then God knows the cosmos. If God is all-powerful *and* all-knowing, why is there evil? If God were not all-knowing, then perhaps God could be excused for not knowing of the existence and preventability of evil.

This chapter examines four analyses of divine omniscience and highlights the more dramatic conjectures of a theistic account of God's supreme, unsurpassable knowledge. After some preliminary groundwork, attention is given to a debate about whether God can know what, for us, is the future in all of its details. This rich debate involves concepts of freedom that are prominent in the philosophy of human nature. Theism and naturalism are contrasted in a final section. A crucial division between these major philosophies is over the concept of intelligence. Theists understand divine intelligence as the ultimate bedrock, the foundation of the cosmos, whereas naturalists contend that there is no God and that intelligent life has emerged through natural, cosmic processes. These two philosophies were principal themes in the last chapter and substantial arguments for each are developed later in the book. It takes time to get acclimatized to debating entire world-views and there is still much ground to cover on diverse religions and values in order for the overall case for naturalism and its alternatives to come into sharper focus.

107

Preliminary Observations About Maximal Knowledge

What is omniscience? An initially plausible analysis of the property of *being omniscient* is as follows:

Analysis 1

Being, B, is omniscient if and only if B knows of everything that is true that it is true, and of everything that is false, that it is false.

If this depiction is right and God is omniscient, then everything is open to God's perspective. There is nothing hidden from God. Richard Swinburne writes: "All God's thoughts are explicit; he does not have partial thoughts, but thinks his thoughts and all their consequences together" (Swinburne 1994, p. 130). One implication of this analysis is that an omniscient being would have an exhaustive grasp not just of the cosmos but of itself. Such a being would not have any aspect of itself – a veiled unconscious for example – that is opaque to its inspection.

Analysis 1 may be given further specificity with an explicit reference to propositions. A "proposition" is a technical term philosophers sometimes use to refer to that which may be stated or expressed in any number of synonymous sentences or translations in different languages. Thus, there is the proposition "It is raining" that is expressed by the English sentence "It is raining," the French "Il pleut," the German "Es regnet," the Spanish "Está lloviendo," the Norwegian "Det regner," the Polish "deszcz pada," and so on. Each of these sentences refers to the same proposition. It is in virtue of their referring to the same proposition that they are deemed successful translations. Propositions, then, have been analyzed as nonlinguistic states of affairs (abstract or theoretical entities) that can be referred to with sentences or simply entertained without using any sentences, e.g. noticing "It is raining" without using any language (see Frege 1956 and Chisholm 1976, or "Proposition" in any standard philosophy dictionary). On one model, there are propositions that are true or false regardless of whether any humans ever existed. Such a construal of propositions is realist and thus distinguishable from a nonrealist view of language as described in chapter 2. Using propositions as a point of reference, one can refine Analysis 1 to make more explicit the object or bearer of truth and falsity. Consider, then:

Analysis 2

A being, B, is omniscient if and only if B knows of every true proposition that it is true and of every false proposition that it is false.

Analysis 2 captures the most common, technical analysis of the property of omniscience, and it will serve to introduce one of the most heated debates in the literature today on divine knowledge.

Can God Know the Future?

If God knows everything that is true or, using the language of Analysis 2, if God knows every true proposition, then God knows all truths about the future. But if the future is known in all its details, then, so it is argued, it seems that the future must in some way be predetermined. If it is true now that you will do something tomorrow – contribute a certain sum to charity, for example – then how could you not contribute such a sum to charity? If you will in fact do it, then you will do it and it will be futile to try to prevent this by setting out to hoard all your money, locking yourself in a room, cutting off all phone lines, notifying all charities that none of your funds are to be given to them, and so on.

The problem is not: if someone foreknows something will occur, then in some fashion this foreknowledge (or the person who has the foreknowledge) causes the future event to occur. One may know that a horse will win a race without having anything to do with fixing the outcome. The problem, rather, is that if a future outcome is foreknown, then it appears to be fixed or determined now that such an outcome will indeed take place. The claim to know something is naturally interpreted as the claim to know that something is true, and, with reference to God, the claim that *God knows the future* is typically understood in the most stringent terms.

Traditional theists have been reticent to suppose that God has to guess or speculate about the future. Instead, God is often thought of as infallible; that is, incapable of error. Richard Sorabji puts the problem of reconciling belief in freedom and God's infallible grasp of the future as follows:

> If God were not infallible in his judgment of what we would do, we might be able so to act that his prediction turned out wrong. But this is not even a possibility, for to call him infallible is to say not merely that he is not, but that

he cannot be wrong, and correspondingly we cannot make him wrong . . . The restriction on freedom arises not from God's infallibility alone, but from that coupled with the irrevocability of the past. If God's infallible knowledge of our doing exists in advance, then we are too late so to act that God will have had a different judgment about what we are going to do. His judgment exists already, and the past cannot be affected. (Sorabji 1983, p. 255)

On this view, the threat to human freedom increases with the enlargement of the scope and exactitude of this supposedly infallible God's eye point of view. In the sixteenth century the Spanish philosopher Luis de Molina held that God knows all of what will take place as well as what would take place under all possible conditions. According to Molina, God knows all possible worlds exhaustively and there are no truths about this world that elude God's knowledge. Can belief in freedom survive if this comprehensive picture of Divine knowledge is adopted?

In order to be gripped by this puzzling question in the philosophy of God, one has to possess at least *some* sympathy with the thesis that persons are free. If it is *obvious* that there is no freedom, then there is no problem with reconciling it with divine foreknowledge.

Freedom, Determinism, and God

For those who are determinists there will not be any special difficulty with countenancing divine foreknowledge. *Determinism* is the view that everything that occurs, occurs necessarily, given the laws of nature and all antecedent conditions. "Determinism" comes from the Latin *determinare,* meaning "to set limits or bounds." If *everything* is so fixed, then appeal to the point of view of a maximum knower can constitute a useful illustration of the thesis that everything is determined. Indeed, some determinists spell out their position by contending that if their view of the cosmos is correct, then, in principle, there could be a being that knows the future in all its details. In a famous statement of the determinist position, Pierre Laplace (1749–1827) explicitly invokes a God's eye point of view:

We ought then to consider the present state of the universe as the effect of its antecedent state, and as the cause of the one which is going to follow. An intelligence which knew at a given instant all the forces at work in nature and the relative positions of the entities which make it up – provided that it were great enough to submit these data to analysis – would comprehend in the same

110

formula the movements of the largest bodies in the universe and those of the tiniest atom. For it, nothing would be uncertain; the future, like the past, would be present to its eyes. (Laplace, cited by Boyle et al. 1976, p. 57)

Determinism has been popular throughout the history of philosophy, theology, and science, and it has sometimes been supported on the grounds of divine omniscience. If one grants that there is an omniscient being, then, so it has been argued, one should grant that the cosmos is determined.

In philosophy of religion, determinism has sometimes been a key notion in understanding the sovereignty of God. Kathryn Tanner advances a vigorous version of divine sovereignty according to which God fixes the limits and boundaries of the cosmos. She describes God's creative power as "all inclusive or universally extensive":

Everything nondivine, in every respect that it is, is dependent upon God's activity, which brings it forth. God's activity calls forth or holds up into being throughout the time of its existence what has its own integrity as a nondivine existence, and this nondivine existence has to be considered the consequence of God's creative calling forth and holding up as a whole, in its order and in its entirety, in every detail and aspect. (Tanner 1994, p. 113)

In this fashion, theistic claims of sovereignty and determinism go hand in hand.

Determinism and freedom may appear to be mutually exclusive, but it has been argued that this need not be so. According to what is customarily referred to as *compatibilism* a person may be free and determined at the same time. Compatibilism is attacked by both stricter determinists and anti-determinists alike, but it is a position of considerable power and widely represented in philosophical literature. Compatibilists construe freedom in accordance with what they take to be solid common sense. For example, a person may rightly be judged to act freely when she performs an act that stems from her own thinking and reflection. To put matters simply, someone is free when she is able to do what she wants. Freedom involves the absence of relevant external constraints like chains (I am not free to leave my chair if I am chained to it), or internal impediments to one's thinking, such as extraordinary pain (I may not be free to think about probability theory if I am in severe pain), or if the person is the victim of hypnotism or other forces such as those described in science fiction (e.g. a mad scientist who has planted an electronic device in my brain to control me). Arguably, freedom from such circumstances and the possession of the power to do what one wants would seem to be *bona fide* freedom and describable without supposing determinism is false. If compatibilism is true, then action under these conditions may be both free and yet determined.

Incompatibilism is the thesis that freedom and determinism cannot both be true. Incompatibilists who are determinists and deny freedom are sometimes called *hard determinists*. Incompatibilists who believe there is freedom are typically called *libertarians* (not to be confused with political libertarians who radically restrict state interference with human liberty). From a libertarian point of view, compatibilism is unable to do justice to our conception of freedom and, more important, to our experience of freedom. The crucial condition that must be satisfied in order for there to be genuine freedom requires the agent's ability to do otherwise – a person performs a free act if and only if she does the act and could have refrained from doing so even if all other conditions (laws of nature etc.) remained constant. Peter van Inwagen advances the libertarian position. He offers the following analysis of what is involved when a thief freely repents:

> There are possible worlds in which things were absolutely identical in every respect with the way they are in the actual world up to the moment at which our repentant thief made his decision – worlds in which, moreover, the laws of nature are just what they are in the actual world – and in which he takes the money. (Van Inwagen 1983, p. 128)

The reason why van Inwagen and other libertarians do not accept compatibilism is because they believe that so long as a person is determined then she has no power to do anything other than what she is determined to do and thus is not free at all. Even if all the conditions cited by compatibilists were met when you thought you freely gave to charity, the act was not truly free if that act was the inevitable, necessary outcome given the prevailing conditions and the laws of nature. In brief, you were not free because you lacked the power to do otherwise.

Figure 5.1 shows the three positions just described: Incompatibilist libertarianism is by no means *the* consensus position in philosophy today, but it has able defenders. These libertarians do not claim that *all* human behavior is free. Our freedom is restricted by a host of factors, social, biological, and perhaps theological. Libertarians nonetheless hold that we make some choices, however limited, and these are genuinely within our power. One reason why libertarianism is less easily dismissed today is due to recent developments in science. The physical sciences are no longer thoroughly deterministic. Quantum me-

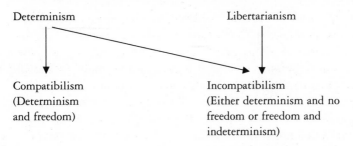

Figure 5.1

chanics recognizes that something may occur that is indeterminate on a sub-atomic level. Allowing for the credibility of the latter has done much to undermine the claim that determinism is necessarily true or that it is in some sense required by science or intuitively obvious.

Historically, an important reason for adopting determinism has been the supposition that determinism may be seen to be necessarily true on the basis of rational insight alone. The claim was that it is self-evident that whatever occurs must necessarily occur given all prevailing and antecedent conditions. It is still possible to muster support for comparatively less ambitious claims such as "There cannot be uncaused events," or "For everything that exists, there must be a reason for its existence," but neither of these (as stated) require that one believe that the cause of events must *necessitate* the event, nor that the reasons or causes for something's existence be *necessitating*. (For an important defense of the view that causation need not always be understood determinis-tically see G. E. M. Anscombe 1971; see also chapter 10 of this book.) Two of the best known defenses of libertarianism rest on an appeal to experience and to moral responsibility.

An appeal to experience.   Some philosophers contend that a proper interpreta-tion of the experience of acting freely supports libertarianism. John Foster defends the view that the apprehension or consciousness we have of ourselves as agents is distinctively positive (Foster 1991; see Campbell 1967 for an earlier statement of this view). That is, for one to experience oneself as free does not involve merely apprehending that we are *free from* certain constraints, but that we are free *to do* one of at least two genuinely open alternative actions. In support of this interpretation of our experience, Roderick Chisholm and others argue that the meaning of the customary ways in which we describe our free action is thoroughly incompatibilist and libertarian (Lucas 1970 and Chisholm 1976).

An appeal to moral responsibility.   Does not determinism entail that all wrong-doing is fixed and, thus, could not have been prevented? Van Inwagen and others argue that if thieves cannot act other than they do, they are not truly free. It may be granted that in a deterministic universe it would still be desirable to punish and blame persons in order to influence their behavior and the behavior of others. It may be useful, also, for society to employ the language of moral responsibility. But in a determinist world, could we properly take full credit for our action as our own when we could not be or do otherwise? Van Inwagen contends that determinism undermines the claim that a person's actions are truly up to him or her:

> If determinism is true, then our acts are the consequences of the laws of nature and events in the remote past. But it is not up to us what went on before we were born, and neither is it up to us what the laws of nature are. Therefore, the consequences of these things (including our present acts) are not up to us. (Van Inwagen 1983, p. 56)

Insofar as moral responsibility rests on the notion that one can control one's actions, then, so it is argued, such responsibility requires libertarianism.

Some critics reply that it is determinism that makes moral responsibility intelligible. It is argued that the libertarian's introduction of indeterminism makes so-called free action random events. If free action lacks necessitating causes then they are random matters and thus not ones for which someone can be held accountable (Ayer 1963). To this, libertarians respond that, on their view, free action is not random; it is comprised of the person exercising a power to choose which course to take where that choice may be prompted by a variety of non-necessitating reasons. The person is the cause of free acts and the bearer of responsibility concerning which act is done (Taylor 1966).

Due largely to the appeal to moral responsibility, many theists have adopted an incompatibilist, libertarian understanding of freedom. One reason why theists are keen to appeal to this account of creaturely freedom is that they think the source of significant evil in the cosmos is directly or indirectly the result of free choices. If Adolf Hitler and other mass-murderers were deter-mined to do what they did, then is not God ultimately responsible for Hitler's actions? Could not God have created Hitler so that he only acted virtuously? J. L. Mackie puts the objection as follows:

> If God has made men such that in their free choices they sometimes prefer what is good and sometimes what is evil, why could he not have made men such that they always freely choose the good? (Mackie 1982, p. 164)

114

Theists who are libertarians reply that God cannot "make" people freely choose the good any more than God can make people freely choose evil. When a person exercises freedom then, in a sense, she becomes the author of her activity in a fashion that is incompatible with God's writing the script for her.

It is due to an appreciation of the relationship between free will and responsibility that many otherwise very strong accounts of Divine creation are hedged. Kathryn Tanner qualifies her powerful, rigorous account of Divine sovereignty cited on p. 111 precisely in order to secure human accountability. She preserves her commitment to a strong view of God's sovereignty on the grounds that doing evil is not so much a matter of positively undertaking something as it is neglecting to do something – evil arises out of a failure of attention, regard, and will power (see Tanner 1994, especially pp. 129–35). God then is credited with authoring all positive, existent things and objects but not the failures of persons to act positively. (Her views closely accord with those of Anselm and Aquinas, reviewed in chapter 3, in which the power to do evil is not a power at all but a warped failure to exercise an authentic power.)

Some theists have qualified their commitment to God's omni-determining will in their articulation of the good of God's relationship with the creation and not as part of a defensive strategy in the face of the problem of evil. The relationship between God and human beings is sometimes pictured as, at best, one of free interplay and shared creativity. This view of divine and human co-creativity is given great prominence in the work of the Russian philosophical theologian Nicholas Berdyaev (1874–1948; see especially his work *The Destiny of Man*). The link between human and divine freedom is noted more recently by Roderick Chisholm in the course of his defense of libertarianism:

> If we are responsible, and if what I have been trying to say is true, then we have a prerogative which some would attribute only to God: each of us, when we act, is a prime mover unmoved. In doing what we do, we cause certain events to happen, and nothing more – or no one – causes us to cause those events to happen. (Chisholm, in Lehrer [ed.] 1966, p. 23)

Such a notion of freedom will be judged as all too mysterious by its critics (such as Dennett 1984, especially chapter four, and Strawson 1991) but as representing a deep, coherent picture by its theistic allies.

There are responses by determinists to each of the above (and more arguments against determinism to which there are additional determinist rejoinders), but rather than consider these here, let us proceed on the assumption – if only for the sake of argument – that humans possess libertarian freedom and see how this fares over and against the belief that there is a God who knows all future human free activity. Convinced theistic determinists may still find this topic crucial to address because they make an exception for God. Thus, while they believe the whole cosmos is determined, they think that God is not determined in some significant ways. It is possible to hold that we do not have libertarian freedom but God does. If so, these theists will have some stake in reconciling libertarian freedom and foreknowledge, for they face this question: If God foreknows what God will do, can God truly be free?

Three Theistic Proposals

Consider the following three ways in which to address the freedom—foreknowledge problem:

(A) *Paradox but no contradiction.* Some philosophical theists contend that there is no contradiction between freedom and foreknowledge but at worst a paradox or mystery. It is often claimed that those who think freedom and foreknowledge are inconsistent do so because they confuse these two claims. The following claim is acceptable:

It is necessarily the case that if God knows that X will happen, then X will happen.

But this claim is not acceptable.

It is necessarily the case that if God knows that X will happen then X happens necessarily.

Compare that claim with the following:

It is necessarily the case that if I take a walk, I will move my legs. Therefore it is necessarily the case that I will move my legs.

The conclusion does not follow in this latter case. I might have decided not to take a walk in the first place, in which case it does not follow that *it is necessarily the case that I will move my legs*. This insistence that the freedom—foreknowledge problem is only paradoxical and not a radical threat to omniscience and freedom may be bolstered by two philosophical maneuvers.

(i) Some philosophers seek support for their dismissal of the freedom—

116

foreknowledge debate by appeal to common experience. Jonathan Kvanvig believes that the compatibility of freedom and foreknowledge is evident in ordinary life. In our own case, "it appears quite obvious that each of us knows quite a bit about our own future actions and the future actions of those around us" (Kvanvig 1986, p. 22). If this does not threaten a recognition of their freedom, why should God's foreknowledge be so threatening?

Some philosophers question this line of defense by challenging the claim that we can indeed *know* future free action (see, for example, Hasker 1989). Libertarians often concede that persons act in ways that are *predictable* and, as it is sometimes put, "in character," though they question whether these predictions can be exact or whether one can rule out as *impossible* a person's acting out of character. By their lights, we may have reasonable beliefs about future free action but this does not amount to knowledge (Campbell 1967, Lucas 1989).

(ii)   A second move is more complex. It is inspired, in part, by Harry Frankfurt (Frankfurt 1969). According to Frankfurt, one can be free even if it is not possible for one to have done otherwise. Linda Zagzebski employs Frankfurt's work in her own project of arguing for the compatibility of freedom and divine foreknowledge. If freely performing an act, X, does not involve the genuine possibility of not doing X, then God can know X, X could not be otherwise and yet X is nonetheless a free act. Consider Zagzebski's version of Frankfurt's thought experiment:

> Suppose that Black is an insane neurosurgeon who wishes to see White dead, but is unwilling to do the deed himself. Knowing that Jones also despises White and will have a single good opportunity to kill him, Black inserts a mechanism into Jones's brain that enables him to monitor and to control Jones's neurological activities. If Jones's neurological activity suggests that he is on the verge of deciding not to murder White when the opportunity arises, Black's mechanism intervenes and causes Jones to decide to commit the murder. On the other hand, if Jones decides to murder White on his own, the mechanism does not intervene at all. It merely monitors, but does not affect Jones's neurological activity. Now suppose that when the occasion arises, Jones decides to murder White without any help from Black's mechanism. Intuitively, it seems that Jones acts freely. He brings about his act in exactly the same way he would have if he had been able to do otherwise. Nonetheless, he is unable to do otherwise since if he had attempted to do so, he would have been thwarted by Black's device. (Zagzebski 1997; for Frankfurt's case see 1969, pp. 835–6)

Does this thought experiment show that freedom does not involve the possibility of doing otherwise? If so, we may come to see that just as knowing the past in all its details does not in any way jeopardize the thesis that persons in the past acted freely, so knowing the future in all its detail does not jeopardize believing that persons will come to act freely in certain specific ways.

Incompatibilists have responded to such Black and White cases on several fronts. A twofold response is to propose either that Jones is not genuinely free because he was unable to refrain from murdering White or that Jones is genuinely free, but not free to do the act described above. On behalf of the latter proposal, one may argue that the mechanism prevents Jones from refraining from the murder and so Jones is not free with respect to that action, but Jones still possesses a modest scope of freedom: the freedom to begin reconsidering whether to commit the murder. The scope is limited, because the mechanism kicks in when Jones is "on the verge of deciding" not to commit the murder, but this capacity *to hesitate in one's plans* may still be thought of as a slender capacity for some free action (see Zagzebski 1991 and 1997 for further development of the debate).

(B) *Eternity*.   A second theistic proposal is to resolve the freedom–foreknowledge problem by challenging the use of the term "foreknowledge" in the way the problem is set up. Arguably, an important factor behind the problem is the thesis that God in some way sees ahead; God knows *beforehand* what will take place. If God is not in time but God is in some sense *eternal*, then strictly speaking, God does not foreknow the future. As Aquinas puts it, God "sees everything at once and not successively" (*ST*, la.14.7). This position is defended today by Eleonore Stump, Norman Kretzmann, Brian Leftow, and others. Stump and Kretzmann cast God's vantage point as God's knowing what for us is the future but for God is in some way simultaneous with God's reality. They introduce the term "ET-simultaneous" to describe God's being eternally simultaneous with all temporal events:

> The short answer to the question whether God can foreknow contingent events is no. It is impossible that any event occur later than an eternal entity's [God's] present state of awareness, since every temporal event is ET-simultaneous with that state, and so an eternal entity cannot foreknow anything. Instead, such an entity considered as omniscient knows – is aware of – all temporal events, including those which are future with respect to our current temporal viewpoint; but, because the times at which those future events will be present events are ET-simultaneous with the whole of eternity, an omniscient eternal entity is aware of them as they are present. (Stump and Kretzmann 1981, p. 247)

The Stump–Kretzmann stance echoes important work by medieval philosophers. Before Aquinas, Anselm entertained a similarly high view of God's overarching reality:

> You were not, therefore, yesterday, nor will You be tomorrow, but yesterday and today and tomorrow You are. Indeed You exist neither yesterday nor today nor tomorrow but are outside all times. For yesterday and tomorrow are completely in time; however, You, though nothing can be without You, are nevertheless not in space or time but all things are in You. For nothing contains You, but You contain all things. (Anselm, *Proslogium*, chapter 19)

According to Anselm, God has a supremely excellent, all-seeing vantage point from which to know all things. Boethius (*c*.475–524) also depicts God's view of the creation as one that is not itself temporal or malleable; God does not observe creation second by second:

> Wherefore since . . . God hath always an everlasting and present state, his knowledge also surpassing all motions of time, remaineth in the simplicity of his presence, and comprehending the infinite spaces of that which is past and to come, considereth all things in his simple knowledge, as though they were now in doing. So that, if thou wilt weigh his foreknowledge with which he discerneth all things, thou wilt more rightly esteem it to be the knowledge of a never fading instant than a foreknowledge as of a thing to come. (Boethius 1918, pp. 403–5)

This may provide theists with what is needed to defeat the charge that one cannot posit both libertarian freedom and foreknowledge. The past and future are open to God. Just as God's knowing the past does not mean that we were not free in the past, then God's knowing what, for us, is the future does not mean that we are not free in the future.

Does it make sense to think that God or anything whatever can transcend temporality? If there is a God, must there be a past, present and future even for God? These are key questions addressed in the next chapter.

(C)   *Temporality and the unknowable future.*   Some philosophical theists today claim that God is in time and that God does not know the future. A popular way to spell out such a thesis while preserving the claim that God is all-knowing is to argue that propositions about future free actions are neither true nor false. Aristotle is attributed with a view like this. In *On Interpretation* he writes:

Propositions about the present or past must necessarily be either true or false . . . But with regard to propositions about the future, and with singular subjects, the situation is different . . . For we can see for ourselves that future events depend on our deliberations and on what we do . . . So it is clear that not everything is or happens by necessity . . . It is necessary that there either will or will not be a sea-fight tomorrow, but yet it is not necessary either that there will be a sea-fight tomorrow or that there will not be. (Aristotle, IX: 18A28–19B3)

It is compatible with this view that there are some necessary truths about the future. "$2 + 2 = 4$" will be true tomorrow and it is true now that either you will freely elect to give to charity or you will not. In matters that are properly contingent, however, in which voluntary action is intermixed, it is not now true that the future will have a given course. It is not true nor false now that you will freely give to charity tomorrow. If there are no true propositions specifying which future free acts will occur, then God's not knowing these propositions does not compromise God's being omniscient (Geach 1977). God may satisfy Analysis 2 and yet not know that you will freely shout "Hello" on 4 July 2010. There are several objections to this alternative.

The surprise objection. On the above account, it would appear that God could be surprised by the outcome of events. This outcome strikes some as absurd. It may be deemed absurd on the basis of a high conception of the perfection of God but also on the grounds that God must be thought of as a supreme, creative artisan. Alfred Fredoso contends that a vital part of Judaism, Christianity, and Islam is the conviction that God is the supreme artisan of all, for whom there cannot be shocking surprises:

> God, the divine artisan, freely and knowingly plans, orders, and provides for all the effects that constitute His artifact, the created universe with its entire history, and executes His chosen plan by playing an active causal role sufficient to ensure its exact realization. Since God is the perfect artisan, not even the most trivial details escape His providential decrees. (Fredoso 1988, p. 3)

Because of the problem of evil, some theists deliberately qualify the claim that God is a supreme artisan of all cosmic history. Still, the theistic affirmation of God's comprehensive, providential care of all things is deeply embedded in Judaism, Christianity, and Islam and (so it is argued) the qualified, Aristotelian approach to the foreknowledge problem is at odds with such an important religious tenet.

The objection from prophesies. There are various prophesies in the Hebrew and Christian Bibles in which God is described as foretelling future free action (e.g. the coming of the Messiah or the fall of Jerusalem). If these are cases of what, for us, is foreknowledge or, for God, is (using the Stump–Kretzmann term) ET-awareness, then this appears to challenge the Aristotelian proposal. A defense of God's being omniscient and yet *not* knowing the future here would involve precise biblical study that is not feasible in this text. See Clark Pinnock et al. (1994) and J. R. Lucas (1989), for a Christian, theological attempt to reconcile biblical testimony with God's not knowing in every detail what will take place.

The Whatever Will Be, Will Be objection. This objection is simply a denial of the Aristotelian thesis that the future is underdetermined on the basis of what seems like common sense. With respect to precisely formulated statements about the future, does it not seem that statements about the future are either true or false? We may not know which are true, but that does not count against the force of assuming the statements are either true or false. This objection may be simply an appeal to "common sense" and it is accepted by some theists who are otherwise sympathetic to the Aristotelian strategy (Swinburne 1994).

The Whatever Will Be, Will Be objection may not seem very forceful to the deeply committed Aristotelian, but it has been faced squarely by a number of philosophers who do not dismiss it and attempt, instead, to defend the thesis that there are truths about future free action and that these are not known by God and yet God is omniscient. The following analysis of omniscience is designed to preserve the claim that God is omniscient and yet does not know future free action. It is a simplified version of a proposal of Swinburne's (1977). (The expression "at time t" is meant to designate any specific time.)

Analysis 3

Being, B, is omniscient at time t if and only if B knows at time t of every true proposition it is possible to know that it is true and of every false proposition it is possible to know that it is false.

The question of whether a philosophy of God should hold that God is within, or transcends, time will be taken up in the next chapter.

The Means and Feasibility of Omniscience

Whether or not omniscience requires knowledge of the future, there are two dimensions of the concept of omniscience that are important to consider.

The means of God's knowledge. Analyses 1 to 3 do not demarcate *how* an omniscient being knows anything. What if a being satisfies the conditions laid out in the analyses and thus knows all true propositions (or all true propositions at some time t it is possible to know) but this knowledge is only achieved by means of some tenuous, circuitous route? Imagine a case in which two beings, Eric and Miriam, know all propositions (or all states of affairs) and thus would both be considered to be omniscient on any one of the standard analyses of the concept, but Eric has this knowledge only by relying on Miriam's testimony. Imagine Eric's evidence is vicarious, and while strong enough so that he may truly be said to have knowledge, he can make this claim with only a minimal degree of justification. Miriam, on the other hand, knows all true propositions directly and immediately. Are the Analyses of omniscience 1–3 all defective because they only outline what an omniscient being knows while ignoring how such knowledge is acquired?

There are several replies. One is to claim that ways of knowing such as Miriam's do not identify *types of knowledge* but *ways of acquiring knowledge*. The way God embodies or realizes omniscience might be closer to Miriam than Eric in the thought experiment, but this is a feature of God's overall excellence and perfection, not God's omniscience (see Kvanvig 1986).

Another option is to amend the original definition, by explicitly building into the analysis of omniscience some conception of how a being comes to acquire knowledge. This strategy receives some support from theories of knowledge which highlight the intellectual virtues. On such a view, to have knowledge is to have a certain kind of excellence, just as to have courage is to have an ethical excellence (Zagzebski 1996). According to this alternative, to attribute supreme knowledge to a being is to attribute to it a supreme way of knowing. In a phrase, when it comes to omniscience, it is not just a matter of *what is known* but *how it is known*. Consider the following attempt to incorporate the means of supreme knowledge:

Analysis 4

Being, B, is omniscient if and only if B has supreme cognitive power and this power is fully exercised.

"Supreme cognitive power" is meant to pick out the highest order of cognitive excellence or virtue. "Virtue" is derived from the Latin *virtus* meaning "power." So, a depiction of an omniscient being would be of a being that is directly, immediately aware of all states of affairs and it would exclude from being omniscient a being whose knowledge is highly precarious, the result of relying upon slender evidence, a series of mediators, shabby equipment (however successful), and so on. Would accepting this analysis render the other depictions of omniscience obsolete? Not necessarily. Unpacking the scope of what would be supremely known still requires considering whether this includes all states of affairs and propositions, only those propositions and states of affairs it is possible to know, and so on. A proponent of Analysis 4 still faces the question: If a being fully exercises supreme cognitive power would it know future free action?

The attainment of God's knowledge.   To know certain things, are not experiences required? If so, then the thesis that God is omniscient seems imperiled. First, consider whether it is necessary to have certain experiences in order to grasp certain concepts. David Blumenfeld insists upon such a necessity:

> There is a host of concepts which require experience for their complete comprehension. Take the concept of the sensation of red. Surely one could not fully grasp this notion if one had never had an experience of redness. . . . The reason for this is that part of the meaning of the concept consists of a certain subjective experience. One who failed to understand fully what this experience is like would thus lack a perfect grasp of its concept. But there is only one way of fully understanding what an experience of redness is like and that is to have it. (Blumenfeld 1987, p. 205)

Given that this is true, several problems arise: God cannot know concepts incompatible with God's omnipotence and goodness, nor can God grasp basic sensation terms. If God is omnipotent, how could God grasp certain concepts like the concept "frustration"? "The experience which is required [to understand frustration] is of such a type which no omnipotent being could possibly have" (Blumenfeld 1987, p. x). Given that God is all-good, how could God grasp the concept *sadism* or *cruel pleasure*? Given that God is without a body and bodily sensations, how could God grasp the idea of *tasting strawberries* or know what it is like? Add to these three difficulties a general picture of God's knowledge, and the outcome begins to look quite chaotic. In order for God to be omniscient must God experience a full, infinite spectrum of experiences that cover the way all things look, feel, taste, and so on for all conceivable creatures? Arguably, this is a bloated, bewildering conception of God's omniscience as an ongoing omnisensory web of cognitive activity.

There are various ways to reply to this complex objection. The simplest is to challenge whether experience is indeed required for grasping the experiential concepts that Blumenfeld identifies. Blumenfeld seems to need more than just the thesis that *we human beings* need experiences to grasp concepts; he needs the thesis that it is necessarily true for all conceivable beings, or at least that it is necessary for God. But is this obvious? Even in our own case, it has been argued that it is not. Thus, David Lewis holds that it is possible for us to have knowledge without experience:

> Having an experience is surely one good way, and surely the only practical way, of coming to know what that experience is like. Can we say, flatly, that it is the only possible way? Probably not. There is a change that takes place in you when you have the experience and thereby come to know what it's like. Perhaps the exact same change could in principle be produced in you by precise neurosurgery, very far beyond the limits of present-day techniques. Or it could possibly be produced in you by magic. If we ignore the laws of nature, which are after all contingent, then there is no necessary connection between cause and effect: anything could cause anything. For instance, the casting of a spell could do to you exactly what your first smell of skunk would do. We might quibble about whether a state produced in this artificial fashion would deserve the name "knowing what it's like to smell a skunk," but we can imagine that so far as what goes on within you is concerned, it would differ not at all. (Lewis 1990, p. 500)

If cases such as those envisioned by Lewis are feasible there is some reason to doubt that Blumenfeld has identified a necessary truth about knowledge that may be used to secure the thesis that the concept of God's omniscience is absurd.

Theists have proposed other ways to respond to Blumenfeld (Beaty 1990). Assume, if only for the sake of argument, that Blumenfeld is right about the necessity of experience. Must an omnipotent being never be frustrated? Monotheistic religions do portray God this way in their scriptures, and many theists today suppose that God is open to feeling sorrow over the world's history (Wolterstorff 1988). If so, God does indeed feel frustration and sorrow over the evil free choices of human beings. Consider Blumenfeld's thesis that omniscience requires experiences that compromise perfect goodness. Let it be conceded that to know what sadism is requires experience. Must it involve experiencing sadism or being sadistic? Some theists argue that this is not obvious. Sadism may be analyzed in terms of pleasure, desire and the like. If one knew pleasure and desire in other, ethically unproblematic contexts, could that not serve as a foundation on the basis of which an omniscient being could form the concept of sadism?

Is possessing a body necessary in order to have sensations and thus to know what seeing red looks like? Blumenfeld's position is supported by essential materialism, and, as noted in the last chapter, this is a philosophical theory which many theistic philosophers address. What a fully successful anti-theistic argument needs here is not the failure to see how God is omniscient, but the more substantial thesis that God cannot be omniscient. As noted in the last chapter, there are many today, and throughout history across radically different cultures, who believe there can be out-of-the-body experiences. Several references to this literature are noted in chapter 4 and additional references are given in chapter 9. Some theists argue for the coherence of these out-of-the-body experiences. Maybe there has never been one, and death is annihilation, but if it is conceded that it is *possible* to survive the destruction of one's body and still have sensory and other experiences then an important part of Blumenfeld's case against theism would be overturned. Consider J. M. E. McTaggart's statement of a dualist point of view. According to McTaggart, while we require our body and bodily organs to perceive the world now, this does not mean that fleshly embodiment is absolutely essential for perception:

> While a self has a body, that body is essentially connected with the self's mental life . . . it might be that the present inability of the self to think except in connection with the body was a limitation which was imposed by the presence of the body, and vanished with it . . . If a man is shut up in a house, the transparency of the windows is an essential condition of his seeing the sky. But it would not be prudent to infer that, if he walked out of the house, he could not see the sky because there was no longer any glass through which he might see it. (McTaggart 1906, p. 105)

If McTaggart is right, Blumenfeld's insistence that bodily life is absolutely necessary for there to be experience, is undermined.

Finally, if it is granted that experience is essential for grasping concepts, are theists committed to believing that an omniscient being must have continuous, infinitely many experiences? Perhaps, though theists have again claimed this is not at all clear. Maybe God could have at any time the full spectrum of experiences. After that, would God need to have these experiences again and again in order to retain the relevant concepts? Michael Beaty and others have claimed that such omni-experiencing would not be required for God to be omniscient. But the debate on all these matters is still very much alive.

An Overview of Naturalism and Theism

In theism, the appeals to power and knowledge are the apex of understanding God and form the heart of the explanation for the existence and continuation of the cosmos. There is a comprehensiveness to theism in its purporting to achieve a unified, ultimate account of the cosmos. This complex, sustained theistic project clashes sharply with a prevalent naturalism that defines much of the current philosophical literature. From a naturalist perspective, there is no need to go beyond nature or the cosmos to account for its existence. The appeal to God is either unintelligible or, if intelligible, clearly false.

In chapter 4 we considered the naturalist critique of theism from the standpoint of essential materialism and positivism. There will be many junctures in what follows (especially in chapters 8 through 10) where naturalism is a key topic. In the final section of this chapter the aim is to take stock of the tension between theism and naturalism, outlining in clear detail the shape of each philosophy.

"Naturalism" does not define a detailed theory of the cosmos. As the term is usually used, naturalism asserts the sufficiency of nature (whatever its limits) and the nonexistence of a transcendental reality beyond nature. One could, then, be a naturalist and adopt essential materialism or substantive dualism, so long as one does not invoke a supernatural God or god. A well-represented form of scientific naturalism rejects theism on the grounds that a scientific investigation of the cosmos reveals a unified spatio-temporal whole that leaves no room for God. Ronald Hepburn and Bertrand Russell have both articulated anti-theistic naturalist positions.

Hepburn once claimed that it makes no sense to appeal to that which lies beyond the universe. The universe as disclosed in science is sufficient to exhaust what we may meaningfully theorize about:

> Compare these sentences – "Outside my room a sparrow is chirping," "Outside the city the speed limit ends," "Outside the earth's atmosphere meteors do not burn out," and finally "God is outside the universe, outside space and time." What of this last statement? The word "outside" gets its central meaning from relating item to item *within* the universe. It . . . is being stretched to breaking-point in being applied to the whole universe as related to some being that is not-

the-universe: its sense is being extended to the point where we may easily come to speak nonsense without noticing it . . . (Hepburn 1958, p. 5)

Bertrand Russell also thought such theistic appeals were nonsense. He did so partly on the grounds that it makes no sense to refer to the universe as a whole, as though it were some kind of "thing" that could have a cause like God. "I think the word 'universe' is a handy word in some connections, but I don't think it stands for anything that has a meaning" (Russell in Hick (ed.) 1964, p. 174). He qualified this judgment somewhat in another statement to the effect that he did not see any reason to suppose there could be a cause of the universe:

> The whole concept of cause is one we derive from our observation of particular things; I see no reason whatsoever to suppose that the total has any cause whatsoever . . . (Russell in Hick (ed.) 1964, p. 175)

Russell likened the inference from *the belief that every part of the cosmos has a cause* to *the thesis that the cosmos itself has a cause* to the following fallacy:

> I can illustrate what seems to me your [the theists] fallacy. Every man who exists has a mother, and it seems to me your argument is that therefore the human race must have a mother, but obviously the human race hasn't a mother – that's a different logical space. (Russell in Hick (ed.) 1964, p. 175)

Is the theistic strategy a sophisticated form of this fallacy? Putting aside for now debate about whether an argument for theism can be convincingly mustered on the basis of causal relations within the cosmos, can theism even carve out sufficient "philosophical space" so that it remains a possible, philosophical option?

In reply, many (though not all) theists take their stand on the supposition that the cosmos is contingent; its structure and constitution are not such that the cosmos exists necessarily. The cosmos is thereby conceived of in profoundly different terms than God. God exists necessarily, without external cause or support, without the contribution of any material reality. According to these theists the universe can be referred to as the totality of contingent things while God is identified as noncontingent, all-knowing, all-powerful, good, and so on. John Findlay highlights the central religious conviction of God's necessary existence:

> Not only is it contrary to the demands and claims inherent in religious attitudes that their object should exist "accidentally"; it is also contrary to these demands

that it should possess its various excellences in some merely adventitious manner. It would be quite unsatisfactory from the religious point of view, if an object merely happened to be wise, good, powerful, and so forth, even to a superlative degree. (Findlay 1964, p. 117)

In theism, God does not exist by chance, the laws of the current galaxy, or by dint of our conceptual and linguistic schemes. In traditional terms, God is said to possess aseity (from *aseitas* for "being for oneself" as opposed to *ab alio* for "being from another"). The existence of the cosmos is derived from God whereas God's existence is not derived from the cosmos or from any external force. In some medieval philosophy of God (Jewish, Christian, and Islamic) it was said that God's very essence or nature is existence – to think of God is to think of a necessarily existing being – whereas this is not true of anything in the cosmos. Unlike the cosmos, God is subsisting being itself (*ipsum esse subsistens*).

For a statement of the extended contingency of the cosmos, consider David Lewis's description below. His depiction of the world may be employed to delimit what is meant by the cosmos as opposed to what traditional theists think of as God:

The world we live in is a very inclusive thing. Every stick and every stone you have ever seen is part of it. And so are you and I. And so are the planet Earth, the solar system, the entire Milky Way, the remote galaxies we see through telescopes, and (if there are such things) all the bits of empty space between the stars and galaxies. There is nothing so far away from us as not to be part of our world. Anything at any distance at all is to be included. Likewise the world is inclusive in time. No long-gone ancient Romans, no long-gone pterodactyls, no long-gone primordial cloud of plasma are too far in the past, nor are the dead dark stars too far in the future to be part of this same world. Maybe, as I myself think, the world is a big physical object; or maybe some parts of it are entelechies or spirits or auras. . . . But nothing is so alien in kind as not to be part of our world, provided only that it does exist at some distance and direction from here, or at some time before or after or simultaneous with now. . . . But things might have been different, in ever so may ways. . . . I might not have existed at all – neither I myself, nor any counterpart of me. Or there might never have been any people. Or the physical constants might have had somewhat different values, incompatible with the emergence of life. Or there might have been altogether different laws of nature; and instead of electrons and quarks, there might have been alien particles, without charge or mass or spin but with alien physical properties that nothing in this world shares. There are ever so many ways that a world might be; and one of these many ways is the way that this world is. (Lewis 1986, pp. 1–2)

The history of the concept of God in Judaism, Christianity, and Islam has been shaped and sharpened over against this concept of a contingent cosmos.

The apparent intelligibility of marking off the God–world relationship along the lines of necessity and contingency is sometimes attested to by naturalists. The naturalist J. J. C. Smart thinks the question, "Why does the cosmos exist at all?" must be put aside as unanswerable. He thinks there is no God and the existence of a physical cosmos must simply be accepted as a fact that is not explained by anything existing outside of it. Nonetheless, he concedes that the contingency of the cosmos leaves him dissatisfied or, rather, in awe. The existence of the cosmos causes him to feel awe and to wonder why it exists:

> Logic seems to tell us that the only answer [to the question "Why does the cosmos exist?"] which is not absurd is to say, "Why shouldn't it?" Nevertheless, though I know . . . [the argument that] God created the cosmos can be pulled to pieces by a correct logic, I still feel I want to go on asking the question. Indeed, though logic has taught me to look at such a question with the gravest suspicion, my mind often seems to reel under the immense significance it seems to have for me. That anything should exist at all does seem to me a matter for the deepest awe. But whether other people feel this sort of awe, and whether they or I ought to is another question. I think we ought to. If so, the question arises: If "Why should anything exist at all?" cannot be interpreted after the manner of the cosmological argument [for God's existence], that is, as an absurd request for the nonsensical postulation of a logically necessary being, what sort of question is it? . . . All I can say is, that I do not yet know. (Smart, in Flew and MacIntyre [eds] 1955, p. 46)

This appeal to feelings like awe suggests that feelings and emotions can have a significant role in one's philosophical theorizing. In the case just cited, Smart resists concluding on the basis of these feelings that the question at hand is reasonable, but these feelings still incline him to doubt whether he is absolutely right in dispatching the question. The same is true for John Hospers, a naturalist who also rejects the theistic enterprise of accounting for the existence of the cosmos in terms of some transcendent, divine reality. In this passage he testifies to the appeal of the question that theists use to sharpen the God–cosmos distinction: Why is it that this contingent cosmos exists replete with its basic laws? Hospers contends that there are basic laws of nature that are not to be explained in any deeper or broader fashion, and that he feels that this is, in some ways (at least psychologically), unsatisfactory:

If a law is really a basic one, any request for an explanation of it is self-contradictory. To explain a law is to place it in a context or network of wider and more inclusive laws; a basic law is by definition one of which this cannot be done. . . . Like so many others, this point may seem logically compelling but psychologically unsatisfying. Having heard the above argument, one may still feel inclined to ask, "Why are the basic uniformities of the universe the way they are, and not some other way? Why should we have just *these* laws rather than other ones? I want an *explanation* of why they are as they are." I must confess here, as an autobiographical remark, that I cannot help sharing this feeling; I want to ask why the laws of nature, being contingent, are as they are, even though I cannot conceive of what an explanation of this would be like, and even though by my own argument above the request for such an explanation is self-contradictory. (Hospers 1956, pp. 116–17)

To many theists, the feelings expressed by Smart and Hospers may be read as stemming from a legitimate, important drive to understand the existence of the cosmos in a broader, explanatory context. According to some theistic philosophers, such feelings are not philosophically irrelevant, like getting a headache when developing an argument in philosophy of law. Rather, it is closer to Albert Einstein's appeal to feeling; he held that "feeling is the strongest and noblest motive for scientific research" (1973, p. 37). Theists aim to foster what they see as this natural drive to explain why the cosmos should exist, as well as to defend the coherence (or at least *apparent* coherence) of appealing to a noncontingent, omnipotent, omniscient, unsurpassable reality that is responsible for the existence of the cosmos.

So, does theism fall into the conceptual pitfalls that are marked by Hepburn and Russell? If there is some credibility to referring to the cosmos as defined by its contingency, then one may well be able to set up the inside–outside distinction that Hepburn critiques. That is, theists may reasonably refer to what lies "outside" the cosmos provided they can secure the ideas that the cosmos is contingent and that, if there is a God, God exists necessarily. From a theistic viewpoint, to construe God's necessary existence as simply a redundant item, the mother of all those who have mothers (as Russell supposed), is wide of the mark, because the God of monotheism is not a supercontingent or hypercontingent being but, rather, one that is profoundly different from the cosmos.

As noted before, the arguments for and against believing theism is true will be taken up later; this section simply outlines the opposing positions of naturalism and theism. Some naturalists have launched important objections to the entire project of thinking that God or anything whatever can exist necessarily. A widely represented objection is that it makes no sense to think there could be a necessarily existing thing; "necessity" pertains to statements, not things. These objections and theistic replies will arise in chapter 10.

In the history of the philosophy of God, sparring over the intelligibility of the God–cosmos relation has been the most heated at precisely the point where theism and scientific naturalism collide. Sometimes the conflict concerns specific claims made on behalf of theism, e.g. certain miracles take place, God made the cosmos in 5000 BCE not 15 billion years ago, God created animal species separately and not solely through evolution, etc. At the end of this section it will be useful to outline further the tension between theism and naturalism as this pertains to the sciences.

Putting to one side (for now) specific theistic claims about miracles and so on, is theism by its very nature in tension with the natural sciences? Naturalism is often advanced in association with scientific claims. What may be called "scientific naturalism" takes its stand with the presumed sufficiency of an explanation of the cosmos that does not involve God. John Barrow writes of the naturalist ideal as ultimately amounting to a "Theory of Every-thing" which "will write all the laws of nature into a single statement that reveals the inevitability of everything that was, is and is to come in the physical world" (Barrow 1991, p. vii). Leaving aside for now whether this project is feasible, the drive to achieve a theory of everything seems to be a scientifically desirable goal. Consider, then, the claim that theism may be shown from the beginning to be not just opposed to naturalism, but opposed to science. Does not recourse to the claim "this occurred because God willed it to be so" seem anti-scientific?

– Theism may be nonscientific insofar as it posits a God that cannot be materially observed through the techniques of the natural sciences, but mak-ing the case that it is incompatible with science is a more ambitious claim that is not easy to secure. Statements and explanations within science are one thing. Do they rule out there being something beyond the spatio-temporal world? Jonathan Kvanvig and Hugh McCann offer the following picture of God's relation to the cosmos. While theism requires that God is the primary cause of the cosmos that science studies, it is not committed to denying the reality of cosmic spatio-temporal causation. Science covers intra-cosmic relations, not the relation between the cosmos and its transcendent creator. Theism is thereby cast as a super-theory that does not compete with, or at least does not *necessarily* compete with, scientific explanations of what occurs within the universe. If some theists are right, appealing to God's creativity can explain the existence of the cosmos, but not why salt behaves as it does in a scientific context:

> As Creator, God is directly and primarily responsible for the fact that there is something rather than nothing: that is, it is His creative activity that is causally responsible for the existence of the physical universe. To say this is not to say He is directly responsible for the states of things in the universe, or the changes they undergo. By contrast, principles of scientific causation are concerned precisely to explain those states and changes, and they do so by relating them to other states and changes. In all cases, the existence of what occupies a state or undergoes a change is presupposed. Indeed, even where the operation of secondary causes produces what may be held to be a substance (salt, for example), the process by which it is produced is conceived scientifically as a transformation of something that predates it (say, sodium and chlorine, or the particles that make up the atoms of these) . . . In no case is it held that the operation of secondary causes is responsible for the existence of something, where the alternative is the absence of anything whatever. (Kvanvig and McCann, in Morris [ed.] 1988, p. 16)

Because theistic explanations of the existence and continuation *of* the cosmos address a different level than scientific explanations *within* the cosmos, some argue that theistic explanations can complement, rather than supplant or compromise, the sciences.

It is well to note, however, that while theism may cohere with the sciences, it does not cohere with certain scientific theories when these are explicitly anti-theistic. Thus, some materialist scientific projects are designed to privilege impersonal, nonintentional, nonconscious explanations of events over explanations that are personal, intentional, and conscious. Some materialists countenance explanations of human consciousness, and indeed of anything whatever, only if they can ultimately be explained without making recourse to consciousness and intentionality. If we are to arrive at a satisfactory, comprehensive account of consciousness, this account must itself be void of reference to intelligence and consciousness. Daniel Dennett writes:

> The account of intelligence required of psychology must not of course be question begging. It must not explain intelligence in terms of intelligence, for instance by assigning responsibility for the existence of intelligence in creatures to the munificence of an intelligent Creator. (Dennett 1978, p. 83)

132

What theists question here is whether the direction of explanation must invariably be from intelligence to nonintelligence, explaining consciousness in terms of nonconscious forces.

Many theists grant that in neuroscience we rightly endeavor to account for intelligent behavior and mental states (at least in part) in terms of underlying physiological objects and processes. But, so it is asked, why must one see this as part of a strategy that displaces intelligence altogether? Why cannot the workings of our own physiology and, indeed, the cosmos itself be seen as a manifestation of supreme intelligence? Richard Swinburne's effort to fill out such a view of supreme intelligence is the mirror opposite of Daniel Dennett's efforts to explain intelligence in terms of ultimately nonintelligent, impersonal forces. Swinburne contends that the laws of nature are subsumed or underwritten by an all-encompassing divine agency:

> Almost all regularities of succession [of nature] are due to the normal operation of scientific laws. But to say this is simply to say that these regularities are instances of more general regularities. The operation of the most fundamental regularities clearly cannot be given a normal scientific explanation. If their operation is to receive an explanation and not merely to be left as a brute fact, that explanation must therefore be in terms of the rational choice of a free agent. (Swinburne 1968, 204)

According to Swinburne, this theistic drive to see intentional explanation as the most fundamental in the cosmos does nothing to displace science:

> If . . . a very powerful non-embodied rational agent is responsible for the operation of the laws of nature, then normal scientific explanation would prove to be personal explanation. That is, explanation of some phenomenon in terms of the operation of a natural law would ultimately be an explanation in terms of the operation of an agent. Hence (given an initial arrangement of matter) the principles of explanation of phenomena would have been reduced from two to one . . . So then in so far as regularities of succession produced by the operation of natural laws are similar to those produced by human agents, to postulate that a rational agent is responsible for them would indeed provide a simple unifying and coherent explanation of natural phenomena. (Swinburne 1968, p. 206)

Some critics dismiss the theistic alternative because they do not accept the coherence of the theistic portrait of the nature and scope of divine intelligence and agency. For example, Brian O'Shaughnessy suggests that the detailed, precise character of the cosmos provides some reason to think that there is not an underlying, supreme intelligence responsible for it:

> Well, four centuries of triumphant advance by the rock-bottom physical sciences of physics cannot but leave some mark on philosophy. When you can predict the wave length of a spectrum line to eight decimal places it is rather more difficult to believe that the underlying reality of everything is spiritual, e.g. an immaterial Deity. After all, should a Deity be so fastidious? (O'Shaughnessy 1980, p. xvii)

But why think a divine intelligence should be so limited? If theists can clarify and explicate the notions of power and knowledge discussed in the early chapters, then theists can juxtapose naturalism with a comprehensive philosophy of nature that, in principle, need not have the limitations O'Shaughnessy proposes.

In future chapters we shall examine in greater detail the plausibility of naturalism and theism. But before doing so, let us explore the nature of more radical, transcendent forms of theism than we have covered so far and consider monist, nontheistic portraits of ultimate reality. How far may we go in thinking of what might exist beyond the physical cosmos, or beyond the naturalist conception of the world? How transcendent can we imagine God or some other religiously significant, ultimate reality? This is the topic of the next chapter.

Suggested Questions and Topics

(1)   Does determinism lead to fatalism? Fatalism is the thesis that what persons do is futile and of no effect on the future. A textbook characterization of fatalism would be: either you will get top marks in a class or you will not. If you will, then nothing you try to do will prevent it. If you will not, nothing you can try to do will change that. It therefore makes no difference what you do.

(2)   Contrast the strongest cases for determinism and libertarianism.

(3)   If God foreknows what you will do, can you do otherwise? If God foreknows what God will do, can God do otherwise? It has been argued that if God is omniscient, God cannot act intentionally. Consider the following argument:

(a) To say that a person is omniscient is to say that he knows all that will happen, including all the decisions he will make and all the actions he will perform.

(b) To say that a person is deliberating is to say that she is trying to decide or make up her mind about her own future, possible actions, given certain beliefs, wants and intentions she has.

(c) But a person at the same time cannot both know that he will do a certain action and deliberate about whether to do the same action.

(d) Therefore, if God is omniscient, he cannot deliberate.

(e) To say that a person is acting intentionally is to say she is acting in a rational, purposive, goal-directed manner to bring about what she desires.

(f) All intentional action necessitates deliberation.

(g) Therefore, if God is omniscient, he cannot act intentionally (from Reichenbach 1984; minor stylistic adjustments mine).

(4) If God foreknows what you will ask for in prayer, why ask for it? Analyze the following argument from R. L. Goldstein:

> Think for example, of all the ink that has been spilled about the alleged omniscience of God, yet it should be clear to anyone who would take a moment to notice that the God who is worshipped by those who approach him in prayer is far removed, indeed, from being omniscient. On the contrary, God's worshippers are forever having to remind him of injustices he has overlooked. The writing on religion is motivated largely by interests developed in logic and metaphysics and has little – or nothing – to do with religion itself. (Goldstein 1983, p. 114; for a reply see Schlesinger 1988, pp. 26–31 and Matthews 1971)

(5) Critically assess the Aristotelian "solution" to the paradox of freedom and foreknowledge.

(6) It has been proposed by J. R. Lucas that there are truths about future free activity but God preserves our freedom by not knowing these truths. Analyze the following stance:

> The real solution to the problem of God's omniscience is to be found by drawing a parallel with his omnipotence. Although God is able to do all things, we do not think he does do all things. . . . We allow that some things happen against God's will. . . . If God is prepared to compromise his omnipotence for the sake of human freedom, surely then he would be prepared to compromise his omniscience also. If he suffers his will to be confined in order that his creatures may have room to make their own decisions, he must allow his understanding to be

abridged in order to allow men privacy to form their own plans for themselves. It seems to me entirely unobjectionable that God should limit his infallible knowledge as he does his power, in order to let us be independent of him. (Lucas 1970, p. 75)

(7)   Do you think there can be cases of knowing a concept like "red" without having any experience of seeing "red"? Some philosophers and theologians propose God knows the world experientially. Consider the philosophical and religious principles at stake in the following two claims, the first by Charles Hartshorne and the second by David Brown:

To fully sympathize with and to fully know the feelings of others are the same relationship, separable in our human case only because there the "fully" never applies, and we never know the feelings of others but only have knowledge about them, abstract diagrams of how in rough, more or less general ways they feel. If we saw the individuality and vividness of the feeling we would have the feeling. As Hume said, without perhaps knowing what a contribution to theology he was here making, the vivid idea of a feeling is in principle coincident with its "impression," that is, with such a feeling as one's own. (Hartshorne 1941, p. 163)

Some children have the misfortune to be born without the ability to experience pain and so unless they are educated in time about the consequences of their actions they end up by doing themselves permanent damage, even accidentally killing themselves. However, if they survive to adulthood, then they will have acquired a good knowledge of the consequences of pain, but even so they will remain without any experiential knowledge of what it feels like to be in pain. Similarly it seems to me with God. Of course, without the Incarnation he already had perfect knowledge of the consequences of pain, but only the Incarnation could have brought him knowledge of what it feels like to be one of us. (Brown 1989, pp. 55–6)

(8)   Analyze the following position of J. C. A. Gaskin:

I do not think it is merely a failure of my anthropocentric imagination that I cannot grasp what it would be like to be a conscious agent everywhere at once. Conscious agents (men, cats, dogs, ghosts and Greek Gods) act from a point of view of the universe. They even have a point of view of their own bodies where a body is present. God, *ex hypothesis* does not. If I imagine myself able, as a basic act, to turn the moon round on its axis so that you could see the other side of it from earth, I would inevitably conceive of myself seeing the moon from some point of view. The supposition of a sight, or an awareness, which embraces all

136

points of view, is not just omniscience, it is dispersal of the agent. It might be like seeing myself from my own fingertip and from everywhere else on my own body simultaneously. I cannot make much sense of even that degree of dispersal of my center of consciousness, let alone understand a dispersal which embraces every view of everything in the universe. (Gaskin 1984, p. 112)

How might a theist reply?

(9)   If God does not know future free action, in what respects, if any, can God be surprised by the future? Peter Geach contends that God can still have complete control over the future even if God does not know precisely what will occur because God "knows all possibilities of development." He thereby contends that his conception of God does not limit God in any way that threatens a high theistic view of God's sovereignty. "I should admit that my account made God's knowledge limited only if I had to ascribe to God such things as surprise, regret, and improvisation: but of course I deny that I ascribe them to God" (Geach 1977, p. 141). Assess the strengths and weaknesses (if any) in Geach's portrayal of God as a "Grand Master":

A parable I have found useful is this: a chess master, without looking at the board, plays a score of opponents simultaneously; his knowledge of chess is so vastly superior to theirs that he can deal with any moves they are going to make, and he has no need to improvise or deliberate. There is no evident contradiction in supposing that God's changeless knowledge thus governs the whole course of the world, whatever men may choose to do. (Geach 1972, p. 325)

Geach develops this further in another work:

God is the supreme Grand Master who has everything under control. Some of the players are consciously helping his plan, others are trying to hinder it; whatever the finite players do, God's plan will be executed; though various lines of God's play will answer to various moves of the finite players. God cannot be surprised or thwarted or cheated or disappointed. God, like some grand master of chess, can carry out his plan even if he has announced it beforehand. "On that square," says the Grand Master, "I will promote my pawn to Queen and deliver checkmate to my adversary": and it is even so. No line of play that finite players may think of can force God to improvise: his knowledge of the game already embraces all the possible variant lines of play, theirs do not. (Geach 1977, p. 58)

(10)   Keith Ward argues against a conception of God and creation that would involve God's nontemporal knowledge of creaturely free action

prior to the creation. Instead he believes theism is better served by believing God to be temporal and subject to change. Analyze the following argument:

> God's creation is consequent upon his knowledge, which depends in part on creaturely acts, which presuppose that creation has already taken place. The only break from this vicious circle is to conceive of divine creation as a gradual and temporal process, depending partly on possibilities in his own being and partly on creatures. In a strictly limited sense, God can be changed from without. (Ward 1982, p. 152)

(11)   Anthony Kenny pinpoints the advantages and disadvantages of versions of theism that treat freedom and determinism as compatible. His specific focus is Calvinism, a religious movement based on the French Protestant theologian John Calvin (1509–64), known especially for its high view of God's will as absolute, unconditioned, sovereign and omni-determining. How might a compatibilist theist (whether a Calvinist or not) respond to the following stance?

> Anyone who accepts the compatibility of determinism with freedom must agree that agents can be justly blamed and punished for acts which they were predetermined to perform, provided only they had the ability and opportunity to refrain from them. But if the Calvinist system is to be tenable, it must be possible to show not only that human beings can be involved in blame for determined sins, but that God can avoid responsibility for them. And this seems to be much more difficult to show. For if an agent freely and knowingly sets in motion a deterministic process with a certain upshot . . . If determinism is true, it is comparatively easy to explain how he can infallibly foresee free action, but impossibly difficult to show how he [God] is not the author of sin. (Kenny 1979, pp. 86–7)

(12)   In his important book, *The Trinity*, Augustine describes God's creation in terms of God's knowledge. Can the following view be articulated in a defensible form?

> But He [God] does not, therefore, know all His creatures, both spiritual and corporeal, because they are, but they . . . are because He knows them. For He was not ignorant of what He was going to create. He created, therefore, because He knew; He did not know because He created. He did not know them differently when they were created, than when they were to be created, for nothing has been added to His wisdom from them; it has remained the same as

it was, while they came into existence as they should and when they should. (Augustine, trans. 1963, p. 485)

(13)   Some philosophers distinguish types of knowledge. As noted in a suggested question in chapter 1, Gilbert Ryle argued that there was a difference between *knowledge that* (as in knowing that a proposition is true) and *knowledge how* (as in knowing how to swim or to tell a joke); see Ryle's *The Concept of Mind*. In the course of considering whether there is an important distinction between these types of knowledge (and others as well, such as *knowledge who*), you may wish to investigate whether these need to be incorporated into an analysis of omniscience.

(14)   Assess the following difficulty with the second and third analysis of omniscience. This problem emerges when omniscience is defined in terms of propositions and their apparent privacy. Consider the sentence "I am in pain" uttered by myself. The use of the pronoun "I" is an indexical term that picks me out. Some philosophers have held that these first-person sentences express propositions that are radically private and can only be accessed by the person whose individual essence these express. In knowing I am in pain, you would know the truth of some other proposition such as "Charles is in pain" or "That fellow over there is in pain" or even "The person who just said 'I am in pain' is saying something true." But none of these get at the proposition that I would express by saying the sentence myself. If so, is there a radical problem with the nature of omniscience? Some think so, for then one would be compelled to admit there are propositions that an all-knowing being would not know (Kretzmann 1966). God cannot know the proposition "I am in pain" when I am in pain, but at best, some other proposition. There are several ways to reply which you may wish to explore. Consider the following. It involves analyzing omniscience in a way that bypasses propositions altogether:

Analysis 5

Being, B, is omniscient if and only if B knows of every state of affairs whether it obtains or not.

On this view, when I know the sentence "I am in pain" is true I know that the same state of affairs obtains which may be described as "Charles is in pain" or "the tallest philosopher in the room is in pain" and so on. When I am in pain I may know this state of affairs immediately and noninferentially, but this does not entail that there are hyperprivate propositions only I can access (see Chisholm 1976 for a defense of private propositions which he later rejected;

see Chisholm 1981 for a criticism of his earlier view; Kvanvig 1986 outlines some of the ways to access propositions in which God may be thought of as accessing all true propositions).

(15)   If God is eternal, can God be a person or person-like? Analyze Robert Coburn's argument as follows:

> Surely it is a necessary condition of anything's being a person that it should be capable (logically) of, among other things, doing at least some of the following: remembering, anticipating, reflecting, deliberating, deciding, intending, and acting intentionally. To see that this is one need but ask oneself whether anything which necessarily lacked all of the capacities noted would, under any conceivable circumstances, count as a person. But now an eternal being would necessarily lack all of these capacities inasmuch as their exercise by a being clearly required that the being exist in time. After all, reflection and deliberation takes time; deciding typically occurs at some time – and in any case it always makes sense to ask, "When did you (he, they, etc.) decide?"; remembering is impossible unless the being doing the remembering has a past; and so on. Hence, no eternal being, it would seem, could be a person. (Coburn 1963, p. 155)

A similar problem is raised by Stephen Davis. Is Davis correct that a timeless being can make no plans, cannot anticipate the future, recall the past, forgive others and so on? How might a defender of divine timelessness respond?

> But the obvious problem here is to understand how a timeless being can plan or anticipate or remember or respond or punish or warn or forgive. All such acts seem undeniably temporal. To make plans is to formulate intentions about the future. To remember is to have beliefs or knowledge about what is past. To respond is to be affected by events that have occurred in the past. To punish is to cause someone to suffer because of something done in the past. To warn is to caution someone about dangers that might lie in the future. To forgive someone is to restore a past relationship that was damaged by offense. (S. Davis 1983, p. 14)

There is more material on God's relation to time in the next chapter.

(16)   Comment on Joseph Albo's (1380–1444) claim: "To know God's nature we would have to be God Himself." It would be useful to consider Albo's thesis in light of Thomas Nagel's work on knowing what it is like to be in certain mental states (Nagel 1974).

(17)   Does it make sense to refer to the universe as a thing?

(18)   Is theism by its very nature, inherently anti-scientific?

(19)   How might one establish or reasonably argue for the claim that the cosmos is contingent? Or that it makes sense to describe God as necessarily existing? This chapter takes note of how Smart and Hospers were prompted by "feelings" to retain awe or wonder about the existence of a contingent cosmos. Wittgenstein, also, is reported to have

> had a certain experience which could best be described by saying that "when I have it I wonder at the existence of a world. And I am then inclined to use such phrases as 'How extraordinary that anything should exist!' or 'How extraordinary that the world should exist!'" (Malcolm 1958, p. 70).

To what extent can experiences bolster or justify the theistic project of distinguishing between a contingently existing cosmos and a necessarily existing God?

(20)   As noted in chapter 2 and this chapter, theists seek to demarcate the divine in terms of maximal levels of excellence with respect to power and knowledge. C. D. Broad raises the following problem of supposing there are upper limits of greatness with respect to some properties. He criticizes the notion that there could be "a being which has all positive powers and qualities to the highest possible degree":

> [T]hat each positive property is to be present in the highest possible degree . . . will be meaningless verbiage unless there is some *intrinsic* maximum or upper limit to the possible intensity of every positive property which is capable of degrees. With some magnitudes this condition is fulfilled. It is, e.g., logically impossible that any proper fraction should exceed the ratio 1/1; and again, on a certain definition of "angle", it is logically impossible for any angle to exceed four right angles. But it seems quite clear that there are other positive properties, such as length or temperature or pain, to which there is no intrinsic maximum or upper limit of degree. (Broad, cited by Wierenga 1979, p. 41)

In your view, does it make sense to attribute to God the greatest possible degree of power and knowledge? Love and happiness? Sorrow?

Further Reading and Considerations

From *A Companion to Philosophy of Religion*, see: "Omniscience"; "Necessity"; "Omnipresence"; "Foreknowledge and Human Freedom"; "Impassibility and

Immutability"; "Providence and Predestination"; "Creation and Conservation"; "The Jewish Tradition"; "The Islamic Contribution to Medieval Philosophical Theology"; "Simplicity"; "Theism and the Scientific Understanding of the Mind"; and "Naturalistic Explanations of Religion." Further readings on free will and determinism have already been referenced in the main text of the chapter. For a defense of determinism, *Freedom and Belief* by Galen Strawson is especially recommended, as is Ted Honderich's *A Theory of Determinism*, which is represented in simpler form in *How Free Are You?* For a powerful defense of libertarianism see *An Essay on Free Will* by Peter van Inwagen. A sophisticated recent contribution to the omniscience–freedom debate is J. M. Fischer's *The Metaphysics of Free Will*. For material on epistemology that may be of assistance in developing accounts of divine omniscience see *A Companion to Epistemology*, edited by Dancy and Sosa. For an interesting book that explores the unity of divine attributes, see Christopher Hughes' *On a Complex Theory of a Simple God*. For additional material on divine necessity, see R. M. Adams' "Divine Necessity," William Mann's "Modality, Morality, and God," and the contributions to *Being and Goodness* edited by Scott MacDonald. For an interesting treatment of the relationship between theism and science, see Peter Forrest's *God Without the Supernatural; A Defense of Scientific Theism* (1996). The more prominent recent naturalists that are critical of theism are J. L. Mackie, Wallace Matson, Paul Durtz, Kai Nielsen, Richard Robinson, Ingamar Hedenius, and Michael Martin. Important anti-theistic earlier work has been done by Ludwig Feuerbach (1884–1900), Sigmund Freud (1856–1939), Max Weber (1864–1920), and Bertrand Russell (1872–1970).

6

The Transcendence of the Sacred

Some philosophers object to theism on the grounds that it is too anthropomorphic (from the Greek *anthropomorphus* for "of human form") in its portrait of God as a supreme reality which, on reflection, looks very similar to a human being or, in Christianity, a committee of three human beings. Christian art has often portrayed God as a bearded old man or as two bearded men (Father and the Son) and a dove (the Holy Spirit) and, to some critics, this appears to be a blasphemous collapse of the distinction between the Creator and creation. The insistence upon a sharp contrast between God and creation has been evident not only among nontheists but among theists as well. Judaism, Christianity, and Islam each have prominent advocates of the profound "otherness" of God. These religions picture God as immanent (from the Latin *immanere* meaning "to inhabit"), or proximate, to the cosmos but God is also believed to be radically transcendent (from the Latin *transcendere* for "to cross a boundary"). In Judaism and Islam a commitment to God's transcendence motivates a staunch prohibition against visually representing God. While it may be thought that Christianity is utterly different on this point because of its central conviction that God became incarnate as a human being, there are also Christian advocates of God's transcendence. There are strands within Christianity that either prohibit depictions of God altogether or, if they are permitted, put a stern emphasis on the profound inadequacy of all such images. Many theists seek to articulate and defend an understanding of the divine as a transcendent reality, a reality not just beyond human form but beyond the boundary of this spatio-temporal world.

This chapter begins by considering the intelligibility of believing that God transcends time; God is eternal or timeless. Next, the radical claim is examined that God is not an individual thing or entity at all. Instead, God is Being.

143

This philosophy of God has led some philosophers to the conviction that human language is not up to the task of describing or directly referring to God. On this view, the divine is ineffable, incapable of being described or referred to in human language (from the Latin *ineffabilis* for "incapable of being expressed in words"). This view of God's transcendence can dramatically check the whole enterprise of philosophy of religion. Consider, for example, T. R. Miles's claim, "To say that God is transcendent is to emphasize the non-applicability of any concept whatever" (Miles 1966, p. 150). If no concepts apply to God, how is a philosophy of God to proceed, if at all? From a religious point of view, it may well seem sacrilegious or arrogant to apply concepts to God philosophically.

The final sections of this chapter consider conceptions of the "otherness" of the divine outside theistic tradition. This includes the monist treatment of the divine in Advaita Vedanta Hinduism. In this tradition, theistic portraits of God as a person are seen as at best provisionally acceptable views of God or Brahman which, in the end, need to give way to (or be seen as an imperfect reflection of) a supreme reality without form, beyond the limitations of personality, space and time. As Eric Lott puts it, "If Vedanta were to be reduced to one key concept, it would be to the concern for Brahman's transcendent nature" (Lott 1980, p. 20). Is it intelligible to posit such a transcendent reality?

God's Transcendence of Time: Arguments from Perfection and Creation

In Judaism, Christianity, and Islam, God is sometimes described as though God is in time; God delivers people from evil, challenges them to be just, calls them into relationship with one another and with God. Such language seems to imply that God is temporal and changeable; God does not "timelessly" or "changelessly" speak to prophets but does so at some times and not at others. These ways of describing God suggest that there is a *before, during*, and *after* for God, or a past, present, and future. God may be infinitely more powerful than any created thing, all-knowing, and exist necessarily and thereby transcend our cosmos on all these fronts, but, for all that, God is not transcendent over time. Does this portray God as too limited, too much like a part of the cosmos rather than its creator? The idea that God transcends time has been backed by two highly influential arguments. The first involves the appeal to God's perfection. The second appeals to the thesis that God created the cosmos from nothing. Consider first the argument from perfection.

If God is a supremely excellent reality, then God is free from the malleable, changeable, limitations of temporality. Historically, some philosophers and theologians have held that construing God in time makes God in some way a captive or prisoner of time. It would mean God cannot enjoy the unity of life that should mark supreme perfection. Brian Leftow contends that a temporal God would have certain limitations that an eternal God would not:

> A life can have two kinds of limit. A life can have outer limits, a beginning or end. A life can also have inner limits, boundaries between parts, e.g. that between one's first and second year. If a life lasts forever in time, always one part of it's past and another is future. So any life in time contains at least one limit, an inner boundary dividing its past from its future. This inner limit is as real a constraint as outer limits are. For it walls us off from parts of our lives. We no longer live what is past, but can only recall it and we do not have even memory's flawed access to our futures. (Leftow 1997, p. 258)

Leftow concedes that such limitations have their advantages, but with God, such limits would mark a splintering and fragmentation that does not befit a conception of the fullness and perfection of the divine:

> Our pasts contain episodes it is good to be done with, and our futures contain events we might dread if we knew of them. But there are also past events we wish we could relive, and future days we are eager to see. Now God is perfect, and so lives a perfect being's life. What is a perfect being's life like? Plausibly, no part of such a life is on balance miserable: each part's balance of good and evil, or the qualities of its specific goods, are such that on balance, the perfect being is better off living that part of its life than not living it. If this is true, having a past and a future would be at best an only partly compensated loss for God. In not living part of His life, God would lose some good involved in living it. If God is on balance better off living than not living each part of His life, the loss of any evils that part of His life brings Him would not wholly compensate for the loss of that good. Thus having a past and a future would limit the perfection of God's life. (Leftow 1997, p. 258)

This position has been well represented historically by prominent Jewish, Christian, and Islamic thinkers.

Peter Bertocci succinctly summarizes an argument akin to Leftow's. It is an argument for the conclusion that God is changeless. If God is outside of time, God is not subject to temporal change. Is this a disadvantage? Arguably not, for a requirement of God's supreme excellence or perfection is that God is not subject to change:

A perfect being, one who is "all finished" cannot be a changing being. Why? Because change, be it in a cabbage or in God must involve either adding or subtracting something, for better or worse. If a being is perfect, what can there be to add or to subtract? He would not allow himself to lose anything good, and being perfect, nothing could be added to his nature. The conclusion is inevitable: God does not change; he is immutable. (Bertocci 1951, p. 309)

God's perfection thereby secures God's changelessness. (Some theists hold that God is changeless and not timeless, but virtually all who believe God is timeless believe that God is changeless.)

The second argument for thinking God transcends time is that this is a crucial presupposition of the thesis that God created the cosmos from nothing. "In the beginning God created the heaven and the earth." So begins Genesis, the first book of the Hebrew and Christian Bibles. This has frequently been read as marking God's act of creating a spatial, temporal world. There was no spatio-temporal stuff out of which God made the cosmos. In fact there was no time at all. God from eternity willed that time and space come into existence. If God is not in time, there was no lengthy time period prior to God creating. But, given that God is in time and caused the cosmos to exist, why did God wait so long to create it? Augustine puts the problem as follows:

What was God doing before he made heaven and earth? If [God] did nothing, why did he not continue in this way . . . forever? If any new motions arise in God, or a new will is formed in him, to the end of establishing creation which he had never established previously . . . then [God] is not truly . . . eternal. Yet if it were God's sempiternal [i.e. everlasting] will for the creation to exist, why is not the creation sempiternal also? (1960, pp. 284–5)

On the supposition that God is eternal, one may respond by claiming there was no time before the cosmos existed; the question of why God did not create earlier does not make sense. It may be odd to think of there being a moment in time and no prior moment (does it not always make sense to ask of anything that occurs, what took place before it?), but some argue that it does not land one in any obvious philosophical absurdity. It would be absurd to claim that there could be, say, a greatest possible number of hours, but it is not clearly mistaken to claim there was a first moment. Arguably, there is no evident logical or metaphysical necessity as to why a temporal period must be preceded by a temporal period, though this is not to claim that imagining a first moment is easily done or possible to picture at all.

William Alston argues that if one maintains that God is in time, one is not justified in positing a creation from nothing. Because most (though certainly not all) theists historically, and today as well, believe God did create the cosmos from nothing, the following objection is designed to move these theists to accept the stance that God is eternal. In what follows, Alston argues that unless they accept the eternality of God, these theists will be forced to maintain that God and creation have always co-existed:

> If God is temporal we have to think of Him as infinitely extended in time. If He began to exist some finite period of time ago, that would call for some explanation outside Himself; He would not be a fundamentally underived being. His ceasing to exist is impossible for the same reason. And if the fact that there is a physical universe is due to an act of divine will, that act, if God is temporal, would have to take place at some time. But then at whatever time it takes place God would have already existed for an infinite period of time, and we would be faced with the Augustinian question of why God chose to create the universe at that time rather than at some other. Thus if we think of God as temporal the most reasonable picture is . . . of God and the world confronting each other throughout time as equally basic metaphysically, with God's creative activity connived to bringing it about, so far as possible that the world is in accordance with His aims. And conversely, if we are to defend the classical doctrine of creation we must come to think of God as nontemporal. (Alston 1989, pp. 132–3)

God's nontemporality is here advanced as crucial to a fundamental traditional teaching about the greatness of God's creativity.

As noted earlier, the thesis that God transcends time may appear at odds with biblical narratives in which God first does one act, then another, but some theologians construe such references to God as highly analogical or metaphorical. The Hebrew and Christian Bibles, as well as the Qur'an, describe God from *our point of view*. Perhaps *we* cannot help thinking of God as acting in successive, time-bound ways, and yet God's action is not successively or temporally executed. Many advocates of God's transcendence over time contend that God eternally wills succession; *God wills that there will be changes but God's will itself does not change*. God's inner being is therefore changeless or immutable, not subject to alteration and flux. God may have a temporal dimension by being "at" all times or (as Christians believe) in the incarnation, as Jesus Christ in first-century Palestine, but God's inner being is transcendent. Boethius (480–524) famously described the unity of God's possessing unending, unlimited life in this way: God's life is *tota simul* or all at once. To examine this topic at closer range, it is desirable to consider the nature of time.

147

The Nature of Time: The "A" Theory and the "B" Theory

What is time? This question is by no means easy to answer and, indeed, there is no current consensus philosophically or theologically as to what the answer is. Augustine's frustration with the question is widely shared:

> For what is time? Who can easily and briefly explain it? Who can even comprehend it in thought or put the answer into words? Yet is it not true that in conversation we refer to nothing more familiarly or knowingly than time? And surely we understand it when we speak of it; we understand it also when we hear another speak of it. What, then, is time? If no one asks me, I know what it is. If I wish to explain it to him who asks me, I do not know. (Augustine, trans. 1948, ch. XIV)

Frederick Waismann has more recently contended that it is a mistake to seek an analysis of time itself. Questions about time only make sense with respect to temporal frameworks as when one asks someone for the time. Allegedly deeper questions about time's nature are not so much deep as they are nonsensical:

> Whoever is able to understand the word "time" in the various examples and to apply it, knows just "what time is" and no formulation can give him a better understanding of it. The question "What is time?" leads us astray, since it causes us to seek an answer of the form "Time is . . . ," and there is no such answer. (Waismann 1959, p. 117)

It is easy to sympathize with the conclusion here, for it is difficult to formulate a noncircular definition of "time."

Perhaps the most plausible, least controversial claim about time is that it involves succession and change. Some scientists use a concept of operational or calendar time, according to which time is defined as a function of the rate of physical change. Thus, one may well use atomic clocks which measure the natural vibration frequency of atomic systems to define temporal periods. Do these operational devices provide the grounds for an illuminating philosophical definition of time? They have a scientific use and as such they can delimit scientifically important frames of reference, but they may not go very far if one then wants a definition of "rate of change." Consider the following exchange:

QUESTION: What is time?

ANSWER: Time is a rate of change.

QUESTION: What is "a rate of change"?

ANSWER: A rate of change is the sequence of when something is in a state at one time and not in that state at another time.

There is an obvious circularity here. It is not bypassed by appealing to atomic clocks, for the question of what constitutes "vibration" leads us back to the question of what constitutes time. A vibration, whether in a beam of cesium atoms or something else, involves variation in motion in which there is an activity (or state of affairs) at one time that is distinct from that at another time. Can we define time without circularity or without having to appeal to experience as when one might define "red" by enumerating cases (e.g. the color of blood)? It is difficult not to admit that at a fundamental level we have little recourse but to appeal to our experience of temporal change to "get at" the concept of time. We are acquainted with temporal change and may simply have to appeal to that experience in unpacking the notion that time involves the past, present, and future, or temporal relations of before, during, and after.

Time, then, is difficult to define without circularity or simply appealing to experience. Other definitions of time, for example "duration," face similar obstacles as the definition of change (e.g. *Question*: What is time? *Answer*: Duration. *Q*: What is duration? *A*: Continuance in time). Time is, in some sense, a foundational feature of our lives and it may be that the best any philosophical analysis of time can do is to try to bring to the surface the features of time as we experience it. Philosophical accounts of time are often delimited in terms of the "A" and "B" series (originally proposed by the British philosopher J. M. E. McTaggart, 1866–1925), and these are valuable to consider in any sustained inquiry into whether God transcends time. What follows is an overview of some of the most difficult concepts at work in the philosophy of God. There is a substantial debate over whether our temporal experiences justify either the "A" or "B" concept of time and, ultimately, over whether, on reflection, our experience leads us to think God can be outside of time.

According to the concept of time labelled "A," events can be properly described in terms of their occurring in the *past*, the *present,* and the *future.* Some event is present now, but eventually it will no longer be present. Arguably, this appears to many of us to be the way we do, in fact, experience time. In the "A" series, the reality of the past is affirmed, though it is not to be construed as a quasi-spatial region some "distance" from the present moment. The events of the past may be said to have ceased to be if that means they have "ceased to be present," but they have not ceased to be if that means they have perished into oblivion and can no longer be referred to. This characterization of time as in "A" series has its defenders (Gale, Lucas, and others), as well as its detractors (McTaggart, J. J. C. Smart, and others). These detractors argue that the "A" series leaves us with too mysterious a picture of the past and future. After the present moment has indeed passed, where did it go? Many "B" theorists claim that time needs to be understood from a more encompassing, less subjective, point of view.

Some philosophers and scientists are drawn to the notion that time is laid out in the "B" series in which objects may be described as occurring in three temporal relations with one another: *earlier than*, *simultaneous with*, and *afterward*. From the standpoint of the "B" series, everything that (for us) has occurred, is occurring or will occur may be described from a changeless point of view. Paul Davies describes a physicist's picture of space–time in terms of the "B" theory:

> The physicist views spacetime as laid out like a map, with time extending along one side. Events are marked as points on the map – some events are linked by causal relations to prior events, others like the decay of a radioactive nucleus, are labeled "spontaneous." It's all there, whether the causal links are incorporated or not. (Davies 1983, pp. 131–2)

Davies contends that, from a physicist's point of view, there is "no past, present and future." This theory of time is sometimes called the static theory as opposed to the dynamic theory. From a God's eye point of view, the whole tract of time may be seen and described.

The "A" theory gives pride of place to a "knife edge," existential sense of time as that which is ever changing. The "B" theory instead construes time in a spatialized, more extended and less existential fashion. It is difficult to illustrate the "A" series in spatial terms, but the "B" theory may be depicted as follows:

"B"

_____

1900   2000   2100

One reason why the "B" theory is preferred by some philosophers is that, on the "A" theory, the extent of the present moment, "now," is either highly

150

subjective or uninhabitable. The subjective nature of "now" is woven into ordinary language. The question "What is going on now?" may be answered with reference to what is going on that day or year or decade or century, e.g. "We are building a city." But if we want a precise reference to what is occurring "now," we seem driven to considering what is occurring at a given instant. How long is an instant? An "instant" is an idealized point in time, not an interval, that itself does not take time or last a while. One cannot say the word "now" in an instant, however quickly one tries. The "B" theorists can posit instants and intervals but they do not rely on our subjective experience of the present to do any more than that. According to some of its advocates the "B" theory captures our experience of the present in a unified, objective framework. Donald Williams illustrates how the "B" series treats the experience of the present:

> Nothing can "move" in time alone any more than in space alone, and time itself cannot "move" any more than space itself. "Does the road go anywhere?" asks the city tourist. "No, it stays right along here," replies the countryman. Time "flows" only in the sense in which a line flows or a landscape "recedes into the west." That is, it is an ordered extension. And each of us proceeds through time only as a fence proceeds across a farm: that is, parts of our being, and the fence's occupy successive instants and points, respectively. There is passage, but it is nothing extra. It is the mere happening of things, their existence strung along in the manifold. The term "the present" is the conventional way of designating the cross section of events which are simultaneous with the uttering of the phrase, and "the present moves" only in that when similar words occur at successively different moments, they denote, by a twist of language essentially the same as that of all "egocentric particulars," like "here" and "this," different cross sections of the manifold. (D. C. Williams, in Gale [ed.] 1978, p. 105)

Williams and other advocates of the "B" series contend that we should not posit the existence of "now" as some brute reality or thing. Just as physicists do not leave references to "here" and "there" in their final descriptions of the cosmos, references to "past," "present," and "future" can give way to reference to space–time coordinates. On their view, all space–time may be cast along "B" lines. Our existential sense of the "reality" of the present moment is part of the way reality is manifested to us. But that does not mean we need to posit "the present" in our basic theory of the cosmos:

> The jerk and whoosh of this moment, which are simply the real occurrence of one particular batch of events, are no different from the whoosh and being of any

other patch of events up and down the eternal time-stretch. Remembering some of the latter, however, and anticipating more, and being in mind that while they happen they are all called "the present," we mistakenly hypothesize *the* Present as a single surge of bigness which rolls along the time axis. There is in fact no more a single rolling Now than there is a single rolling Here along a spatial line – a standing line of soldiers, for example, though each of them has the vivid presentment of his own here. (D. C. Williams, in Gale [ed.] 1978, p. 110)

The "B" theory has been supported by an interpretation of the theory of relativity in physics, according to which the identification of an event as past or future is relative to certain frames of reference. Because, on this view, whether an event is properly described as "past" depends on one's point of view, some philosophers have concluded that the "A" series is a too subjective, experientially molded way of seeing things.

Some philosophers reply that to dispense with the "A" theory and opt only for "B" amounts to a radical denial of experience and clear common sense. Time can be described in "B" terms but it cannot supplant or defeat the conviction that *the present is now* and that this refers to an important, irreducible fact about reality. It is "irreducible" in the sense that it cannot be explained away in other terms. The statement "The average plumber has 2.5 children" can be reduced or analyzed in terms of statistical generalizations about lots of individual plumbers and children. Arguably, "the present is now" is something that cannot be broken down into "B" coordinates. Richard Gale thinks that it is because of our temporality as understood in "A" terms (past, present and future) that a question like "When are you?" is absurd:

[I]t is meaningful to ask "Where are you?" to which the answer could be "I am here": herein it is the direction that the voice comes from that constitutes the answer. However there is no use for the question "When are you?": "I am now" has no use in our language. The reason why it is meaningless to ask this question is that it is a precondition for the asking of an A-question that the communicants share the same present, although not the same here, and obviously this precondition cannot itself be the subject of an A-question, as it is when we ask someone "When are you?" (Gale 1968, p. 215)

Gale seeks to highlight the temporal nature of our experience. His point can be accentuated if we pose this problem: If all you knew were "B" facts, would there not be an important fact that you would not know, namely that *the present is now*? If so, then "B" advocates appear to leave out a fundamental feature of time. Consider an analogy. Imagine you develop amnesia and find yourself in a hospital room. You are heavily bandaged and unsure of your age, gender, race, size, and so on. Someone describes to you the only two people in the room, but all by proper names and descriptions: "Eric is in such and such shape, Miriam in another . . ." and so on. You might know an enormous amount of information, but not know the answer to a highly important question: Are you Miriam or Eric? Advocates of the "A" theory argue that there is a similar gap in the "B" description of reality. If the "B" theory is intelligible one could, in principle, know all that occurs at all times and still not know that it is *now*, say, the year 2000.

Defenders of the dynamic "A" theory also contend that theories of relativity do not support the "B" account. The theory of relativity relies on operational definitions of time (where time is defined operationally in terms of atomic clocks, the speed of light, and other ways to measure change) that do not bear on questions of absolute simultaneity, and relativity theory also allows that some events are truly past irrespective of the frame of reference employed.

Most theists who believe God is temporal argue for the primacy of the "A" series, whereas most theists who believe God is eternal argue for the sufficiency of the "B" series and God's changeless grasp of all that occurs in time.

The Temporality of God: Replies to Arguments from Perfection and Creation

Consider how those who embrace the temporality of God respond to the arguments cited earlier – the arguments from perfection and the argument from creation.

In contrast to Leftow, who claims that there is more unity in God as an eternal being than as a temporal reality living from moment to moment, Alan Padgett proposes that God is both temporal and enjoys a "lordship over time" (Padgett 1992; see also Swinburne 1994). In human consciousness we do not experience time instant by instant, but as a process. In William James' colorful language, we ride through time on a saddle back. This is sometimes called "the specious present" and refers to the supposed fact that the present moment for us cannot exist all at once in a present instant; that which is present to us is an interval. Could it be that God extends over an interval of extraordinary magnitude, altogether above metric division? J. R. Lucas holds that God is

"the master of events, not their prisoner; time passes, but does not press". All time is present in the divine mind, in the sense that no-one is remote or far away or absent, but not in the sense that all is simultaneous, nor that eternity is a timelessness in which nothing ever happens nor can be conceived of as happening. (Lucas 1973, p. 307)

This might go some of the way to accommodate Leftow's thesis, though Leftow thinks it will be of little use:

> Some suggest that . . . God's "specious present" holds His whole past and God has perfect predictive knowledge or literal prevision of His future. But as time passes, we regret losing not just the vivid experience of events but the events themselves – losing parts of our own lives. A continuing hallucination of the past would content nobody who knew that what seemed to be happening really was not. This holds a fortiori for a future one has yet to live at all. And what would it say about God if it made no difference to Him whether we lived with Him or ceased to exist, as long as His memory/prevision was intact? (Leftow 1997, pp. 258–9)

In reply one may argue that transcending time in the way Leftow describes is metaphysically impossible for God or any being whatever and thus it is no defect of God's perfection or omnipotence if God does not do so. As noted in chapter 3, many theists contend that God is not imperfect or defective if God cannot do what is impossible. Additionally, if God is able to grasp the past as a specious present, as though it were all spread out before God, why would that count as an "hallucination"? God would have an hallucination of the past if God were to have a false visual representation of it. But, presumably, grasping the past as past could be part of the divine consciousness without falling prey to such fabrication. Presumably, too, Padgett, Lucas, and others can claim that their view does just as well (or better) at securing the view that it makes a difference to God whether or not we live or perish. A God who transcends time enjoys an eternal view of created, temporal persons. A temporal God who prizes relationships with creation would at least appear to be equally or more motivated to preserve the creation in an ongoing successive relation.

As we shall see in the next chapter, some advocates of the "A" theory stress God's continuous affective presence in the cosmos, taking pleasure in its goods and sorrowing over its ills. God's perfection is thereby understood in terms of God's loving presence in a changing, valued cosmos. If plausible, this may provide the basis of a reply to the argument represented by Bertocci according to which any change in God would amount to an imperfection.

Let us now consider replies to the argument from creation. For those who think God is in time, there may well be some motivation to believe God has always had a created order – the creation of this cosmos had no beginning. One thereby avoids having to posit any empty time prior to creation. If the cosmos has always existed this need not undermine the monotheistic teaching that the cosmos is dependent upon God. Some theists have held that the cosmos has always existed though they have been a minority voice in monotheistic tradition. In Islam, for example, Al-Farabi (tenth century) and Averroes (1126–98) held that the cosmos was eternal, though this stance was vigorously opposed by other Islamic philosophers. In Hinduism, Ramanuja and Madhua both thought the cosmos was without origin and yet perpetually dependent on Brahman or God. Recently Richard Taylor has articulated a view of God's creation that does not require that there was a first moment of creation:

> People tend to think that creation – for example, the creation of the world by God – *means* creation *in time*, from which it of course logically follows that if the world had no beginning in time, then it cannot be the creation of God. This, however, is erroneous, for creation means essentially *dependence*, even in Christian theology. If one thing is the creation of another, then it depends for its existence on that other, and this is perfectly consistent with saying that both are eternal, that neither ever came into being, and hence, that neither was ever created at any point of time. Perhaps an analogy will help convey this point. Consider, then, a flame that is casting beams of light. Now there seems to be a clear sense in which the beams of light are dependent for their existence upon the flame, which is their source, while the flame, on the other hand, is not similarly dependent for its existence upon them. In this sense, they are the creation of the flame; they derive their existence from it. And none of this has any reference to time; the relationship of dependence in such a case would not be altered in the slightest if we supposed that the flame, and with it the beams of light, had always existed, that neither had ever *come* into being. (Taylor 1974, p. 107)

On this view, the cosmos depends on God for its ongoing existence, notwithstanding the fact that there was no origin or first moment of the existence of the cosmos.

Alternatively, one may argue that while there was a beginning of creation and there was time before creation, God's time is profoundly different than we can imagine. The extraordinary level of cognitive power that theists like Padgett, Lucas, and others attribute to God may well compel one to shed anthropomorphic pictures of God as a being of limited ability putting off creation in endless procrastination. If one grants that theists may avoid positing some lifeless picture of a pre-creation, temporal God, is there still the problem with what may be called the rationality of creation? If God was, is, and will be in time, why did God choose to create this cosmos 15 billion years ago or 900 billion years ago, as opposed to some other time? Arguably, the absence of a sufficient reason is not enough to conclude God would be irrational for electing to create at all. If one believes that God has a reason to create (e.g. it is good for there to be a creation), why must one also think that there must be a reason why God creates *at some particular time rather than another*? If one adopts a determinist view of God according to which all divine action is fixed by necessitating reasons then there is a serious question of identifying a reason why God created at a specific point rather than another. But it is difficult for theists to avoid positing *some* form of freedom to God. For example, must theists suppose God had reasons necessitating God to create some exact number of stars? Presumably not. So, it has been held that if God did not have an overriding reason to create at one instant rather than another, God's actions are not thereby irrational or unintelligible. Thomas Senor argues: "The fact that God has no reason to prefer to create at one moment as opposed to any other does not mean that his creating at a particular time is not perfectly rational" (Senor 1993, p. 91). On this view, it can be rational to create at some time without it being rationally required that the creation occur at a specific time.

Four Reasons for Believing God Does Not Transcend Time

Here are four important arguments against the thesis that God transcends time and a brief review of replies to each. Some of these will draw on the debate about the "A" and "B" theories of time.

(1) *An argument from temporal knowledge.* God is omniscient. If God is omniscient, God knows what time it is now. If God is outside time, God cannot know what time it is now. Hence God is not outside time. Arguably, there is a fact of the matter that now is now. That it is now, say, 1999, is an important fact. But if God is outside of time, how can God know this? God could know that in 1999 various people thought (accurately) that, for them, it is now 1999, but would God know that it is now 1999 as opposed to 1980 when many people thought (accurately) that, for them it is 1980? Richard Sorabji puts the problem as follows:

For if he [God] has not a position in time, he cannot know any tensed propositions such as that there will be a sea battle. For someone who has this thought must be thinking of the battle as later than his thought, and God's thoughts, on the present view, are not in time. God would at best know the tenseless proposition that there is (tenselessly) a sea battle on such and such a date, and that was argued to be a different proposition from the tensed one . . . If he cannot know that a sparrow is falling to the ground now, he cannot know that it needs his concern now. Nor again could he know when to intervene in human affairs, when for example, to send his son, or to answer a prayer. (Sorabji 1980, pp. 125–6)

If omniscience requires such existential awareness, can God be omniscient of the present and yet be eternal?

REPLY: One may elect simply to deny that such beliefs about "Now" in the "A" series represent facts that must be recognized as ultimately real. Williams contends that if there were a supreme intelligence that occupied an exclusively "B" series view of the cosmos and, as it were, "entered" our "A" series point of view, it would learn nothing new. To embrace the "B" series does not mean denying that there is a manifestation or appearance of the present moment; one can acknowledge those appearances and yet promote "B" over "A":

Let us hug to us as closely as we like that there is real succession, that rivers flow and winds blow, that things burn and burst, that men strive and guess and die. All this is the concrete stuff of the manifold, the reality of serial happening, one event after another . . . What does the theory allege except what we find, and what do we find that is not accepted and asserted by the theory? Suppose a pure intelligence, bred outside of time, instructed in the nature of the manifold and the design of the human spacetime worm, with its mnemic organization, its particular delimited but overlapping conscious fields, and the strands of world history which flank them, and suppose him incarnated among us: what could he have expected the temporal experience to be like except just about what he actually discovers it to be? How, in brief, could processes and experiences which endure and succeed each other along the time line appear as anything other than enduring and successive processes and a stream of consciousness? (Williams, in Gale [ed.] 1978, pp. 110, 111)

Williams thinks there is no fact of the matter expressed in the "A" series that cannot be absorbed and reinterpreted in terms of the "B" series.

If one does wish "to take temporality seriously" and yet contend that God transcends time, one might acknowledge the reality of the dynamic "A" series and yet propose that God's eternal awareness of the creation is fully able to grasp the reality of each "now". This is due to the richness of God's awareness, not an impoverishment. William Alston describes God's knowledge of the cosmos as radically distinct from ours. While we need to formulate specific beliefs and propositions that refer to various states of affairs, God cognitively takes in all features of all things with a comprehensive, all-encompassing, immediate awareness:

> It seems plausible to suppose that the propositional character of human knowledge stems from our limitations. Why is our knowledge parceled out in separate facts? For two reasons. First, we cannot grasp any concrete whole in its full concreteness; at most we cognate certain abstract features thereof, which we proceed to formulate in distinct propositions. Second, we need to isolate separate propositions in order to relate them logically, so as to be able to extend our knowledge inferentially. Both these reasons are lacking in the divine case. God can surely grasp any concrete whole fully, not just partial aspects thereof. And God has no need to extend His knowledge, inferentially or otherwise, since it is necessarily complete anyway. (Alston 1986, p. 291)

According to Alston, God knows the presentness of each present moment (to put it awkwardly) but God does so from an overriding vantage point to which all that occurs is disclosed. It is for these reasons that Alston proposes that a propositional account of God's omniscience should be rejected and, instead, theists ought to construe God's knowledge of the cosmos in terms of "direct intuition":

> If God's knowledge simply consists in an intuition of one or more concrete realities, and does not involve a segregation of these realities into abstract propositions, this issue [the problem of God knowing temporal events] does not arise. I see the sun shining and register this fact by assenting to the indexical proposition that the sun is shining here and now. If the knowledge of a timeless or immutable deity is propositionally structured, we have to ask whether that deity knows just the proposition that I expressed by the words "the sun is shining now." And that will lead us into the question of whether some non-indexical proposition which that deity can know is the same proposition as the one I just expressed. But on the non-propositional account of divine knowledge the question is as to whether an immutable or timeless deity can have an intuition of the same concrete reality that I registered one abstract aspect of by assenting to the position "The sun is shining now." And there would seem to be no problem about that. What is there in that concrete hunk of space–time that would be unavailable to an immutable or timeless deity? If God is not con-

fronted with the task of analyzing reality into distinguishable propositions He will have no traffic with either indexical or non-indexical propositions concerning the current state of affairs. That being the case, we cannot specify some bit of knowledge that is unavailable to Him by focusing on indexical propositions. A deity that enjoys a direct intuition of the concrete reality has slipped through this net. (Alston 1986, p. 305)

On this view, "A" theorists appear to cling to some feature of space–time which can be cognitively grasped as whole and complete from God's more engrossing, comprehensive vantage point. (Alston's depiction of God's knowledge seems closest to Analysis 4 of chapter 5.)

(2) *An argument from simultaneity.* It appears that simultaneity is transitive. That is, if I am writing at the same time as you are running and, in turn, you are also running at the same time Martha is singing, I am writing at the same time Martha is singing. But if God exists simultaneously with Nero burning Rome and God is likewise simultaneous with your whistling, then it follows that Nero's burning Rome is simultaneous with your whistling (Kenny 1979, pp. 38–9). This objection has been advanced by Richard Swinburne:

> The inner incoherence can be seen as follows. God's timelessness is said to consist in his existing at all moments of human time – simultaneously. Thus he is said to be simultaneously present at (and a witness of) what I did yesterday, what I am doing today, and what I will do tomorrow. But if t1 is simultaneous with t2 and t2 with t3, then t1 is simultaneous with t3. So if the instant at which God knows these things were simultaneous with both yesterday, today and tomorrow, then these days would be simultaneous with each other. So yesterday would be the same day as today and as tomorrow – which is clearly nonsense. (Swinburne 1977, pp. 220–1)

Swinburne and others contend that to suppose God is timeless is conceptually absurd and adopt, instead, the view that God is in time.

REPLY: Technical moves have been introduced here to avoid such absurdities. Norman Kretzmann and Eleonore Stump propose that God's simultaneity involves God's being "at" all times but that all times remain distinguishable and not simultaneous with each other:

> Although the stipulation that an eternal entity completely possesses its life all at once entails that it is not part of any sequence, it does not rule out the attribution of presentness or simultaneity to the life and relationships of such an

entity, nor should it. Insofar as an entity is, or has life, completely or otherwise, it is appropriate to say that it has present existence in some sense of "present"; and unless its life consists in only one event or it is impossible to relate an event in its life to any temporal entity or event, we need to be able to consider an eternal entity or event as one of the relata in a simultaneity relationship. (Stump and Kretzmann 1981, p. 434)

They use the following concept of God's presence to override the problem of simultaneity. God exists simultaneously with all temporal events but this is a special kind of simultaneity – an eternal simultaneity that they abbreviate as *ET-simultaneity*. They illustrate how this concept works in the course of analyzing God's relation to Richard Nixon:

ET-simultaneity cannot be taken to mean that the temporal entity Nixon exists in eternity, where he is simultaneously alive and dead, but rather something more nearly like this. One and the same eternal present is ET-simultaneous with Nixon's being alive and is also ET-simultaneous with Nixon's dying; so Nixon's life is ET-simultaneous with and hence present to an eternal entity, and Nixon's death is ET-simultaneous with and hence present to an eternal entity, although Nixon's life and Nixon's death are themselves neither eternal nor simultaneous. (Stump and Kretzmann 1981, p. 443)

Stump and Kretzmann thereby describe God's eternal simultaneous presence to all things in a fashion that parts company with our use of the term "simultaneous" when used to describe mere temporal beings. They insist that God's eternity is not a static or frozen instant; "the eternal present is not instantaneous but extended" (Stump and Kretzmann 1981, p. 225). God is thus described as present to all things without all the history of things collapsing into a single instant. Brian Leftow similarly stresses God's eternal duration, "An eternal God is God present with the whole of time by His life's being stretched out alongside it" (Leftow 1991, p. 117).

(3) *An argument from divine causality.* If God is outside of time, God could not create or interact with the cosmos. God does create and interact with the cosmos, hence God is not outside of time. Grace Jantzen poses this problem:

A timeless and immutable God could not be personal because he could not create or respond, perceive or act, think, remember, or do any of the other things persons do which require time. Thus within the framework of a theology of a personal God, the doctrines of divine timelessness and immutability cannot be retained. (Jantzen 1988, p. 574)

160

This is a position shared by Lucas (1973), Wolterstorff (1982), and Swinburne (1977). Nelson Pike advances the difficulty as follows:

> Let us suppose that yesterday a mountain, 17,000 feet high, came into existence on the flatlands of Illinois. One of the local theists explains this occurrence by reference to divine creative action. He claims that God produces (created, brought about) the mountain. Of course, if God is timeless, He could not have produced the mountain yesterday. This would require that God's creative-activity and thus the individual whose activity it is have position in time. The theist's claim is that God timelessly brought it about that yesterday, a 17,000 feet high mountain came into existence on the flatlands of Illinois . . . [But:] The claim that God timelessly produced a temporal object (such as the mountain) is absurd. (Pike 1970, pp. 104–5)

Production of something at a time would appear to require that the producer do so at that moment rather than from some eternal vantage point.

REPLY. Brian Davies defends the atemporal, eternal position against such objections. He argues that divine action may be understood to have temporal effects without having a temporal cause. He uses an analogy from teaching to bring home his point.

> Suppose we ask how people manage to teach. It seems natural to say that they do it by uttering words or by using blackboards and so on (and therefore by undergoing various changes in time). For that is how teaching is effected by people. But teaching cannot be defined as going through certain motions. I can utter true statements until I am blue in the face. I can fill a thousand blackboards with letters and diagrams. But none of these processes will count as teaching unless somebody actually learns something . . . Teaching occurs when learning occurs . . . In a similar way . . . God's bringing things about need be understood only in terms of things coming about, not in terms of something happening at some time in God. It is a condition and a limitation of my nature that I can only bring about in you the change we call "learning" by, as a matter of fact, changing myself as something in time. But there is nothing in the notion of teaching that requires such a change in the teacher. There is thus no reason why God should not teach you by bringing about a change in you without in any way changing himself. And, more generally, there is no reason why God should not bring about changes and, in so far as times depend on changes, times without himself changing or being in time. (Davies 1993, pp. 146–7)

According to this schema, God may be understood as acting sequentially but, from the standpoint of eternity, God nonsequentially wills that there be a temporal and sequential series of events or divine acts. God thereby nonsuccessively wills there be various successions and (so it is argued) these may capture what Jantzen notes as God's responsiveness, creativity, thinking, and remembering. God would not have a memory on this view in any strict sense of recalling that which was God's past but God could be said to have an exhaustive grasp of what, for us, is the past. Consider, for example, how Thomas Aquinas treats the attribution of passions to God. In the Hebrew and Christian Bibles God is described as having passions like anger. According to Aquinas, these passages must be treated metaphorically or analogically:

> When certain human passions are predicated of the Godhead metaphorically, this is done because of a likeness in the effect. Hence a thing that is with us a sign of some passion is signified metaphorically in God under the name of passion. Thus with us it is usual for an angry man to punish, so that punishment becomes an expression of anger. Therefore punishment itself is signified with anger, when anger is attributed to God. (Aquinas in *ST*, I. Q. 19, art. 11)

In this same way, scriptural descriptions of God suggesting God alters and is in time may be read as highly metaphorical. God appears to alter but, strictly speaking, God does not do so. An (imperfect but classic) analogy that may be of some value is if we imagine the sun remained perfectly fixed and yet our planet continued in its orbit. From our point of view, the sun would still seem to change in position constantly (rising and setting) while all along it remains changeless.

(4) *The personal God argument.* Even if God can timelessly and non-sequentially will sequences, can such a God rightly be considered a person? If God is timeless, could God be conscious? A popular argument may be given the following form: If God is outside of time, God is not a person nor conscious. God is a person and conscious. Hence God is not outside of time. John Lucas claims that "To say that God is outside time, as many theologians do, is to deny, in effect, that God is a person" (Lucas 1973, p. 300). Swinburne adopts a similar position. For religious believers who are deeply committed to viewing God not just as person-like or personal, this constitutes a substantial problem:

> If God had thus fixed his intentions "from all eternity" he would be a very lifeless thing; not a person who reacts to men with sympathy or anger, pardoning and chastening because he chooses to there and then . . . if God did not change at all, he could not think now of this, now of that. His thoughts would be one thought which lasted for ever. (Swinburne 1977, p. 214)

162

REPLY: The belief that God is a person has a complex history. In the next section we will consider some arguments that God is not a person but Being. Here I simply note that many theists within Jewish, Christian, and Islamic traditions do not accept the thesis that God is a person. According to these thinkers, God may still be said to be "personal" in the sense of creating, knowing the cosmos, and so on, but God would thereby only be describable as a person in a highly qualified, metaphorical fashion.

The debate goes on. Philosophers sometimes focus on different areas in the philosophy of time depending upon the religious tradition they are addressing. Thus, Christian philosophers who believe God is eternal face a difficult task in defending the intelligibility of the incarnation. Does not the traditional view of the incarnation entail that there was a time before God became incarnate and then a time during which God was incarnate, and afterwards? If so, this would seem to secure that God is subject to the "A" series, however much God's knowledge might also encompass the "B" series. Some defenders of divine eternity have suggested that while God entered time in the incarnation this was a true "entering," but God is otherwise eternal. St. Bernard adopted such a position. By his lights, in the incarnation God learned about the cosmos in a temporal fashion what God knows of the cosmos eternally. More on this in the appendix to chapter 9.

Arguments for Thinking God is Not an Individual Object

Having canvassed some of the key arguments about God's relation to time, let us consider whether God might be even more transcendent, even further beyond the boundary of created, cosmic categories. In this section several arguments are raised that God is best thought of as Being, and not as an individual object or person.

One reason advanced for thinking God is not an individual is owing to God's uniqueness. Being an individual appears to entail that God could be one of many Gods or gods. If there is a God, arguably, there could not be more than one. Thomas Aquinas and many other theists describe God as *sui generis*, in a class of its own. Based on this and the view that God is not subject to the categories of creation, Brian Davies concludes that God is not a being:

> God cannot be classified as a member of the world; he will be no possible object
> of research for biologists, zoologists, physicists and chemists. Nor can he share

with things in the world certain of their essential features. He cannot, for instance, be confined in a space, for that presupposes bodily existence and location. Nor can he be something changing or changeable, where "change" is ascribable to a thing precisely in virtue of its materiality. So God cannot move around. Nor can he be altered in other ways that depend on or involve bodily changes. We can also deny that God is an individual. By this I do not mean that God is in no sense a subject or an agent. I am not denying the reality of God. But suppose one concentrates on the sense of individual (arguably its most common sense) according to which to call something an individual is to imply that there could always be another of the same kind. In that case . . . we would be right to deny that God is an individual. (Davies 1987, p. 61)

Davies goes on to argue that God is not a person:

For people are also commonly associated with, for example, bodies and parents and food and drink and sex and society and death. Yet God is said to be above such things. He is said to be bodiless and immortal or eternal . . . If people are our models for persons, then in an obvious sense God, it would seem, is not a person. (Davies 1987, p. 65)

Because human persons differ so radically from the way God is conceived of in theistic tradition, Davies contends that it would be a mistake to construe God as a person. Davies' view is compatible with the thesis that God is properly described analogically as a person or personal but this falls short of any literal attribution (see also Robinson 1967 and Thatcher 1985 for a qualified thesis that God is personal but not a person).

Consider a reply. In chapter 4 some central issues in the philosophy of human nature were covered (dualism versus materialism) and more will be addressed later. If it can be plausibly argued that the very concept of being a person involves the concept of being materially embodied, then it would be nonsense to think of God as a person and immaterial. If, on the other hand, it can be successfully argued that it is coherent to suppose that there could be a person that is not materially embodied, then at least one of Davies' points can be met. It can be argued, then, that the way the word "person" works in human affairs is to refer to embodied beings, but it need not be so restricted. In fact, Davies does not seem to insist on any sort of essential materialism, for his notion that God is Being does not amount to claiming that God is material or physical. Perhaps his point may be put as a linguistic one. If being a person requires being materially embodied, then God is best not described as a person.

164

Davies' argument for divine uniqueness may be responded to in at least two ways. First, it may be contested whether the bare fact that God is unique and there cannot be more than one God (if that is a fact) entails God is not an individual. One may argue for God's unique status on the basis of an argument from God's omnipotence. The argument may be put as follows, employing Analysis 3 of omnipotence outlined in chapter 3:

1 God is an omnipotent individual.
2 An omnipotent individual is such that there cannot be any other being with a greater scope of power.
3 There cannot be two omnipotent individuals, A and B, because either A or B existing alone without the other would have a greater scope of power than the two of them together. When both exist together each is limited by the action of the other (e.g. A cannot will that something occur and it occur unless B acquiesces; in a case where their actions are contradictory, presumably nothing would occur).
4 There cannot be more than one God.

If successful, this would enable theists to argue that God is an individual and there cannot be more than one.

While arguments like these have currency in philosophy of religion, they have also been challenged. (For a classic version of the above argument see Duns Scotus' entry in Urban and Walton [eds] 1978; see Werner, same volume, for a current discussion.) Some argue that not only can there be more than one omnipotent being, there are three. While Jews and Muslims are deeply committed to there being a single divine reality, some Christian philosophers and theologians propose that there can be more than one individual in the Godhead. The Christian Trinity will be discussed briefly in the appendix to chapter 9. Here I simply record one description of the Trinity according to which there is a singular divine nature borne by three centers of consciousness, three individuals, that are each omnipotent, omniscient, and so on. This view is sometimes called the Social Theory of the Trinity, while some of its accusers call it Tri-theism or polytheism. How would this fare in relation to the above argument from omnipotence? One route is to question premises two and three. Analysis 3 of omnipotence makes no reference to values. Recall the fourth analysis of omnipotence in chapter 3:

(i) Being, B, is omnipotent if and only if it possesses perfect or supremely excellent power, and (ii) Being, B, possesses perfect or supremely excellent power if and only if there is no other being that could have a greater scope of power and possesses a greater compossible set of excellent properties.

If one believes there are three individuals that are essentially perfect and thereby jointly coordinate in all their activities, it does not appear that they would be any less excellent than just one of them existing alone (Swinburne 1994). There would be perfect harmonious action, on this view, and no conflictual competition.

So, a defender of the thesis that God is an individual could either argue that the individuality of God does not compromise supposing that God is unique or, failing that, challenge Davies' assumption that there cannot, in principle, be more than one being satisfying the characterization of divinity.

Whether or not Davies' argument succeeds, there are other reasons for thinking the divine is not an individual. One such reason is religious experience. We shall consider the evidential force of religious experience in chapter 8. For now, let us focus on the meaning and intelligibility of the claim that God or a divine, ultimate reality is not an individual. Does it make sense to think the divine could be radically different from our world of individual objects?

The Intelligibility of Believing God is Being

Our language that describes objects and individuals supports the view that the world is divisible, and capable of fracture. This conflicts with a strong religious impulse to see an inner unity that binds all things together. "Object" comes from the Latin *ob* ("over against") and *jacare* ("to throw") and "individual" from the Latin *individuus* ("undivided" or "indivisible"). Such ways of carving up the world into separable atomic parts has not always been deemed a definitive mark of the way things are. From a practical point of view, viewing the world in terms of distinguishable individuals may be unavoidable and perhaps unassailable religiously and philosophically. Nonetheless, perhaps such individuation should only be recognized as having legitimacy for certain purposes. Could there be something that some philosophers and theologians refer to as "Being" that is below or deeper than our world of individual objects, a reality which is not itself a substantive individual or object?

Paul Tillich (1886–1965) was an important advocate of the thesis that God is Being and not an object:

The being of God is being-itself. The being of God cannot be understood as the existence of a being alongside others or above others. If God is a being, he is subject to the categories of finitude, especially to space and substance. Even if he is called the "highest being" in the sense of the "most perfect" and the "most powerful" being, this situation is not changed. When applied to God, superlatives become diminutives. They place him on the level of other beings while elevating him above all of them . . . Whenever infinite or unconditional power and meaning are attributed to the highest being, it has ceased to be a being and has become being-itself. (Tillich 1951, vol. I, p. 235)

Tillich endeavors to locate talk of God on a plane that is deeper than that arena of disputes between theists and atheists.

Grave difficulties attend the attempt to speak of God as existing . . . The question of the existence of God can be neither asked nor answered. If asked, it is a question about that which by its very nature is above existence, and therefore the answer – whether negative or affirmative – implicitly denies the nature of God. It is as atheistic to affirm the existence of God as it is to deny it. God is being-itself, not a being. (Tillich 1951, pp. 236–7)

Our term "existence" (from the Latin *ex* and *sistere*, "to step forth" or "emerge") is adequate for negotiating everyday affairs, but (if Tillich is right) in a fully mature religious conception of God we must seek that ground behind individual objects, the place from which specific objects emerge. Because God is not accessible to us in the language of individuals and objects, our talk of God in any direct fashion as an object is oblique at best, and at worst gravely misleading.

Tillich's thesis is very different from those of some contemporary philosophers of religion. Swinburne, for example, seems decidedly to favor thinking of God as an object:

If you mean [by saying of God that he is an object] God is something of which properties are true, which causally interacts with other recognizable observable objects, which can be distinguished from others as the subject of certain predicates which he has and they don't: well, that is the case with God, and therefore on any natural understanding of "object", God is an object. (Swinburne, cited by R. Messer 1993, p. 21)

But, as we see with Tillich, this object-oriented approach to God is not universally accepted. And as philosophers and theologians have gone on to examine the repercussions of thinking that God is not an object, they have questioned the feasibility of any direct, literal descriptions of God.

This recognition of the inadequacy of our speech in describing God or the ultimate, sacred reality, is well noted by many representatives of all five world religions. The great Jewish philosopher Maimonides (1135–1205) argued strongly for what is sometimes called *via negativa* at precisely this point. According to the *via negativa* (the negative way), we may know God through knowing what God is not. Our awareness of God is thereby indirect. In *The Guide for the Perplexed* Maimonides writes:

> There is no necessity at all for you to use positive attributes of God with the view of magnifying Him in your thoughts . . . I will give you . . . some illustrations, in order that you may better understand the propriety of forming as many negative attributes as possible, and the impropriety of ascribing to God any positive attributes. A person may know for certain that a "ship" is in existence, but he may not know to what object that name is applied, whether to a substance or to an accident; a second person then learns that a ship is not an accident; a third, that it is not a mineral; a fourth, that it is not a plant growing in the earth; a fifth, that it is not a body whose parts are joined together by nature; a sixth, that it is not a flat object like boards or doors; a seventh, that it is not a sphere; an eighth, that it is not pointed; a ninth, that it is not round shaped; nor equilateral; a tenth, that it is not solid. It is clear that this tenth person has almost arrived at the correct notion of a "ship" by the foregoing negative attributes . . . In the same manner you will come nearer to the knowledge and comprehension of God by the negative attributes . . . I do not merely declare that he who affirms attributes of God has not sufficient knowledge concerning the Creator . . . but I say that he unconsciously loses his belief in God. (Maimonides, trans. 1956, p. 86)

The *via positiva* (the positive way) is thereby relinquished as both philosophically inadequate and religiously offensive. A philosophy of God adopts the *via positiva* when it directly attributes properties to God either univocally (from the Latin *unus* for "one" and *vocare* for "to call") when words are used of God and creatures with the same meaning (God *knows* X, you *know* X) or analogically (from *ana* for "according to" and *logos* for "proportion") when terms are used of God and creatures based on some believed resemblance (God's knowledge is similar to but not the same as your knowledge). Thomas Aquinas endorsed analogical references to God but he so qualified this that some of his contemporary commentators such as Brian Davies describe him as largely agnostic about God's nature (Davies 1993). Muslim writers have

168

referred to the "hidden essence of Allah." In Vedanta philosophy, Brahman has been characterized as being beyond discursive thought. Consider Shankara's portrayal of Brahman:

> There is no class of substance to which the Brahman belongs, no common genus. It cannot therefore be denoted by words which, like "being" in the ordinary sense, signify a category of things. Nor can it be denoted by quality for it is without qualities; nor yet by activity, because it is without activity . . . neither can it be denoted by relationship for it is without a second. Therefore it cannot be defined by word or idea, as the scripture says, it is the one "before whom words recoil." (Shankara from Huxley 1950; see also (rest-Jewel of Discrimination p. 129))

In his important investigation *The Varieties of Religious Experience*, William James (1842–1910) cites "ineffability" as a crucial dimension of the overwhelming experience of the divine. The ineffability of the divine seems extoled in both monotheist as well as monist religious traditions.

The belief that God is ineffable has had an important impact on the perceived limits of philosophy and also on religious practice. Nicholas of Cusa defined wisdom as "learned ignorance," in which one keenly appreciates the limits of human cognition. Could it be that there is an ultimate reality – what Shankara refers to as Brahman and Tillich as Being – that is ineffable? Some think not. Consider two arguments.

The first may be termed the *Argument from Contrasts*. In essence, objection is that meaningful reference requires contrasting terms. Because "Being" has no proper contrast or contrary, it is without meaning. Kai Nielsen uses it in criticizing Tillich's position:

> "Being itself," "ultimate reality," "wholly other source and unity of all beings," "Unconditional Transcendent" are all supposedly referring expressions. That is, it is assumed they stand for something and can make an identifying reference. But then they must have an intelligible opposite. Consider, for example, "being in itself". If such obscurantist talk helps characterize what "God" actually means, i.e. gives us something of the cognitive import of the term, it must in some way indicate something about God, something about how God is a different kind of reality, or what it means to say that God is ultimate reality. But, to do this, "being itself" must contrast with something else. But in turn, to do this we must be able to distinguish being itself from something else; being itself must make an identifying reference. Yet how is being itself to be identified? We seem at least simply to have the phrase and nothing else. (Nielsen 1973, p. 54)

If Nielsen is correct, then the religious drive to shed references to an individual God and to embrace, instead, a deeper notion of Being is not to strive after something more meaningful but something that is conceptually meaningless.

But why is a contrast term needed? Some things appear to be true and yet it is not possible for anything to exemplify their opposites. Take the claim that "Everything is itself and not something else." This is a thesis that is so general and abstract that it can hardly have any role in ordinary affairs. Still, the thesis that everything is itself and not something else strikes many as necessarily true. As Alvin Plantinga phrased it: "Everything is self-identical is true in every possible world" (Plantinga 1974a, p. 57). Nothing can exemplify the opposite – that is, there cannot be something that is not itself, and yet it appears that the statement is meaningful. The opposite of *everything being itself* could never be realized and thus we could never in principle face a problem of differentiating between objects that are self-identical and those that are not.

This case may not satisfy Nielsen. The denial of the necessary truth (everything is self-identical) is intelligible in the sense that one can understand that its negation is necessarily false. But how might we understand the opposite of Being? Is it nonbeing or nothing at all? A defender of the Being-tradition might well consider "nonbeing" or "nothing" the contrast term. Nielsen and other critics are vexed by some of the ways in which Tillich and the philosophers Tillich relies upon (such as Martin Heidegger 1889–1976) use the term nothing. (See suggested question 9 at the end of this chapter.)

But is it so obvious that it is nonsense to suppose the opposite of Being is nothing? Perhaps it is not surprising that talking of nothing *seems* absurd because we thereby treat it as a kind of thing, but does this mean that it makes no sense at all for there to be a proper contrast between Being and Nothing, *viz.*, if there is nothing, there is no Being; if there is Being is it false that there is nothing? Tillich's view may well be defensible against Nielsen's objection.

Consider a second argument against positing an ineffable reality on the grounds that to do so is self-refuting. By describing God as Being or referring to Brahman as the ultimate reality, are we doing something that would be impossible if God or Brahman is actually ineffable? Alvin Plantinga articulates some of the difficulties for theists in general and Christian theists in particular who adhere to divine ineffability:

> It clearly makes no sense at all to say that there is such a being as God but that none of our concepts apply to God. We cannot coherently suppose that there is a being to which none of our concepts apply, because such a being would be neither wise nor nonwise, neither good nor nongood. Indeed, the concept of

existence or "there-ness" would not apply to it, so that if there were such a being, our response to God should be incredulous puzzlement, rather than the Christian's reverence, awe, worship, trust, and gratitude. Why trust God, if the concept of being trustworthy does not apply? Why worship God, if God is not an adequate object of worship? In this view, the Christian life becomes a complete shambles. (Plantinga 1981, p. 119)

According to Plantinga, one cannot posit such an ineffable reality, for positing it would require some kind of description. A. J. Ayer advances a similar point, claiming that advocates of ineffability either contradict themselves or fail to advance anything meaningful:

To say that something transcends the human understanding is to say that it is unintelligible. And what is unintelligible cannot be significantly described. . . . If one allows that it is impossible to define God in intelligible terms, then one is allowing that it is impossible for a sentence both to be significant and to be about God. If a mystic admits that the object of his vision cannot be described, then he must also admit that he is bound to talk nonsense when he describes it. (Ayer 1952, p. 118)

How might a defender of Tillich or Shankara reply? One response would be to qualify the ineffability thesis. W. T. Stace points out the difficulty of securing the *absolute ineffability* of the Being revealed in religion:

Absolute ineffability . . . would mean that the something called ineffable would be outside our consciousness altogether, in the same sense in which God is presumed outside the consciousness of a dog . . . If the mystical consciousness were absolutely ineffable, then we could not say so because we should be unconscious of such an experience; or, in other words, we should never have had such an experience. (Stace 1960, p. 291)

So, one may concede that the ineffability of the divine is not absolute or strict, but that does not rule out that Being or God is radically distinct from creation. Ninian Smart treats religious claims that God is ineffable or transcends experience as dramatic ways of insisting upon the uniqueness of God:

If we say that God transcends human experience, in the religious context, we cannot mean that he is beyond all possible human experience. It is axiomatic that the believer thinks that he has or can have some experience of God . . . A God who could never enter into human experience would *a fortiori* have no interpersonal relations with men. This would be flatly contrary to both the

A fortiori ?

Christian revelation and to the beliefs of other theistic faiths . . . Similar remarks apply to the notion that God is beyond comprehension [totally] or that he transcends thought . . . "God transcends existence" – to say this is a way of showing that God is not a finite being, like a star. Yet it is a paradoxical thing to say. What it can scarcely mean is that, by transcending existence, God does not exist. To assert this is to assert the thesis of atheism . . . Suffice it to say that the analysis of transcendence here presented should make it clear that God is not something like a star. Nor is he, for the believer, an entity additional to the furniture of the world; for the believer's universe already includes God. (Smart 1966, pp. 478–9)

On this view, then, the religious claim that God is ineffable or transcends existence is reinterpreted as an insistence upon God's radical dissimilarity from all we observe in the world but not as an instance that no sense at all can be made of references to the divine.

If one allows that the divine can be experienced in some fashion, another revised ineffability thesis may be feasible. We define many things by ostension where our key reference point is experience. Seeing the color red may be analyzed in terms of wavelengths, stimulus objects and such, but it may be argued that a key reference point is simply a person's color experience. Indeed, the other factors (wavelengths et al.) may plausibly be construed as the conditions that bring about our seeing red, rather than as an analysis of what it is to see red. One may argue that for us, given our nondivine cognition, it is difficult to define or describe the experience itself. One may chart how red functions on the color spectrum, but for the meaning of "seeing red" to be satisfactorily grasped, one must simply experience it. As noted in chapter 5, perhaps God may not require such experience, but (for all that) maybe we do, and possibly a parallel ineffability thesis can then be employed in the case of the divine. (For further suggestions on ineffability, see questions 7 to 9 at the end of this chapter.)

Let us now consider at closer range what it would mean to think of the divine as radically different from the world of discrete individual, separable objects.

Monism

According to monism, there is only one reality as opposed to two (such as Creator and creation) or a plurality of irreducibly different things. Religiously

172

the most prominent form of monism is the Advaita Vedanta school of Hinduism of which the main exponent is Shankara (788–820).

In Shankara's view, Brahman is the supreme reality. The empirical, sensory world in which we seem to find ourselves is not the fundamental and final reality. Rather, this world may be described as a world of appearances. Brahman is in the world of appearances in that these appearances are the result of Brahman, but Brahman also transcends this whole empirical domain and exists beyond any distinction, division or change. The changes we observe and the distinctions we seem to draw with ease around the boundaries of objects (here is a person, there is a mountain) are the outcome of our limited point of view. "The world can be produced out of Brahman just as snakes are produced out of ropes and bent sticks are produced by water (by refraction)" (Koller on Shankara, p. 90 1985). A properly trained person who is not ignorant of the ultimate nature of things may see past or through the illusion of plurality to the ultimate unity holding all things together.

An analogy may be drawn from Alston's theistic portrayal of God's nonpropositional grasp of all things, outlined above under "Four Reasons For Believing God Does Not Transcend Time," pp. 158–9. Imagine going considerably beyond Alston's theistic framework. Consider the possibility that not just our propositionally based approach to reality is a reflection of our limitations, but that our very tendency to divide this world (this "concrete hunk of space–time," in Alston's colorful phrase) into discrete individuals is a reflection of human limitations – limitations that can and should be left behind when pursuing a more comprehensive understanding of reality.

In monist religion, is this ultimate unity of all things, this comprehensive whole, conscious or personal? For Shankara and most advocates of Advaita Vedanta, ultimate reality transcends consciousness and personality altogether. As noted in chapter 1, Hindu tradition includes important strands in which ultimate reality is described in theistic terms and there is an acknowledged distinction between Brahman, conceived of as the Creator of the cosmos, and the cosmos itself. Ramanuja sought to affirm the reality of that which was below Brahman, while Radhakrishnan (1888–1975) sought to harmonize these two strands of Hinduism, monist and theist, holding out for both for the unity and distinguishability of objects. His views are certainly monist in the end, however – "There is nothing else than the Absolute which is the presupposition of all else" (Radhakrishnan 1960, p. 119):

So far as the Absolute is concerned, the creation of the world makes no difference to it. It cannot add anything to or take anything from the Absolute. All the sources of its being are found within itself. The world of change does not disturb the perfection of the Absolute. (Radhakrishnan 1958, p. 502)

While in theism the principle mode of understanding the cosmos is in terms of creation (from the Latin *creare* for "to produce, bring forth, beget"), monist systems, such as those advanced by Radhakrishnan, describe the visible world as more of a manifestation or emanation (from the Latin *e* for "from" and *mano* for "flow") or, if you will, a divine evolution (from the Latin for "to roll out," *volvere*).

There is not a singular form of monism in the history of philosophy and religion, but different types. Competing forms of monism can be found outside of Hinduism, in work by Western philosophers Spinoza (1632–77) and Hegel (1770–1831), for example, and in some Jewish, Christian, and Islamic mysticism as well. While the three main monotheistic religions emphasize the reality of and difference between Creator and creation, some mystics in each tradition have advanced views which admit of a monist interpretation. A. C. Ewing notes how theism is so close to monism and the boundary between them so tenuous that one may even describe theism as a moderate version of monism:

> Theism, as ordinarily believed, may be regarded as a form of monism since it admits that the world is created and controlled by a single all-powerful mind. But it stops short of more thorough-going forms of monism in that it gives human minds a kind of relative independence, holding them not to be included in, though created by and dependent on, the divine mind. But orthodox Christianity itself, since it asserts the absolute dependence of everything on a single omnipotent mind and a single purpose, goes very far in the direction of monism, even when this is toned down by the admission of the undetermined, though very limited, freedom of the human will. (Ewing 1985, p. 207)

Some of the Christian mystics like Eckhart are thought to have pushed theism almost to the breaking point in their championing the unity and comprehensiveness of God.

Many, though by no means all, analytically minded philosophers of the twentieth century dismiss monist claims about transcendence as incoherent, relegating them to "mere" poetry. As O. K. Bouwsma commented in a related context: "What poets revel in gives the philosopher a bad night" (Bouwsma 1982, p. 7). Is this philosophical wariness justified? Perhaps not. Gilbert Murray and others commend more poetic treatments of God than philosophers customarily tolerate: "We must notice the instinctive language of the poets, using the word *theos* [Greek, usually translated "God"] in many subtle senses for which our word God is too stiff, too personal, and too anthropomorphic" (Murray 1943, p. 12). A chief concern in this and the last section is whether monism can be plausibly described in coherent terms (with or without poetry).

At least at the outset, monism appears to be radically false. It appears that individual persons are indeed different (I am not you) and that diverse spatio-temporal objects are diverse. Recall the claim that everything is itself and not something else. As Bertrand Russell once commented: "The universe is all spots and jumps, without unity, without continuity" (Russell, cited by Ewing 1985, p. 207). Must all versions of monism be seen as completely undermined by this perspective?

Some monists are prepared to think of their views as truly in opposition with common sense and no worse off because of it. In Advaita Vedanta Hinduism the justification for monism is built principally on the authority of the Vedic scriptures and on religious experience. This provides a way of liberation for the soul that comes to understand itself as not wedded to the illusions of this world but at one with that which is truly ultimate. This is certainly not a repudiation of using "common sense" in "common circumstances," but a rejection of thinking of such common sense as revelatory of the deepest levels of reality (there are deeper accounts of why things are as they are and deeper, greater values). Do such monist accounts or others need to be seen as radically at odds with common sense? In the rest of this section a strategy is outlined to accommodate common sense within monism.

In recent philosophy there is considerable debate as to how to weigh competing conceptual schemes each of which may be used to describe what exists. This is sometimes called "the division problem." How should reality be divided? Why do we group some objects together in one category as opposed to another?

> Our language divides up reality in a certain way, though we can apparently describe an indefinite number of other ways this might be done. This fact may not in itself be seen as generating a philosophical problem, for it may merely suggest the need for an empirical explanation, in terms of psychology or sociology, of why our division practices are as they are. A philosophical problem is generated, however, by certain normative intuitions which we seem to have about these practices. Intuitively, it seems that there are good reasons why we ought to have essentially the division practices we do have; it seems that it would be in some sense incorrect or irrational for us to employ a language that divides reality in some way significantly different from our ordinary way. The philosophical problem is to explain what these normative intuitions amount to,

and to determine whether they can be properly defended. What, if anything, makes our division practices more correct or rational than various alternative practices we seem able to describe? This is what I am calling the division problem. (Hirsch 1993, p. 3)

Much argument in the philosophy of science, language, and mind is focused on this division problem. Clearly the division problem calls for a sophisticated response. Some of our classifications seem straightforward reflections of human desires (e.g. consult any dictionary definitions of "garbage" or "weed" or "pollution"), others do not (e.g. geometric shapes). Let us focus entirely on monism and its problem, not of division, but of unification.

Consider the following move by a monist. Let it be granted that the best of the natural scientific schemes of the world should be adopted, but adopted, not as true in their formulation of "ultimate reality," but instead as pragmatic, useful ways of ordering our experiences, making predictions, and controlling outcomes. The strategy here is similar to the nonrealist position outlined in chapter 2. The point is that monists need not deny that separable, distinct persons "exist" in the sense that contexts arise in which referring to them as distinct, nonidentical objects is fully justified. What monists may then seek to do is reinterpret these pragmatic claims as intelligible in light of a deeper, transcendent unity.

One way to spell out this position is by a grammatical illustration. Imagine a shift in grammar. In English we distinguish between subjects, adverbs and adjectives. "Adjectives" modify subjects and do not stand for objects in their own right. There is no such object "big" but there can be a "big tree." We routinely refer to a host of things which are granted honorary subject status that can be reinterpreted as adjectives. Thus we may speak of the swiftness of a dance or the pain in a leg or the minty taste of tea, but these may all be understood as *ways people move, the way one's leg feels* and *the way mint tea tastes*. We may so keenly reify references to dances as "things" that it seems odd to insist that what we are referring to are not "things" but modes or ways of being or acting or sensing. It seems quite natural to think of there being an odor in a basement, for example, as though it is one thing among others – the odor is over there! But none of this way of talking gives one serious pause when it comes to reinterpreting one's claims in terms of what the basement smells like to someone who goes there.

Let us consider the following thought experiment: think of individual objects (the mountain, river, you and me) not as subjects pure and simple, but as ways in which the universe is at various stages. The universe is mountaining, to put it very awkwardly. On this analysis, the things we take to be subsistent objects (subsistence comes from Latin *subsistere* for "to continue") become something similar to waves, that are configurations of something deeper, something more unified, something that binds us together. Individual objects are thus continuous ways (modes or manners) of something else. Back to the charge that "everything is itself and not something else"; does monism fly in the face of this dictum? Not necessarily. The monist can argue that the modes of God or Brahman are distinct and not identical, notwithstanding the fact that each mode is a reflection of a singular reality.

An analogy with ethics may be useful. A series of ethical views will be outlined in the next chapter, and the following is only meant as an illustration. It appears to many of us as though there are many disparate duties and rights. What of the possibility that all these may be derived from only a singular principle of good and evil? According to hedonism, the only good state that exists is pleasure, the only bad state is pain. This theory has many critics. But, even if false, it may be a useful way to illustrate monism. If hedonism were true, the appearance of many distinguishable values might well be reduced to different degrees or modes of a single value.

The promise of this monist strategy may be tested by considering the following objection, advanced by Pierre Bayle (1647–1706) and revived recently by Chisholm (1976, pp. 212, 213). Bayle argued that monism leads to absurdity. His specific target was Spinoza's monism but his argument applies to other forms of monism as well:

> When we say that a man denies, affirms, gets angry, caresses, praises, and the like, we ascribe all these attributes to the substance of his soul itself, and not to his thoughts as they are either accidents or modifications. If it were true then, as Spinoza claims, that men are modalities of God, one would speak falsely when one said, "Peter denies this, he wants that, he affirms such and such a thing"; for actually, according to this theory, it is God who denies, wants, affirms; and consequently all the denominations that result from the thoughts of all men are properly and physically to be ascribed to God. From which it follows that God hates and loves, denies and affirms the same thing at the same time. (Bayle 1965, pp. 309–10)

Does monism involve such incoherence?

Monists may be able to avoid the charge of incoherence if they clearly distinguish between the modes of God or Brahman. If Peter affirms X and Susan denies X we need not think of God affirming and denying X at the same time in the same sense. Rather, one may think of God affirming X in the mode

177

or role of Peter and denying X in the mode or role of Susan. This may evoke a view of the cosmos which is profoundly at cross-purposes, but such a picture is in fact what some monists endorse. The ills of the cosmos are sometimes depicted as the outcome of our loss of coherence, our failure as Peters and Susans to realize the ultimate unity of which we are modes or distinct configurations.

The Individual, Brahman, and Nirvana

As noted in the last section, some monists redraw the map of personal identity, construing individuals as modes of ultimate reality, God or the One. What are the ethical repercussions of this? The unity that is espoused in monist religions obviously involves more than tinkering with grammar or coming up with unified accounts of ethics. As the nonrealists are quick to point out, religious ideas are usually not born of mere academic scheming alone but form part of a way of life. T. L. S. Sprigge describes how monism offers what he takes to be a broader, deeper account of our experience of the physical world and of each other:

> Gazing with awe at the starry heavens, the monist who is imbued with the sense that all things belong together in an inconceivably comprehensive unified experience can make a sense of his emotional response which is closed to the materialist, and which is not quite what an orthodox theist will make of it. One is not responding to something answering to the incoherent conception of a vast unconscious system quite alien in its inner being to what one feels within oneself, but to a phenomenal presentation of the ocean of unified feeling in which one is one drop . . . The sense, on the other hand, that the one is present in each of the many makes of, and reinforces, the ethically basic sense one has when looking into another's eyes that somehow what looks out at one from thence is oneself again, and that its difference is not that of some ultimately distinct bare particular such that there is a difference in the fact that it rather than oneself feels something not reducible to the difference in what it feels. (Sprigge 1983, p. 278)

The recognition of a unity among persons can serve to fill out and undergird an ethic of respect. It can also assist in challenging what appears to be, by contrast, a narrow-sighted egoism. Monism can, however, run into ethical qualms here.

A. C. Ewing notes how monism can lead to washing out vital differences between persons, though he also argues that this is not at all necessarily so:

178

Monism has often, though by no means always, been associated with views which exalt the state at the expense of the individual and do not look kindly on individual freedom in political life. This connection must not, however, be regarded as a necessary one. For it does not follow that because the individual is absolutely dependent on the universe as a whole, therefore the ties which bind him to the state compared to the ties which bind him to other human individuals or to societies other than the state should be particularly strong. We cannot, from a general proposition about the unity of everything that is, conclude that unity ought to be realized in a particular way in human life, thus deducing our politics from our metaphysics. There is nothing in the nature of things which entails that the national state is not a mere piece of political machinery but the representative of the Absolute on earth. If everything is really a close unity metaphysically, it is obvious that this unity is compatible with great disunity in the political sense, since such disunity is often an empirical fact. And I do not see how we can draw an inference from the supposed ultimate metaphysical unity as to just how much of this disunity we ought to tolerate in the political sphere. (Ewing 1985, pp. 210, 211)

Ewing rightly notes how monists can respect the differences between persons politically and ethically. As Vinit Hasksar observes, a Hindu monist can distinguish between ordinary life and life as observed and experienced at the deeper levels of mystical awareness:

But it is wrong to claim that in fact the average Hindu sees himself in his ordinary life as one with Brahman. The view that he is one with Brahman is one that he may aspire to comprehend; with the exception of the sages and the mystics it is a truth that people are, at best, only dimly aware of. His ordinary life is so full of his egoistical drive, which is why he needs to be reminded by himself and by others of deep truths which stress his identity with the cosmos. According to the doctrine of *Advaita* there is indeed just one Brahman or the cosmic self pervading us all, but as long as the people are in the grip of *Maya* or illusion they will believe that they have separate egos and attach themselves to illusory goals. (V. Hasksar 1991, p. 89)

At the mystical stage of perception, however, monists in Hindu as well as Buddhist traditions highlight the absorption of the individual into Brahman or Nirvana. Consider this passage from the Hindu *Brihadaranyka Upanishad*:

[A]s a lump of salt cast in water would dissolve right into the water . . . so, lo, verily, this great Being (*bhuta*), infinite, limitless, is just a mass of knowledge. Arising out of these elements (*bhuta*), into them also one vanishes away . . . For

179

where there is a duality, as it were, there one sees another . . . Where, verily, everything has become just one's own self . . . then whereby and whom would one see? (2, 4, 12 and 14)

Consider, too, Suzuki's description of the ultimate absorption into that which is ineffable:

The individual shell in which my personality is so solidly encased explodes at the moment of satori. Not necessarily that I get unified with a being greater than myself or absorbed in it, but that my individuality, which I found rigidly held together and definitely kept separate from other individual existences . . . melts away into something indescribable, something which is of quite a different order from what I am accustomed to. (Suzuki 1933, p. 18)

But it may be argued that this vision need not be reflected in a denigration of nonabsorbed, individual life.

Having pointed out that monists can supplant certain egoistic views of the world without necessarily denigrating all aspirations of individual persons, it needs to be noted that this is an area of ongoing debate and concern. The focus of some of this controversy is Hindu and Buddhist accounts of reincarnation. I close this chapter by outlining the issues at stake.

In much of the traditional teaching about reincarnation or the transmigration of souls in Hinduism and Buddhism, there is a central concern with karmic justice according to which goodness is rewarded and evil punished. Those who act ethically receive a reward, while the wicked are punished. M. Hiriyanna describes the implications of the Law of Karma as it is borne out in practice:

The law of karma accordingly is not a blind mechanical law, but is essentially ethical. It is this conviction that there are in reality no iniquities in life which explains the absence of any feeling of bitterness – so apt to follow in the wake of pain and sorrow – which is noticeable even among common people in India when any misfortune befalls them. They blame neither God nor their neighbour, but only themselves for it. In fact, this frame of mind, which belief in the karma doctrine produces, is one of the most wholesome among its consequences. Deussen refers thus to the case of a blind person whom he met once during his Indian tour: "Not knowing that he had been blind from birth, I sympathized with him and asked by what unfortunate accident the loss of sight had come upon him. Immediately and without showing any sign of bitterness, the answer was ready to his lips, 'By some crime committed in a former birth.'" (Hiriyanna 1951, pp. 48–9)

180

This justice across lives is an important element in accounting for evil. But a key difficulty, much debated, is how justice can in fact be served in this way because it is not clear what would count as the same person being reborn again and again. Putting the worry in first-person terms: What would make it true that I am the reincarnation of some person who lived, say, in the nineteenth century? What account of personal identity is required if reincarnation is accepted?

At least initially, it appears that reincarnation requires that there be an individual person, call him "Peter," who successively animates or comes to have distinct material bodies. Reincarnation is typically described in ways that do not involve the physical transfer of any stuff (a brain or part of the brain, say) and so it is natural to think of reincarnation involving Peter or his soul as some nonphysical thing that migrates from one body to the next. If so, reincarnation may well be describable in a coherent fashion that does not require as a condition of personal identity that persons actually remember their past lives. The problem with relying on memory is that many of us simply have no evident recollections of our former lives. But just as a person, Peter, may be the same person over time in a single life (e.g. Peter was born in 1952 and is now in his forties) despite his not remembering large tracts of his past, so Peter might be the same person as Napoleon despite the fact that he has no memories of his former, imperial existence. Difficulties arise, however, in some Hindu and Buddhist traditions according to which the individual person has only an apparent or provisional individual identity. We have already noted how some Hindus describe the absorption of the individual into Brahman. Consider briefly some Buddhist and related teaching.

While most Buddhists do not look to union with Brahman as the goal of enlightenment, many of them describe Nirvana as a release of the illusion that one is a substantial individual thing. The Buddha is recorded as claiming that ". . . there is nothing that can be called an 'ego,' and there is no such thing as 'mine' in all the world . . . Everything is impermanent and passing and egoless" (from *The Teachings of the Buddha*). The doctrine of the no-self (*anatta*) has a crucial role in Buddhist views of both human nature and ultimate fulfillment. This view of the self is not restricted to Asian Buddhism. David Hume's (1711–76) view of the self is often cited as similar to the Buddhist no-self theory (see question 11 at the end of this chapter). Today Derik Parfit has defended a view of the self he sees as both Humean and Buddhist. Parfit cites with approval the Buddha's teaching: "O Brethren, actions do exist and also their consequences but the person that acts does not" (cited by Parfit in *Reasons and Persons* 1984, p. 302).

181

The problem is that if the individual person does not exist over time, how can it make sense for that person to be the subject of karmic justice over many lives? Bruce Reichenbach concludes his recent study of karma with this summation:

> To conclude, we have argued that there is an ambiguity in the Buddhist account of the human person. On the one hand, personal identity is merely ascribed; selfhood is a fiction. We are easily misled into thinking that there is personal identity and continuity when in fact there is nothing but series of events. This perspective entails that rebirth is a fiction, as are the doctrines of karma and liberation. On the other hand, the doctrine of karma is held to have empirical content; karma and liberation are experienced realities. This perspective entails that the person is reborn. We have seen that it falls to karma to provide the objective ground for the personal identity and continuity found in rebirth. These two hands are not consistent. Is the self a fiction or not? (Reichenbach 1990, p. 132)

The dilemma may be put this way: If the self is not a fiction, then reincarnation and karma may be coherently described, but then a fundamental teaching of Buddhist tradition and some Hindu tradition (Advaita) is in jeopardy. But if the self is a fiction, then the process of reincarnation is difficult to defend consistently.

This debate over the nature of the self is an exciting, fruitful area in which the philosophy of mind and value theory converge in the philosophy of religion. Much work needs to be done in exploring these concerns in which competing thought experiments are marshalled either to defend or responsibly and sensitively to evaluate these monist themes. (See suggested question 10 and further suggested readings below.)

We shall consider additional aspects of monist ethical teaching in chapter 9 in the context of addressing the problem of evil. The next chapter covers ethical theory in general, theistic theories of value, and the challenge of religious ethical pluralism.

Suggested Questions and Topics

(1) There are several general worries about time which are useful to address: Where is the past? Does the future exist in front of us, as it were? How long is the present "now"? Is time made up of instants, extensionless points of time?

If so, are there infinitely many instants in, say, a second? If they take up no time interval whatever, how can any number of instants constitute an interval? Is time essentially one-dimensional? Is time travel possible? What are the similarities and differences between spatial and temporal relations?

(2) Irrespective of whether you think it makes sense to believe God or Brahman exists outside of time, do you think other entities can so exist or do so exist? For example, do you think that propositions or mathematical entities exist timelessly? Consider the following claim by William Kneale:

> An assertion such as "There is a prime number between five and ten" can never be countered sensibly by the remark "You are out of date; things have altered recently." And this is the reason why the entities discussed in mathematics can properly be said to have a timeless existence. (Kneale 1960–1, p. 98)

(3) Do you think God could create more than one time frame and exist simultaneously with each? Consider the following proposal by Keith Ward:

> God can create different . . . space–time systems which cannot be spatially or temporally related to one another. He will relate himself to each of those systems, in such a way that he will exist simultaneously with each event in each system, as it occurs. But those different time sequences will not be temporally relateable to each other . . . God is temporal, in that he does some things before he does others; and in changing, he projects his being along one continuous temporal path. But there may be many such paths . . . in different universes . . . which are not absolutely correlatable with each other. So God must be conceived as moving along all such paths, as existing in a number of different times. To the extent that this is so, there cannot be causal relations between those times, for each such point of correlation would establish a simultaneity. We may speak of God, then, not just as temporal but as multi-temporal. (Ward 1982, p. 166)

(4) Analyze the following claim by Stewart Sutherland:

> A timeless being cannot utter, but neither can he represent to himself. He cannot physically make or create, but neither can he deliberate, reflect, anticipate or intend, for these are all essentially temporal notions . . . He cannot, of course, remember or predict, suspect or confirm; nor is it easy to grasp what timeless love really can be. (Sutherland 1984 p. 56)

(5) J. R. Lucas contends that Christian theism is best served by the belief that God changes and is affected by the goods and ills of the world. In a

chapter entitled "The Vulnerability of God" in *The Future* Lucas writes against the thesis that God is impassible (that is, not able to suffer):

> If individuals are valuable in their own right, as children are in the eyes of their father, the traditional doctrine of impassibility loses its appeal. It was thought to be incompatible with the ultimacy of God that He should be moved by anything outside Himself. But if God has created independent centers of value, He is not being constrained by some external force, if He then values them for what they are and what they become, independently of any further choice of His. Having created men in His own image, He has endowed their choices and predilections with a value in their own right. A father does not merely leave his children free to make up their own minds for themselves on occasion: he so much respects their choices that the fact that they want something is valuable in his eyes too. Likewise God is guided in the things He wants to happen by the things we want to happen. But this is not the constraint of external necessity, but the free first-personal choice of creative love. (Lucas 1989, p. 232)

How might an advocate of God's eternity reply to this objection? In what respects, if any, might defenders of divine eternity like Brian Davies or Brian Leftow accommodate the thesis that God is vulnerable? See chapter 5 for material on divine passibility and impassiblity.

(6)   Paul Helm objects to theists who argue that although God is spaceless, God cannot be timeless. He first formally analyzes the argument that God is timeless as follows:

(1)   God exists timelessly.

(2)   God exists simultaneously at all moments of human time.

(3)   God is simultaneously present at what I did yesterday, am doing today and will do tomorrow.

(4)   If time t_1 is simultaneous with time t_2, and t_2 is simultaneous with t_3, then t_1 is simultaneous with t_3.

(5)   If God is simultaneously present at what I did yesterday and am doing today then yesterday and today are simultaneous (from 3 and 4).

(6)   But the idea that yesterday and today are simultaneous is absurd.

(7)   Therefore (1) is incoherent (Helm, "God and Spacelessness" in Cahn and Schatz [eds] 1982, p. 103; I have adjusted the enumeration for ease of reference but not the sequence of steps in the argument).

He then constructs a parallel argument to show that if the earlier argument is sound, then so is the following:

(8)   God is spaceless.

(9)   God is wholly spatially present at different places.

(10) God is wholly spatially present at what I am doing here and you are doing there.

(11) If an individual is wholly spatially present with another individual, and that individual is wholly spatially present with a third individual then the first individual is wholly spatially present with the third individual.

(12) Thus if God is wholly spatially present at what I am doing here and you are doing there then where you are and where I am are the same place.

(13) But the idea that this place and that place are the same place is absurd.

(14) Therefore (8) is incoherent. (Helm, in Cahn and Schatz [eds] 1982, p. 103)

Assess the validity and soundness of each argument. How might one defend the thesis that while God is temporal, God is nonetheless spaceless? Is the thesis that God is spaceless the same as the traditional theistic thesis that God is omnipresent?

(7)   Are there plausible religious reasons for a restricted treatment of ineffability? One thesis to consider is that while there are no philosophical barriers to applying conceptual categories to God (e.g. God is a being, an agent, and so on), there are nonetheless important religious reasons grounded in respect and reverence for restricting such conceptualization. Martin Buber (1878–1965) held that God may be spoken to but not about. An interesting paper might be written exploring positions like Buber's that advance a qualified treatment of ineffability.

(8)   There appears to be a contradiction involved in the claim "God is nameless," for one is thereby naming as "God" that which one claims is nameless. Stace suggests a solution you may wish to consider:

> As every logician knows, any name, any word in any language, except a proper name, stands for a concept of a universal . . . Neither God nor Nirvana stand for concepts. Both are proper names: It is not a contradiction that Eckhart should use the name God and yet declare Him nameless. For though He has a proper name, there is for Him no name in the sense of a word standing for a concept. (Stace 1952, p. 24)

(9)   William Alston constructed an extended dialogue on the concept of ineffability. Consider the adequacy of the reply of the character Mysticus to the charge of Philologus:

Philologus: Let's see what is left after the purge. "'To say that God is ineffable is to say that no concepts apply to Him, . . . that any statement of the form 'God is *x*' is false." "Thus you cannot attach any predicate to Him." But if in saying "God is ineffable" we are making a true statement, haven't we applied a concept of ineffability? Haven't we attached a predicate to Him, viz., "ineffable"? Haven't we made a true statement of the form "God is *x*"? Aren't we in the position of being able to make a true statement only by doing the very things which the statement declares impossible, thereby falsifying it? Is this like a man saying "I can't speak English"? (Cf. the case of a town crier who cries that crying has been outlawed.)

Mysticus: Surely you aren't serious. When I say, "God is ineffable," I am not attempting to apply a concept to Him or attach a predicate to Him, and so if the statement is true it would not be correct to say that I have succeeded in doing these things. I am denying that any concepts of predicates can be applied to Him. Of course, the grammatical form of "God is ineffable" is misleading. It looks like a positive statement, such as "Jones is ill" or "Susie is pretty," but actually it doesn't involve attaching any predicate to anything. Its logical form would be more clearly exhibited if it were formulated: "It is not the case that any predicate can be attached to God." This shows that "God is ineffable" is not really the *logical* form "God is *x*," although it looks as if it were. Similarly, saying "King Arthur is factitious" does not constitute attaching a predicate to King Arthur, although it looks as if it did. Hence to say truly "God is ineffable" we are not required to do what we are declaring to be impossible. (Alston 1972, pp. 79, 80)

(10)   Analyze the following claim by David Hume:

For my part, when I enter most intimately into what I call *myself*, I always stumble on some particular perception or other, of heat or cold, light or shade, love or hatred, pain or pleasure. I never can catch *myself* at any time without a perception, and never can observe any thing but the perception. When my perceptions are remov'd for any time, as by sound sleep; so long am I insensible of myself, and may truly be said not to exist. And were all my perceptions remov'd by death, and cou'd I neither think, nor feel, nor see, nor love, nor hate after the dissolution of my body, I shou'd be entirely annihilated, nor do I conceive what is further requisite to make me a perfect non-entity. . . . But setting aside some metaphysicians of this kind, I may venture to affirm of the rest of mankind, that they are nothing but a bundle or collection of different perceptions, which succeed each other with an inconceivable rapidity, and are in a perpetual flux and movement. Our eyes cannot turn in their sockets without varying our perceptions. Our thought is still more variable than our sight; and all our other senses and faculties contribute to this change; nor is there any single power of the soul, which remains unalterably the same, perhaps for one moment. The mind is a kind of theatre, where several perceptions successively make their appearance; pass, repass, glide away, and mingle in an infinite variety of postures and situations. (Hume 1988, Book 1, Part IV)

(11) Contrast the saying of the Buddha (cited in the text, p. 181) with Thomas Reid's claim: "I am not thought, I am action. I am not feeling; I am something that thinks and acts and suffers" (Reid 1941, chapter 4).

Further Readings and Considerations

From *A Companion to Philosophy of Religion*, see "Eternity"; "Immutability and Impassibility"; "Being"; "Hinduism"; and "Buddhism." For good anthologies on the philosophy of time see *The Philosophy of Time* edited by R. M. Gale, *The Nature of Time* edited by R. Flood and M. Lockwood, and *Problems of Space and Time* edited by J. J. C. Smart. A superb treatment of the history of competing conceptions of time and eternity is Richard Sarabji's *Time, Creation and the Continuum*. Brian Davies' work on God as Being is developed in the course of his analysis of Thomas Aquinas' philosophy of God. See his "Aquinas on What God is Not." Among the most useful introductions to the philosophy of time are *Aspects of Time* by George Schlesinger, *The Structure of Time* by W. H. Newton-Smith, and *An Introduction to the Philosophy of Time and Space* by Bas van Fraassen. For interesting arguments in the philosophy of both God and time see David Braine's *The Reality of Time and the Existence of God*.

While I have maintained in this chapter that the appeal to experience is essential to get us launched in the philosophy of time, such an appeal does not provide us with any neat escape from various puzzles. For while we may be forced to appeal to our experience of time to get us started, it is not obvious how to proceed in articulating a comprehensive theory of time. Richard Gale comments on the difference between ostensively (from the Latin *ostendere* meaning "to make manifest" or "to show") defining a color by pointing to it and defining time by pointing:

There are many words, such as "yellow," which stand for simple unanalyzable (indefinable) properties. There are, however, good reasons why no one ever asked in anguish, "What, then, is yellow . . . ," for at least we can ostensively (demonstratively) define yellow: we can point to an instance of yellow. Time unfortunately, admits of no such straightforward ostensive definition. Obviously there is nothing we can point to and say, "*This* is the past (or future)." (We must not confuse a photograph or memory with the *past* event it depicts.) Neither is it possible to point to the present, since it is, as Aristotle claimed, a knife-edge without thickness which serves merely to connect the past with the future. (Gale 1978, p. 4)

So experience may be a good beginning but it only opens us up to a larger theoretical project.

Theists sometimes construe time as more fundamental than space, because there cannot be spatial change (a shift in spatial locations) without temporal change but there can be temporal change without spatial change (e.g. a state of affairs in which there are no spatial objects at all but, instead, a temporal, changing deity and a multitude of spirits). It is for reasons such as this that J. R. Lucas argues that "Time is more fundamental than space. Indeed, time is the most fundamental of all categories" (Lucas 1973, p. 3).

For valuable contributions on the character of religious language see Janet Soskice's *Metaphor and Religious Language*, and William Alston's *Divine Nature and Human Language*. A superb classical work on how to render biblical imagery of God is Moses Maimonides' *The Guide for the Perplexed*.

For recent work on the nature of individual persons in Buddhist and Hindu traditions, see work by David Kalupahana, Donald Swearer, S. Collins, Joanna Macy, Gunapala Dharmasiri, Bruce Reichenbach, and Paul Griffiths.

7

God, Values, and Pluralism

All extant religions address the nature of good and evil and each commends human fulfillment, whether this is understood in terms of salvation, enlightenment, liberation, happiness, tranquility or Nirvana. This chapter focuses on some important ways in which fulfillment and frustration, good and evil are treated religiously.

The chapter begins by introducing some terminology in ethical theory. The focus is on the question of whether moral judgments are objectively right or wrong. Much of the material is then used later in the chapter to outline different religious treatments of values. Because theistic religions play the largest role in the political and ethical dispute in the contemporary English-speaking world, there is an emphasis on theistic ethics. A final section concerns the role of religion in political life. Many societies today face a dramatic challenge in upholding a commitment to democracy in the wake of some religious movements. How should this challenge be addressed? In what ways can world religions support toleration and respect for one another and for secular practices?

At least two challenges face the project of this chapter: the difficulty of addressing two animated, expansive fields (ethics *and* philosophy of religion) and the difficulty of addressing issues that have generated such enormous, heated debate. In an effort to stabilize and balance the material to be covered, considerable attention is given to investigating the general methods of moral reflection. This is then utilized in a specific account of moral reflection in light of religious beliefs. By first taking on board more general, structural matters, my hope is that the ground will be laid for further, more specific work for readers to pursue. The British philosopher H. H. Price once said, "In philosophy, the longest way around is often the shortest way home" (Price 1969,

189

p. 24). In this chapter, I am proposing a longer walk through the issues than in other chapters in order to get a clearer picture of the terrain and to help to locate areas for more focused philosophical study.

Preliminary Distinctions

Many of us assume there are certain actions that are morally right and morally wrong, good and bad. The terms "morally right" and "morally wrong" apply principally to actions as in *Acting with integrity is morally right*, and *Killing the innocent is wrong*, or omissions as in *Failing to prevent famine is morally wrong*. The terms "good" and "bad" can be used in assessing actions, but they can also be used more extensively. "Good" and "Evil" can describe states of affairs in which there may or may not be moral or immoral action. The state of affairs *The death of thousands* may be deemed bad and *The happiness of thousands* may be deemed good even if neither involves any moral action or omission. The first state of affairs may be bad and the second good regardless of whether either is the result of moral or immoral action (e.g., they are brought about by volcanic eruptions, droughts, tidal waves). So, the state of affairs *There being a beautiful island* may be deemed good but not morally right, as islands cannot be morally right or wrong. *John Doe acts justly*, on the other hand, may refer both to a good state of affairs and to a morally right action.

Following current practice, the terms "ethical" and "moral" will be treated synonymously. (In the past, the English term "moral" would be used to refer to assessing the rightness or wrongness of action whereas "ethical" would be used when matters of character are highlighted, e.g. integrity, courage and cowardice.) "Value theory" names the general area in which one reflects on ethics along with other values and disvalues such as beauty and ugliness, knowledge and ignorance.

The view that there is no such thing as moral rightness and wrongness, or good and evil, is called *nihilism* (from the Latin *nihil* meaning "nothing"). Nihilists may grant that it makes sense within a given society to utilize the categories "good" and "bad" in relation to various conventions. They may acknowledge prevailing social laws and think it prudent to conform to them, but nihilists do not think that there is a fact of the matter as to whether some action is truly right or wrong. Following the laws and conventions of one society rather than another is neither morally right nor wrong.

A *moral skeptic* does not affirm or deny objective moral codes and values, but withholds judgment about their status. A moral skeptic is like the agnostic who neither affirms nor denies theism.

Ethical relativists maintain that there are moral rights and wrongs but that these are relative to different conditions. This thesis is close to nihilism, but distinguishable from it insofar as relativists think there are facts that do count as establishing moral rightness and wrongness. An *individual relativist* claims that judgments of moral rightness and wrongness are relative to the individual making the judgment. On one version of this view, *individual relativism*, for me to claim "X is wrong" means the same thing as "I disapprove of X." A *cultural relativist* claims that the legitimacy of moral judgments is relative to cultures. According to this view, to claim that "Y is wrong" means the same thing as "Y is disapproved of by or in some culture."

In contrast with nihilism and relativism there are different forms of moral realism according to which there are bona fide moral facts. Moral realists hold that certain acts are truly wrong (such as torturing the innocent) and truly right (such as acting courageously to protect the innocent) regardless of social conventions, or individual approval or disapproval. Moral realism is sometimes referred to as moral or ethical objectivism. I am using the term "moral realism" very broadly to encompass *any* view that upholds objective moral values.

One may be a stringent moral realist and claim that there are moral rules and principles of an absolute, universal kind that do not admit of variation in application. On this view there may be rules such as *lying is always wrong*, *theft is always bad* and so on, that hold in all contexts. More qualified forms of moral realism may claim that there are some bedrock absolutes (for example: murder, rape, torture are absolute wrongs and always prohibited) but that certain contexts can permit actions that are otherwise wrong. Thus, someone may claim that lying is wrong but only *prima facie* (literally "at first glance"). That is, the fact that some action is a lie counts as a reason not to do that act and yet, all things considered, it may be morally required for a person to lie if it is reasonable to believe that doing so will prevent catastrophic harm. Consider the following thought experiment. You live during a fierce persecution of innocent people whom you protect, hiding them from their brutal pursuers. You are asked by a belligerent army officer whether you are indeed harboring such people. A moral realist may deem you morally required to lie, deliberately deceiving the pursuer, even though, if conditions were otherwise, lying would be wrong. Such a qualified position might well be called *contextual moral realism*. What marks a moral realist (whether a contextualist or a more stringent realist) is that she does not think that the bare approval of a human being

191

or a culture automatically makes something right or good for that person or culture. While moral realism allows that an individual could, in principle, approve of actions that are wrong, and so could whole cultures, relativism does not. For the relativist who claims that what a culture approves is what defines moral rightness in that setting, it cannot be the case that what a culture approves of is not morally right.

One reason for adopting moral realism is based on an appeal to common experience and judgments. This may amount to appealing to what philosophers variously call intuition, reason, insight, common sense, or experience. To this end, some philosophers advance moral realism simply by describing cases that they hope will bring to light the plausibility of moral realism. Consider, for example, this description of atrocities from Dostoevski's novel *The Brothers Karamazov*:

> They burn villages, murder, outrage women and children, they nail their prisoners by the ears to the fences, leave them so till morning, and in the morning they hang them all – all sorts of things you can't imagine. People talk sometimes of bestial cruelty, but that's a great injustice and insult to the beasts; a beast can never be so cruel as a man, so artistically cruel. The tiger only tears and gnaws, that's all he can do. He would never think of nailing people by the ears, even if he were able to do it. These Turks took a pleasure in torturing children too; cutting the unborn child from the mother's womb, and tossing babies up in the air and catching them on the points of their bayonets before their mother's eyes. Doing it before the mother's eyes was what gave zest to the amusement. Here is another scene that I thought very interesting. Imagine a trembling mother with her baby in her arms, a circle of invading Turks around her. They've planned a diversion; they pet the baby, laugh to make it laugh. They succeed, the baby laughs. At that moment a Turk points a pistol four inches from the baby's face. The baby laughs with glee, holds out its little hands to the pistol, and he pulls the trigger in the baby's face and blows out its brains. Artistic, wasn't it? (Dostoyevsky, trans. 1950, p. 283)

Moral realism is served insofar as one feels (or senses or judges or intuits or simply reasonably believes) that such action must be objectively wrong. Nihilists are committed to holding that nothing objectively evil takes place in the events described by Dostoyevsky. Relativists can condemn such atrocities from the standpoint of individual victims (a victim's crying out "that is wrong" would mean he or she does not approve of it), or cultures (the action took place in a culture that did not approve of it). But, from the standpoint of the person inflicting the suffering, the behavior may be permissible.

There are, as will be noted later, many forms of moral realism. But first let us consider some of the reasons behind the rejection of moral realism. Moral realism is not the most popular of philosophical positions. William Lycan writes: "Moral facts are right up there . . . in the ranks of items uncordially despised by most contemporary philosophers" (Lycan 1988, p. 198). It is not obvious that *most* contemporary philosophers reject the category of objective moral facts, but certainly many do and it is important to consider some of the reasons why this is so before we consider competing accounts of values in religious contexts.

Reasons For and Against Moral Realism

What follows are four arguments commonly employed against recognizing objective values. Replies to each will then be considered.

(A)   Perhaps the most common complaint against moral realism is the charge that if it were true there would be less diversity of moral practices and beliefs. There is widespread variation of moral codes both between societies and within most societies. Therefore moral realism is false (Benedict 1934; Mackie 1977).

(B)   Following from the first objection is the charge that moral realism is not borne out by any evident, stable moral methodology. Granted, if only for the sake of argument, that there are objective values, how can we discover what these are? If there is a stable method for identifying moral facts, then they can have a rightful place in our deliberations and practical affairs. But if we have no reliable way to determine what they are, they seem to be useless. *Moral facts* can do no work in our deliberations. We are better off ignoring claims to objectivity and simply regarding moral disagreements as the reflection of different individual or cultural preferences. For arguments against moral realism on the grounds that it lacks a proper methodology, see Mackie (1977) and Harman (1977).

(C)   An argument against moral realism has been advanced by J. L. Mackie that he calls, "The Argument from Queerness." "Queerness" is the term Mackie employs in his case for "the metaphysical peculiarity of the supposed objective values" (Mackie 1977, p. 49). From Mackie's point of view, empirical propositions about the world and our feelings and judgments can be accommodated in a reasonable theory about nature. Objective values, on the other hand, are comparatively peculiar objects. Moral facts cannot be seen or weighed or felt. Moreover, when a person judges an action to be morally required she appears to be committed to believing she has a reason to do the act. Judgments about colors, shapes, and so on do not have a parallel structure. According to Mackie, theories explaining objective moral facts as basic features of the world leave one with more mystery than concluding that they are merely reflections of our subjective projections.

(D) The belief in moral facts, objective rights and wrongs, has had a horrifying role in colonialism and other oppressive practices. Many of the world's atrocities have been justified on the basis of their serving what is believed to be a great, objective good. Along these lines one may take note of the title of one of Bertrand Russell's essays: "The Harm that Good Men Do," or Karl Popper's chronicle of the harms done in the name of utopian ideals: *The Open Society and its Enemies.*

Consider a series of replies on behalf of moral realism.

REPLY TO (A): Two replies are often marshaled in response to the objection from moral diversity.

(i)   The first is to acknowledge that there are indeed widespread differences between societies and within societies in terms of moral belief and practice but to argue that such differences have no bearing on the status of objective moral facts and values. This strategy is akin to that used by the logician Gottlob Frege (1848–1925) in his reply to an objection against an objective account of logical relations. He considered the possibility of there being cultures in which people embraced what are, for us, absurdities like "1 + 1 = 3." Should discovering such cultures weaken our commitment to an objective account of mathematical and logical relations? His conclusion was that unless these foreign symbols are different from ours (for example, their "1" means "1.5" in our system, while "3" stays the same as "3" for us) such cultural beliefs are simply mistaken. Just as Frege contended that the abandonment of an objective account of logical and mathematical relations lands us in absurdity, it may be argued that the abandonment of an objective account of values lands us in moral absurdity. According to some moral realists, moral experience can itself deliver assurance that, for example, torture, rape, and so on, are morally wrong. Anyone who fails to see that torture is evil is morally blind (see Elizabeth Anscombe and Dietrich von Hildebrand).

(ii)   Another reply to argument (A) is more elaborate. One can question the thesis that there is indeed widespread diversity of moral codes across cultures. Some moral realists contend that there is more consensus and considerably fewer differences than appear at first. It is argued that while an initial review of the anthropological and sociological data may lead one to believe there are radically different views of morality across cultures, these differences

194

should not obscure the massive amount of agreement between societies and cultures. Peter Singer, a leading contemporary ethicist, summarizes his overall assessment of the spectrum of moral practices as follows:

> For ethics is *not* a meaningless series of different things to different people in different times and places. Rather, against a background of historically and culturally diverse approaches to the question of how we ought to live, the degree of convergence is striking. Human nature has its constants and there are only a limited number of ways in which human beings can live together and flourish; indeed . . . some of the features common to the nature of human beings in different societies are common to the nature of any long-lived, intelligent social mammals, and are reflected in our behavior as they are reflected in that of other primates. Hence what is recognized as a virtue in one society or religious tradition is very likely to be recognized as a virtue in the others; certainly, the set of virtues praised in one major tradition never make up a substantial part of the set of vices of another major tradition. (Exceptions tend to be short-lived, societies in the process of decay or self-destruction.) Moreover within each tradition, the same oscillating currents can be observed: there are periods in which the emphasis is on the performance of conventional duties, obligations or roles; then a great reformer will appear, urging that we have become so far steeped in obedience to the rules, so conventional in our ways of thinking and acting, that we have forgotten the higher goods by which the moral conventions themselves must be justified. Thus Buddha stressed egolessness rather than observance of the Hindu rituals of his day, as Mozi argued that we should follow universal love, not the particular duties specified by Confucianism, and as Jesus taught that love of God and neighbour was more important than following the letter of the prevailing Jewish moral law. (Singer [ed.] 1991, pp. 553, 544)

Moral realists such as Ralph Linton have argued in substantial detail for the common moral bond between cultures concerning many ethical precepts (see Linton 1954, especially pp. 145–68). If Singer, Linton, and others are correct, then the objection from diversity does not succeed.

This highlighting of the uniformity of ethical principles may be reinforced by noting the ways in which moral disagreements arise. Many moral disagreements seem to rest on differences about nonmoral matters, namely one's grasp of what may be called the nonmoral facts, one's abilities to effectively be apprised of the points of views of others, and one's ability to be impartial. I briefly note the importance of each and how variation of abilities in each area can shape one's moral reasoning. This material will be used later in theistic treatment of a God's eye view of moral disagreements.

Nonmoral facts. Consider some of the ways in which moral disagreements stem from empirical disagreements. A disagreement about whether a war is justified may rest upon different judgments about who started it. A disagreement over the permissibility of nuclear power may rest upon divergent assessments of the probability of highly destructive radiation. A disagreement over the ethics of famine relief may rest upon competing assessments of whether such relief will be successful in overturning famine in the long run. All these areas of moral divergence rest upon matters that one may call "nonmoral facts" in the sense that they can be described without any explicit use of moral terminology. Thus, one can describe different famine relief policies without using terms like "right," "wrong," "evil," "good," "cruel," and the like. It is often on the basis of one's view of what I am referring to as "nonmoral facts" that a view of the moral facts is derived.

Affective appraisal. Moral disagreements may stem not just from divergent assessments of nonmoral facts, but from different assessments of the relevant feelings involved. Two parties may know the same facts about, say, famine relief (they know the numbers involved, the likely survival rate if certain relief projects are funded, and so on), but have radically divergent views of the affective repercussions of either giving or withholding such relief. This condition of affective appraisal might well be seen as simply one more nonmoral fact of the matter, but I distinguish it to highlight the role of feelings in moral reflection. The base for our moral judgments is often not just clinical, abstract beliefs about various states of affairs, but borne out in an understanding of how things feel to those involved. Different levels of experience and exposure to such feelings can fuel different moral judgments. A disagreement about the ethics of famine relief may not stem from disagreement about some of the statistical facts of the case (both parties know that 20,000 die per day from famine-related causes), but from the fact that one person has not affectively grasped what it is like to be a victim of famine while the other has.

Impartiality. Some moral disagreements seem to arise from the failure of competing parties to achieve impartiality. Impartiality is often seen as an essential condition of moral reasoning (see, for example, Immanuel Kant and Stephen Darwell). It is frequently professed but less frequently practiced. The widespread appeal across cultures of the Golden Rule of "Do unto others as you would have them do unto you" is evidence of the widely recognized thesis that moral reasoning needs to stand the test of hypothetical role reversal of some kind, a putting yourself in the other person's shoes, so to speak. (It is called "Golden" because of its presumed worth and is often found alongside the so-called "Silver Rule" of "Do not do unto others as you would prefer that they not do unto you.")

If divergences with respect to the above three areas are taken seriously, then much of what counts as moral disagreement may be seen to rest on the failure to agree on these other matters. It may be that parties can agree on the ethical principles that are binding while disagreeing on how they are to be applied. For example, people could agree that one ought not to kill innocent persons, while disagreeing about the nonmoral fact of whether the human fetus is a person, or diverging in the ability affectively and impartially to grasp the points of view of involved parties.

REPLY TO (B): True, there is not a universally agreed list of sufficient conditions for moral reasoning. But the observations made in reply to Objection (A) about the importance of knowing the nonmoral facts, being apprised of the points of view of involved parties, and impartiality, do name what many believe to be essential conditions in moral reflection, even if other factors should be included as well. Thus, it would be paradoxical, if not incoherent, to claim that proper moral reasoning on some topic, X, involves relying on faulty data about the nonmoral facts, a faulty sense of the ways the different parties are affected by X, and only involving the immediate desires of what the so-called moral reasoner wants (Singer 1972). This may not be *sufficient* for an account of what constitutes moral reasoning, but it is at least a start.

As noted above, the fact that there are many moral disagreements within societies and across societies need not be seen as a sign of deep discord on all moral matters, including moral methodology. In fact, one test of the degree of moral accord between cultures and between groups within cultures is the extent to which moral arguments are even possible. An argument between parties requires some agreement. If one's beliefs and values differ entirely from another party, there can be little hope of a common language in which to carry out debate. So while apparent disagreement across cultures on moral matters is a significant obstacle to the claim that all reasonable people know what is right and wrong, disagreement itself and the ability of competing parties to argue with one another can be evidence of a deep, common accord (Rachels 1986).

REPLY TO (C): Moral rightness and wrongness may be no more strange or "queer" than other items that make up plausible accounts of the world. Compare moral realism with a standard account of evidence on the theory of knowledge. It may be argued that ethics is no more strange or queer than standard accounts of the justification of our beliefs. Many philosophers recognize that some beliefs are better justified or more evident than others, and that such justification amounts to a normative constraint on one's beliefs. Thus, if you have sufficient justification (evidence) for some position, you ought to believe it. On this view, one may be held accountable (blameworthy or praiseworthy), depending upon how one weighs evidence. If one acknowledges that there are objective, normative constraints about what ought and ought not to be believed, why think these are any less odd than thinking there are objective, normative constraints about what one ought and ought not to do? (Brink 1984) (For further reflection on the nature of justification and evidence, see chapter 8.)

REPLY TO (D): Undoubtedly, great harms have been done in the name of what is believed to be the morally right thing to do. But if there are no objective moral facts or principles, then it is difficult to condemn these harmful acts as immoral or to blame societies for unfairly imposing their standards on others. One can condemn imperialism and international belligerence on the basis of the United Nations Universal Declaration of Human Rights (1948), but unless the Declaration is believed to reflect that which is objectively right and valuable about human life, such condemnation has little worth except as an expression of power and threat of punishment. From a relativist position, it is unclear why the Declaration should have any moral significance for a culture that fails to see the Declaration as binding. For the relativist and nihilist there can be no condemnation of what is believed to be, objectively, morally wrong practices, such as female circumcision in Africa, or the old practice in Japan of *tsujigir* ("crossroads cut") in which a Samurai tests his new sword by cutting a person in two (Midgley 1981). Those who reject objective values might find such practices repellent, and appeal to our felt dispositions or instincts to reject them. So, for example, Bertrand Russell signals his own preference for Buddhist ethics as opposed to what he sees as a cruel view of life advanced by Nietzsche:

> For my part, I agree with Buddha as I have imagined him. But I do not know how to prove that he is right by any arguments such as can be used in a mathematical or a scientific question. I dislike Nietzsche because he likes the contemplation of pain, because he erects conceit into duty, because the men whom he most admires are conquerors, whose glory is cleverness in causing men to die. But I think the ultimate argument against his philosophy, as against any

198

unpleasant but internally self-consistent ethic, lies not in an appeal to facts, but in an appeal to the emotions. Nietzsche despises universal love; I feel it the motive power to all that I desire as regards the world. His followers have had their innings, but we may hope that it is coming rapidly to an end. (Russell 1957, p. 800)

Moral realists may also appeal to emotions as well (love of persons, affective sympathetic identification with the oppressed) but they would see these as responding to objective values (it is a fact that persons ought to be loved) rather than mere expressions of emotion. But to relativists who do not share Russell's emotions or Buddhist compassion, there may be no ideological barriers to very cruel practices. Note the way in which the Italian fascist Mussolini used relativism:

> In Germany relativism is an exceedingly daring and subversive theoretical construction (perhaps Germany's philosophical revenge) which may herald the military revenge. In Italy, relativism is simply a fact . . . Everything I have said and done in these last years is relativism by intuition . . . If relativism signifies contempt for fixed categories and men who claim to be the bearers of an objective and immortal truth . . . then there is nothing more relativistic than Fascist attitudes and activity . . . From the fact that all ideologies are of equal value, that all ideologies are mere fictions, the modern relativist infers that everybody has the right to create for himself his own ideology and to attempt to enforce it with all the energy of which he is capable. (Written in 1921, cited by Veatch 1962, pp. 32–46)

Mussolini's relativism is, of course, radically dissimilar to the "live and let live" attitude that is popularly associated with relativism. I cite him only to note how versions of relativism can be used for (what appears to be) profoundly intolerable ends. Some of the ways in which objectivists seek to secure principles of tolerance are explored in a final section of this chapter.

The debate over moral realism is far from resolved and there are certainly responses to the above arguments and counterpoints. My aim is simply to represent some of the major *pro* and *contra* arguments (see Singer [ed.] 1991, for a review of further arguments). The defense of moral realism above does not involve any explicit appeal to God or God's will. If we do invoke God, God's will or a God's eye point of view, does the case for moral realism improve? Alternatively, is theism required to secure moral realism? If there are no objective moral values, what authority does God's will have?

199

Divine Command Theories

Consider first the significance of God's will if nihilism is true. In such a world, God's commands might give rise to *prudential* values but these would not count as objective moral facts. Thus, if God commanded that everyone do X and God threatened to punish those who did not, everyone would have some reason to do X. The kind of obligation that this theistic picture generates would be thoroughly pragmatic. Consider the role of the term "ought" in these two instances: "You ought to avoid harming others" where this is meant to be a straightforward moral claim, and "You ought to give me your money" as uttered by a thief with a gun pointed at you. The second incident is practical – provided you do not wish to be harmed, you should give the thief what he wants – but it fails to be ethical. Similarly, it would be intelligent or wise to obey a nihilist God, but this falls short of claiming that it would be ethically required.

Peter Geach is by no means a nihilist, but his conception of God's power would fit into this schema in which God's authority is grounded in power. Geach believes that the power of God is a key feature in God's moral authority. It makes no practical sense to defy an all-powerful God. In reply to the question "Why should I obey God's Law?" Geach writes:

> This is really an insane question. For Prometheus to defy Zeus made sense because Zeus had not made Prometheus and had only limited power over him. A defiance of an Almighty God is insane: it is like trying to cheat a man to whom your whole business is mortgaged and who you know is well aware of your attempts to cheat him, or again, as the prophet said, it is as if a stick tried to beat, or an axe to cut, the very hand that was wielding it. (Geach, in Helm [ed.] 1981, p. 172)

In response to the accusation that his analysis of God and goodness comes down to mere power worship, he writes:

> I shall be told by [some] philosophers that since I am saying not: It is your supreme moral duty to obey God, but simply: It is insane to set about defying an Almighty God, my attitude is plain power worship. But since this is worship of the Supreme Power, it is as such wholly different from, and does not carry with it, a cringing attitude towards earthly powers. An earthly potentate does not compete with God, even unsuccessfully: he may threaten all manner of

afflictions, but only from God's hands can any affliction actually come upon us. (Geach, in Helm [ed.] 1981, pp. 172–3)

This position is very much like Thomas Hobbes' (1588–1679), who used a high view of God's power and sovereignty to establish some basic duties. In Hobbes' view, "God is King, though the nations be angry . . . Whether men will or no they must be subject always to the divine power" (Hobbes, cited by Geach, p. 172).

The difficulty with this approach, however, is that it seems to fly in the face of what many take to be essential features of moral life. Geach's terminology suggests ethics is like a business arrangement (cheating on someone who owns your mortgage). It is widely believed that moral relations are very different from mercantile, bargaining arrangements. On this view, sometimes one's ethical duty is not in one's best interest. There is also the problem (which he recognizes and seeks to address) that Geach's picture of divine authority appears to saddle one with a dangerous preoccupation with power. Recall the various analyses of "omnipotence" in chapter 3 and the danger of interpreting God's "power" in a value-free context. There would not be anything objectively wrong or bad if God were to act inconsistently, break promises, torture the innocent, and so on. After all, if God commanded murder and rape, would those acts then become right? Arguably not. So, an important reason why many theists resist the Hobbesian move today is that they wish to secure nonarbitrary standards of value.

Many theists today seek to secure moral realism and still ground morality on divine commands. "Divine Command Theory" names any theory which grounds objective values and moral facts on the will or character of God. Could it be that there are objective rights and wrongs, goods and bads, because God made them so? They are not right simply because God is powerful and promises rewards in return for obedience and punishment for disobedience, but because God in some way creates an objective array of duties and rights. According to theism, the laws of nature are explained, ultimately, through the creative power of God. If it is coherent to believe God is the author of the objectively existing laws of nature, why not also the laws of good and evil, right and wrong?

One version of the divine command theory may be formalized as follows. Let "L," "M," and "N" stand for actions:

L is morally right because God commands L
M is morally wrong because God prohibits M

N is neither morally right nor morally wrong because God neither commands nor prohibits N

The "because" in these claims is meant to capture a causal relationship whereby what is asserted is that it is *in virtue of* God's commands and prohibitions, that there are such objective values. (The theory may be refined to account for the value of states of affairs and not just actions, e.g. Q is a good state of affairs because God approves of it.)

At least four objections face such a divine command theory. In exploring possible replies to each, I suggest ways in which the theory may be modified.

(A) OBJECTION: The first objection is perhaps the most important. Why should God's commanding that an action take place make it right? This is essentially the same worry that hounds the Hobbesian view of divine commands. It might be granted that a divine command theory can provide an account of objective moral laws in the same way that theism can provide an account of objective laws of nature. But just as many philosophers assume that the laws of nature could have been otherwise (in our cosmos the speed of light is a fixed, determinate rate, and yet God could have made it otherwise), it appears that the divine command theory allows that God could have made the moral laws differently. Cruelty is wrong in our world, but could God have made cruelty not just permissible but praiseworthy? Allowing for such a possibility strikes many as dangerous, for it makes objective moral laws subject to arbitrariness and caprice.

REPLY TO (A): Consider two moves.

(i) The first reply concedes that morality and values in general are arbitrated by God and these could have been otherwise. However, the point is that God did not do otherwise and that objective moral values and rights are as they are because of God's will. If God is viewed as eternally willing all objective values and moral truths then there was no time when God did not will that certain things are good and evil. The fact (if it is one) that God could have done otherwise is therefore of no consequence. This strategy may be satisfactory for some but significant numbers of philosophers deem it unsatisfactory because of the conviction that ethics and objective values simply could not be otherwise (Moore 1996).

(ii) A second reply to (A) introduces a modification on the divine command theory. According to a *modified* divine command theory, God in some way had to will what God did; God of necessity willed that justice and courage are good, cruelty and malice evil. This is very much like the new Cartesian strategy outlined in chapter 3, according to which the necessary truths of metaphysics and logic are necessary because God willed that they be so and yet God could not have willed otherwise. Arbitrariness in ethics is avoided because of the supposition that God's will is itself necessary.

This view has an important role in the history of theistic accounts of value. God has often been considered essentially good (Augustine, Aquinas, for example), and this has blocked the presumption that God is somehow remote from goodness, as if God needs to check God's behavior over and against some external measure or standard. God's essential goodness has sometimes been described as God being "the good" or "goodness itself" (Dionysius, Augustine, Aquinas, and others). Identifying God as "the good" may seem peculiar from a logical, grammatical point of view. It makes no sense to talk of "the large" or "the small." Things are large or small; there is no "the large." Similarly, things are good; there is no "the good." However, these conceptual snares may be avoidable. The identification of God as "the good" may be interpreted as thinking of God as supremely excellent or good and the source of all created goods. God's being marked out as "the good" may thereby be understood as an affirmation of God's essential goodness and creative power in bringing into existence all other goods. In creating a cosmos, God creates something of value and in God's loving creation and possessing such excellences as knowledge and perfect power, God is the highest good. Thomas Aquinas worked hard to identify God as goodness itself, analyzing this identity in terms of God's preeminent claim to being good and the author of created goods:

> This thing is good and that good, but take away this and that, and regard good itself if thou canst; so wilt thou see God, not good by a good that is other than Himself, but he is good of all good. For in all these good things, whether those which I have mentioned, or any else that are to be discerned or thought, we could not say that one was better than another, when we judge truly, unless a conception of the good itself had been impressed upon us, such that according to it we might both approve some things as good, and prefer one good to another. (Aquinas, *De Trinitate* 8.3)

An appeal to the essential goodness of God is part of a classic response to a dilemma that Plato put forward in his dialogue *Euthyphro* (at 9e). Plato advances the question: Is something good (or holy) because God approves of it, or does God approve of good things because they are good? To take the first option is to risk arbitrariness while the latter risks seeing God as subservient to something higher or more important than God. Augustine and Aquinas seek to understand God as essentially good and thus not remote from goodness in the least, thereby avoiding arbitrariness and the threat of being subject to that which is outside of God.

If one is going to develop a divine command theory of values, this second alternative seems to me the more promising. It may still seem open to criticism on various fronts. Is a will that is necessary still a will? Perhaps not. But here the crucial point for a defender of the theory to note is that the will of God is not some kind of "thing." The Augustine–Aquinas understanding of the goodness of God does not lead one to think of God in terms of sheer will, but in terms of a supremely good nature. Reference to God's will, then, may be interpreted as a reference to the intentionality of a supremely good God. This is at odds with some twentieth-century treatments of "the will," but perhaps no worse for it. I briefly note why this may be so.

Modern Western philosophy includes theories of human nature that put enormous weight on "the will." From the mid-twentieth century on this has been prominent among the existentialists. According to existentialism one's identity is achieved not on the basis of fulfilling one's nature, but in the exercise of a self-determining, self-creating will. This is seen in especially dramatic terms in the work of Jean-Paul Sartre (1905–80), in which human freedom has a profound self-constituting role bordering on the notion of *causa sui* considered in chapter 3 in the Morris–Menzel project. Emphasis on the will can also be seen in Friedrich Nietzsche's philosophy of the will to power and in Arthur Schopenhauer's use of the will in his vast metaphysical scheme of the world. Some theological texts which give center-stage to the power and will of God sometimes refer to God's will in highly reified ways that tax our language and concepts. Consider this statement by the Swiss theologian Karl Barth (1886–1968): "God confronts us with a specific meaning in intention, with a will which has foreseen everything and each thing in particular" (Barth 1948, p. 663).

To think of one's identity as primarily a matter of the will risks not only celebrating some bare notion of power and, thus, being prey to the charge of ethical capriciousness, it also runs into general philosophical trouble. Talk of "the will" makes sense in ordinary contexts, though it may be forcefully argued that its intelligibility rests, in the end, in an overall account of human nature. As John Locke once put it in his discussion of freedom, the proper question is not "whether the will is free" but whether *a person* is free (Locke 1689, edition 1979, II:21). Does it make sense even to think there could be a will (whether free or determined) without there being a person or some kind of being that is willing? Consider again Barth's claim, cited above. His statement can be given a charitable interpretation according to which Barth is referring to God intending something in light of what God foresees; but, if read literally, in which "the will" itself is said to foresee something, his account seems conceptually absurd. Presumably a will cannot think or feel or sense. The concept of the will is not easy to analyze philosophically, but it may be best viewed in terms of the deliberate intentions of agents. Someone acts with *will power* or *wills* such and such when he or she does something with conviction and determination or he or she intentionally does something. Here the reference to "the will" has intelligibility, but taken alone in a conceptual vacuum, so to speak, it does not.

Consider further the prospects of a divine command theory of ethics over and against three objections.

(B) OBJECTION: It is fully intelligible to make moral judgments without having any belief in God. Indeed, there seems to be nothing contradictory about claiming some act is morally wrong and believing there is no God whatsoever.

REPLY TO (B): Let it be granted that it makes perfect sense to make such judgments without invoking God at all, and even while denying God's existence. It does not follow that God is not the cause of objective values and moral laws. By analogy, someone who denies God's existence might consistently and coherently use the laws of nature in explaining natural events but that, alone, does not establish that God did not create the laws of nature and nature itself.

The objection seems to presuppose that the meaning of moral discourse has to be analyzed in terms of God's commands. If a divine command theory that holds "L is morally right" means "God commands L," then it would be committed to holding that it is a contradiction to claim "L is morally right but it is false that God commands L." Analyses of the meaning of synonyms must involve agreement, for if "Grandmother" means "A female whose child has a child," then it is contradictory to claim "There is a Grandmother whose child does not have a child." So, while the second objection may work in terms of arguing that talk of morality and talk of God have different meanings, it does not show that objective values are independent of God's will.

(C) OBJECTION: There are suitable alternative explanations for the existence of objective moral values. These may be biological or social. According to biological accounts, we may be genetically programmed to engage in social activity. Socially, we may be shaped and trained to act in ethical ways. It may also be better to explain ethics in terms of sheer rationality or intuition or claim they exist independently, rather than grounding them in speculative assumptions about God's attitudes (see Moore 1996).

205

REPLY TO (C): This objection will have to be taken up in chapter 10 when the moral argument for theism is considered along with other arguments for and against the existence of God. For present purposes it should be noted that the existence of other nontheistic explanations of ethics need not displace a role for theism. For example, if one were to account for ethics by appealing to evolutionary biology, it would not follow that theism is not needed to explain the workings of evolutionary biology.

(D) OBJECTION: There are many different conceptions of God and God's will. There is no clear, objective way of determining the will of God and thus no clear, objective way of determining what is ethical.

REPLY TO (D): Granted that there are different conceptions of God and God's will, it may be replied that this does nothing to undermine the thesis that the existence of objective values is in virtue of God's will. The divine command theory of ethics does not rest on the supposition that we possess independent access through revelation of God's creativity. What is supposed instead is that objective values themselves stem from divine activity. On this scheme, one may hold that the way in which one comes to know God's will is by coming to know what is objectively valuable. If God is necessarily good and we properly grasp certain essential, objective goods, then, arguably, we have a way of sifting through some of these alternative conceptions of God and rejecting those views in which God approves of what we know to be bad. Imagine justice is necessarily good, and good in virtue of God's necessarily willing that it be so. Under those conditions, to know justice is good is to know what God wills. The parallel with omniscience may be useful – if you know anything and God is omniscient, you know what God knows.

This fourth objection raises an issue of deep significance and compels us to consider moral methodology at greater length. Here both theists and nontheists may find value in what is commonly called *the ideal observer theory* of ethics.

The Ideal Observer Theory

While the earlier version of the divine command theory does not analyze the meaning of moral discourse, I think it is promising to claim that moral discourse does in fact imply an appeal to a "God's eye point of view." The ideal observer theory presents an account of moral discourse and an outline of moral methodology. I shall first set forth the theory and then draw out its theistic implications.

Versions of the ideal observer theory have been advanced by David Hume, Adam Smith (1723–90), Henry Sidgwick (1838–1900), and, more recently, by Roderick Firth, R. M. Hare, and Thomas Carson. I offer a version of the theory that I take to be the strongest (or, if you like, the least implausible). According to the ideal observer theory, the meaning of our moral language can be analyzed in terms of the hypothetical approval and disapproval of an ideal observer.

Let me begin laying out this theory by focusing on three features of what appears to count as ideal observation of values. These three features are developed from the observations cited earlier under the section "Reasons For and Against Objectivism." If getting nonmoral facts wrong, being unable to apprise affectively the points of view of involved parties and failing to be impartial, can account for inadequate moral reasoning, perhaps an ideal realization of knowing all nonmoral facts, affective appraisal, and impartiality can account for ideal moral reasoning.

Omniscience of nonmoral facts.   Our moral judgments typically seem to rest on what we believe to be the facts of the nonmoral case. The reasoning behind our judgments about euthanasia, abortion, nuclear power, economic justice, and so on, seems grounded on beliefs about human desires, origins, physics, history, and so on. Many of these involve facts which may be called "nonmoral facts," a term introduced earlier, which refers to those facts that can be described without explicitly introducing moral and other value-laden terms. The first thesis about ideal observation then, is that an observer would be ideally situated if she were in command of all the facts of the case so that she could form her approval or disapproval free of ignorance.

The reason for having to specify the ideal observer as knowing all the "nonmoral facts" is to avoid having the theory collapse due to circularity. If one were to identify the ideal observer as simply one who knows the facts, including all the facts about morality, then the theory would be as unilluminating as one that claimed that the ideal mathematical judge knows all the facts of mathematics or the ideal historian knows all history. In ethics it is important to appreciate that many judgments rest on that which can be grasped without any sort of ethical categories; an ideal observer would be one that was supremely situated to know all such facts that undergird and inform ideal moral judgments.

Omnipercipience.   This is Roderick Firth's term for being affectively appraised of the position and feelings of all involved parties. Arguably, ideal observation consists not just in knowing the facts but being affectively or emotionally apprised of what is at stake. One can see the appeal to affective appraisal at work in much ethical debate in which various parties are urged to take the role of others seriously. In part, this is why literature has had the moral role it does in ethics and even politics. Rather than just listing morally relevant features of situations, literature enables one to appreciate those features "from the inside" of those involved. By securing this affective dimension separately, the ideal observer theory highlights the vital roles of imagination and feeling in ethics. J. C. F. Schiller (1759–1805) exposes the moral problems of failing to use both imagination and affective appreciation. He laments the person who "has a narrow heart, since his imagination, imprisoned within the unvarying confines of his own calling, is incapable of extending itself to appreciate other ways of seeing and knowing (Schiller, trans. 1962, pp. 91–3; see also Janet Soskice's fine essay "Love and Attention", in McGhee [ed.] 1992).

Impartiality.   As noted earlier, impartiality is a widely recognized feature of moral reasoning. To judge any ethical matter it is essential to achieve a certain measure of impartiality rather than acting simply to advance one's preferences irrespective of the consequences. "Impartiality" should not be confused with "indifference" or "disinterest" insofar as these suggest an ideal observer is not interested in the outcome of its observations. "Impartiality" is also distinguishable from "neutrality" if the latter suggests that an ideal observer cannot have any judgments at all. A judge can be impartial and yet contend that John Doe did something both morally wrong and illegal. The judge is not, then, "neutral" over John Doe's behavior, but neither is he or she partial in the sense that she is biased or acting unfairly.

The ideal observer theory draws on each of the conditions just outlined. An ideal observer who would assess morality and immorality, good and evil would be as follows:

An Ideal Observer is omniscient of all the nonmoral facts, omnipercipient, and impartial.

An ideal observer's vantage point thereby reflects a dismissal of egotism. The resultant point of view is one that many philosophers have prized and sought. Schiller underscored the desirability of developing a moral sensitivity that is informed by impartiality and an affective appreciation of others: .

It would be . . . difficult to determine which does more to impede the practice of brotherly love: the violence of our passions, which disturbs it, or the rigidity of our principles, which chills it – the egotism of our senses or the egotism of our reason. If we are to become compassionate, helpful, effective human beings, feeling and character must unite, even as wide-open senses must combine with wide-open intellect if we are to acquire experience. How can we, however laudable our precepts, be just, kindly and human towards others, if we lack the power of receiving into ourselves, faithfully and truly, natures unlike ours, of feeling our way into the situation of others, of making other people's feelings our own? (Schiller, trans. 1962, pp. 91–3)

An ideal observer with such powers would be ideal at least in the sense that it would achieve unsurpassable ideals of knowledge, affective appraisal, and impartiality. Presumably none of us are ideal observers. But, according to the theory, what is at work when we make moral judgments or value judgments is that we invoke such an ideal point of view. The thesis is not that in moral judgments we are committed to holding that *there actually exists an ideal observer*, but that we are committed to holding that *if there were an ideal observer*, its judgments could be analyzed as follows (let "IO" stand for "ideal observer"):

L is morally right = L would be approved of by an IO
M is morally wrong = M would be disapproved of by an IO
N is neither morally right nor morally wrong = N would be neither approved of nor disapproved of by an IO

Unlike the ideal observer theory, the divine command theory articulated in the previous section did not rest on an analysis of meaning. The divine command theorist can concede that it is not a contradiction to claim "L is morally right and yet it is false that God commands L." Is it a contradiction to claim "L is morally right and it is not the case that L would be approved of by an IO"? It may not be readily apparent, but there are some reasons for thinking that this would be contradictory or at least reflect an unconventional use of English. If someone claims that an act is indeed good – an act of courage, for example – it would be paradoxical at best to claim that an act of courage is good yet not approved of if one knew all the nonmoral facts of the case, one were affectively apprised of the points of view of all involved, and one were truly impartial. If the ideal observer theory is true then we implicitly allude to an idealized vantage point when we make moral judgments, betting (as it were) that we are holding beliefs that would be vindicated rather than undermined if we could see matters more extensively and clearly. We are committed to holding that our views are those that would be matched from an IO point of view.

The IO theory has its critics and some of their objections to the theory are noted among the suggested questions at the end of this chapter. If the theory can be defended, it has some advantages. Though highly abstract, the theory does highlight principles that are commonly at work in everyday moral reasoning. Insofar as empirical study of facts, affective appreciation of others, and impartiality are ideals we seek in practice, the IO theory singles these out as vital conditions in moral reasoning. The IO theory may be of use to theists, as I note below, but one can also be an atheist and embrace the theory and, indeed, one can be a moral skeptic and yet hold the theory. A skeptic could uphold the theory and then argue that because none of us can achieve IO status, we should suspend our own, considerably less ideal judgments. But assuming such skepticism is too severe (we may be uncertain about the moral status of euthanasia, yet surely we know torture is wrong), theists may use whatever gains are made by the IO theory to fill out their conception of God and moral methodology. The IO seems to mirror closely the concept of God as recognized in theistic religious tradition.

Consider how theistic notions of God resemble the IO, and then how religious and ethical discourse may then be seen to accord with one another. As noted in chapter 5, theists contend that God is omniscient and, therefore, that God knows all nonmoral facts. Omnipercipience may or may not involve God having to undergo experiences, but a mark of divine omniscience is that God would have such an affective grasp of all creation. God, as envisioned in traditional monotheism, is also believed to be impartial. Judaism and Christianity recognize God as singling out some individuals for special blessings and the like, but all this is understood within a providential care for all. It is customary to understand such special dispensations as leading to the overall good, a good that would be approved of impartially. Of course theists believe God is more than an ideal observer. Perhaps a theistic view of God would more accurately be described as the portrait of what is believed to be an ideal agent. But if God is more than an IO, theists seem committed to holding God is not less.

If this theistic portrait is acceptable, then moral reflection may be read as trying to mirror or achieve a God's eye point of view. Just as Newton spoke in terms of the scientist's role of trying to think God's thoughts, the ethicist may be thought of as trying to identify the approval or disapproval of God, or, putting the point in a more qualified form – trying to identify what would be the approval or disapproval of an IO, if there were one.

For further reflection on whether theism can account for morality see chapter 10. For now, let us consider the repercussions of theism on values in general and then consider theistic reflection on specific moral problems.

Theism and Values

Here are three ways in which theism may serve to intensify or extend one's commitment to values and to introduce new values as well.

(A)   Granting an affective understanding of God called passibilism and a fairly basic moral precept, it may be argued that if God exists then the goods of the cosmos are even more good and the evils of the cosmos even more evil than if God does not exist. This may be termed the "intensity of theism" argument. A first step in the argument is unpacking what is meant by passibilism.

Passibilism is the thesis that God sorrows and feels pain over the world's ills and takes pleasure in the world's goods. It is distinguished from impassibilism (from the Latin *impassibilis* meaning "without passion"), the thesis that God does not suffer or feel pain. Reasons for adopting impassibilism include the following: (a) Passion involves change, and if God is changeless, God does not undergo passion. (b) Similarly, it is argued that to suffer requires being in time. God is eternal, hence God does not suffer. (c) It is also argued that suffering is an imperfection. If so, then there is reason to think that a supremely excellent, all-perfect being would not suffer. A passibilist theism has been defended on the grounds that it is more plausible to believe (a*) God does change, and (b*) God is in time (see the exchange in chapter 6). (c*) While some suffering is seen as an imperfection, suffering or feeling sorrow can also stem from a great excellence. It can be argued that loving another person is an excellence and that this involves feeling sorrow over the beloved's ills, and joys over the beloved's welfare and flourishing. For these reasons, plus the appeal of some revelation claims (Hebrew and Christian Bibles) and religious experience, a range of theists have adopted a passibilist version of theism, (see Creel 1986 for a defense of impassibilism, and Clark [ed.] 1992 for a defense of passibilism).

The intensity of theism argument may be formulated succinctly. A principal premise in the argument is that there are goods and ills, rights and wrongs, and among these, causing someone sorrow can be both evil and wrong, while causing someone pleasure can be both good and right. I state this in terms of "can be," rather than "always is," because of the following important caveat.

There is no need to commit the intensity of theism argument to an exclusively hedonistic view of values, according to which *all* pleasure is good and *all* sorrow is evil. One may run the intensity of theism argument and grant that it is not necessarily the case that all pleasures are good, and all pain *ipso facto* bad. (Anti-hedonistic moral judgments strike many as very forceful in certain cases. Thus, it is plausible to judge that pleasure in wickedness is not at all good, but, rather, that such pleasure is itself supremely wicked. It is part of what makes a person paradigmatically cruel and malicious; to take pleasure in evil is, as Schopenhauer once termed it, a "malignant joy.") Still, having acknowledged the difficulties with an unfettered hedonism, it may plausibly be argued that certain pleasures are in themselves good. Thus, a person's taking pleasure in caring for others, in friendships, and in the beauty of good relationships is itself good. Similarly, sorrow and pain under many conditions can constitute something bad. Thus, if Eric cruelly tortures George, it is reasonable to think that part of what makes this bad, and thus part of what makes such torture torturous, is the fact that he brings about a state of pain and sorrow. There may be many evils other than sorrow and pain, but it may still be argued that there are plausible cases when sorrow and pain are indeed bad states and it is wrong and evil to bring them about.

A further assumption in the argument is that there are straightforward cases when the degree of evil and the gravity of wrongness involved in a state of affairs is directly related to how much sorrow or pain is caused. Why is it that we might assess Eric's deliberately tormenting George to be worse than his deliberately causing George some lesser injury, such as stealing George's ticket to an opera? Many factors might enter our judgment at this stage, but, arguably, we are safe in assuming that when Eric's actions are morally unwarranted, and George is morally innocent in all the relevant respects (he is not a wicked tyrant, a murderer, etc.), then the gravity of the wrong done to him is a dimension of the degree of sorrow caused.

According to theistic passibilism, God's sorrow and pleasure over the world's goods and ills is morally fitting. God's affective responsiveness to the world is neither malicious nor cruel; God takes pleasures in values, not in wickedness. Similarly, God's sorrow does not stem from any wicked designs or aims, as it would if God's sorrow was prompted by the fact that even more evil has not occurred. God's affective responsiveness is also not something epistemically deviant. We might feel sorrow over what we *believe* to be some cruel act and hardship, and this sorrow actually manifest goodness, and yet there still be something deeply amiss in our sorrow. Imagine that I feel great compassionate sorrow and seek to assist people who, as it turns out, are not at all in any danger, nor afflicted by any ills. Perhaps I am in such poor shape cognitively that I am forever misjudging the plight of others, going about my honest, but inept and undesirable compassion-based projects. As an omniscient being, God would not be subject to such impairments, however benignly motivated.

The intensity of theism argument claims that if God exists, then the wrongs we do cause more sorrow than if God does not exist, and that this sorrow is morally relevant. We could perhaps discount its relevance, if God's sorrow stemmed from ill motives or, if God was not morally innocent in some other respect. But given God's goodness and omniscience, this discounting is not available. God's resultant sorrow may be termed morally unjustified sorrow because, while the sorrow is morally fitting in the sense that it stems from God's goodness, it is unjustified in the sense that it is caused by a morally wrong act and all morally wrong acts are unjustified. The latter, presumably, is part of what it means for an act to be wrong. The intensity argument may be cast in a formal way as follows:

(1)   Causing unjustified sorrow is wrong.

(2)   Other things being equal, if two wrong acts, X and Y, are indistinguishable from the moral point of view in all respects except that X causes more unjustified sorrow than Y, then X is more gravely wrong than Y.

(3)   If God exists, then any wrong act causes God unjustified sorrow.

(4)   If God does not exist, then no wrong act causes God unjustified sorrow.

(5)   If God exists, then wrong acts cause more unjustified sorrow than if God does not exist.

(6)   Therefore, if God exists, then wrong acts are even more gravely wrong than if God does not exist.

This argument may easily be fashioned in terms of evil states of affairs. Premise (2) may be reformulated as follows: Other things being equal, if two evil states of affairs X and Y are indistinguishable from an axiological point of view in all respects except that X causes more unjustified sorrow than Y, then X is more evil than Y. Premises (3)–(6) may then be reformulated to yield the conclusion that if God exists then evil states of affairs are even more evil than if God does not exist.

A complementary argument may be fashioned with respect to right action and good states. If passibilism is correct, then right action and good states of affairs bring about Divine pleasure. It is plausible to believe that pleasure (delight, appreciation, enjoyment) in right action and good states is itself right and good. In modern philosophy, G. E. Moore, and before him Franz Brentano (1838–1917), have ably identified the high value of pleasure in the good (see Chisholm 1986 for a more recent defense). Consider good acts and states such as acts of courage, compassionate service, just institutions, friendships, the beauty of romantic love. If God exists, then in addition to the evident right action and states of affairs themselves, there is the good of pleasure in these acts and states. Let me underscore here, as I sought to earlier, that this does not assume an unqualified hedonism in that one need not assume that all pleasure is *ipso facto* good. The pleasure may be thought of as befitting moral innocence and a constituent part of God's love of the world.

If passibilism is accepted, theists may give greater weight to the proximity of the God–cosmos relationship than many philosophers assume. Thus, William Rowe's depiction below may be seen to be an accurate theistic description of God's metaphysical independence of the world, but not an accurate depiction of God's affective, intimate concern with the cosmos:

> According to the Judeo-Christian and Islamic conception of God, the world is entirely distinct from God; everything in it could be entirely annihilated without the slightest change in the reality of the divine being. (Rowe 1993, p. 12)

On a passibilist construal of the God–world relation, the annihilation of creation would profoundly affect "the reality of the divine being." To write off such annihilation as not causing the slightest change in the reality of God would be either wrong or misleading.

Passibilists emphasize both the sorrow and pleasure of God. According to passibilism, just as sorrow may be a part of an intimate God–world bond, so may pleasure. A distinction is sometimes made in ordinary English between *being pleased that*, or *feeling pleasure that*, such and such took place, and *feeling pleasure in* something, where the latter marks off a more intimate, engaged feeling. It is one thing for me to be pleased that you achieved some goal and another for me to take pleasure in your achievement. Current word-use may not always carry this subtle difference in meaning, but I note here that on certain passibilist accounts God may be more accurately described as taking pleasure *in* the goods of the cosmos, and not just pleasure *that* such goods exist.

(B) Theism has also led to an expanded conception of goods and ills in virtue of the claim that because God created the cosmos and sustains it in existence, God therefore owns the cosmos or, putting it somewhat differently, the cosmos belongs to God. Divine ownership of the cosmos is upheld in the

Hebrew and Christian Bibles (1 Chronicles 29:11–18; Psalms 24:1; 50:12; Ezekiel 18:4) and the Qur'an ("To God is the personal ownership [*mulk*] of the heavens and the earth," from "The Light"). The thesis that the cosmos is owned by or belongs to God is a key claim in medieval philosophical theology and much modern theology. It has led both to an amplified sense of duties (i.e. do X not just because it is good in itself but also because you belong to God and God commands X) but also to new duties such as the duty not to commit suicide (with possible rare exceptions).

Among modern philosophers, probably the most well-known advocate for divine ownership is John Locke who developed his stance in the *Second Treatise on Civil Government*. Locke held that "we owe our body, soul, and life – whatever we are, whatever we have, and even whatever we can be – to Him [God] and to Him alone. . . . God has created us out of nothing and, if He pleases, will reduce us again to nothing" (Locke, in Idziak 1980, p. 182). Locke's position has been defended by Richard Swinburne, Baruch Brody, and others. Swinburne writes:

> The other characteristic among those traditionally ascribed to God which makes his commands impose moral obligations which would not otherwise exist is that he is the creator of the rest of the universe other than men; he brought it into existence and keeps it in existence, and so is properly judged its owner. What greater claim could one have to property than having created it *ex nihilo*, and kept it in being by one's free choice, unaided? The owner of property has the right to tell those to whom he has loaned it what they are allowed to do with it. Consequently God has a right to lay down how that property, the inanimate world, shall be used and by whom. If God has made the earth, he can say which of his children can use which part. (Swinburne 1977, pp. 206–7)

It is because of this ownership that it would be conceptually impossible for God to steal from creation. None of us have a right to property over against God's rights. Thomas Aquinas held this: "What is taken by God's command, who is the owner of the universe, is not against the owner's will, and this is the essence of theft" (Aquinas, *ST*, Ia2ae., 94.5). Swinburne draws the following conclusion: "It follows from this that it is logically impossible for God to command a man to steal – for whatever God commands a man to take thereby becomes that man's and so his taking it is not stealing" (Swinburne 1977, p. 207).

Appeals to divine ownership have often been used by theists to undermine what is believed to be excessive individualism and to foster a greater sense of the duty to aid others. Historically, the theistic appeal to give to others in need has often been preceded by advancing the thesis that all one's possessions are conferred as a gift by God. This theme of the creation as a gift runs through Jewish, Christian, and Islamic traditions. Lenn Goodman singles it out in his summation of Jewish philosophy:

> Through all the change of style and structure, and all the seeming change of paradigms, the thematic content [of Jewish philosophy] remains remarkably steady, anchored in tradition and text: God offers love and demands justice and generosity. Life is a gift; truth, a sacred and inescapable responsibility. (Goodman 1995, p. 431)

A divine ownership ethic has its critics. A chief objection is that such an ethic seems to make human beings slaves to God and this offends a mature view of our autonomy and dignity (Young 1977 and Lombardi 1984). One defense of divine ownership maintains that being owned by God is not pernicious. Another defense is to revise the divine ownership ethic so that it is significantly different and amounts to a weaker claim of persons belonging to God.

As for the first defense, it may be argued that God is essentially good and thus not subject to capriciousness and injustice. Any analogy with human enslavement is therefore wide of the mark. Consider the second possibility – In English the term "belonging" can be used both to indicate property but also to make a value judgment. When someone reports that "Jane Doe belongs in this school" or "John Doe belongs in this family" there is a suggestion that there is a fitting propriety to being in certain relationships. It is good or in some way deserved for Jane and John to be in school and in the family. The ownership of God thesis can be modified to make the claim that persons belong to God in the sense (a) that they exist, in part, because God conserves them in being (life is a gift); and (b) a life of fulfillment and welfare is to be found in relationship with God (for further material on divine ownership see Brody 1974 and Avila 1983). This later view of belonging brings us to as third area where theists claim to find new values and goods.

(C) Theism has given rise to alternative pictures of the meaning of life, involving what are believed to be values that stem from a relationship with God. At the most general level, the good of a divine–human relationship is believed to be forged in part by how one thinks God sees oneself. Here the appeal of the ideal observer theory may come into play. I briefly note this general character of what theists believe to mark a relationship with God, and then turn to more specific concerns.

Our self-image is often grounded upon only what we *think* we are and not what we *know* we are. Many of our own desires seem predicated on assuming we are right about the details of the world around us. Thus, I might point to what I believe is a glass of water and say: "I want that." Unknown to me the glass is actually filled with poison. Do I really want *that liquid*? Upon learning its contents it would make ample sense to claim something like: "I do not really want *that*, I want a glass of water!" If there is an omniscient observer or God, then (s)he knows us thoroughly. Given an ideal vantage point, one would have a transparent, clear notion of one's own desires and identity. We are often interested in things which we do not realize are not in our interests. Theistic construals of our self-image in the context of a relationship with God often focus on the importance of honesty and shedding self-deception.

But theists tend to attribute more to God's role in defining the meaning of life than just this general appeal to an omniscient vantage point. There is also the conviction that God is involved in individual lives. This may involve religious experiences (the topic of chapter 8) in which "a person" feels herself to be conjoined to a greater purpose, the fellowship and friendship with God. Marilyn Adams describes this good in terms of a relationship with God:

> For each created person, the primary source of meaning and satisfaction will be found in his/her intimate personal relationship with God. This relationship will also be the context in which a created person can be best convinced of his/her worth, because it is the place where God's love for the individual is most vividly and intimately experienced. Christians naturally see it as to everyone's advantage to enter into this relationship as deeply as one can in this world, as soon as possible. (Adams 1991, p. 291)

Brian Hebblethwaite also notes that theists believe the relationship with God places one in an enlarged context, a shared life:

> Forgiveness, reconciliation, peace and justice sound much the same when advanced as ideals of life by theists and non-theists alike. But in fact these qualities and ideals of life turn out rather differently when they are experienced and embraced as effects of gratitude, grace and the divine indwelling. (Hebblethwaite 1988, pp. 15–16)

Traditional theism includes this expanded concept of goodness and relationships.

This theistic picture of the divine–human relationship seems very different from the way some of its critics portray it. Consider, for example, Kurt Baier's description of God's relationship with creatures:

> The Christian world picture . . . sees man as a creature, a divine artifact, something halfway between a robot (manufactured) and an animal (alive), a homunculus, or perhaps Frankenstein, made in God's laboratory, with a purpose or task assigned him by his Maker. (Baier, in Hanfling [ed.] 1988, p. 22)

While there certainly have been theists who view the divine–human relationship in something like these terms, this portrait is considerably distant from that of Adams, Hebblethwaite, and many others who emphasize human freedom and shared love in religious experience.

In the context of what some theists take to be their relationship with God, new values can be realized and other values transformed. Thus, there may be a value of worship that is realized in a theistic world view. One form of worship may be understood as taking delight in the holy, and privileging this delight so that other things are enjoyed, in part, because of this overarching pleasure in God (Smart 1972). The transformation of values would come into play in the course of religious teaching about forgiveness, mercy, atonement, and the like.

Theistic Ethics in Practice

If one believes there is an all-good God and believes that God's commands are always good and right, then to discover God's commands will be to discover what is good, and to discover what is good is to discover what God approves. In a theistic philosophy, there will be a balance between revelation claims and independent moral reflection, depending upon theistic convictions about nature, reason, and revelation.

Nature. Some theists believe that nature is fundamentally good. Evil is essentially the twisting of something valuable. Fulfilling the nature of persons, for example, counts as a basic good. This is not the same as holding that whatever is, is good. Rather, it is the stance that persons and animals (perhaps plants too) have natural ends and states, so that it makes sense to talk of their fulfillment, flourishing or health, and these count as genuine goods. On this view, discovering the will of God and discovering what fulfills a being's nature

218

are commensurate. Stump and Kretzmann depict this position in terms of what it is natural to desire:

> Desirability is an essential aspect of goodness. Now if a thing is desirable as a thing of a certain kind (and anything at all *can* be desirable in that way, as a means, if not as an end), it is desirable to the extent to which it is perfect of that kind – i.e., a whole, complete specimen, free from relevant defect. But, then, a thing is perfect of its kind to the extent to which it is fully realized or developed, to the extent to which the potentialities definitive of its kind – specifying potentialities – have been actualized. And so, Aquinas says, a thing is perfect and hence desirable (good of its kind) to the extent to which it is in being. (Stump and Kretzmann, in Morris [ed.] 1988, p. 283)

This link between goodness and being leads some theists to believe that evil consists in the destruction of something good – evil is parasitic on the good and thus properly seen as a privation of being and not some force in its own right:

> Evil is always and only a defect in some respect to some extent; evil can have no essence of its own. Nor can there be a highest evil, an ultimate source of all other evils, because a *summum malum*, an evil devoid of all good, would be nothing at all. A human being is defective, bad, or evil not because of certain positive attributes but because of privations of various forms of being appropriate to his or her nature. And, in general, the extent to which a thing is not good of its kind is the extent to which it has not actualized, or cultivated dispositions for actualizing, the potentialities associated with its nature. Every form of privation is covered by that observation – from physical or mental subnormality, through ineptitude and inattention, to debauchery and depravity. In each case some form of being theoretically available to the thing because of its nature is lacking. (Stump and Kretzmann, in Morris [ed.] 1988, p. 288)

Not all theists believe that nature in its present state is fundamentally good, however. Some believe that there has been a fall in which nature, which was created as essentially good, has become profoundly marred and broken. For someone who holds such a position, discovering what fulfills a being's nature will not count as heavily for marking off what is good or establish a reliable guide to what is morally right. On this view, even a person's nature can be twisted.

Reason. While considerations of nature may provide one route in constructing an ethic, some theists believe that we have reflective abilities enabling us to grasp moral truths (e.g. promise-keeping is good, etc.). Such abilities may be referred to simply as "reason" – abilities that include the power to reflect impartially and affectively in light of nonmoral facts. If one has a high view of our capacity to use reason (or, if you like, "insight," "judgment," "intuition") to discover moral truths, then this will serve as an important reference point both in determining one's general ethical outlook as well as in forming one's conception of God's will. While some theists have such a high view of reason, others are convinced that our reflective faculties are too often corrupted by the effects of evil. Putting the point in terms of the IO theory, there is disagreement about the human capacity to approach, let alone achieve, an ideal observer point of view.

Revelation.   According to some theists, God's commands and prohibitions are revealed in religious experience itself and preeminently in sacred texts (the Bible, the Qur'an). To employ the terminology of this chapter, the ideal observer exists and has disclosed itself in human history. According to the Christian and Hebrew Bibles and the Qur'an God condemns murder, cruelty, rape, and injustice, and approves of justice and compassion, for example. Insofar as obedience to God is held to be paramount, such revelation claims are of pivotal concern in theistic ethics.

To see how theistic ethics work in practice, consider a topic in medical ethics such as theistic views of voluntary euthanasia – the practice of someone believed to be gravely ill ending his life voluntarily either by active means or by cessation of life support. For those who argue on theistic grounds that active euthanasia is permissible, there may be an appeal to nature (perhaps it is natural to die and also natural to assist the process), reason (this seems like an act that a reasonable person can make), and religious experience (revelation claims, either permit or encourage the act). Theists on the other side typically argue for the unnaturalness and irrationality of the act, as well as its being prohibited in revelation. A common theistic prohibition against active voluntary euthanasia is that it is essentially suicide and this involves an illicit, unauthorized destruction of a life that belongs to God. To destroy God's property without God's consent is sacrilege. The Roman Catholic Papal Encyclical, *Evangelium Vitae*, declares: "Man's life comes from God; it is His gift, His image and imprint, a sharing in His breath of life. God therefore is the sole Lord of his life: Man cannot do with it as he wills . . . the sacredness of his life has its foundation in God and in His creative activity" (1995, p. 703).

One can see this same strategy of appealing to nature, reason and revelation in nearly all the debates about abortion, suicide, capital punishment, political

220

responsibility, sexual ethics, and so on through the standard list of moral issues. Thus, for theists who have a high view of nature, the ethical permissibility of, say, same-sex relationships would be secured if it is evident that such relationships are natural. For those who believe nature is fallen or at least not a stable reference point ethically, such reasoning would be irrelevant or at least carry less weight.

In assessing moral issues in light of revelation claims and views of nature and reason, theists draw on different moral theories. I note three main approaches that have been widely represented in theistic traditions. These may also be construed as matching what would be approved of by the ideal observer.

Natural law theory and virtue theory. On this view, there are real goods in human flourishing and development. Persons, perhaps some nonhuman animals as well, have a character or nature and its fulfillment counts as a good. This fits the appeal to nature sketched earlier. In the tradition of Aristotle, most advocates of natural law understand this good and proper fulfillment of human persons as coming about through a life of virtue. The virtues mark certain excellences of character and typically include justice, courage, temperance and prudence, and the avoidance of vices.

Deontology. Deontologists hold that there are duties such as the duty to protect the innocent and duties not to murder, lie, inflict suffering on the innocent, and so on. "Deontology" is derived from the Greek *deon* for "necessity" or "obligation." Deontologists hold that the rightness or wrongness of acts are not entirely determined by consequences. On this view, there may be a duty not to kill even if killing would produce good consequences (happiness).

Consequentialism. According to this view, the consequences of an act determine its rightness or wrongness. A popular form of this is called *act utilitarianism*, according to which an act is morally right if and only if there is no other act available to the agent that will produce greater utility. "Utility" is sometimes construed as happiness, pleasure or preference satisfaction. A commonplace consequentialist precept is that one ought to produce the greatest happiness for the greatest number.

There are many movements within theistic traditions that highlight different dimensions of moral reflection. I believe that some of these may be seen as refining a comprehensive ideal observer theory. Thus, *narrative ethics* highlights the importance of using first-person accounts and literature in ethical

221

reflection. Novels by Jane Austen, Henry James, Fyodor Dostoevski, Leo Tolstoy, George Eliot, and others are increasingly being explored for ethical insights. Such efforts to explore these narrative pictures of character, virtue and vice may be seen as contributing to knowledge of the nonmoral, refining one's powers of affective appraisal, and compelling one to take seriously points of view other than our own (in some cases, challenging our biases). *Communitarian ethics* conceives of the moral life as defined by a community identity, the shape of a group's ethical ideals and reflections as this is borne out historically. On the surface, such a school of ethics appears to eschew the comparatively abstract, seemingly nonhistorical vantage point of ideal observation. This need not be seen as incompatible with the ideal observer theory, however, which should treat as morally relevant the points of view of *all* traditions and communities. Thus, communitarian ethics could be used to fill out what a truly comprehensive ideal vantage point would include.

Feminism. Feminism names a broad array of positions, ranging from the political and legal position that women and men should be treated fairly and equally to radical views affecting every area of social relations. While some feminists explicitly repudiate what may appear to be the detachment of the ideal observer theory, it is not clear why any of the extant feminist ethic projects could not be seen as respected and endorsed from an ideal observer vantage point. Thus, some feminist concerns with narrative, first-person points of view may be seen as filling out affective and nonmoral awareness. The experience of oppression, stereotyping, rape, empowerment, love, rage, hate, and so on should all be taken seriously in the ideal observer framework. Karen Warren's (and others') appreciative work on the "loving gaze" brings to light the importance of an empathetic, affective way of seeing the world (Warren 1990). Much of this insightful, illuminating work can be integrated into a description of ideal observance. IO awareness would also include apprisal of the nature of gender: Are differences of gender entirely constructs of society or based, in part, on biological differences? Scientific studies vary here, as do feminist theories. Ideally, the IO vantage point would be one in which the natures of gender and sex are elucidated. Some have claimed that the IO vantage point is essentially male; but arguably it represents what would ideally encompass the points of view of males and females without obscuring or unfairly melding the views at stake.

Environmentalism. In order more closely to consider applied theistic ethics, it will be useful to concentrate on a specific area of concern. Environmental ethics is an area of considerable debate and can serve as a useful reference to exhibit some of the principles employed in theistic ethics outlined in this chapter. Theists often distinguish between the *dominion* and *stewardship* models of environmental responsibility. According to the dominion model, humans have primacy of worth and rights over other animals. This primacy, justified by an appeal to revelation (Genesis), has also been advanced on the basis of reason. In the most stringent form of the dominion model, nonhuman nature does not count as intrinsically important and morally relevant in itself; its only relevance is in how nature affects human beings. A more qualified dominion model holds that nonhuman nature consists of some goods, but that these goods are not to be weighed with the same significance as human desires and projects. A stewardship model, on the other hand, understands nonhuman nature as intrinsically valuable and not simply as instrumentally good. Something is intrinsically valuable if it is valuable for its own sake, whereas something is instrumentally valuable if it is valuable because of its promoting that which is intrinsically valuable. The dominion model typically sees the nonhuman environment as instrumentally valuable, while the stewardship model sees nature as both intrinsically and instrumentally valuable. In a stewardship ethic, human beings should not just use the environment, but care for it. On this view, human beings may still have some primacy over other life-forms and yet other forms of life are deemed to be morally worthy of protection because of their own value and importance.

The dominion model has been criticized as an exaltation of pure power. This critique recalls discussion earlier in this chapter of divine command theories which allow for caprice and theories of ethics that secures divine authority in virtue of sheer power. Some philosophers argue that the dominion model has produced (or been used to justify) serious environmental damage. Fraser Darling accuses monotheism of siphoning off the human from the rest of creation, thereby introducing a dangerous partition between humanity and God on one side and the rest of life on the other:

> Monotheism was a powerful thrust forward for the human being, concentrating spiritual force, especially when man identified the image of God with his own – though he puts it the opposite way, that God created him in His own image. Now comes a process of dissociation with other living things . . . Here is enormous strength – at a cost usually unimagined and perhaps unseen until our own era. Western man, having adopted the Judaic-Christian religion, has not only banished all living things other than his own species from the partnership of God and himself, but has developed the convenient conviction that God created

223

the rest of living things for the *use* and delectation of man. (Darling, in S. J. Armstrong [ed.] 1993, p. 299)

Along similar lines, Mary Midgley contends that the allure of an exclusive God–human relationship has tended to promote a power-based ethic. She argues that the allure and systematic abuse of technology has been undergirded by the myth of omnipotence. Because we have a culturally embedded notion that supreme power is divine and desirable in and of itself, we have sometimes pursued technology for its own sake and with perilous consequences:

> The sense of omnipotence which expanding technology generated has proved a misleading one, and it has now become clear that technology itself has no tendency to make people behave better, only to distract them more effectively from what they are up to. The notion of psychological omnipotence was itself a myth. Abandoning it does not commit us to fatalistic resignation, but makes realistic attempts at change more possible. (Midgley 1984, p. 68)

It is because of such ill-effects, that some theists reject an unqualified dominion theory.

The dominion model still has its representatives and can be defended against some of the more common objections against it. Often the environmental degradation that has been carried out in the name of the dominion model can also be attributed either to straightforward human greed or to the use of alternative dominion pictures. As Donald Hughes observes, much of the damaging application of the dominion model stemmed not from monotheism but from the outlook of ancient Rome. "The Romans treated the natural environment as if it were one of their conquered provinces" (Hughes, in S. J. Armstrong [ed.] 1993, p. 168). And Lewis Moncrief argues that the complex forces behind ecological degradation are too diverse all to be linked to Judeo-Christianity:

> The forces of democracy, technology, urbanization, increasing individual wealth, and an aggressive attitude toward nature seem to be directly related to the environmental crisis now being confronted in the Western world. The Judeo-Christian tradition has probably influenced the character of each of these forces. However, to isolate religious tradition as a cultural component and to contend that it is the "historical root of our ecological crisis" is a bold affirmation for which there is little historical or scientific support. (In Pojman [ed.] 1994, p. 19)

Despite this effort to disentangle a dominion form of theism from environmentally destructive ends, many theists now seek an alternative in the stewardship model.

In the stewardship literature, one can see all the workings of the theistic ethical framework outlined in this chapter: The appeal to nonmoral facts, omnipercipience and impartiality (of the IO theory), to reason, nature, and revelation, to virtue, duty, and consequences. Jay McDaniel appeals to an affective approach to environmental concerns in ways that echo the affective concerns of the ideal observer theory:

> Openness to the world as known and loved by God is a contemporary and ecologically minded version of what Paul conceived as putting on the mind of God. It is feeling the presence of the world as God feels it. In a process context this feeling need not be understood simply as a mirroring by humans of God's way of feeling, as if God were "up there" and humans and the rest of nature "down here." Rather it can be understood as an actual internalization within the human psyche: a lived participation in the divine consciousness. (McDaniel, in S. J. Armstrong [ed.] 1993, p. 511)

"Putting on the mind of God" may be read here as aiming to reflect, if only in part, the omnipercipience of God. Other themes in this chapter are at work in the stewardship literature. Mawil Deen Samarrai construes the Islamic environmental ethic as very much grounded in the duty to the God to whom creation belongs. "The environment is God's creation and to protect it is to preserve its values as a sign of the Creator" (Samarrai, in S. J. Armstrong [ed.] 1993, p. 528). Sensitive to the religious repercussions of ethical practices, D. Z. Phillips notes the difficulty of holding a high view of creation and Creator alongside a practice of environmental exploitation:

> Could hills declare the glory of God once gold has been discovered in them? Well, they might. The gold may be regarded as untouchable no matter how great the needs of the people. But if the hills are mined, could the hills declare the glory of God? Again, they might. If the hills are only mined in face of real need, the hills might come to be regarded as the Great Providers. But what if the hills are mined because of the greed for gold? It is hard in these circumstances to see how the very same hills could declare the glory of God, since the act of exploitation, the utilitarian attitude to the hills, would jar with regarding the hills as belonging to God. (Phillips 1981a, p. 71)

One can see how theistic critiques of technology have gone hand in hand with theists rethinking their conception of the power of God. If theists are able to secure a value-based understanding of omnipotence such as the Anselmian model in chapter 3, then they can explicitly repudiate the glorification of pure power that can occur in highly technological societies (for further arguments on theistic notions of technology and power see Ferre 1988 and 1993).

The most difficult of live debates among theists in the stewardship tradition concerns the status of nonhuman animals. The two most distinctive stewardship positions may be described as individualism on the one hand, and holism on the other. Both have been supported by appeal to ideal observation, with specific appeals to reason, nature, and revelation.

On the view of individualism it is the individual that counts, not groups or systems. Species and ecosystems are valuable but chiefly because of the individual life-forms within them. Moreover, some individuals claim that some of the individual animal life-forms (more developed mammals, for example) have rights, such as the right to life or the right not to be harmed.

This view appears meritorious to many insofar as it breaks down the presumption that moral considerations, rights and duties are limited to the human species. Some ethicists contend that to attribute rights only to human beings is an instance of *speciesism*, a preference of one individual over another chiefly due to species membership. To Peter Singer, Tom Regan and others, this is on a moral par with racism and sexism. The difficulty with this view, however, concerns the precise determination of which nonhuman animals (henceforth: NHAs) have rights or morally relevant interests. On a common ranking, dolphins, whales, and chimpanzees are placed high, followed by pigs, dogs, and cats, then chickens, eagles and so on down to ever simpler life-forms. According to Singer, whatever we have good reason to believe has sentience (can undergo pain or pleasure) has moral considerability. Regan does not deny this rightful moral considerability, but he places greater emphasis upon whether the NHA is a self or self-like. Difficult debate focuses on both the level of criterion (self or sentience) and on how different NHAs meet the criterion.

There are problems here for the theist, but they are not insuperable. Some theists adopt a rights-based approach and others take up the criterion of sentience. Either can serve as justifying a moral condemnation of much current animal factory farming today. But theists face a pressing difficulty when it comes to assessing natural relations. If some NHAs do have rights or they have such moral considerability, what of the animal suffering that appears to be built into nature itself? J. B. Callicott observes the natural role of predation:

226

The living channels – "food chains" – through which energy courses are composed of individual plants and animals. A central, stark fact lies at the heart of ecological processes: Energy, the currency of the economy of nature, passes from one organism to another, not from hand to hand, like coined money, but, so to speak, from stomach to stomach. Eating and being eaten, living and dying are what make the biotic community hum. (Callicott, in S. J. Armstrong [ed.] 1993, p. 393)

So, is NHA suffering built into the creation and willed by God or is it something that is the result of a fall or aboriginal wickedness? The Problem of Evil is the focus of chapter 9, but here I note a popular theistic move in the stewardship tradition, which is holism.

According to a *holist* approach to the environment, NHAs and other natural goods such as wilderness areas are to be assessed not so much as individuals, but as complex natural systems. Aldo Leopold, a theist and environmentalist, advanced the position that: "A thing is right when it tends to preserve the integrity, stability, and beauty of the biotic community. It is wrong when it tends otherwise" (Leopold 1987, pp. 224–5). This has become a hallmark of the so-called "deep" ecological movement with its construal of the whole of life as a community. Theists who take this wider, systemic viewpoint sometimes describe their stance as being life-centered, holistic or biocentric. It has been defended on the grounds that it is able to offer a better account of the good of species diversification and that it leads to a defensible, rich wilderness policy. As for the first area, it is charged that individualists have difficulty accounting for why we (often) think it good that there be multiple species and not just more individuals. As for the second, individualists who adhere to a high view of NHAs may be led to very aggressive, radical interference with natural processes. If NHA suffering is bad, do we not have an obligation to prevent NHA predation? But to do so would seem to require widespread interference with NHA habitats and so on.

We will return to the topic of NHA suffering in chapter 9. But before proceeding to the final section, it may be useful to outline the topics covered thus far in this chapter.

Theories of Value

Nihilism   Relativism   Moral Realism

Two Theistic Accounts of Value

Divine Command: theory in which	*Modified Divine Command*: theory in which God creates

God freely creates moral values but God does
moral values. so as informed by God's all-
good nature, *viz.*, God could
not have made murder good.

The Ideal Observer Theory

A theory of moral reflection that can assist theists to articulate a God's eye
point of view. It can also be accepted by atheists for the theory outlines a
hypothetical ideal point of view.

Theism and Values

The Intensity of *Divine Ownership* *Theism* may inform
Theism: argument claims may be conceptions of the
that theism can used to justify meaning of life.
magnify values. obligations.

Theistic Ethics in Practice

Nature
Reason Can inform beliefs of God's will.
Revelation

Natural law Three main theories utilized by theists
Deontology in articulating good and evil.
Consequentialism

Narrative ethics Recent contributions to moral
Communitarianism reflection.
Feminism

Theistic Environmentalism Dominion vs. Stewardship Models.
Ethics Individualism vs. Holism.

In this last section, let us consider the ramifications of religious ethics for
political relationships.

Religious Pluralism and Politics

A religiously pluralist society is one in which there are distinguishable religious bodies (churches, temples, ashrams, synagogues, or simply movements)

which are in some sense incompatible. The incompatibility need not be strict. Thus, there can be a pluralist society made up of Christians and Buddhists, notwithstanding the presence of some who believe one can be a Christian Buddhist (or Buddhist Christian), as long as significant numbers believe the religions are distinct and not part of a singular religion made up of both.

Many modern nation-states that are religiously pluralistic face the challenge of addressing tensions between religious bodies. Within some religions there are strong political aims and these often compete with other religions. Recently, radical groups within Islam have used force in advancing their cause. In orthodox Islam the function of the state is to apply Islamic law (*sharia*). God's law should prevail politically and radical groups such as the Islamic Jihad and Hamas aim to establish such laws. ("Jihad" is often translated as "holy war," but it is derived from the Arabic *jhd* for "struggle" and is better translated as "struggle on behalf of the faith.") The aims of these groups are sometimes in fundamental tension with other religious factions within a society – Hindu, Buddhist, Jewish, Christian – as well as with secular forms of liberalism, socialism, and Marxism.

In the United States there is currently a substantial debate on the government's role in religious matters. The Constitution of the United States (1789) appears to insure freedom of religion in its First Amendment:

> Congress shall make no law respecting an establishment of religion or prohibiting the free exercise thereof; or abridging the freedom of speech, or of the press; or the right of the people peaceably to assemble, and to petition the government for a redress of grievance.

But this declaration has hardly settled matters. Religious ideals seem to run through many layers of the United States government and society at large, and court cases continually challenge prohibitions of prayer at school, the government's use of religious symbols and objects (the "In God We Trust" motto on currency, swearing to tell the truth on a Bible in courts of law, the oath of allegiance), the government's support of religiously affiliated schools and institutions (whether by direct contributions or by tax relief), the recognition of some religious holidays, and so on. There have also been pivotal debates over the extent to which religious groups should be tolerated in refusing to take oaths (Seventh Day Adventists), participating in the military (Amish, some Quakers, Mennonites, Seventh Day Adventists), receiving standard medical treatment (Christian Scientists and Jehovah's Witnesses), using illegal substances in religious ceremonies (some native American groups), and keeping dietary restrictions (such as the designated ways that some religious Jews and Muslims kill animals).

The political philosophy of John Locke was a key influence on the framers of the United States Constitution. In *A Letter Concerning Toleration*, Locke construes the Church as "absolutely separate and distinct from the Commonwealth. The boundaries on both sides are fixed and immovable. He jumbles Heaven and Earth together, the things most remote and opposite, who mixes these Societies . . ." (Locke [1689] 1985, p. 33). The resulting picture here is that there should be a state-enforced tolerance of alternative religions.

Locke's case for tolerance is built on several grounds. He argued for tolerance by appeal to human fallibility. We simply do not have sure and certain knowledge of the truth of religions and so should not enforce any. Another reason for tolerance is due to the irrationality of persecution. Religious conversion is a matter of voluntary consent; beliefs are not the sort of thing anyone can coerce. Locke also appealed to the isolation of individuals from one another: one's neighbors' damnation will not affect oneself. Because of all such reasons, Locke claimed toleration to be the chief mark of the "True Church" (Locke [1689] 1985, p. 23). Locke thereby sought to foster a secular state, without endorsing a secular society. Religions are left alone by government in order to flourish as voluntary organizations.

Arguments supporting this separation of state and religion have been advanced recently by Robert Audi, Richard Rorty, John Rawls, Ronald Dworkin and others. Here the goal is to restrict the reasons that are acceptable in political decision making only to those that are capable of being appreciated independent of recourse to comprehensive, religious conceptions of the cosmos. Jeremy Waldron states the aim of liberalism as follows: "Liberals demand that the social order should in principle be capable of explaining itself at the tribunal of each person's understanding" (Waldron 1987, p. 149; see also B. Ackerman and C. Lamore). In the same spirit, Audi countenances only secular reasons in public, political deliberation. "A secular reason is, roughly, one whose normative force, that is, its status as a prima facie justificatory element, does not (evidentially) depend on the existence of God (for example, through appeals to divine command) or theological considerations (such as interpretations of a sacred text), or on the pronouncements of a person or institution *qua* religious authority" (Audi 1989, p. 278). John Rawls adapts a similar position. In public life, when making political decisions which affect society at large,

230

we are to appeal only to presently accepted general beliefs and forms of reasoning found in common sense, and the methods and conclusions of science when these are not controversial . . . We are not to appeal to comprehensive religious and philosophical doctrines – to what we as individuals or members of associations see as the whole truth – nor to elaborate economic theories of general equilibrium, say, if these are in dispute. (Rawls 1993, pp. 224–5)

Rawls and other liberal political theorists thereby seek to secure a sharp distinction between religious and political discourse.

There are several difficulties, however. First one may challenge the delimitation of "comprehensive religious and philosophical doctrines" from "common sense." It may be argued either that "common sense" can itself count as a comprehensive doctrine or that some comprehensive doctrines (such as religious views of life) can count as "common sense." Moreover, it may be argued that if we are to banish from political decision making all theories of the cosmos and values unless they are held by *every reasonable person*, then very little will be left standing. Is there any consensus in the United States about consequentialism, deontology, natural law, the ideal observer theory, etc.? Arguably not. As R. M. Adams writes: "nothing in the history of modern secular ethical theory gives reason to expect that general agreement on a single comprehensive ethical theory will ever be achieved – or that, if achieved, it would long endure in a climate of free inquiry" (Adams 1993, p. 97). If we allow any of the ethical theories just cited to count as worthy of use in political decision making, why cannot the divine command theory or Buddhist ethics also have a role to play?

Against the secularism of Locke, Stephen Macedo points out that "Locke does not really succeed . . . in fashioning arguments capable of convincing those who regard a supportive social and political environment as crucial to salvation" (Macedo 1993, p. 623). A key difficulty that faces contemporary political liberalism is that many in society define themselves in religious terms. For those who do, the liberal ideal seems not only unmotivated but based on a suspect account of the individual. Our individual identities are shaped by the communities in which we live and are at radical odds with a religiously barren secularism. Paul Morris laments the religious cost of liberalism:

My own Jewish tradition becomes largely unintelligible when viewed in a liberal light. The first words of my Bible "In the beginning God created the heavens and the earth" are unproved and unprovable and so it can only be a

231

private opinion, and an opinion that runs counter to the scientific principle that matter is self-creating, self-sufficient, and eternal. A little later in the same chapter we read "And God saw that it was good"; the public realm of matter is neutral, without value, according to the canons of liberalism. And finally, at the end of the very first chapter of my Bible, it is stated that man is created in "God's image and likeness", as opposed to the modern claim that man is an accidental product of evolution. It is not that liberalism presents my tradition with unanswerable challenges but that it trivializes it and renders it unintelligible. My tradition does not hold knowledge to be neutral and makes important distinctions concerning the "public" sphere, for example, between just and unjust wages, fair and unfair prices, and pure and impure wealth. The liberal model of creativity, individual originality, is hostile to my tradition of commentary. The liberal emphasis on the value of spontaneity challenges my tradition's overriding concern with routine. Our religious traditions, traditions that are made up of cosmologies, politics, epistemologies, soteriologies, eschatologies, and mythologies are genuine and total world-views. These world-views are reduced by the liberal state to private spirituality. "Spirituality", one of the most often used words in contemporary religious discourse, refers to the acceptance of the liberal reduction of religion to the private sphere. (Morris 1990, pp. 187–8)

Similar complaints may readily be given from representatives of virtually all the major traditions.

Because of the religiously embedded identity of so many of us, a pure liberalism with an absolute division between state and religion is virtually unachievable. Perhaps the most prudent position is Larmore's *modus vivendi* (way of living or getting along) form of liberalism, which sees itself as trying to establish cooperation between parties that are deeply at odds (Larmore 1987, p. 129).

In articulating what such a *modus vivendi* might look like from a religious point of view, I close by sketching three features of some of the world religions that may contribute to tolerance and respect in pluralistic societies.

(A) Each of the world religions has important representatives who highlight the qualified nature of their religion's picture of "the truth." Within Judaism, Christianity, and Islam there have been strong endorsements of God's otherness and transcendence (Maimonides, Thomas Aquinas, al-Ghazali), as well as within Hinduism and Buddhism. Accentuating the limited nature of our beliefs and language about ultimate reality can help foster efforts to learn from otherwise competing world-views. Keith Ward suggests that this acknowledgement of such limitations can help clear the way to see different religions as providing partial insights into reality:

If such an agnosticism is an authentic religious insight, it is bound to qualify any of the truths any tradition affirms of God. So, if Christians say that God is a morally judging and gracious saviour, the Buddhist, who has no God, can say that the universe is morally ordered by the law of karma so that our good and evil acts issue in their due rewards and punishment, and that the compassionate Bodhisattvas help us towards our ultimate goal. And if Buddhists say that the self is to be extinguished in nirvana, the Christian, who believes in an endless continuance of the human personality, can say that we must be so transfigured by the indwelling presence of Christ that all those self-centered desires which form our present personalities must fall away and we shall be sharers in the beatitude of eternity. Taken strictly, the ideas contradict. But qualified by an ultimate agnosticism about the fundamental character of reality and our relation to it, they can be seen as partial insights into a common goal which is unlike any of our presently available concepts. This is not an agnosticism which leaves us with a total blank; rather, it functions to qualify all our present, restricted concepts in the direction of a goal which we cannot fully comprehend. (Ward, in Hamnett [ed.] 1990, p. 17)

Some ways in which Buddhism and Christianity may be seen to collaborate are in sharing a high view of compassion, their opposition to narrow self-interested practices, and their endorsement of the objectivity of morality in general (promoting courage, justice, and wisdom, condemning cruelty, vanity, exploitation and the like). This need not be seen as collapsing the distinction between religions but rather as each contributing some insights into the nature of reality. Indeed, if any one of the world religions is true then at least some aspect of each of the others must also be true. With the increased awareness of this bond, there may be less tension between religions.

(B)   There has been progress recently in identifying shared values between religions not just on the general level of applauding justice and compassion, but in terms of religious views of salvation, fulfillment or ultimate enlightenment. This development signals a promising opportunity for even greater harmony among world religions.

One may readily see how some religions can incorporate aspects of other religious teachings. Thus, Hinduism may readily conceive of various nonHindu religions as providing portraits of God or Brahman that are legitimate, provisional pictures of Brahman. The Baha'is also have a considerable legacy of endorsing other world religions as valued, authentic paths to a God-filled life. Perhaps the world religion thought to be most at odds with tolerance and respect towards other religions is Christianity. For this reason, I offer an overview of contemporary efforts by some Christian theologians and philosophers to show how Christianity may not just tolerate and respect other religious teachings about salvation (fulfillment, deliverance, enlightenment) but see these as authentic, viable ways in which salvation is achieved. This focus on Christianity may allow one to appreciate how a specific religious tradition can provide an enlarged picture of religious fulfillment while not departing from its core beliefs.

Christians have proposed various theories of how salvation is brought about, but the chief teaching of the religion is that salvation involves the work of God incarnate, Jesus Christ. On this view, through Jesus' birth, teaching, miracles, suffering, death, and resurrection, God graciously offers forgiveness of wrongdoing, an opportunity for reformation, and, ultimately, healing of harms. The latter is composed, in part, by God's not allowing the bodily death of persons to count as our absolute annihilation. According to most Christian traditionalists, there is an afterlife in which God's love and justice reign. Here I simply consider the question of whether Christians must insist that in order for this salvation to be achieved, a person must explicitly know of Jesus Christ, his teaching and life, and have explicit faith in Jesus' atoning work. While there is some scriptural testimony often interpreted as requiring such an explicit commitment (especially in the Gospel of John in the Christian New Testament), a significant number of Christian thinkers today believe that this interpretation is by no means binding.

A common strategy of these thinkers is to contend that while the work of Jesus Christ makes salvation possible, this by no means entails that God is at work only in the historic Jesus Christ of the first century. Core ideas of Christian teaching about the incarnation (God's grace, God's becoming incarnate) can be found, at least in part, in some other religions. For example, Raimundo Panikkar's book *The Unknown Christ of Hinduism* locates narratives and teachings in Hindu tradition that can be read as promoting Christ-like practices. He writes that "recognizing the presence of God in other religions is equivalent to proclaiming the presence of Christ in them, for in him all things subsist" (Panikkar 1981, p. 169). According to Panikkar and others, God reaches people in different terms and contexts in order to draw all parties ultimately (though perhaps only in the next life) to a fuller union with God in Christ.

Jacques Maritain advanced this inclusive picture of Christ's saving work. According to Maritain, persons may be deemed Christian even if they explicitly deny the truth of Christianity. In this passage he underscores how God may well reach others, even those who are firmly committed to atheism:

The speculative refusal of God as a final end and as the supreme rule of human life does not necessarily imply, for a mind so blinded, a practical refusal to order one's life with regard to that same God, whose name is no longer known. The Christian knows that God has infinite resource; and that the possibilities of good faith stretch farther than men imagine. Under many names, names which are not that of God, in ways only known to God, the interior act of a soul's thought can be directed towards a reality which in fact truly may be God. For, as a result of our spiritual weakness, there can easily be a discordance between what in reality we believe and the ideas in which we express to ourselves what we believe, and take cognizance of our beliefs. To every soul, even to one ignorant of the name of God, even one reared in atheism, grace offers, at the moment when the soul deliberates with itself and chooses its final end, grace offers as an object, as something to be loved above all things, under whatever name the soul describes such an end to itself – but it is then a case (and this is the whole question to which God alone knows the answer) of its thinking under that name of *something other* than it signifies, of going beyond the false name – offers that Reality of absolute goodness, which merits all our love and is able to save our life. And if this grace is not rejected, the soul in question, in its choice of that reality, believes obscurely in the true God and really chooses Him, even when in good faith it is in error and adheres, not by its own fault, but by that of the education it has received, to a philosophical system of atheism, and conceptualizes this faith in the true God under formulas which deny Him. An atheist of good faith would thus, against his own apparent choice, really choose God as the true end of his life. (cited by Baillie 1959, pp. 93–4)

While Maritain identifies Christ as the saving agent in bringing about atonement or reconciliation with God, other Christian theologians and philosophers have sought an even more inclusive picture of salvation. John Hick has adopted a radical approach which may be termed pluralism:

We have moved to a pluralism which sees the other great world faiths as authentic and valid contexts of salvation/liberation, not secretly dependent upon the cross of Christ. Each tradition has its channel of revelation or illumination, expressed in its sacred scriptures and responded to in distinctive forms of worship or meditation and in its own unique history of individual and communal life. Muslims, Hindus and the rest are not anonymous Christians, nor are Christians anonymous Muslims, Hindus and so on. Each constitutes a uniquely different (though overlapping) awareness of the ultimate transcendent Reality, as perceived through the "lens" of a particular religious tradition. (Hick 1993b, p. 143)

To many Christians, this later move by Hick may be too extreme, making Christianity more Hindu than classically Christian. But the point here is that in the Christian tradition one can see a movement to widen its understanding of salvation using the categories of its tradition. This development may be seen as contributing to a wider scope of respect, tolerance, and collaboration with others' commitment to good as each religion sees it.

(C)   Ideal Observation in world religions. Each of the world religions underscores features that are captured in the ideal observer theory discussed earlier. These features include the prizing of impartiality and a readiness to be apprised affectively of the points of view of others. This can serve to promote a spirit of respect and consideration for others. I note two traits of world religions that can contribute to ideal observer virtues: Belief in reincarnation can be of assistance in endeavoring to be impartial, and belief in theism can help to block certain postmodern deconstruction projects. I outline these briefly.

First, belief in reincarnation has many forms and, in Hinduism and Buddhism, it is linked to a rich theory of Karma. I note only one feature of it here: it involves imagining oneself (or one's soul) in a radically altered environment. At times it has involved imagining even that one has crossed species. Insofar as such beliefs make sense, simply the bare thought experiment of imagining such reincarnation can bring into clearer terms a fundamental aspect of much moral reasoning, namely the enhancement of our powers to see moral problems through other eyes, imagining various roles are reversed and so on.

Secondly, theism also has an important role to play in promoting tolerance in a pluralistic culture. Because the "God's eye point of view" is supposed to be impartial, it can serve as a reminder of the importance of seeing things from the points of view of other parties. Here, theism may serve as a check on some forms of what is often referred to as "postmodernism."

Defining what is often referred to as "postmodernism" is no easy task, but common to most characterizations of it is the thesis that there is no unified point of view or perspective by which to explain, let alone describe, the cosmos and our human social and political life. In his essay "What is Postmodernism?" Jean-François Lyotard described it as the thesis that there is no magisterial discourse or ultimate language by which to describe the world. Lyotard sums up postmodernism as "incredulity toward metanarratives" (Lyotard 1984, p. xxiv). The reason postmodern thinkers are called *post*modern is because they are at odds with the modern era's preoccupation with objective truth (the modern era is typically dated from the European Enlightenment or, roughly, the eighteenth to the twentieth century).

Lyotard's postmodernism stands in sharp contrast to theism. If there is a God of all creation and if God's knowledge extends over all, this marks some unity in the way things are. If theism is adopted, then there is some overarching point of view of reality. Michael Dummett writes:

> Without a belief in God, we must conclude that to which we can attribute truth holds only of *our* world. We know confusedly that there are other worlds; but, not only do we know nothing of them, but we cannot really speak intelligibly of them. If all creatures are truly creatures, however, that is, the work of one Creator, then and only then, there must be a single world of which all their worlds are aspects. (Dummett 1992, p. 147)

Dummett does not say why he believes that theism is *necessary* here, but it is clear that in the West there has been a close link between invoking a Creator and believing in the ultimate coherence and unity of the cosmos. Indeed, as Martin Jay has contended, one can document a close connection between the loss of belief in realism and loss of belief in God. As some intellectuals lost their religious moorings, declaring God to be a dead hypothesis, the death of realism soon followed. "The death of God meant the end of a God's-eye view" (Jay 1993, p. 190). An appreciation of the contextualized, historically conditioned nature of personal life without an overall point of view is prominent in postmodernism. Jay writes:

> No retrospective total knowledge of history would ever be possible, no sovereign, God's-eye would ever be granted to other pretenders to the role of subject/object history. The flesh of history is unsurveyable as the flesh of the natural world; we are always in the middle of a multilayered process. (Jay 1993, pp. 318, 319)

Perhaps here, then, a defensible form of theism can be part of a rebuttal to this fragmentary outlook. Arguably, theism provides a rationale for thinking an impartialist point of view is in some measure achievable (and if not achievable then at least approachable). Without some underlying theory accounting for the unity of persons a fragmented picture looks inviting.

Michael Fishbane underscores the difficulty of supporting a liberal ideal of rights without an undergirding treatment of persons in the cosmos: "All concerns for human rights will flounder as so much idealism and cheap legality, if they are not grounded in a strong and shared sense of personhood" (Fishbane 1988, p. 31). He thinks Judaism has an important contribution to make here: "The fundamental presupposition of the rights of the person in

Judaism is a belief in the absolute and uncompromisable worth of human life" (Fishbane 1988, p. 17). Similar claims can be made in other world religions. G. Tinder argues that the religious teaching that persons are made in the image of God provides a firmer foundation for tolerance than many of its secular alternatives (Tinder 1976).

While this last section began with a citation of Islamic groups that seem firmly opposed to competing nonIslamic nation-states, it needs to be appreciated that Islam has historically had an important legacy of tolerance. Islamic countries have sometimes protected nonIslamic groups (Jews and Christians) and allowed them to practice their faith. When Jews were evicted from Spain in 1492, some resettled in Istanbul and Palestine where they were free to practice their faith.

The world religions have often faired well in pluralistic cultures, and, as I hope to have shown, there are distinctive religious resources which may serve democratic ideals of tolerance, respect, and even, at times, collaboration.

I end the chapter by noting how such debate is by no means new and that religious and secular pluralism have been an important catalyst to religious life and philosophy. Harold Coward underscores how pluralism has been a party to religious development from the very beginning of the history of religions:

> Religious pluralism is a special challenge facing the world religions today, yet in another sense religious pluralism has always been with us. As the history of religions shows, each religion arose in a religiously plural environment and shaped itself in reaction to that pluralism. The creative tension pluralism occasions has often been the catalyst for new insight and religious development. It was out of the welter of views, the Brahmanical/Jain/Materialistic/Agnostic pluralism of his day, that the Buddha's enlightenment arose. It was in the midst of the Meccan admixture of Jews in the Christians, Zoroastrians, Manicheans and others that the prophecy of Allah through Muhammad burst forth. It was in the midst of the numerous territorial gods of the ancient Near East that God covenanted with Abraham and Moses. It was the challenge of Gnosticism and Greek philosophy that helped early Christians to identify their separateness from Judaism. And it may be said of Hinduism that plurality has been its strength right up to the present day. Certainly there were times in the history of each of these religions when the pluralistic challenges receded to the background, often signaling a period of spiritual stagnation, for example, Christianity through the Middle Ages or Islam just prior to Sufi encounter with Hinduism. And when the challenge of pluralism reasserted itself, it usually infused new life into the tradition confronted. Thus, although the challenge of religious pluralism is in one sense the crisis of our age, it is at

the same time its opportunity for spiritual growth. (Coward, in Dean [ed.] 1995, pp. 45–6)

It is also an opportune time for philosophical growth.

Suggested Questions and Topics

(1)   Granted a basic theistic outlook (Judaic, Christian, Islamic or some combination, or a more general, philosophical theism), what do you think is the best reply to the Euthyphro dilemma (taken from Plato's dialogue *The Euthyphro*)? Does God approve of acts because they are good or are acts good because God approves of them? A similar question may be formulated in the context of the discussion of power in chapter 3: Are some logical and metaphysical truths true because God knowingly wills that they be true or does God know and approve of such truths because of their truth? Compare the question "Is God good because God makes things that are good or is God good in Himself?" with "Is water wet because it makes things wet or is it wet in itself?"

(2)   Consider some of these objections or challenges to basing ethics on theism, taken from John Arthur's paper "Does Morality Depend on Religion?":

(a)   It seems to me that most of us, when it really gets down to it, don't give much of a thought to religion when making moral decisions.
(b)   How can anybody be sure his or her religion is the right one? After all, if you had been born in China or India or Iran your religious views would almost certainly not be the ones you now hold. And even if we can somehow convince ourselves that the Judeo-Christian God is the real one, we still need to find out just what it is He wants us to do.
(c)   If we are to use revelation as a guide we must know what is to count as revelation – words given us by God, events, or both? Far from providing a shortcut to moral understanding, looking to revelation for guidance just creates more questions and problems. It is much simpler to address problems such as abortion, capital punishment, and war directly than to seek answers in revelation.
(d)   Certainly the expressions "is commanded by God" and "is morally required" do not *mean* the same thing; atheists and agnostics use moral

words without understanding them to make any reference to God. And while it is of course true that God (or any other moral being for that matter) would tend to want others to do the right thing, this hardly shows that being right and being commanded by God are the same thing. Parents want their children to do the right thing, too, but that doesn't mean they, or anybody else, can make a thing right just by commanding it!

(e) Since God is all-powerful, and since right is determined solely by His commands, is it not possible that He might change the rules and make what we now think of as wrong into right?

(3)   In this chapter, it is noted how theistic ethics is often shaped by competing views of nature, reason, and revelation. You may wish to consider a specific moral problem and how you think a plausible theistic account may be constructed: How should one balance the appeal to nature, reason, and revelation?

(4)   How would you analyze the Abraham and Isaac story, Genesis 22 (the Hebrew Bible and the Christian Old Testament)?

(5)   Consider the ramifications of the right to privacy. Do you think God can violate your right to privacy? Along similar lines, do you think we have a right to life over and against God? Does God have a duty to keep persons in existence? Do you think we have a right to property over against God? Could God steal from you?

(6)   In outlining the ideal observer theory it was noted that in theism God is pictured as impartial. Divine impartiality is recorded in much theistic tradition. Do you think it is contradictory to the very nature of God to suppose God could have favorites? Is some preferential treatment – whereby God confers some goods to some people and not to others – compatible with God's being just or fair? Some ethicists explicitly repudiate all partiality. Thus, Jeremy Bentham (1748–1832) held that, "I would have the dearest friend know that his interests, if they come in competition with that of the public, are nothing to me" (cited by E. Johnson 1992, p. 28). Could a fair, good God think otherwise?

(7)   James Rachels develops the following argument, which you may wish to assess:

(a)   If any being is God, He must be a fitting object of worship.
(b)   No being could possibly be a fitting object of worship, since worship requires the abandonment of one's role as an autonomous moral agent.

240

(c) Therefore, there cannot be any being who is God. (Rachels, in Helm [ed.] 1981, p. 45)

(8) How might the ideal observer theory be defended against some of the following charges:

(a) IOs might disagree. If so, the theory cannot account for objective values.
(b) At most the theory provides a conditional analysis of values: If there were an IO it would approve of this or that. But just as a hypothetical promise is not a promise, hypothetical approvals are not genuine approvals.
(c) The IO theory is so abstract, it cannot confer a plausible account of ethical motivation.
(d) It is possible there could be an IO that approves of wickedness, hence the theory cannot serve as an analysis of goodness.
(e) The IO theory extolls detachment and is thus both male-biased as an ethical theory as well as at odds with moral reasoning itself which is action-oriented.

(9) It was suggested in this chapter that theism secures a reference point for its believers, whereby persons may understand their true identity in terms of how God sees them. Does it make sense to refer to a person's "true self," and if so, can one's understanding of a true self be secured in terms of what and how one is from a God's eye point of view?

(10) Consider Roland Puccetti's description of nonhuman animal suffering:

> A rabbit lives by foraging for food in the fields. One day he is caught by a farmer's cat, who carries him back to the farmhouse relatively unharmed. Then the cat bites his hindquarters, partially hamstringing the rabbit. He lets the rabbit hop a few steps, then pounces on him again, tearing at his flesh. This is repeated several times. When the cat tires of this he settles down and begins to gnaw at the back of the rabbit's head. The rabbit lies there, beating, its eyes still open until death comes. (Puccetti, in Peterson [ed.] 1992, p. 232)

How do you think this is best addressed within a theistic framework, if at all? (See chapter 9 for more material on natural evil.)

(11) Some theists construe the duty owed to God in terms of a duty of gratitude like the gratitude owed a parent from a child. Is this adequately conceived in terms of parent–child relations? Raymond Belliotti has proposed a model of the parent–child relationship that may be of use to theists in

exploring the values at work in the God–human relationship. Belliotti defends two principles:

> *The Contribution to Self Principle*:
> If person N either has made or is making a contribution to person P's personal identity either by (a) a genetic contribution or (b) being an attachment or commitment or (c) contributing a property constitutive of P's personal identity, then P owes a prima facie moral requirement to care for N. The relative strength of the requirement owed is proportionate to the extent of N's contribution to P's personal identity at the time of calculation.
> and *The Metaphysical Proximity Principle*:
> If person N is metaphysically closer to P (N is "like" P) than the metaphysical proximity of person X to P (X is not like P), then P is morally permitted to advance the interests of N rather than the interests of X. (Belliotti 1986, p. 156)

You may find it interesting to articulate a theistic ethic working with some version of these principles.

(12)   According to passibilism, God has feelings, sorrowing over the evil in the cosmos and taking pleasure in its goods. Is it a defect, or somehow less than perfect, for God to have certain needs? Consider Anselm's statement: "You are only one supreme good, altogether sufficient unto Yourself, needing nothing else but needed by all else in order to exist and to fare well (*Proslogion*, ch. 22).

(13)   Assess T. D. J. Chappell's argument for the conclusion that God is not a consequentialist moral agent:

(1)   If God exists and is a consequentialist moral agent, then God will act only so as to make it true that the predominance of happiness over unhappiness in existence is maximized. (*Definition*)

(2)   If God exists, then in God's own existence, the predominance of happiness over unhappiness in existence is maximized. (*Metaphysical Premise*)

(3)   Therefore, if it is true that God acts, then God will act only so as to make it true that God exists. (1, 2)

(4)   Therefore God will not create anything. (3)

(5)   But (4) is false: God *has* created things. (*Premise of Observation*)

(6)   Therefore God, if He exists, is not a consequentialist moral agent (4, 5).

(7)   If God exists, then necessarily, "God believes p" entails "p is true". (*Definition*)

(8)   If God exists, then "God is not a consequentialist moral agent" entails "God believes that consequentialism is not true". (*Definition*)

(9)   Therefore, if God exists, "consequentialism is not true" is true. (6, 7)

(10) Therefore, if God exists, consequentialism is not true. (9) (Chappell 1993, p. 240)

(14)   Does liberalism lead to a homogenized, religiously insensitive view of world religions? Consider Kenneth Surin's charge:

> Traditional liberal intellectuals pride themselves on acknowledging heterogeneity and plurality, but this acknowledgement is always fatally compromised by a deployment of homogeneous logic – a logic which irons out the heterogeneous precisely by subsuming it under the categories of comprehensive and totalizing global and world theologies . . . (Surin, in D'Costa [ed.] 1990, p. 210)

In reply you may wish to distinguish types of liberalism. Are there nontraditional forms that might avoid Surin's account?

(15)   Michael Slote has recently argued that virtues and vices should be measured and gauged in terms of a person's stage of life. What counts as a virtue for a child is different than for an elder man or woman. Is it plausible to believe there are different virtues and vices of a distinctively religious kind depending upon one's religious development or maturation? (Consult Slote's *Goods and Virtues* for relevant material.) Slote also argues that the significance of a life is partly a matter of the pattern or distribution of good and evil over time. He contends that it is plausible to regard "the characteristic goals and successes of certain life periods (e.g. adulthood or the prime of life) as having greater significance for life overall than those of certain others (e.g. childhood)" (Slote 1983, p. 2). Do you find this plausible? What might its implications be theistically? You may wish to consider such a question of significance not just for individuals but for periods of human history.

Further Readings and Considerations

Relevant entries from *A Companion to Philosophy of Religion* include: "Goodness"; "Immutability"; "Moral Arguments"; "Theism and Scientific Understanding of the Mind"; "Theism and Technology"; "Divine Command Ethics"; "Natural Law Ethics"; "Virtue Ethics"; "Narrative Ethics"; "Agapeistic Ethics"; "Theism, Law and Politics"; "Theism and Medical Ethics"; "Theism and Environmental Ethics"; "Atonement"; and "Theism and Toleration."

Nihilism is sometimes classified together with relativism as both share the denial of objective values. Certain forms of relativism seem indistinguishable from nihilism, as seen in the following remark of Ernest Hemingway: "So far, about morals, I know only that what is moral is what you feel good after and what is immoral is what you feel bad after" (cited by Pojman, in Audi 1995, p. 690). Relativism is also sometimes called "conventionalism" insofar as it matches the claims of ethics to the prevailing conventions.

Historically, those either advocating or sympathetic to a divine command theory of ethics include: Augustine; Ambrose; Gregory the Great; Isidore of Seville; Hugh of St. Victor; Anselm; Duns Scotus; William of Ockham; Andrew of Neufchateau; Peter of Ailly; Jean Berson; Gabriel Biel; Martin Luther; John Calvin; Karl Barth; Emil Brunner; and Carl Henry. Its opponents include: Ralph Cudworth; Thomas Chubb; George Ruse; Anthony, Earl of Shaftesbury; Francis Hutcheson; Richard Price; and Jeremy Bentham. See Janine Idziak's very fine anthology for more information, *Divine Command Morality: Historical and Contemporary Readings*. Philip Quinn's *Divine Commands and Moral Requirements* offers a sophisticated, formal treatment of a divine command ethic. I defend the ideal observer theory in "The Environmental Ethics of an Ideal Observer" and "Relativizing the Ideal Observer Theory." I believe that an ideal observer theory can be defended that analyzes both ethical as well as aesthetic judgments (see "The Ideal Aesthetic Observer"). On this front, I follow Francis Hutcheson (1694–1746) and, even more so, follow the Cambridge Platonists of the seventeenth century (Cudworth, Henry Moore, and Whichcote).

Robert Oakes has developed a formal analysis of God's affective, all-knowing presence to the cosmos in these terms: "N is affectively infallible = df. Necessarily, for any emotion E, intensity of emotion I, and situation S of which N is aware, E of I-intensity constitutes the perfectly appropriate affective response to S if E of I-intensity constitutes (is qualitatively identical to) N's affective response to S" (Oakes 1990, p. 138). There is a rich tradition in Christian religious ethics emphasizing rightful, fitting, and effective responsiveness to values. This draws on work by Plato and Aristotle. It can be seen in Augustine's emphasis on the order of love (*ordo amoris*), Pascal's (1623–62) notion of the order of the heart (*l'ordre du coeur*) and in the work of Max Scheler (1874–1928).

Some feminists and other philosophers (preeminently Jean-Paul Sartre) worry about whether exalting an ideal observer will inevitably threaten subjectivity. Here I note that particularly important work on this problem has been prominent among twentieth-century Jewish thinkers such as Franz

Rosensweig (1886–1929) and Emmanuel Levinas (1906–95). These philoso-phers have been especially keen to address the problem of reconciling an objective, realist God's eye point of view with the vital importance of subjec-tivity and experience. In this context, Levinas, for example, has written in moving terms about the ethical and philosophical significance of how we address each other face to face. And before him, Martin Buber highlighted the radical difference between I–it (impersonal) and I–you (personal) relations in his effort to articulate a theistic philosophy that gave enormous weight to diversified personal life and relations (see Buber 1923; Levinas 1961 and 1974).

For works on pluralism and world religions, see *Human Rights and the World's Religions* edited by L. Rouner. *War and Peace in the World's Religions* edited by J. Ferguson; and *Religious Pluralism and Unbelief* edited by I. Hamnett, are especially useful.

For further work on the atonement, see Grensted's *A Short History of the Doctrine of the Atonement*; Hare's *The Moral Gap: Kantian Ethics, Human Limits and God's Assistance*; and Swinburne's *Responsibility and Atonement*.

It has not been feasible to cover religious conceptions of aesthetic values (beauty and ugliness), though this has been an area of growing interest and work. See, for example, *Religious Aesthetics* by F. B. Brown. For an intriguing examination of theological issues in an aesthetic context see "The real or the Real? Chardin or Rothko" by Anthony O'Hear, in *Philosophy, Religion, and the Spiritual Life*.

8

Evidence, Experience, and God

Today there is a concentrated debate in philosophy of religion and in the discipline of philosophy at large over the nature and requirements of evidence. What is evidence? What are the implications of the current theories of evidence for the justification of the belief that there is a God? Do religious views of God and the cosmos require evidence in order to be intellectually respectable? Where does the burden of proof lie in religious matters? Some philosophers charge that any religious conception of reality that goes beyond atheistic naturalism faces a weighty burden of proof. On their view, if one does not have compelling evidence for God's existence, one should embrace atheism. This chapter addresses these charges with special attention on the role of religious experience in justifying claims about the divine.

These topics constitute an important juncture where philosophers focus on what appears to be the very soul of religious tradition. A significant number of religious believers in different traditions appeal to experience to justify their convictions. Sarvepalli Radhakrishnan singles out the experience of God as central to a robust and pervasive recognition of the divine. Such experiences, on his view, constitute the most reliable and reasonable approach to God:

The possibility of the experience [of God] constitutes the most conclusive proof of the reality of God. God is "given", and is the factual content of the spiritual experience. All other proofs are descriptions of God, matters of definition, and language. The fact of God does not depend on mere human authority or evidence from alleged miraculous events. The authority of scripture, the traditions of the Church . . . may not carry conviction to many of us who are the children of science and reason, but we must submit to the fact of spiritual experience, which is primary and positive. We may dispute theologies, but cannot deny facts. The fire of life in its visible burning compels assent,

246

though not the fumbling speculations of smokers sitting around the fire. (Radhakrishnan 1959, pp. 22–3)

According to Radhakrishnan, other philosophical or scientific arguments for God's existence pale in contrast to an experiential awareness of the divine. Radhakrishnan and others contend that a proper philosophy of God must be informed by the experience of God either directly or through the rites and practices of religious tradition, or by relying on the testimony of those who have had such experience of God. This chapter assesses the merits of this experientially-based philosophy of God.

The development of an account of religious experience is important for many religious believers not just as part of a defense of the reasonability of their beliefs. It is also vital in articulating religious conceptions of salvation and human fulfillment. Grace Jantzen highlights the place of religious experience in theistic religions:

> Salvation is not (or at least not primarily) about our future destiny but about our relationship to God and the gradual transforming effect of that relationship in our lives. . . . If religious experience is centrally the sense of the loving presence of God, gradually helping people to reorient and integrate their lives in accordance with their love for him, is this not precisely what salvation is? Salvation must, surely, be religious experience if anything ever is: not in the sense of being a single climactic experience . . . but in the sense of a gradual opening of all life, all of experience to the wholemaking love of God. (Jantzen 1987, pp. 128–9)

If Jantzen is right, religious experience has a vital role in securing religious values and maturity.

A defense of the intelligibility and coherence of religious experience is as important to many theists as a critique of religious experience is for nonreligious naturalists. Many critics of theism put great emphasis on explaining away purported experiences of God. By their lights, claims to experience God or Brahman are either irrational or unreliable. Let us begin with a general overview of philosophical reflection on the nature of evidence and then proceed to the philosophy of religious experience.

The Nature and Sources of Evidence

This section surveys some of the current accounts of evidence, a delimitation of what many philosophers take to be the sources of evidence, and three theories about the structure and requirements of evidence.

As noted in the Introduction to this book, the word "evidence" is derived from the Latin *ex videre*, meaning "to see." Typically the term is used to mark off considerations that justify beliefs, or, if you will, justify that what persons believe they see to be true. Normally, a question about why a person holds some belief calls for the presentation of what counts as evidence. "Evidence" generally refers to reasons of a justificatory sort, reasons why one's beliefs may be said to be properly warranted, entitled or deserved. The question of why one holds a belief may sometimes be used more broadly than to request evidence. I may report that the reason why I have a belief is due to the fact that I was brought up a certain way, when this report is not intended to count as evidence as to why I (or anyone else) *should* think the belief is true. But to believe something on the basis of evidence is to have grounds, a foundation, basis or reason, which is typically thought of as strong or weak, depending on the quality of evidence.

The crucial reason why evidence should be taken seriously is that it appears that there is an important distinction between a justified belief and a belief that is simply a lucky guess or backed by outrageously faulty reasoning. If one's sole evidence for thinking an ant is in a room is that –

(1)   There is an animal in room X

and

(2)   An ant is an animal

– one is not entitled to the conclusion. For even if (2) is right, one lacks a sufficient reason to believe that the animal in room X is an ant, rather than a cat and so on. The conclusion would be earned with the help of other premises such as: If there is an animal in room X, it is an ant. The possession of evidence has sometimes been thought of as establishing that one has "a right to be sure" of one's beliefs (A. J. Ayer).

At least at the outset, it appears as though we can distinguish between good and bad evidence, and that what constitutes good and bad evidence is not a matter merely of individual decision. Can one simply decide, arbitrarily, that some particular experience is evidence for a given belief? This seems doubtful. Consider, for example, whether one can simply make it the case by an arbitrary decree that seeing yellow is evidence that the ant population in Minnesota is currently one trillion. One can *imagine* an electronic ant-counting device such that its display of a yellow light is triggered by the appropriate expansion of ants and, thus, one's seeing a yellow light would count as proper evidence. But short of something bizarre like this, merely seeing yellow is of no evidential support for the belief about ants. George Mavrodes proposes that there is an important difference between a belief being made evident as opposed to a belief simply being triggered or brought about:

> In general, the fact that a certain circumstance, event, and so on – call it "C" – activates a disposition to form and hold a certain belief, B, does not at all make C evidence for B. Some men, for example, apparently have a disposition to believe that they are wonderful entertainers, and this disposition is activated by drinking two or three cocktails. That fact, however, does not make the existence of alcohol *evidence* that these people are great entertainers. We need not deny either the disposition or its triggering mechanism in order to maintain that the resulting belief is groundless . . . But the triggering relation and the evidential relation are not identical. (Mavrodes 1983, p. 199)

A major preoccupation within the theory of knowledge is to analyze the nature of such evidential relations.

Perhaps the most widely agreed, general condition for something to count as evidence for believing something, X, is that the occurrence of the evidence is plausibly believed to be a condition for or a result of X. Seeing a shoe-print in some mud is deemed evidence that John Doe was present if it is deemed likely that there would be such a print if and only if John Doe had indeed been present. The quality of the evidence is then measured, in part, by the plausibility (or likelihood) of the print being caused by others, the reasonability of assuming John Doe would have been wearing the shoes, and so on. But while a schema appears to be plausible, it is highly abstract and there is fierce debate about the concepts of reasonability, likelihood, plausibility, and so on. As will be noted later, there is a wide spectrum of accounts of these notions, from the *laissez-faire* position of anything goes to the highly restrictive.

What sources of evidence are typically appealed to in justifying claims about ourselves, the world, and God or some other ultimate religious reality? Our sensory abilities are often delimited as our principle sources of evidence. The so-called five senses involve:

Seeing   Feeling
Hearing   Smelling
Tasting

These sensory modes or powers are often thought of as providing our chief source of evidence about the nature of the world. We typically ground our beliefs about ourselves and the objects around us on the basis of what we see, hear, feel, smell and taste. Some features of objects appear to be available to more than one sense (shape can be felt and seen) while other features appear to be accessible through one sense rather than another (claims to hear the smell or the taste of an object are puzzling).

The senses are sometimes described by philosophers in terms of pure sensory states (e.g. color sensations) and sometimes as a combination of judgments and sensations (e.g. forming the belief "I see the blue ball"). "Perception" is usually thought of as a matter of judgment *and* sensation, in which one judges or believes that one visually sees the thing one assumes that one sees. Consider John's report:

I saw Jane Doe

According to a perceptual use of the term "to see," John visually sensed Jane Doe *and* judged or believed that the person he saw was indeed Jane Doe. Alternatively, on a sensory (nonperceptual) use of "to see," John might visually have seen her but failed to make the judgment that he saw her. In this respect, it would make sense to claim: John saw Jane Doe but did not realize it.

Two further faculties are often singled out as providing evidence for our beliefs:

Reason
Memory

The use of reason and memory appear to many philosophers to be essential in the structuring of our sensory and perceptual experiences. It is because of reason and memory that we take ourselves to be sensorially aware of a world of enduring objects and aware that we ourselves endure over time. Reason and memory may or may not involve the use of visual imagery. Someone may rightly claim to recall some past event without this involving any visual picture of what occurred.

"Reason" is a term that is often used to refer to the ways in which persons reflect critically on experience (inductively inferring conclusions based on sense experience, for example) or on conceptual matters such as mathematics that do not involve sensory experience. Some philosophers think that we can know some truths without relying upon any experience at all. This is sometimes said to be *a priori* (from the Latin term for "from the preceding"). If one knows that $1 + 1 = 2$, for example, and the justification for one's belief does not require sensory evidence, one may be said to have *a priori* knowledge. Thought experiments often come into play in testing what one can grasp *a priori*. Thus, one reason for claiming that $1 + 1 = 2$ is the unimaginability of any alternative; a stronger reason involves grasping that it is impossible for $1 + 1$ not to be the same as 2. (Arthur Pap highlights the role of imaginative thought experiments in *a priori* reflection; see Pap 1958.) The *a priori* contrasts with what we may know *a posteriori* (from the Latin for "from the later"). *A posteriori* knowledge involves recourse to experience. Some philosophers claim that one can only know *a posteriori* such things as "Swans exist" but one may know *a priori* such things as "squares are four sided," "There cannot be more green balls than balls," "Nothing can be taller than itself," "If all humans are mortal then no immortal is human," and so on. The division between *a priori* and *a posteriori* is under debate now, and we need not agree at this point on the strict character of each. It will suffice for present purposes simply to note a rough and ready, apparent difference between believing something on the basis of experience and on the basis of conceptual reflection.

Other faculties that are sometimes delimited in the theory of knowledge include:

Introspection
Intuition
Insight
Imagination
A moral sense
A religious sense
An aesthetic sense

More will be said about some of these later.

Still other faculties have been posited but these are often considered suspect. Some parapsychologists argue that we possess powers of telepathy (from the Greek *tele* for "at a distance" and *pathein* for "to experience"), the ability to be aware of states of affairs or receive messages in ways that do not rely on five senses or other "ordinary" faculties, precognition or clairvoyance (awareness of the future), and postcognition (past events known without the use of memory or other ordinary means). There is a significant philosophical literature on parapsychology well worth researching (Beloff 1993).

Without making a decision now as to whether some of these latter, more controversial faculties may legitimately be relied upon, consider how any (or all) of our faculties may be classified as providing evidence for our beliefs, whether these be garden-variety beliefs about ourselves and surroundings or more exotic beliefs about the origin and nature of the cosmos. There are three main theories of evidential relations popular today: internalism, externalism, and theories that seek to bridge the internalism and externalism divide.

Internalism

Evidence is internal if it is available to the person relying upon it. On this view, for some experience or the use of some faculty to provide evidence for a belief, the person must either be aware of the justificatory reasons for her belief or it must be such that she could be aware of them. Your seeing a yellow sphere may be evidence that there is a yellow sphere in front of you if indeed you seem to see it and are capable of grasping the fact that seeming to have such visual experiences confers such justification. Earl Conee is an internalist who holds that "A person has a justified belief only if the person has reflective access to evidence that the belief is true" (Conee 1985, p. 15). Ernest Sosa describes the internalist account of evidence succinctly: "What does matter for justification is how the subject performs with respect to factors internal to him . . . it does not matter for justification if external factors are abnormal and unfavorable" (Sosa 1988, p. 369). Some internalists are strict foundationalists, others are either weaker foundationalists, critical cognitivists, or coherentists. These may be delimited as follows:

Foundationalism. If foundationalism is right, what one knows can be justified as either part of a well-grounded base of beliefs or derived from such a base. On a strict version of this position, for a person to have a properly justified set of beliefs, these must form what the person may grasp as either self-evident or known indirectly by being justified by their relationship to these bedrock, self-evident or justified evident beliefs. Historically prominent foundationalists include René Descartes and John Locke.

Critical cognitivism. According to this view, the justificatory relations between one's beliefs need not be strict or foundational, but the justificatory relations must nonetheless be normative. The reasons are still, in principle, accessible. Critical cognitivists like Roderick Chisholm allow for normative justificatory relations that are considerably more relaxed than a strict foundationalist. Thus, on Chisholm's view, you may be justified in believing something on the grounds that it simply seems to you to be true and you know of no reason to think it is not true. To some foundationalists, this stance is *too relaxed*, while to some critical cognitivists, foundationalism is sterile and lands one in an inescapable skepticism.

Coherentism.   Various views are pertinent here, but they are united by the thesis that the justification of a belief is a matter of its connection with a network of other beliefs. This connection is sometimes analyzed in terms of overall reasonability or consistency or explanatory comprehensiveness. Laurence BonJour is a prominent coherentist. According to each of these views – foundationalism, critical cognitivism, and coherentism – the justificatory process may be interpreted as working from the inside (what is available to the subject) to the outside (to beliefs about the world).

Externalism

Externalism is the opposite of the internalist theory of evidence. Its most common form is reliabilism. According to *reliabilism* a belief is justified if it is produced by a reliable, truth-producing mechanism or process. If the process is likely to result in a preponderance of true beliefs then it confers justification. Alvin Goldman and Fred Dretske are prominent defenders of reliabilism. According to Goldman, "The justificational status of a belief is a function of the reliability of the process or processes that cause it, where . . . reliability consists in the tendency of a process to produce beliefs that are true rather than false" (Goldman 1979, p. 10).

An example may help to clarify the distinction between internalism and externalism. The example is rough and should be read as a case where internalists and externalists *tend to differ*, not an instance where they are *compelled* to do so. Imagine John Doe has studied English History, but as time goes by he does not rehearse what he learned and even forgets he undertook his history studies. One day he is given a surprise exam on English History. Feeling dismayed, he sets out to guess the answers and, much to his surprise, he gets all the answers right. An internalist is disposed to think he was not justified in believing the answers he submitted, for he thought he was merely guessing and not capable of reviewing the evidence for his answers. An externalist may construe the matter otherwise. Even if John Doe was incapable of recalling the evidence he had for his various beliefs, so long as he was relying on a reliable procedure for answering the question (memories operative on a subconscious level, perhaps), he may be deemed justified in submitting his answers. A reliabilist may even conclude that John knew the answers though he did not realize it. (I have adopted the example from one that is discussed in Lehrer 1974; for a recent overview and attack on internalism see Dancy 1985.)

A Combination of Externalism and Internalism

Some philosophers seek to bridge these dominant schools of thought. Today, the most widely discussed combination is typically considered a form of virtue theory. It will prove useful first to take note of virtue theory in ethics and then observe how it is applied in theories about evidence.

Virtue theory. Historically, the theory of virtues in ethics has been used to combine internal and external factors. That is, according to virtue theory, the determination of whether a person is virtuous covers both excellence from an internal vantage point (the person's intentions, motives, desires), and from an external vantage point as well (the person's actions and their effects). Consider, for example, whether our current classification of virtues today would be retained if these "virtues" produced horrible results. Imagine that John Doe is, from an internal point of view, courageous, just and prudent, but due to no fault of his own, he regularly brings about disasters, accidentally killing people, and the like. Standard virtue theory stipulates that there is an accord or fit between the internal and external. Similarly, so it is argued, a reasonable assessment of our cognitive virtues (relying on sense experience, perception, reason, memory, and so on) has credibility to the extent that persons take themselves to be responsible, careful and attentive as well as to the extent that, by doing so, persons wind up with a preponderance of true beliefs. Linda Zagzebski is a leading exponent of such a virtue theory. These theories of evidence may be represented as follows:

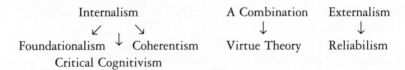

Each of the above theories of evidential relations has important proponents. And each is used by naturalists to build an argument that religious beliefs should be considered suspect unless bolstered by good evidence. The next section employs the three main categories of evidence – internalism, externalism, and virtue theory – to build a case against theistic beliefs. A range of replies are then considered, including the radical claim that religious beliefs do not require evidence in order to be intellectually respectable.

Religious Claims and the Burden of Proof

Burden of proof arguments involve arguments that a given position should be rejected unless it can be established by good evidence. In American criminal law, persons are presumed innocent until proven guilty. The government has the burden of proving someone guilty. If no proof is forthcoming, persons are presumed innocent. Some philosophers advance a burden of proof argument against religious convictions. They argue that religious claims should be presumed guilty from an intellectual point of view until proven to be justified by evidence. The most common form of such a burden of proof argument against religious convictions has involved arguing that the starting point for any respectable philosophy must be naturalistic. Religious claims are then cast as claims that are acceptable if and only if they are warranted by forceful evidence. Claims that go beyond naturalism are, as it were, guilty until proven innocent.

The force of this burden of proof argument may be made clear by considering the following kinds of cases. If there is no positive evidence to believe in goblins, unicorns and elves, should one suspend judgment that there are such entities or, rather, deny they exist? Arguably, one should simply deny they exist. N. F. Hanson lays out a burden of proof argument using such analogies:

> [I]f looking and not finding does not constitute grounds for denying the existence of God, then looking and not finding does not constitute grounds for denying the existence of goblins, witches, devils, five-headed Welshmen, Unicorns, mermaids, Loch Ness monsters, flying saucers, Hobbits, Santa Claus . . . etc. *But there are excellent grounds for denying the existence of such entities.* They consist not simply in the failure to find and identify such remarkable creatures. Rather, these grounds consist largely in the fact that there is no good reason whatsoever for supposing that such creatures *do* exist. (Hanson 1971, p. 323)

Hanson, Antony Flew, Michael Scriven, Keith Parsons, and others argue that skepticism about religious claims in general, and especially theistic religious claims, is the preferred, natural starting point.

Each of the theories of evidence sketched in the previous section has been employed in developing such a naturalist starting point that places theists (and others who advocate non-naturalist religious outlooks) at a disadvantage. The strategy outlined below involves articulating a naturalist starting point, and then sticking to it. Consider, then, three versions of a burden of proof argument.

Internalism

The base of available, noncontroversial evidence is free of any religious objects – God, Brahman, the Tao and so on. There is no good reason (so it is argued) to believe people have a religious sense or faculty that makes a divine reality directly or indirectly evident. Going beyond our sensory experience, and the material world disclosed to us in such experience, requires good reasons. Positing powers to perceive God is in the same category as positing powers of precognition and telepathy. People have claimed to possess such powers but these claims are not confirmed by empirical, statistical studies (i.e. predictions based on them are no better than good guess-work), and their uneven distribution among people should lead us to suspect their credibility.

Internalists may sharpen their critique as follows. If a foundationalist theory of evidence is adopted, it is arguable that no base, nor evident rules of evidence, can warrant such abstract notions as "There is a God." While critical cognitivists might rejoin that some people are justified in believing "God exists" on the grounds that such a belief appears to be true to many people, it can be objected that this loose justification may accommodate all sorts of absurdities (the belief in elves, unicorns, Santa Claus). It may also be argued that coherentism favors naturalism insofar as naturalism is better grounded as an overall coherent philosophical schema. While theism (and other non-naturalist religions) might be coherent, at first glance theism seems like extravagant speculation, or it is at least at an apparent disadvantage in comparison with naturalism. Theists are required either to provide good evidence for believing that a theistic philosophy of God is both coherent and justified, or to abandon their beliefs.

Externalism

Here the case for a burden of proof argument is strongest if it is part of a comprehensive case for naturalism. If naturalism may be articulated as a simple, coherent way of describing and accounting for the cosmos, then one may well depict competing religious schemes as systems of belief that are dramatically (and thus precariously) beyond what is reasonable to accept without substantial evidence. This burden of proof argument may work with significant force against some versions of theism. Some theists hold that the naturalist view of the cosmos is substantially correct (e.g. the natural sciences provide a reasonable description and account of the cosmos) with one exception: it leaves out God. But if naturalists and theists agree about the substantial, initial credibility of naturalism, it appears that theists are then comparatively suspect. In the absence of good reasons to believe there is more to the cosmos than accounted for naturalistically, one should deny that there is more.

Combinations

A virtue theory of evidence can be formulated that applauds naturalist virtues of resisting superstition and speculative theories that go beyond evidence. William Clifford (1845–79) is often credited with developing the most well-known naturalist account of cognitive virtue. Clifford claimed: "It is wrong always, everywhere, and for anyone to believe anything upon insufficient evidence" (Clifford 1879, p. 186). Clifford applauds the intellectual virtues of restraint and of criticism:

> Whoso would deserve well of his fellows in this matter will guard the purity of his belief with a very fanaticism of jealous care, lest at any time it should rest on an unworthy object, and catch a stain which can never be wiped away. . . . [If a] belief has been accepted on insufficient evidence, the pleasure is a stolen one. Not only does it deceive ourselves by giving us a sense of power which we do not really possess, but it is sinful, because it is stolen in defiance of our duty to mankind. That duty is to guard ourselves from such beliefs as from a pestilence, which may shortly master our body and spread to the rest of the town. (Clifford 1879, pp. 183, 184)

Clifford contends that this virtue-based approach to justification prompts us to classify the religious believer as reckless, negligent, and irresponsible (the host of an intellectual pestilence) as opposed to the more reasonable, intellectually healthy, level-headed naturalist.

All three versions of the burden of proof argument employ a version of Ockham's razor to the effect that if one has no good reasons to believe there is a God, one has reason not to believe in God. Antony Flew casts the debate between theists and naturalists as follows:

> It is up to the theist: first, to introduce and to defend his proposed concept of God; and second, to provide sufficient reason for believing that this concept of his does in fact have an application. (Flew 1992, p. 20)

Flew thinks that this requirement to justify matters is even more stringent because of the moral consequences involved:

> It is . . . not only incongruous but also scandalous in matters of life and death, and even of eternal life and death, to maintain that you know either on no grounds at all, or on grounds of a kind which on other and comparatively minor issues you yourself would insist to be inadequate . . . It is by reference to this inescapable demand for grounds that the presumption of atheism is justified. If it is to be established that there is a God, then we have to have good grounds for believing that this is indeed so. Until and unless some such grounds are produced we have literally no reason at all for believing . . . [O]ur concern here . . . is with the need for opinions to be suitably grounded if they are to be rated as items of knowledge, or even probable belief. (Flew 1992, p. 25)

Michael Scriven adopts a similar stance. He construes the theist and naturalist as possessing a similar grasp of the structure of the world (both accept the existence of the cosmos, the reliability of science and so on) except for the theist's further claims about a transcendental God:

> Every sane theist . . . believes in the claims of ordinary experience, while the reverse is not the case. Hence, the burden of proof is on the theist to show that the further step he wishes to take will not take him beyond the realm of truth. (Scriven 1966, p. 101)

Scriven thinks that in the absence of positive beliefs, one should disbelieve theism and not simply remain agnostic. Like Hanson, Flew, and Clifford, Scriven argues as follows:

> Now even belief in something for which there is no evidence, i.e., a belief which goes beyond the evidence, although a lesser sin than belief in something which is contrary to well-established laws, is plainly irrational in that it simply amounts to attaching belief where it is not justified. So the proper alternative, when there is no evidence, is not mere suspension of belief, e.g., about Santa Claus; it is disbelief. It most certainly is not faith. (Scriven 1966, p. 103)

Should this stance be vindicated, it would have considerable force for it can be advanced on the basis of each of the three major theories of evidence.

258

Naturalism and the Burden of Proof

A dramatic way to contest the above naturalist argument is to propose that the burden is on the shoulder of the naturalist rather than the religious believer. Can there be occasions when a religious view of the world should be preferred unless naturalism can be given a plausible defense? Consider first the comparatively more modest claim that the burden of proof is shared equally by the religious believer and skeptic. For ease of reference, let us contrast naturalism and theism. Later we shall consider nontheistic claims based on religious experience, as well as the claim that no evidence at all is required for religious beliefs to be intellectually tenable.

Scott Shalkowski contends that it is not at all clear whether the atheist or theist bears the burden of proof. Both positions may be considered substantial theories of the way things are and, as such, both positions need justification:

> Of course, if the task is to show in a debate that "God" properly applies to some object, the onus [burden] is on the theist. But, if the context is inquiring about who, if anyone knows the correct propositions about the application of "God," then both sides have work to do. Flew's point about knowledge is if anyone knows anything it is in virtue of having good grounds for believing it. This applies to atheism and theism equally. (Shalkowski 1992, p. 60)

The parity between theism and atheism becomes apparent, according to Shalkowski, when one appreciates that atheism is a positive thesis, not a negative one. Atheists contend that a certain description and account of the cosmos is all there is; there is no divine reality:

> Suppose one fully delineated all the things in one's ontology and added that these are all the individuals there are. Is such a claim a positive claim, since it says only what there is and does not directly say anything about nonexistence, or is it a negative claim by virtue of the fact that it says the given list is exhaustive? By saying that the list is complete, one can certainly infer that many things do not exist. (Shalkowski 1992, p. 61)

As noted earlier, Hanson, Scriven and others develop the burden of proof argument using analogies such as the belief that there are goblins and that Santa Claus exists. Shalkowski thinks these analogies are unsuccessful:

> The reason adults disbelieve in Santa Claus is not simply that there is no good reason to think that he exists, but because we have good reason to think he does

not. At some point in our lives we found that those who let us in on the myth were conscious of the fact that they were telling us a falsehood. Our parents knew that they were telling us a lie and later we found this out. We disbelieve rather than suspend belief because at some point we learned of the wilful deception, participate in the process of decorating trees . . . But, this is not the situation with belief in God for most atheists. Atheists do come to hold the belief that theism is false and that there is some deception present in religious teaching and practice, but in the vast majority of cases this is not because someone like a parent confesses deceiving them at an early age, nor do atheists typically begin to participate in the production of the phenomena that is allegedly explained by the activity of God. (Shalkowski 1992, p. 63)

If Shalkowski is right, theists and atheists face the same task of providing some evidence or justificatory reason as to why we should accept their position.

But what about the prospects of a more radical reply to the naturalist burden of proof argument? Consider the plausibility of contending that the burden of proof is borne by the atheistic naturalist, not the theist. Many people approach the world religiously, believing that they do experience God or God's works. Might it be the case that for such persons, the charge that God does not exist would itself require considerable evidence in order to be justified? I note briefly how such a shifting of burdens might work with respect to the three theories of evidence.

Internalism

What follows is a range of considerations that may be marshaled according to foundationalist, critical cognitivist, and coherentist accounts of evidence.

Many people believe that they do experience God. Such experiences are sometimes described as direct, unmediated experiences of God or as mediated by experiences of nature, religious rites, other people, holy scriptures, dreams, art, profound good or ill fortune, and so on. Alvin Plantinga and others argue that the belief that God exists may be a fundamental, basic belief that is often involuntary and as fixed and stable as any of our other basic beliefs about ourselves and the world. Given the forceful, involuntary character of religious beliefs, Plantinga argues that religious beliefs may not be the sort of thing that religious believers can be under moral obligations to give up:

The suggestion [of Flew's and others] is that I now have the *prima facie* duty to comply with the following command: either have evidence or do not believe [God exists]. But this may be a command I cannot obey. I may not know of any

260

way to acquire evidence for this proposition [God exists]; and of course if the objector is right, there is no adequate evidence for it. But it is also not within my power to refrain from believing this proposition. My beliefs are not for the most part directly within my control. If you order me now, for example, to cease believing that the earth is very old, there is no way I can comply with your order. But in the same way it is not now within my power to cease believing in God. So this alleged *prima facie* duty is one such that it is not within my power to comply with it. But how can I have a duty, *prima facie* or otherwise, to do what it is not within my power to do? (Plantinga 1983, p. 34)

According to Plantinga, some persons may rightly hold theism as a basic tenet, a fundamental truth which (if theists are right) God led them to accept. As a basic tenet, it may well be a foundational belief that is not justified in terms of any deeper set of beliefs.

In Plantinga's view, the fact that not all persons accept theism as a basic tenet need not lead one to conclude that theists are unjustified or unentitled to their convictions:

[T]here is no reason to assume, in advance, that everyone will agree on the examples [of basic beliefs]. The Christian will of course suppose that belief in God is entirely proper and rational; if he does not accept this belief on the basis of other propositions, he will conclude that it is basic for him and quite properly so. Followers of Bertrand Russell and Madelyn Murray O'Hare [*sic*] may disagree; but how is that relevant? Must my criteria, or those of the Christian community, conform to their examples? Surely not. The Christian community is responsible to *its* set of examples, not to theirs. (Plantinga 1983, p. 77)

This proposal opens the door to competing views of the world and God (theistic and atheistic) being equally justified as starting points depending upon one's basic beliefs. But if plausible, Plantinga has articulated an account of beliefs and justification in which naturalists may face a burden of proof. In a theistic community in which persons take theism to be foundational and where there are no known reasons against theism, it may well be that naturalists face the charge of having to justify their position rather than vice versa.

Plantinga's sustained project on the warrant of religious belief has led him to think that belief in God may be properly basic and fully warranted without having to be justified in relation to standard arguments for God from the design of the cosmos, miracles and so on. Plantinga argues that the tendency to believe in God follows natural tendencies of the human mind:

> There is in us a disposition to believe propositions of the sort *this flower was created by God* or *this vast and intricate universe was created by God* when we contemplate the flower or behold the starry heavens or think about the vast reaches of the universe . . . Upon reading the Bible, one may be impressed with a deep sense that God is speaking to him. Upon having done what I know is cheap, or wrong, or wicked, I may feel guilty in God's sight and form the belief *God disapproves of what I have done.* Upon confession and repentance I may feel forgiven, forming the belief *God forgives me for what I have done.* A person in grave danger may turn to God, asking for his protection and help; and of course he or she then has the belief that God is indeed able to hear and help if he sees fit. When life is sweet and satisfying, a spontaneous sense of gratitude may well up within the soul; someone in this position may thank and praise the Lord for his goodness, and will of course have the accompanying belief that indeed the Lord is to be thanked and praised. (Plantinga 1983, p. 80)

This stance comprises what is now commonly referred to as *Reformed Epistemology*. Plantinga, Nicholas Wolterstorff and others appeal to the Reformed theologian John Calvin's thesis that we have a sense of God (*sensus divinitatus*) leading us to see God in the world around us. This sense of God does not simply trigger beliefs, as in Mavrodes' example cited earlier of how consuming alcohol may trigger someone's belief that he is witty. Rather, it makes belief in God warranted. Plantinga has thereby couched issues of justification within the larger arena of metaphysics. By advancing an intricate, comprehensive picture of how beliefs can be warranted when they function as God designed them, he has provided what some believe to be a combined metaphysical and epistemic case for the rationality of religious convictions.

While the above observations are grouped under the category of an anti-naturalist, internalist burden of proof argument, they are readily cast in terms of a reliabilist or virtue theory strategy as well.

Reliabilism and Virtue Theory

A burden of proof argument against naturalism may be developed using reliabilism and virtue theory. If theists are able to fill out an account like Plantinga's as to how one may reliably come to believe God exists through the exercise of a *sensus divinitatus*, it may be argued that it is the naturalist who needs to account for why such a belief-producing process is unreliable. Imagine one appears to experience or apprehend God. In such circumstances (so it is argued) claims to sense God may well be considered reliable until shown otherwise.

This appeal to the experience of God has captivated many philosophical theists. John Hick provides the following overview of an experientially-based, reasonable belief in God. He contends that the justification that we experience God is analogous to the justification we have for relying on sense experience:

> This, then, I suggest, is the way in which belief in the existence of God is to be justified. It is justified in basically the same way as our beliefs about "what there is and how things are" in our total environment: namely, by the impact of that environment upon us . . . In order for it to be rational for us to believe in the reality of entities which are ostensibly given in our experience, whether directly (as when we experience what is before us as a chair) or indirectly (as when we experience our lives as being lived in the unseen presence of God), two conditions have to be fulfilled. One is that we have responsibly judged (or reasonably assumed) it to be possible for such an entity to exist. The other is that it seems to be given in our experience in a powerful, persistent, and intrusive way which demands belief in its reality. When someone believes in the existence of God on the basis of compelling religious experience, his or her belief is accordingly a case of rational or reasonable or well-founded belief. (Hick, in Geivett and Sweetman [eds] 1992, p. 312)

Hick challenges the thesis advanced by Scriven, Flew, and others, that the theist and naturalist share the same body of beliefs about the world.

> There is a sense in which the religious man and the atheist both live in the same world and another sense in which they live consciously in different worlds. They inhabit the same physical environment and are confronted by the same changes occurring within it. But in its actual concrete character in their respective "streams of consciousness" it has for each a different nature and quality, a different meaning and significance; for one does and the other does not experience life as a continual interaction with the transcendent God. (Hick 1974, p. 281)

From a religious point of view the "virtue" of a naturalist like Clifford will appear more like a vice (failure of proper trust). If this is right, then the naturalist use of Ockham's razor will not be as easy to apply as Scriven et al. suppose.

Reliabilism may also serve to secure religious beliefs even if persons are not able to provide evidence for them. William Alston contends that to know something does not require that one know that one knows it or can provide grounds upon request:

263

[I]f I cannot show that my ground for believing that God is speaking to me at time t, or that God has promised salvation to those who repent and follow the way of the cross, is an adequate ground, is sufficiently indicative of the truth of the belief, it may *be* adequate nonetheless, and if it is, and if the other conditions for knowledge are satisfied, I will know that God is speaking to me at time t, or whatever, even though I may not know that I know this or be able to show that I know it. We must always be alive to the point that just as I may be resentful or witty without realizing that I am or being able to show that I am, so I may know that p without knowing that I do or being able to show that I do. At least, that is true on the relatively externalist approach to knowledge I am adopting, where the satisfaction of the conditions for knowledge does not depend on the subject's knowing or being able to show that they are satisfied, an approach I am prepared to defend. . . . And so it is quite possible that knowledge of God extends more widely than many of us suspect. (Alston 1991b, p. 285)

Reliabilism can thereby be used to deflect the charge that religious believers lack knowledge simply on the grounds that they cannot provide an explicit account of their evidence.

Central to much of this burden of proof argument in naturalism and Shalkowski's argument cited earlier, is the claim that religious experience is intelligible. Flew, Scriven, and others work with the assumption that religious experience is of no worth. Let us consider at closer range the status of religious experience in justifying beliefs about God or Brahman. In my view, it is only after a focused examination of the nature of religious experience that one can make further progress in considering whether naturalism has primacy or an initial advantage over non-naturalism. Can one reasonably (justifiably, reliably or virtuously) rely on what may be interpreted as the experience of God to justify one's belief that there is a God?

The Role of Religious Experience

An argument from religious experience may take the form of advancing a case for a specific religion or for a general religious thesis such as theism which is compatible with a wide range of religions. More generally still, the argument may simply take aim at naturalism. C. D. Broad held that religious experience vindicated this more modest aim:

The claim of any particular religion or sect to have complete or final truth on these subjects seems to me to be too ridiculous to be worth a moment's consideration. But the opposite extreme of holding that the whole religious experience of mankind is a gigantic system of pure delusion seems to me to be almost (though not quite) as farfetched. (Broad 1953, pp. 200–1)

Whatever its conclusion, most arguments from religious experience employ an analogy between religious experience and our ordinary experience of the world that will be important to consider.

John Hick, Keith Yandell, Richard Swinburne, and others argue that just as perceptual experience justifies our beliefs about the material world around us, religious experiences warrant beliefs about the divine or sacred. The argument is thus *a posteriori* as opposed to *a priori*. Yandell offers one version of this argument from religious experience, employing the term "numinous" to describe the experience of God. ('Numinous" is derived from the Latin *numen* for divinity or divine will.) As Yandell uses the term, a numinous experience may or may not involve sensations; it refers principally to sensing, perceiving, or the apprehending of God:

> A standard term for alleged experience of God is *numinous* experience, and its classic characterization goes something as follows. The subject, on the one hand, has a sense of being in some manner in the presence of a being who at least seems to have certain properties; on the other hand, the subject has certain responses to this sense of being in the presence of a being who at least seems to have these properties. The former is the core of the experience; the responses are conditioned by, or are functions of, the at least apparent existence of a being who seems worthy of attention. (Yandell 1984, p. 9)

In a numinous experience, *a person seems to apprehend a divine reality independent of oneself*. Subsequent experiences of, say, the desire to worship, venerate, delight in or fear the object of experience follow from this prior experience of what is assumed to be the reality of the divine:

> Numinous experience, then, is a complex phenomenon; the subject seems to experience a being which it would be laughable to regard as somehow the product, and not the object, of the experience; whatever the facts of the matter, the subject seems to be aware of something – more carefully, someone – distinct from and independent of himself or herself. (Yandell 1984, p. 10)

So, according to Yandell, sensations may be involved in such numinous experience with visual (colors, shapes, dimensions), auditory (noise or even speech), somesthetic (heaviness or hotness), gustatory (sweetness), or olfactory (fragrance) features. On the other hand, the experience of God may not have these sensory features.

Consider a report of the experience of God taken from the work of the twelfth-century monk St. Bernard of Clairvaux. This report appears to fit what Yandell would classify as a numinous experience:

> The Word [Jesus Christ] has visited me – indeed, very often. But, though He has frequently come into my soul, I have never at any time been aware of the moment of His coming. I have felt Him present, I remember He has been with me, I have sometimes even had a premonition of His coming, but never have I felt His coming or departure. . . . It is not by the eyes that He enters, for He has no colour; nor by the ears, for His coming is silent; nor by the nostrils, for He is blended with the mind, and not with the air; nor again does He enter by the mouth, for His nature cannot be eaten or drunk; nor lastly can we trace Him by touch, for He is intangible. You will ask then how, since His track is thus traceless, I could know that He is present? Because He is living and full of energy, and as soon as He has entered me, has quickened my sleeping soul, and aroused, softened and goaded my heart, which was torpid and hard as a stone. He has begun to pluck up and destroy, plant and build, to water the dry places, light up the dark places, throw open what was shut, inflame with warmth what was cold, straighten the crooked path and make rough places smooth. . . . In the reformation and renewal of the spirit of my mind, that is my inward man, I have seen something of the loveliness of His Beauty, and meditating on these things have been filled with wonder at the multitude of His greatness. But when the Word withdrew, all these spiritual powers and faculties began to droop and languish, as if the fire were taken from beneath a bubbling pot; and this is to me the sign of His departure. Then my soul must needs be sad and sorry, till He comes back and my heart again warms within me as it is wont; for this is to me the sign that He has returned. (Cited by Underhill 1975, pp. 86, 87)

Such testimonies are neither rogue nor merely intermittent in the history of human spirituality. See Evelyn Underhill's *Mysticism* for a good overview of the scope of religious experience, and for its sweeping and eloquent character (also see the references at the end of this chapter).

The analogy between religious experience and perceptual experience has been articulated by Yandell. He uses the word *phenomenology* (from the Greek *phenomenon* for "appearance" and *logos* for "knowledge of") to refer to the experiential character of appearance:

> If there is experiential evidence for any existential proposition, perceptual experiences provide evidence that there are physical objects; it is arbitrary not to

add that perceptual experience provides evidence that God exists, unless there is some epistemically relevant difference between sensory and numinous experience. The crucial similarities are that both sorts of experience are "intentional" and have phenomenologies, or can be expressed via "intentional" phenomenological descriptions. That perceptual experiences have sensory fillings or phenomenologies, and numinous experiences do not, by itself seems no more reason to think that numinous experience in no way supports the proposition *There is a God* than does the fact that numinous experiences have theistic fillings or phenomenologies, and perceptual experiences do not, by itself provides reason for thinking that perceptual experience in no way supports the proposition *There are physical objects.* (Yandell 1984, p. 11)

The analogy between perceiving God and perceiving material objects in one's immediate environment has been endorsed by a range of philosophers. C. S. Peirce treated religious experience as a kind of perception. "As to God, open your eyes – and your heart, which is also a perceptive organ – and you see him" (Peirce 1931–68, 6.493).

The argument from religious experience is rarely advanced to the effect that it secures infallible (incapable of error), incorrigible (incapable of correction) certainty about the divine. Rather, the most common claim by defenders of the argument is that religious experience provides *some* evidence for its conclusions about the divine. The ostensible experience of God is thereby described as *defeasible* in that it provides some evidence for its conclusion albeit the evidence is not decisive and so it is capable of being defeated or overridden by conflicting evidence.

The possibility that beliefs formulated on the grounds of numinous and other religious experiences could be mistaken is often held to be important but not a decisive objection to relying on such experiences in justifying religious beliefs. As Yandell writes: "It is logically possible that all numinous experiences are nonveridical; it also is logically possible that all sensory experiences are nonveridical" (Yandell 1984, p. 19). Is it possible that all our sensory experience could be mistaken? Scott Sturgeon considers whether one could be mistaken in the belief that one is now reading a book:

What is your evidence for this? Well, you seem to be reading. You have certain perceptual evidence of a page in front of you. You seem to see a book, and perhaps also to feel pages. This is the evidence which makes you justified in believing that you are reading. Hence this is the evidence on the basis of which you know that you are reading. This much is undeniable. But does your evidence rule out the *possibility* that you are not reading? Certainly not. Perhaps you are dreaming that you are reading, or perhaps hallucinating that you are reading, or perhaps your brain has been placed in a machine by evil scientists and manipulated to make you think you are reading. None of these possibilities is ruled out by the evidence on the basis of which you now believe that you are reading. But this doesn't mean that you actually fail to know whether you are reading. *Of course* you know that you are reading. (Sturgeon 1995, p. 16; the classic thought experiment highlighting the possibility of perceptual error is Descartes' *Meditations* of the seventeenth century)

If the bare possibility of error does not undermine the authority of our perceptual claims about the world, then (so it is argued) it should not erode perceptual claims about the divine. This strategy of putting religious and ordinary judgments about the world on an even playing field marks a common move by defenders of the argument from religious experience.

In assessing below the prospects of an argument from religious experience let us consider whether it provides some evidence for what Caroline Davis terms "broad theism." This position is useful as it stands roughly midway between tradition-specific arguments (in which a religious experience is held to justify beliefs that are specific to a single religion) and much less ambitious uses of the argument (e.g. securing Broad's comparatively more modest thesis cited earlier that naturalism may not be true). Davis summarizes what she takes to be the conclusion of a plausible version of the argument from religious experience in six areas:

(i)   The mundane world of physical bodies, physical processes, and narrow centers of consciousness is not the whole or ultimate reality.

(ii) In particular, the phenomenal ego of everyday consciousness, which most people tend to regard as their "self", is by no means the deepest level of the self; there is a far deeper "true self" which in some way depends on and participates in the ultimate reality.

(iii) Whatever *is* the ultimate reality is holy, eternal, and of supreme value; it can appear to be more truly real than all else, since everything else depends on it.

(iv) This holy power can be experienced as an awesome, loving, pardoning, guiding (etc.) presence with whom individuals can have a personal relationship, to whom they are profoundly attracted, and on whom they feel utterly dependent; it may be described positively in terms of goodness, wisdom, and so forth, but all such descriptions are ultimately inadequate.

(v)   Though introvertive mystical experiences cannot in themselves show that union with something else has been attained, since only the unity is experienced, the evidence of numinous experiences and the fact that

268

experiences of awe before the numen and love of the numen can easily slip into mystical experiences when all sense of self has been annihilated make it probable that at least some mystical experiences are experiences of a very intimate union with the holy power, however that is spelled out. (Other mystical experiences may nevertheless be no more than the integration or purification of the meditator's mind.)

(vi) Some kind of union or harmonious relation with the ultimate reality is the human being's *summum bonum*, his final liberation or salvation, and the means by which he discovers his "true self" or "true home." (Davis 1989, p. 191)

Davis's description of broad theism is intended to capture a host of factors that are found in diverse religious traditions and yet to give primacy to "theism" in an overriding account of religious experience. Thus, at (ii) the discovery of one's deeper self (as opposed to one's apparent or phenomenal self) and the testimony to be united with the numen or divine at (v), may suggest the Hindu teaching that each individual self is a manifestation of Atman which, in turn, is a manifestation of Brahman. Here, Davis is not invoking such a framework as a rival nontheistic model, but seeking to show how theism can appreciate and embrace important features of religious experience found outside explicitly theistic traditions. She notes that broad theism can allow for mystical experiences in which one feels united with the divine, albeit in a theistic understanding of God and human persons. Such a unitive experience would not involve a complete absorption of the person into God or a complete metaphysical collapse of the God–creature distinction.

A helpful way to consider whether broad theism (or any religious worldview) can be warranted on the basis of religious experience will be to organize a series of objections and replies. Consider the following six objections and replies to the thesis that broad theism is made evident in religious experience.

Objections and Replies

Some of the objections are closely related and may be seen as building on one another. In summary form, these are the objections that will be outlined below: (A) By their very nature, religious experiences alone are unable to count as evidence; (B) Religious experiences cannot be properly tested or checked for reliability; (C) Religious experiences are contradictory and are thus of no

269

evidential value; (D) The fact that many people do not have religious experiences is evidence that such experiences are unreliable; (E) Even if religious experiences provide some evidence for religious convictions, for those lacking them the reliance upon the testimony of these believers is negligible; (F) There are naturalistic explanations as to why persons report religious experiences and these explanations should be preferred unless a religious hypothesis (God or Brahman exists) is vindicated.

Just as the objections may be appreciated as forming a cumulative case against arguments from religious experience, the replies delimited below may be seen as part of a comprehensive strategy bolstering a case for broad theism. The replies are of different length, with the most attention weighted in response to (B) and (C).

(A) OBJECTION: Religious experiences cannot justify broad theism nor any substantial religious claims about the divine, for they are best regarded as bare feelings, sensations or undergoings that do not allow one to draw any such substantial conclusions. The experience of a sensation (hot/cold) might give one reason to reach conclusions about the world around one but this is because we operate with a secure, justified view about how our experiences are shaped by the objects around us. Thus, from my experience of heat I may come to learn that I inadvertently left the stove on, but the sensation of heat taken alone does not entitle me to reach such conclusions. Similarly, arguments from religious experience can, at best, provide additional evidence for one or more of Davis's conclusions only after the central case for "broad theism" has been established independently. To put the objection in a condensed form: Religious experiences do not have an evident, reliable referential content. Just as heat, by itself, does not refer to the stove but only serves as a sign or evidence of the stove in light of our vast, complex "commonsense" view of sensations, so religious experience alone cannot serve as evidence or a sign of God.

REPLY: While some religious experiences may plausibly be read as bare sensory states which subjects then interpret as stemming from God or the sacred (just as I might sense heat and then infer that it came from a stove), the experience itself is often described by subjects as including an explicit disclosure of the divine. That is, reports of experiencing the presence of God are often cast as occasions where God is apprehended as truly present. A better analogy for many religious experiences may be that in such experiences people feel themselves in the presence of God much like one feels an object pressing against one's skin and apprehends its shape, texture and temperature. This analogy may be more successful at suggesting the referential force (and possibly the passionate nature as well) of religious experience as opposed to suggesting religious experience is like a sensation of heat which one then infers must have come from a remote object.

Here is a passage from St. Teresa's account of experiencing God. This description suggests St. Teresa apprehends God experientially without having to rely on an independent belief that God is present:

> It is as if a person were to feel that another is close beside her; and though, because of the darkness, he cannot be seen, she knows for certain that he is there. This, however, is not an exact comparison, for the person who is in the dark knows that the other is there, if not already aware of the fact, either by hearing a sound or by having seen him there previously. But in this case nothing of that kind happens: though not a word can be heard, either exteriorly or interiorly, the soul knows with perfect clearness who is there, where he is and sometimes what is signified by his presence. Whence he [God] comes, and how, she cannot tell, but so it is, and for as long as it lasts she cannot cease to be aware of the fact. (Teresa of Avila, trans. 1946, p. 326)

St. Teresa's account has some similarities to St. Bernard's cited earlier. Consider one other description of the experience of God. This is recorded in William James's famous *Varieties of Religious Experience*:

> I was in perfect health: we were on our sixth day of tramping, and in good training. . . . I felt neither fatigue, hunger, nor thirst, and my state of mind was equally healthy. . . . I can best describe the condition in which I was by calling it a state of equilibrium. When all at once I experienced a feeling of being raised above myself, I felt the presence of God – I tell of the thing just as I was conscious of it – as if his goodness and his power were penetrating me altogether. The throb of emotion was so violent that I could barely tell the boys to pass on and not wait for me. I then sat down on a stone, unable to stand any longer, and my eyes overflowed with tears. . . . I think it well to add that in this ecstasy of mine God had neither form, color, odor, nor taste; moreover that the feeling of his presence was accompanied by no determinate localization. It was rather as if my personality had been transformed by the presence of a *spiritual spirit*. But the more I seek words to express this intimate intercourse, the more I feel the impossibility of describing the thing by any of our usual images. At bottom the expression most apt to render what I felt was this: God was present, though invisible; he fell under no one of my senses, yet my consciousness perceived him. (James 1958, pp. 62–3)

Like Yandell, Nelson Pike analyzes such experiences in terms of their ostensibly mediating an independent reality:

In this passage [just cited from James's work], the reporter seems clearly to be saying that the experience he is reporting was one in which he perceived himself to be in the presence of another, a "not-me" – someone whose goodness and power penetrated him completely. Further, Tramper [a term referring to the subject of James's report] says that the not-me in question was *God* – adding that this is to "tell of the thing just as I was conscious of it." On the most natural reading of the passage it would appear that Tramper is reporting an experience that was phenomenologically of God. In other words, it looks as if Tramper had a theistic experience. (Pike 1992, p. 117)

If Pike, Yandell and others are correct, then religious experiences may well at least appear to have God as their object.

Many defenders of the argument from religious experience contend that taking such awareness seriously is part of the structure of our very rationality. According to Richard Swinburne, it is a bedrock, rational assumption that we should trust appearances until we have good reason not to:

It is a principle of rationality that (in the absence of special considerations) if it seems (epistemically) to a subject that x is present, then probably x is present; what one seems to perceive is probably so. (Swinburne 1979, p. 254)

This principle is akin to a principle of testimony that is fairly widely embraced. H. H. Price advances this principle as: "Accept what you are told, unless you see reason to doubt it" (Price, in Chisholm [ed.] 1973, p. 115). If we have positive reasons for thinking broad theism is false then we may well have sufficient reason to place to one side the reports of religious experience. But, in the absence of such reasons, it is argued by Yandell, Swinburne and others, that one should trust appearances.

(B) OBJECTION: In ordinary perceptual experience there are ways of checking whether the conditions of perception are apt to be reliable. In religious experiences we lack such testability. There is no clear, objective way in which to determine, say, whether fasting or the use of drugs will enhance or compromise religious perception. C. B. Martin contends that for religious experiences to provide evidence for theistic conclusions one must possess a stable, reliable means of checking when the experiences are veridical. While we have such checks on perceptual experience, we do not possess them in a religious framework.

The presence of a piece of blue paper is not to be read off from my experience of a piece of blue paper. Other things are relevant: What would a photograph reveal? Can I touch it? What do others see? It is only when I admit the relevance of such checking procedures that I can lay claim to apprehending the paper, and, indeed, the admission of the relevance of such procedures is what gives meaning to the assertion that I am apprehending the paper. (Martin, in Flew and MacIntyre [eds] 1955, p. 77)

Richard Gale, Michael Martin, William Rowe, and others concur that while such checks are in good working order when it comes to perceptual claims about the world, they are woefully lacking when it comes to religious experience.

REPLY: In response it has been argued that it is not clear that there are objective, independent ways of checking for reliability even with respect to ordinary perceptual evidence. Is it conceivable that our whole perceptual system of beliefs could be mistaken? As noted earlier, it is very difficult to rule out such possibilities as impossible and, if so, then the bare impossibility of checking religious perception does not cast aspersions on it as a window on reality.

This reply, alone, will need some further extension however. If religious experience is largely capricious in its conflicting details and one is without any recourse in identifying proper conditions for experiencing (or sensing or becoming aware of) God, then arguments from religious experience will seem to have negligible force at best.

In the reply to the next objection, more will be said on the apparent difficulty that religious experience justifies conflicting pictures of ultimate reality. But here notice should be taken about the importance of describing the object of religious awareness in sufficiently broad terms so that it may cover (and show to cohere) a large array of features. This is partly why Caroline Davis's notion of *broad* theism is valuable.

It has been argued by Brand Blanshard and some other philosophers that an important reason why we trust our sensory, perceptual faculties is not so much because we can place them to one side and then check their reliability "independently," but because of the vast coherence of the picture of the world that we achieve when we rely upon them. In determining the fundamental reliability of the senses we distinguish between dream experiences and our experiences while awake, our being prey to hallucinations (from the Latin term for "to wander in mind") and our clear-headed, wide-awake view of things. Blanshard draws attention to the basis of our distinguishing between dream and waking states:

When we are suddenly roused from a vivid dream, we may be momentarily dazed, not knowing the dream from the actuality. How do we establish which

273

is which? Mere vividness does not decide the matter; the dream may be of nightmare intensity while the perception of our familiar surroundings may be comparatively dim. The deciding factor in the battle is what may be called the mass and the integration of the household troops. The bureau and windows of our familiar bedroom and the sound of a familiar voice throw out innumerable lines of connection that bring our everyday world around us again in irresistible volume. Against the great bulk of this world, and without any lodgment in it, the figures of our dream appear unsubstantial and fugitive, quickly dissolving for want of support. (Blanshard 1939, pp. 278–9)

Similarly, broad theists may defend their thesis that religious experience should be taken seriously as disclosing a divine reality by arguing that the great bulk and volume of religious testimony is coherent and vastly more substantial than vivid yet fugitive dreams, mirages, after-images, and so on. (More on this in the next objection and reply.)

Among the particular conditions for reliable religious experience, honesty and attentiveness are often singled out as necessities. Alan Donagan has specified the dual importance of avoiding carelessness and dishonesty as marking a duty in all our belief formation (Donagan 1977, p. 134). I. M. Crombie emphasizes honesty in his account of religious experience:

> All that is necessary is that he [a person who believes he has had an experience of God] should be honestly convinced that, in interpreting them, as he does, theistically, he is in some sense facing them more honestly, bringing out more of what they contain or involve than could be done by interpreting them in any other way. . . . There is a partial parallel to this in historical judgment. Where you and I differ in our interpretation of a series of events, there is nothing outside the events in question which can over-rule either of us . . . (Crombie, in Flew and MacIntyre [eds] 1955, p. 112)

Evelyn Underhill has emphasized how one's apprehension of the divine can be self-correcting, just as one can continually correct one's vision as one sees objects from different angles and in different lights.

As for whether drugs can facilitate religious perception, some philosophers have argued they can. For a fascinating portrait of how they might, see Aldous Huxley's splendid *The Doors of Perception*. Psychedelic (from the Greek for "soul" and "manifest") substances have been used in a range of religious contexts, famously the Aztec Peyote Cult and in various Native American traditions. There is an amusing reply to Huxley by R. C. Zaehner in his *Mysticism, Sacred and Profane*. In an effort to refute Huxley, Zaehner took an hallucinogenic and then recorded his subsequent conversations (see especially Appendix B: The Author's Experience with Mescalin). Alister Hardy strikes a conciliatory note as far as drug-use goes:

> It should not worry us if it is shown that altered states of consciousness may be produced by chemical means; the chemicals themselves do *not* produce the divine ecstasy, but affect the brain in such a way that a rarely accessible region of the sub-conscious mind becomes available to those who already have, perhaps unknown to them, a mystical streak within them. (Hardy 1979, p. 97)

Overall, though, perhaps Caroline Davis's position is the most widely represented and prudent:

> The use of drugs to induce religious experiences cannot be recommended, partly because of the dangers of drug use, and partly because experiences produced in such a way tend to be regarded as something separate from normal life and so may not become properly integrated into the subject's religious, psychological, and cognitive development. Most importantly, one must wonder how experiences which can be so easily manipulated can be reliable sources of knowledge about an uncontrollable, autonomous reality. (Davis 1989, p. 220)

It is due to this susceptibility of manipulation that drug-induced religious experiences are customarily underplayed as providing evidential force.

(C) OBJECTION: Religious experiences radically conflict with one another. They cannot all be true. Any evidential force they have is thereby compromised. This objection may be seen as directly challenging Caroline Davis's project of articulating a broad, coherent description of the object of religious awareness. Michael Martin advances the objection:

> Religious experiences . . . tell no uniform or coherent story, and there is no plausible theory to account for discrepancies among them. Again the situation could be different. Imagine a possible world where part of reality can only be known through religious experiences. There religious experiences would tend to tell a coherent story. Not only would the descriptions of each religious experience be coherent, but the descriptions of the experiences of different people would tend to be consistent with one another. Indeed, a religious experience in one culture would generally corroborate a religious experience in another culture. When there was a lack of corroboration, there would be a plausible explanation for the discrepancy. (Martin 1990, p. 159)

And he offers some of the following as marks of discrepancy:

275

> In the Western tradition, God is a person distinct from the world and from His creatures. Not surprisingly, many religious experiences within the Western tradition, especially nonmystical ones such as the experience of God speaking to someone and giving advice and counsel, convey this idea of God. On the other hand, mystical religious experience within the Eastern tradition tends to convey a pantheistic and impersonal God. The experience of God in this tradition typically is not that of a caring, loving person but of an impersonal absolute and ultimate reality. To be sure, this difference is not uniform: There are theistic trends in Hinduism and pantheistic trends in Christianity. But the differences between East and West are sufficiently widespread . . . and they certainly seem incompatible. A God that transcends the world seemingly cannot be identical with the world; a God that is a person can apparently not be impersonal. (Martin 1990, p. 178)

Because neither God nor any object can have contradictory properties, religious experience cannot serve as reliable evidence for theism or other religious hypotheses.

Martin's thesis may be bolstered by evidence that religious experience is profoundly shaped by independent social conditioning. Stephen Katz contends that all religious experiences are mediated by the conceptual schemes that give them life. As such, the experiences themselves are evidence of a person's background and training, but fail to function as clear channels of evident awareness of an external divine reality. The competing social context of different religious experiences can both explain why they are so diverse as well as further the general naturalistic project (to be considered below as the sixth objection) of explaining why persons have religious experiences without having to invoke God, Brahman et al.

> *There are no pure* (i.e. *unmediated*) *experiences*. Neither mystical experience nor more ordinary forms of experience give any indication, or any grounds for believing, that they are unmediated. That is to say, *all* experience is processed through, organized by, and makes itself available to us in extremely complex epistemological ways. The notion of an unmediated experience seems, if not self-contradictory, at best empty. This epistemological fact seems to me to be true, because of the sorts of beings we are, even with regard to the experiences of those ultimate objects of concern with which the mystics have intercourse, e.g. God, Being, nirvana, etc. (Katz 1978, p. 26)

It is because of our training in different cultural, religious contexts that some of us come to think we experience God or achieve Nirvana or harmony with the Tao. Because of the socially embedded character of these claims, they cannot be taken as quasi-scientific evidence that, say, God exists or Nirvana is possible.

REPLY TO C: As Martin suggests, religious experiences are not so limited to cultures that there are *no* similarities in a wide range of cultural settings. Moreover, as noted earlier, the prospects of "broad theism" are more promising here than comparatively more narrow conceptions of God's character, especially as one takes stock of the many religious traditions that have theistic strands. Arguably, broad theism is sufficiently extensive to describe or accommodate much of the central reported religious experiences in Judaism, Christianity, and Islam, and theistic traditions within Hinduism, Buddhism, African religions, Sikhism, aboriginal or primary religions, theistic Confucianism, and other religions.

Some of the differences Martin cites may be seen as less radical than they first appear. Martin notes the discrepancy between those who claim to experience a God that is identical with the world and a God that transcends the world. To be sure, there is no middle ground between thinking that God is identical with the world and thinking that God is not identical with the world. But some theologians have articulated a view of God that is at once embodied or immanent as well as transcendent. On this view, insistence upon the transcendence of God secures the conviction that God is more than the material, created cosmos. But having said that, it does not mean that God is less than the created cosmos or that the cosmos could not function in some way like a divine embodiment. The difference between God being "a caring loving person" and "an impersonal absolute and ultimate reality" may at first also seem a stark, uneliminable difference. But even here the contrast need not be strict. Could God be at once personal and yet also appear to have an impersonal aspect? God might be adequately described as a person insofar as God has intentions, knowledge and acts, and yet God may be described as impersonal in that God necessarily exists or that as an essentially good being God can function as a moral reference point (divine laws or principles) and thus appear as an abstract entity of sorts.

In harmony with Davis's emphasis on breadth, John Hick notes that the object of religious experiences is often thought of by those who report them as more general, rather than as having a narrow construction specific only to a given religion.

> The universe of faith centers upon *God*, and not upon Christianity or upon any other religion. He [God] is the sun, the originative source of light and life, whom all the religions reflect in their own different ways. (Hick 1980, p. 52)

Hick appeals to the role of conceptual schemes in shaping religious experience but in a way that does not undermine the evidential role of such experiences. In brief, his point is that even if religious experiences are conceptually forged by training and social setting (as supposed by Katz) this does not dispense with the vast, interconnected ways in which these different experiences of God or Nirvana or ultimate reality may be seen to converge.

> Because different ways of being human have produced a variety of such conceptual systems with their associated spiritual practices, the transcendent reality . . . postulated by a religious understanding of religion is experienced in a variety of ways which have become enshrined in the different religious traditions. (Hick 1993b, p. 21)

This view is not antithetical to the expressed beliefs and practices of religious traditions to the extent that they stress that the transcendent Being revealed in experience is greater than any given, narrow conception of it (Hick 1980, p. 81).

This strategy of trying to harmonize or accommodate the conflicting attributes of God is similar to the replies some philosophers offer to the argument of conflicting properties in sense perception. Faced with the quandary of how to explain how two persons may see the same object despite the fact that one person sees it as red and the other as nonred, we sometimes appeal to perspectives. On one common analysis, an object may be truly red but appear nonred under certain lighting conditions. If you correctly see the book as red whereas I see it as green we need not infer that I fail to see the book. There is no need to imagine that I am having an hallucination or seeing a hologram, for example. I may be seeing the red book *as it appears to me under different conditions or from a different point of view.* When it comes to colors we typically identify the "true color" of an object in relation to its appearance in sunlight. The reason for this is, in part, because that under such conditions we maximize our ability to discriminate between colors. John Hospers states the position as this bears on our ordinary judgments about colored objects. It may also be used in an analogy for religious experience:

> In daily life, we say that a thing has the quality it *appears* to have *under certain conditions.* We say the curtains in the room are blue; they look blue now, with the sunshine coming in through the windows. In artificial light they may look black. And in the dark they surely look black, as everything else does in the dark. Yet we don't say that at night everything – the curtains, the chairs and tables, and so on – have all *become* black. We say the curtains are blue all the time

278

even though they look black in the dark. We take the way they look in sunlight to be the color they "really have." Is this because sunlight is the condition in which we see them most of the time? No, sometimes it isn't: People who sleep during the day and are awake at night seldom see the "true color" of the curtains. It's not because it's the most usual condition, but because sunlight is the condition in which the *maximum color discrimination* is possible. A black dress and a dark blue dress may both look black in artificial light, but in sunlight we can tell the difference. We want to be able to describe that difference, which we all perceive, and so we take that as the *standard condition*. Thus we say "It's really dark blue, but it looks black under artificial light," and we do not say "It's really black, but only looks dark blue in sunlight." (Hospers 1988, pp. 54–5)

John Hick's model may provide a suitable analogy for this grasping of "true colors." According to Hick, the wide spectrum of religious conceptions of God, ultimate reality, or "the Real," would capture a maximal view of the diverse ways in which God or ultimate reality may be seen under various conditions. Gary Gutting's conclusion about the merits of the argument from religious experience comes close to this position (Gutting 1982). It is in lieu of what Gutting takes to be the diversity of religious experiences that he thinks the argument from religious experience cannot generate sufficient reasons for concluding that a specific religion is true rather than another. However, it is still enough evidence to believe that a broadly theistic outlook is justified.

In the previous chapter several reasons were posited as to why persons may come to ethical disagreements. A similar strategy may be employed here. Just as persons might agree about ethical principles but disagree about how these are to be applied, there may be agreement about certain general features of the divine or ultimate reality, though these will be articulated in very different terms depending upon one's social, cultural, religious context. Consider what might be the hardest case: correlating Buddhist religious experience with theism.

As noted in chapter 1, Buddhism is a fertile, diverse tradition with many strands. It is often considered atheistic, especially in its Theravada form, but this, it has been argued, is not obvious. Edward Conze writes:

Buddhist tradition does not exactly deny the existence of a creator, but it is not really interested to know who created the universe. The purpose of Buddhist doctrine is to release beings from suffering, and speculations concerning the origin of the universe are held to be immaterial to that task. (Conze 1975, p. 39)

Certainly Buddhism has produced philosophers who have been atheistic and committed to arguing against Hindu, Muslim and Christian conceptions of Brahman, Allah, and God. But if Conze is right this is not an *essential* mark of Buddhist tradition. Moreover, one can interpret some Buddhist concepts of Nirvana as very similar to a theistic notion of God.

> The ultimate reality, also called Dharma by the Buddhists, or Nirvana, is defined as that which stands completely outside the sensory world of illusion and ignorance, a world inextricably interwoven with craving and greed. To get somehow to that reality is the supremely worthwhile goal of the Buddhist life. The Buddhist idea of ultimate reality is very much akin to the philosophical notion of the "Absolute", and not easily distinguished from the notion of God among the more mystical theologians, like Dionysius Areopagita and Eckhart. (Conze 1975, pp. 110–11)

John Hick presses this point further in his own survey of Buddhist teachings of Nirvana. Far from Nirvana functioning as the name for something that may only be characterized in negative terms (such as loss of self), Hick proposes that it may also be read as naming a positive reality, not entirely dissimilar to a theistic picture of God:

> In the Pali scriptures of the Theravada, *nirvana* (*nibbana*) is certainly sometimes presented in purely negative terms as simply the cessation of the grasping self and its attendant anxieties. It is the "blowing-out" of the ego with its inevitable sorrows. But there is also in the tradition a strong element of positive and indeed supranaturalistic teaching about *nirvana*. Thus the Buddha declares, in a famous passage, "Monks, there is a not-born, a not-become, a not-made, a not-compounded. Monks, if that unborn, not-become, not-made, not-compounded were not, there would be apparent no escape from this here that is born, become, made, compounded." Again, in the *Majjhima-Nikaya nirvana* is described as "the unborn . . . unaging . . . undecaying . . . undying . . . unsorrowing . . . stainless", and in the *Samyutta-Nikaya* as "the further shore . . . the unfading . . . the stable . . . the invisible . . . the taintless . . . the peace . . . the deathless . . . the excellent . . . the blissful . . . the security . . . the wonderful . . . the marvellous . . . the free from ill . . . the island . . . the cave of shelter . . . the stronghold . . . the refuge . . . the goal". This sounds more like supranaturalistic-religious than naturalistic-humanist language. And it is, I think, so understood by most of the leading Theravadins of today. (Hick 1993b, pp. 172–3)

A recent study that backs up Hick's latter claim is Nerada Mahathera's commentary on *The Dhammapada*. Mahathera describes Nirvana as "the permanent, immortal, supramundane state which cannot be expressed in mundane terms" (Mahathera 1972, pp. 24–5). This would stand in for a theistic description of God, albeit theists would go on to claim much more, just as a Buddhist account of Nirvana would involve much more as well. The point is, though, that some overlap or family resemblance may be seen between these portraits of God and Nirvana.

But what if the difference between religions is indeed more radical than Hick grants and one cannot formulate a composite picture of them all? On such grounds one faces the question of whether or not it would be reasonable to adopt a religion even if there are equally good reasons to adopt a different religion. In some contexts, if the evidence is equally in favor of some proposition and equally against it, it is reasonable to withhold judgment and believe neither. Is agnosticism called for if experience is equally in favor of competing religious conceptions of reality?

William Alston maintains that it can be reasonable to adhere to one's own religious tradition even though other religious practices seem equally well grounded and secure in their own articulation of how things are on the basis of religious experience. Alston recognizes the challenge of competing mystical perceptions:

> Each of our rival (religious doxastic) practices is confronted with a plurality of uneliminated alternatives. Thus in the absence of sufficient independent reason, no one is justified in supposing her own practice to be superior in epistemic status to those with which it is in competition. (Alston 1991b, p. 270)

Alston concedes that the existence of these competing practices can lessen the justificatory force of religious experiences, but he believes that it does not compel one either to give up one's particular religious practice or to concede that one's own practice has no internal justificatory force. With specific focus on Christianity, Alston contends that while from the outside it may appear no more justified than an alternative practice, from within it may be seen to have a coherence and confirmation that gives its adherents additional justification:

> For given the equal social establishment of a number of mutually incompatible practices each with its built-in system of belief it is at least arguable that the most reasonable view, even for a hitherto committed participant of one of the practices, would be that the social establishment in each case reflects a culturally generated way of reinforcing socially desirable attitudes and practices, reinforcing these by inculcating a sense of the presence of a Supreme Reality and a way of thinking about it. That would imply that the justificatory efficacy of any of

these practices has been dissipated altogether. But . . . that is not the whole story. For both secular and religious practices, though in different ways, there are also significant forms of self-support that rightfully shore up the participants' confidence that the practice gives them at least a good approximation to the truth. In the case of CMP [Christian mystical practice] we say [earlier], that this significant self-support amounts to ways in which the promises God is represented by the practice as making are fulfilled when the stipulated conditions are met, fulfilled in growth, in sanctity, in serenity, peace, joy, fortitude, love, and other "fruits of the spirit." This, I submit, markedly changes the picture. In the face of this self-support it is no longer the case that the most reasonable hypothesis is that none of the competing practices provide an effective cognitive access to the Ultimate. It is by no means guaranteed that a social establishment of a religious system for the sake of desirable social goals will bring in its train a fulfillment of putative divine promises in the spiritual life of the devotees; the fact that this happens is a significant point in favor of the epistemic claims of the practice. Given the "payoffs" of the Christian life of the sort just mentioned, one may quite reasonably continue to hold that CMP does serve as a genuine cognitive access to Ultimate Reality, and as trustworthy guide to that Reality's relations to ourselves, even if one can't see how to solve the problem of religious pluralism, even if one can't show from a neutral standpoint that Christianity is right and the others are wrong on those points on which they disagree. (Alston 1991b, p. 276)

More will be discussed in the next section of this chapter and in chapters 9 and 10 about the limits of justification and pragmatic arguments for and against theism.

(D) OBJECTION: Religious experiences may or may not admit of the convergence suggested by Hick and others, but there are many people who fail to have any religious experience whatever. The fact that only some have such experiences suggests that religious awareness is very different from perceptual awareness. While some lack sensory organs and therefore are not capable of apprehending some of the sensible aspects of their environment, it is odd that some persons lack religious abilities or religious faculties or organs by which God may be grasped. Is such disparity the result of some persons lacking a nonphysical religious organ or faculty? There is a further problem in positing such disparity in religious powers and abilities in terms of the problem of evil. If there is an all-good God, and the felt experience of being in God's presence is a great good, surely God would ensure that there is maximal experience of God. The fact of there being such disparity and failure of uniformity in this area is a reason for thinking that there is no stable religious cognition as required by the argument.

REPLY: There are serious issues at stake here in terms of the problem of evil. A defense of God's goodness in the face of there being an uneven distribution of experiential awareness of God may well have to appeal to many factors. These may include arguing that while experiencing God is a great good, it is not something that any created being has a right to and therefore not something God has a duty to produce. Perhaps this stand may be bolstered by arguing that God, as the Creator and thus the owner of the cosmos, is not bound to produce the greatest possible goods for all beings. It may also be contended that while the experience of God is good, there may be a good to be gained by living life in some autonomy from God without a felt awareness of God. In some religious contexts, this may be thought of as a necessary condition for the development of faith. Many atheists stress the good of living courageously without a reliance upon God. It may be that by God not being overwhelmingly evident to people experientially, there is an arena in which a host of virtues are possible that would be obscured otherwise. More on these concerns later in chapter 9.

Some theists have contended that differences in the ability to sense God need not amount to differences in some mystical or religious organ – like a spiritual eye or nonphysical ear. Some of our other faculties like memory, the imagination, and reason do not seem to require positing organs and it is not clear why a defender of religious experience should have to do so either. A. E. Taylor compares the variation in the ability to experience the world religiously with variation of aesthetic appreciation and perception:

> A man with the artist's eye, we very rightly say, "sees beauty" everywhere, while a man without it goes through life not seeing beauty anywhere, or at best seeing it only occasionally, where it is too prominent to be missed. . . . however truly beauty may pervade the whole of things, there are special regions where its presence is most manifest and obvious. What is characteristic of the artist is that he makes just these elements of experience a key to unlock the meaning of the rest. So the religious man, no doubt, means the man who sees the whole of reality under the light of a specific illumination, but he has come to see all things in that light by taking certain arresting pieces or phases of his experience as the key to the meaning of the rest. (Taylor, in Hick [ed.] 1990, pp. 153–64)

C. D. Broad adopts a similar approach:

> Let us, then, compare tone-deaf persons to those who have no recognizable religious experience at all; the ordinary followers of a religion to men who have some taste for music but can neither appreciate the more difficult kinds nor

compose; highly religious men and saints to persons with an exceptionally fine ear for music who may yet be unable to compose it; and the founders of religions to great musical composers, such as Bach and Beethoven. (Broad 1953, p. 190)

Differences in religious awareness are thereby cast in terms of differences in the development of certain skills or of practices such as developing appreciative hearing and seeing in the arts.

(E) OBJECTION: Even if religious experiences confer evidence for the existence of God or Brahman for the person who has these experiences, their evidential weight for those who do not is considerably diminished if not rendered negligible. Testimony on such matters that go beyond the basic, commonsense naturalism of everyday experience, should be considered untenable until proven to be justified. Religious experience is too rare to provide substantial evidence for religious claims.

REPLY: It is true that testimony will introduce another stage or step between oneself and the object of the testimony and thus introduce a new concern for evidence, *viz.*, one needs evidence both for the integrity and honesty of witnesses as well as for the reliability of their experiences. A defender of the argument from religious experience may nonetheless first argue that reliance upon the extant testimony is eminently reasonable and, second, that religious experience is more widespread than often supposed.

First, then, it can be argued that the appeal to testimony is radically bound up in the justification of many of our beliefs. If the evidence of the testimony of others were eradicated, our lives would be shaken to the core. Elizabeth Anscombe describes the role of testimony in vivid terms:

Nor is what testimony gives us entirely a detachable part like the thick fringe of fat on a chunk of steak. It is more like the flecks and streaks of fat that are often distributed throughout good meat; though there are lumps of fat as well. (Anscombe, cited by Kenny 1983, p. 41)

The second point theists have made is that the existence of religious experience may be far more pervasive than is typically recognized. H. D. Lewis has lamented how religious experience is often treated as a highly exalted, discrete, ecstatic undergoing, whereas, on his view, the sense of the divine is far more prevalent as an elusive awareness of a higher power or transcendent reality:

We certainly do an ill service to religion if we smother or alienate or underestimate the vague and inarticulate and much bewildered sense of something elusively and irretrievably "beyond" which is also intertwined with present reality, the sense of ultimate but sustaining mystery in which all religion begins. (Lewis 1962, p. 48)

Perhaps the attention given to more "exotic" reports of religious experience has led us to a diminished view of the pervasiveness of religious experience and its forming a large part of many people's lives.

A new move by some feminist philosophers is important to note in this context. Grace Jantzen has critiqued the current treatment of religious experience in the philosophical literature for its depicting religious, mystical experiences as largely private and personal: "Contemporary philosophers of religion have a clear presupposition that mystical experiences are private, subjective, intense psychological states" (Jantzen 1994, p. 192). According to Jantzen, religious and mystical experience may be understood as more widespread and much more bound up with issues of social justice, moral experience, social relations and other public matters. Indeed, many mystics in all the extant world religions have understood their pursuit of justice as part of their responsiveness to God, Brahman, the sacred, the vital compassion of Buddha, the call of Allah, and so on. Jantzen laments the failure to take seriously this aspect of mysticism as well as the more commonplace, public, political and ethical dimensions of many reported religious experiences:

> In the philosophical study of mysticism, with its assumption that mystical experience is an essentially private, subjective matter which, as such, does not connect with issues of social justice, feminism has yet to make an impact. If this amounted only to there being a small academic enclave which had not taken feminist scholarship into account and which insisted on defining and studying mysticism in male-dominated ways, that would be bad enough, though feminists might well decide that in a world of starving children, battered women, and rising fascism we had more important things to do than to spend energy trying to change the minds of philosophers of religion. But the situation is very much more serious. (Jantzen 1994, p. 199)

So, while many people may not have religious experiences, and thus (if the argument works) have to rely on the testimony of others, it can be argued that religious experiences are far more pervasive than is often noted in the philosophical literature. And, if Jantzen is right, there are overriding ethical reasons to treat with greater seriousness the more embedded, politically important role of religious experience.

    (F) OBJECTION: Even if it is granted that religious experience can provide *some* evidence for broad theism, shouldn't a naturalistic hypothesis still always be preferred? Michael Martin advances the naturalist position as follows:

> The problem . . . is that there is a rival hypothesis. One might suppose that a person's religious experience is caused not by some external reality but by the workings of the person's own mind. On this theory, a religious experience would have an origin similar to that of delusion and delirium. But then religious experience would have no objective import and would not be trustworthy at all. (Martin 1990, p. 158)

Given that one can fashion a reasonable explanation of religious experience from a naturalist, scientific point of view, will it not always be the simpler hypothesis and thus the one we should elect rather than the comparatively more ambitious theistic theory? There are many naturalist projects designed to explain the emergence and persistence of religious experience and belief. Sigmund Freud (1856–1939) held that theism was the fruit of deep psychological causes which led people to project a heavenly Parent to placate infantile needs, while Karl Marx (1818–83) argued that theistic religious belief and experience was explainable in terms of economic, social and political development. Independent of the details of either explanatory scheme, should some naturalist account not always be preferred over a more flamboyant, supernaturalist account?

REPLY: It is easy to sympathize with this strategy. But, as with the reply to the burden of proof arguments above, some philosophers argue that privileging naturalism from the outset is question begging and fails to take seriously the natural, basic ways in which the world may be experienced (described and explained) in religious categories. And it is argued, too, that many of the accounts used to explain the origin of religion can be used to explain the origin of religious skepticism. Richard Purtill writes:

> Some of the specific mechanisms described by Freudians seem equally apt as an explanation for a lack of religious belief. If the Oedipus complex is as basic as Freud thought it to be, any rejection of God can surely be explained on good Freudian grounds as the desire to reject and abolish the father and have undisputed possession of "mother" earth. (Purtill 1974, p. 36)

Those opposed to naturalism such as Purtill argue that explanations of theism require a substantial theoretical context. That is, if naturalism is assumed to be established, these specific naturalist arguments carry significant weight. But, by the same token, if theism is assumed to be true, then there are ample explanations theists can resort to in explaining why there are not more theists.

What constitutes the simplest or most reasonable account of why religious believers report the experiences they do? This will depend, in part, on one's assessment of the overall weight of evidence and the coherence of religious and nonreligious views of the cosmos. Consider, then, the way in which different arguments for a philosophical position can form part of a cumulative case for or against a comprehensive view of God, Brahman, the cosmos, and ourselves.

Cumulative Arguments for Comprehensive Philosophies

I begin with an analogy. It is a common (though certainly not universal) practice in painting a landscape to make a sketch to secure the composition first, otherwise one risks an entirely disjointed picture. In developing a coherent painting, one may well aim to produce first what amounts to a skeleton or the outline of a structure, which one then gradually builds up in the course of painting objects in the painting's composition rather than, say, painting the objects as separate objects and then sticking them into the painting. The various parts of a painting taken by themselves may seem aesthetically flat and uninteresting, but taken together form an overall dynamic picture with its own interesting content. Similarly, when considering the coherence of a world-view and the reasons for it, it is important to take into account its overall structure and evidence. Like producing a coherent painting, it is crucial to take into account the composition as a whole, the size and depth of its components as they work together, and not just focus on the parts in isolation.

Another artistic analogy may help to accentuate the role of an argument from religious experience as part of a cumulative case for theism. Some artists use underpainting. A whole canvas may first be painted a color which one then paints over. One may paint a canvas burnt umber, say, and then paint a landscape. While the burnt umber may not directly be seen, the color yet works with the other colors and shapes to give the painting as a whole a given character (tone, mood) that it would otherwise lack. Similarly, some theists argue that if the argument from religious experience carries some weight (albeit not decisive), it may function as a background source of justification that can inform and assist other arguments. Thus, imagine that an argument from the apparent design or purposive character of the cosmos provides some evidence of a divine designer, but not sufficient by itself to vindicate broad theism. If an argument from religious experience is also taken to provide some evidence for theism, there may be a cumulatively stronger case for theism given both arguments rather than either considered alone.

Clearly we have moved some distance from the confident claims of earlier philosophers to have proved God exists. But there are still philosophers, theists and naturalists alike, who see their work in a broad context for which evidence does not come in piecemeal bits but must be weighed in a comprehensive, synthetic fashion. To describe the current philosophical climate in a fanciful way, there is now a more ecological approach to arguments, an appreciation of how arguments may be mutually supportive or form parts of larger theories.

I believe that it is only in light of this bigger project that we can come to terms with the question of whether evidence is a purely intellectual requirement for religious or naturalist beliefs. If one's religious beliefs are sufficiently radical and would greatly risk evident harms for the sake of nonevident goods, then it seems natural and plausible to demand that such beliefs receive considerable evidential justification. For example, a belief that God commands one to injure another person would be a prime case of a belief that should not be held without weighty evidence. But matters may differ when the case concerns religious beliefs that appear to cause no harm or appear to bring about goods, goods that are appreciated from an independent, naturalist point of view. Consider a religious belief that God commands one to be compassionate, help the vulnerable, relieve famine, fight environmental degradation, and so on. Imagine the belief is in fact true but not known to be true by Jane Doe who has a "feeling" it is true but nothing she believes amounts to evidence. Does she do something wrong by holding this belief about God? Blaise Pascal (1623–62) and William James (1842–1910) argued that in certain cases when the evidence is not clear, it is reasonable to wager on the truth of religious beliefs. A similar wager argument is outlined in chapter 10. Prior to taking up this argument, I propose here that one's views about Jane Doe's intellectual responsibilities are best seen in light of an overall assessment of the intellectual and ethical costs and benefits of theism, naturalism, and other world views.

A common move by some theists in their cumulative argument for God's existence is to spell out respects in which theism is fundamentally more simple and provides what they take to be a more elegant explanation of the cosmos than its alternatives. Richard Swinburne is perhaps the best known advocate of this stance, and it will be useful to reference his work here to set the stage for discussing the theistic and atheistic arguments of the next two chapters.

According to Swinburne, theism is a profoundly simple, though comprehensive world-view, beginning with its positing a supremely great being:

> To start with, theism postulates a God with capacities which are as great as they logically can be. He is infinitely powerful, omnipotent. That there is an omnipotent God is a simpler hypothesis than the hypothesis that there is a God who has such-and-such limited power (e.g., the power to rearrange matter, but not the power to create it). It is simpler in just the way as the hypothesis that some particle has infinite velocity rather than a velocity of 301,000 km/sec. A finite limitation cries out for explanation of why there is just that particular limit, in a way that limitlessness does not . . . There is . . . a neatness about zero and infinity which particular finite numbers lack. Yet a person with zero capacities would not be a person at all. So in postulating a person with infinite capacity the theist is postulating a person with the simplest kind of capacity possible. (Swinburne 1979, p. 94)

Swinburne contends that this ultimately simple view of God stands in sharp contrast to the complexity of the cosmos. By his lights, the power of theism to explain the complex material world counts as a great advantage:

> A complex physical universe (existing over endless time or beginning to exist at some finite time) is indeed a rather complex thing. We need to look at our universe and meditate about it, and the complexity should be apparent. There are lots and lots of separate chunks of it. The chunks each have a different finite and not very natural volume, shape, mass etc. – consider the vast diversity of the galaxies, stars, and planets, and pebbles on the seashore. Matter is inert and has no powers which it can choose to exert; it does what it *has* to do. There is just a certain finite amount, or at any rate finite density of it, manifested in the particular bits . . . There is a complexity, particularity, and finitude about the universe which cries out for explanation. (Swinburne 1979, p. 130)

While theists argue that this explanation must be located in God, naturalists and other atheists either locate it in the cosmos itself or deny that the cosmos does indeed cry out for such an explanation.

The last chapter of this book surveys some of the key theistic arguments now under debate, but first we shall consider what is probably the strongest argument against theism. Some naturalists and other atheist philosophers charge that the problem with theism is precisely its simplicity in positing God as all good, omnipotent and omniscient. As the author of the cosmos, why did

God allow evil? In the eyes of many philosophers and nonphilosophers, the horrors of the world cry out for an explanation, and theism is found wanting. To use the art analogies cited earlier, many naturalists argue that theism fails to provide us with a coherent painting of the way the world is. Moreover, the underpainting (as it were) of religious experience simply intensifies the unsatisfactory character of theism. Perhaps some persons are justified in thinking there is a God of love on the basis of apparent experiences of God. But there is no doubt at all that we are subject to great evils and that enormous numbers of innocent persons have met with cruel, agonizing deaths. How can there be an all-good, all-powerful God in the face of such evil?

Suggested Questions and Topics

(1)   One of the most prominent defenders of the notion that we have strict duties never to hold beliefs beyond persuasive evidence was W. K. Clifford. Do you agree or disagree with Clifford's ethics of belief as laid out in the passage cited in this chapter?

(2)   As noted in this chapter, Swinburne adopts a principle of rationality according to which one should trust appearances until one has good reason to do otherwise. William Alston likewise holds that all socially established doxastic practices are "innocent until proven guilty," "they all deserve to be regarded as prima facie rationally engaged . . . pending a consideration of possible reasons for disqualification" (Alston 1991b, p. 153). Do you agree or disagree with Swinburne and/or Alston?

(3)   Does it make sense to suppose that one can perceive God or Brahman in a nonsensory fashion? In a phrase, is such nonsensory perception nonsense?

(4)   General questions on evidence and justification: Can one rightly be said to know something if one cannot provide evidence as to why one believes it? If you know something, do you know that you know it? You may wish to consider the religious repercussions of each of the accounts of evidence outlined in this chapter. If there are normative, evidential relations, do you believe these may be altered by God? Granted that certain experiences make some belief evident (seeing what appears to be a swan is justification for believing you see a swan), can God alter these such that these experiences do not justify the belief? To structure such an essay question, you may wish to consider how William Mann's portrait of God's determining what counts as

good in general might be applied in considering whether God can fix what counts as good in the pursuit of evidence and knowledge:

> God's will does not operate by acknowledging the good-making intrinsic properties of things; his will establishes what properties *count* as good-making. Analogous remarks apply to badness or evil. God could have created a world whose inhabitants are incapable of scientific discovery, aesthetic appreciation, and moral sentiment, who are exquisitely sensitive to the pain to which they are perpetually subjected, and who rise above that pain solely to inflict torture on helpless animals. Had God declared that world to be good, *ipso facto* it would have been good. Had he "seen" that the actual world, the world he did create, was very rotten, it would have been very rotten. Any world God picks can have any dimension of value he declares it to have, just in virtue of his act of declaration. The pursuit of wisdom is a good thing, but it might have been replaced by the practice of sadism. Charity is a virtue, but in some possible worlds hardness of heart is the summum bonum. (Mann, in MacDonald [ed.] 1991, p. x; in this passage Mann presents what he takes to be Scotus' position)

You may wish to consider the prospects of a Euthyphro dilemma in the theory of knowledge (see Plato's dialogue the *Euthyphro* for details). Is X evidence for Y because God wills that it be so, or does God will that X is evidence for Y because such a relation is binding?

(5)   Imagine the grounds for believing that God exists are not accessible universally (to the majority of reflective persons, for example). Assess J. C. A. Gaskin's argument about the implications of this state of affairs. Do you agree or disagree?

> If we have grounds other than the experiences themselves for believing that God exists, then his selective revelation of himself would account for the solitary and frequently unshared experiences which people have of him. On the other hand, if we do not have other grounds for believing in his existence, then it will remain a more simple and obvious explanation for the selective experiences if we take them to be internal, and caused by social and psychological factors. (Gaskin 1984, p. 100)

(6)   Consider Anthony O'Hear's critique of religious experience as a source for justified beliefs about the divine. How would you either elaborate and defend O'Hear's thesis or, rather, defend the appeal to religious experience?

> The likelihood of an objective reality being causally related to certain experiences will be very much increased if (i) we are able to predict accurately further

experiences of our own or others due to our assuming the existence of the reality, (ii) some of these future experiences of our own are experiences of senses other than the original sense involved, and (iii) other people can corroborate what we are perceiving . . . Condition (iii) reflects the not unreasonable presumption that if something is objectively real, it will have similar effects on other similar observers similarly placed . . . The religious interpretation of religious experience, however, comes off quite badly under all three conditions . . . The judgement that one has had a divine experience is quite unlike the judgement that one has seen a table in that it appears to lead to no testable independent predictions. Moreover, in many religious traditions, it is a key aspect of religious experience that it is unpredictable. Christians, for example, tend to explain this unpredictability by saying that these experiences are a gift of God. This may be so, but saying it certainly weakens the attempts to argue form the experience to the reality. (O'Hear 1984, pp. 44–6)

(7) Anthony Kenny develops this argument against there being a sense experience of God. According to Kenny, God cannot be seen or sensed because God (if God exists) is omnipotent. You may wish to consider possible replies to this argument or ways in which it may be further strengthened.

If there is a God with the attributes ascribed to him by Western theism, then He is everlasting, unchanging, and ubiquitous. In relation to such an object there cannot be any activity of discrimination resembling the discriminatory activities of the senses: we cannot have a sixth sense which detects that God is here and not there, as we can see that something is red at one end and not at another, or which detects that God was a moment ago and is not now, as we can hear a noise which suddenly stops. If God is everywhere always, there can be no sense to discriminate the places and times where he is from those where he is not; the whole nature of a sense is an ability to tell differences of this kind. A sense of God would be as absurd as a sense of sight whose only function was to detect a uniform unchanging whiteness or a sense of hearing whose only function was to listen to a single unchanging middle C. Seeing whiteness only makes sense amid telling one color from another; hearing middle C involves telling it from other notes. One cannot get nearer to or get further from God as one can get nearer to or further from a source of light or sound: one cannot be too early or too late to encounter him as one might be to see or hear something. The whole context within which talk of sense-experience makes sense is lacking in the case of alleged sense-experience of God. (Kenny 1983, p. 60)

(8) Helen Keller (1880–1968) was blind, deaf, and could not speak. She eventually learned language and communication skills through the assistance of A. M. Sullivan. Consider how Keller's description of her self-awareness

might be cast in a religious context of coming to understand oneself over against or in relation to the divine, highlighting the philosophical issues at stake. You may wish to consider how this discovery of one's identity may have an analogy in Caroline Davis's account of "broad theism," condition (ii). Alternatively, you may wish to build a case for the profound disanalogy between Keller's self-awareness and self-awareness in a religious context.

> Before my teacher came to me, I did not know that I am. I lived in a world that was a no-world. I cannot hope to describe adequately that unconscious, yet conscious time of nothingness. I did not know that I knew aught, or that I lived or acted or desired. I had neither will nor intellect. I was carried along to objects or acts by a certain blind natural impetus . . . I had a power of association . . . After repeatedly smelling rain and feeling the discomfort of wetness, I acted like those about me: I ran to shut the window. But that was not thought in any sense. It was the same kind of association that makes animals take shelter from the rain. When I learned of the meaning of "I" and "me" and found that I was something, I began to think. Then consciousness first existed for me. (Keller 1904, pp. 141–3, 145)

(9)   Can the moral and spiritual flourishing of those who claim to have religious experiences lend credibility to their claims? Alston notes how the Christian mystical practice is tied in with the development of a life of compassion and virtue. You may wish to utilize Alston's thesis here in considering whether character development can serve in some way to authenticate religious claims about God's existence.

> CMP [CP], including the associated Christian scheme that has been built up over the centuries, generates, among much else, the belief that God has made certain promises of the destiny that awaits us if we follow the way of life enjoined on us by Christ. We are told that if we will turn from our sinful ways, reorder our priorities, take a break from preoccupation with our self-centered aims long enough to open ourselves to the sanctifying work of the Holy Spirit, then we will experience a transformation into the kind of nonpossessive, nondefensive, loving, caring, and sincere persons God has destined us to become. (Alston 1991, p. 252)

(10)   How might drug-use affect the argument from religious experience? Assess Yandell's treatment of drugs and evidence. What, if anything, might allow drug-induced experience to count as evidence for religious claims about God or the divine?

293

From all this, it seems to follow that if Ralph has been given the right sort of drug dosage to produce a numinous, or near-numinous, experience, the occurrence of that experience will not do much to epistemically enhance the claim that there is a numinous being or that God exists, for we (and he) will be in a good position to explain that experience without our making any reference to God, just as it follows that if Ralph has had enough alcohol to produce the perceptual, or near-perceptual, experience of seeming to see vermin, the occurrence of that experience will not do much to epistemically enhance the claim that the walls are covered with vermin, for we (and he) will be in a good position to explain that experience without our making any reference to vermin. Ralph, in these cases, may experience God or the vermin, but the experiences (numinous in the former case, perceptual in the latter) will not be *evidence* that this is so. But it is not clear why any of this should affect the epistemic status of cases in which numinous experience occurs without drugs having been taken, or walls are seen as vermin-infested without any white lightning having been imbibed. (Yandell 1984, p. 20)

(11)   What are the limits of what may be revealed in religious experience? John Hick advances this question:

How can you tell from the voice alone that the being you heard was omnipotent, omniscient, and completely free? How can you distinguish the voice from an enormously powerful but finite being – a being with, say powers 1,020,000 times greater than any human? . . . Answers in terms of the pitch, volume, intensity, and other typical qualities of voices would hardly be adequate. (Hick 1966, p. 181)

You may wish to consider different replies to the above passage or to the following statement of the problem:

God is described in Christian theology in terms of various absolute qualities, such as omnipotence, omnipresence, perfect goodness, infinite love, etc., which cannot as such be observed by us, as can their finite analogues, limited power, local presence, finite goodness, and human love. One can recognize that a being whom one "encounters" has a given finite degree of power, but how does one recognize that he has *un*limited power? How does one observe that an encountered being is *omni*present? How does one perceive that his goodness and love, which one can perhaps see to exceed any human goodness and love, are actually infinite? Such qualities cannot be given in human experience. (Hick 1966b, p. 189)

(12)   Terence Penelhum construes fideism (literally faith-ism) as follows:

Philosophical defenders of faith have commonly tried to show that it is not at odds with reason: that it is internally consistent, that it accords with scientific knowledge, or even, more positively, that some of its tenets can be established independently by philosophical reasoning. Fideists reject this mode of apologetic argument, and maintain, in contrast, that faith does not need the support of reason, and should not seek it. (Penelhum 1997, p. 376)

Assess what you take to be the best defense of fideism. Tertullian (155–222) is often celebrated as a premier fideist. His dictum was "I believe because it is absurd" (*credo quia absurdum est*). Is it even coherent to believe something is true that you take to be absurd (not only unjustified but at odds with what you take to be nearly decisive reasons for thinking it false)?

(13)   You may wish to consider the strength and weakness of an argument for naturalism based on the appeal to experiencing the absence of God.

(14)   Swinburne contends that the argument from religious experience is crucial in his cumulative argument for theism.

I concluded the last chapter [of his book, *The Existence of God*] . . . with the claim that unless the probability of theism on other evidence is very low indeed, the testimony of many witnesses to experience apparently of God suffices to make many of those experiences probably veridical. That is, the evidence of religious experience is in that case sufficient to make theism overall probable. The argument . . . was that the testimony of many witnesses to experiences apparently of God makes the existence of God probable if it is not already on other evidence very improbable. I believe that I have shown in this chapter that that condition is well satisfied and hence . . . on our total evidence theism is more probable than not. (Swinburne 1979, p. 289)

What is your view of the evidential contribution of religious experience? You may wish to consider the function of religious experience in either supporting or challenging some other theistic or atheistic arguments (e.g. the problem of evil – the cosmological argument to be reviewed in chapter 10 – and so on).

(15)   Basil Mitchell offers the following analogy of cumulative arguments. You may wish to assess it critically or to devise your own analogy of how cumulative reasoning is credible.

In a ship at sea in stormy weather, the officer of the watch reports a lighthouse on a certain bearing. The navigating officer says he cannot have seen a lighthouse, because his reckoning puts him a hundred miles away from the nearest land. He must have seen a waterspout or a whale blowing or some other marine phenomenon which can be taken for a lighthouse. The officer of the watch is satisfied he must have made a mistake. Shortly afterwards, however, the lookout reports land on the starboard bow. The navigating officer, still confident in his working, says it must be cloud – and it is indeed very difficult to distinguish cloud from land in these conditions. But then a second cloud-looking-like-land or land-looking-like-cloud appears on another bearing. It really does begin to look as if the navigator might be out in his reckoning. He has, perhaps, underestimated the current, or his last star sight was not as good as he thought it was. The reported sightings are consistent with one another and indicate that he is approaching land. . . .

The question whether there was a lighthouse there and the question whether the officer of the watch saw it or saw something else, or just imagined that he saw it, can only be answered in relation to some overall appraisal of the situation. The navigator's original appraisal, based on his dead reckoning, led him to say there was no lighthouse and the officer of the watch did not see it; and this was reasonable enough at that stage. But the other reports, although their evidential value, taken singly, is as slight and as controversial as the first, do cumulatively amount to a convincing case for reading the whole situation differently. (Mitchell 1981, pp. 112–13)

(16)   It has been argued that we do not see remote physical objects directly or immediately because there is a time delay between our seeing such objects and the way the objects are at that time. Thus, for me to see the moon directly or immediately I would have to see it as it is at the time of my observations. But because light travels at a finite rate, what I see when I see the moon is the state of the moon some four minutes earlier. Analyze this argument or a related version, considering its applicability to the claim to experience God or Brahman.

(17)   In the novel *Roger's Version* by John Updike a divinity school professor is confronted by a character who believes that there is growing evidence of God's existence. You may wish to write a philosophical review of the arguments at play in the novel. Alternatively you may wish to write a short story or longer dramatic work in which theistic and anti-theistic arguments have a role. The history of art offers various imagery worth noting which depicts the relation between faith and reason. Compare the ways in which reason is depicted in Dante's *Divine Comedy* and Spenser's *The Faerie Queene*. In addition, belief and doubt about God's existence is dealt with in Ingmar Bergman's films. One or more of these would make a fruitful essay in philosophy and film criticism. For a lighter treatment of these themes, one may wish to focus on Woody Allen films or epic films such as "The Ten Commandments."

(18)   Assess William Wainwright's claim: "Passion, sentiment, and affection may be necessary conditions of using our cognitive faculties correctly" (Wainwright 1995, p. 154).

(19)   Contrast David Pole's analysis of disgust and aversion (Pole 1983) with some of the reports of religious experience in *The Varieties of Religious Experience*.

Further Readings and Considerations

From *A Companion to the Philosophy of Religion*, see: "The Reformed Tradition"; "Fideism"; "Reformed Epistemology"; "Naturalistic Explanations of Theistic Belief"; "The Presumption of Atheism"; "Religious Pluralism"; and "Comparative Philosophy of Religion." In addition to the material already cited in the text on burden of proof arguments and material on religious experience, see also Timothy Beardsmore *A Sense of Presence*, Thomas Wood's *Mind-Only*, Paul Griffith's *On Being Mindless*, as well as his *On Being Buddha* and *An Apology for Apologetics*, Thomas Wood's *The Mandukya Upanishad and the Agama Sastra*, Eric Lott's *Vedantic Approaches to God* and his *God and the Universe in the Vedantic Theology of Ramanuji*, Rudolph Otto's classic *The Idea of the Holy: An Inquiry into the Non-rational Factor in the Idea of the Divine and its Relation to the Rational*, John Bowner's *The Religious Imagination and the Sense of God*, and Edward Schoen's *Religious Explanations*. There are many texts on the relation of faith and reason. For a recent, brilliant treatment, see William Wainwright's *Reason and the Heart*. There is a repository of accounts of religious experience at The Religious Experience Research Unit, Manchester College, Oxford University. The Paulist Press has a wonderful series of translations of great mystical works, from East and West. Crossroad Publishers have a magnificent series, *World Spirituality, An Encyclopedic History of the Religious Request*, which has valuable original essays and dictionaries on religious experience (25 volumes). Many of these explore the relation between tradition and religious experience. For a very fine recent treatment of the role of critical reflection in the life of a religious tradition see Basil Mitchell's *Faith and Criticism*.

This chapter emphasizes cumulative reasoning. There is a corporate aspect to this in philosophy of religion. Insofar as one appreciates that philosophical reflection draws on many elements one can appreciate further how individual philosophers often draw on each others' work. Ian Barbour aptly notes the collective nature of religion and science; philosophy of religion could easily be included. "Neither religion nor science is an individual affair. Religion is corporate; even the contemplative mystic is influenced by a historical tradition. No one adheres to science or religion in general; the initiate joins a particular community and adopts its modes of thought and action . . ." (Barbour 1974, p. 133).

9

The Problem of Evil and the Prospects of Good

While the acknowledgment of both evil and an all-good God is at the heart of traditional monotheistic faith, the denial that there can be both is at the heart of much religious skepticism.

There are some philosophers who argue that an all-good God would not allow any evil at all. From their standpoint the existence of even a single instance of evil, no matter how trivial, is sufficient to demonstrate that theism is false. After all, if God is all-knowing *and* all-powerful *and* all-good, not only would God have the knowledge of how to prevent each and every evil and be powerful enough to be able to do so, but God would also be good enough to assure that no evil occurred at all, at any place and at any time. This is often called the *deductive* version of the problem of evil, for it purports to deduce the conclusion that God does not exist. According to this version of the problem of evil, if one grants the traditional understanding of God's omnipotence, omniscience and goodness along with the existence of evil, then the conclusion *God does not exist* necessarily follows. A more qualified anti-theistic argument grants that it is possible that an all-good God may permit *some* evil, but it is not possible (or at least highly improbable) that an all-good God would allow what appears to be the enormity of evil that exists. This version of the problem of evil is often called *probabilistic* or *inductive* as it is grounded in estimates of the likely magnitude of evil and estimations of what an all-good being would tolerate.

The pervasiveness of evil appears to be the most widely held objection to theism in both the Western and Eastern philosophy of religion. Historically, an important part of much Buddhist philosophy of religion has been a critique of theistic forms of Hinduism on the basis of the problem of evil. The problem is addressed both within religious traditions and without. In the Hebrew

Bible (Christian Old Testament), the Book of Job has been valorized for its dramatic formulation of the problem of evil for theists. Many commentators interpret the message of the Book of Job as an appeal to the mystery and otherness of God. According to a popular interpretation of that book, we must put to one side the attempt to understand why evil occurs and simply trust in God (see Job, chapters 38 to 42). Today some theists are so repelled by proposed solutions to the problem of evil that the appeal to mystery seems more attractive than articulating possible solutions. At this juncture, religious believers and skeptics may be in agreement about the prospects of resolving the problem of evil. Antony Flew comments "The Problem of Evil . . . seems to attract bad arguments as jam-making attracts wasps" (Flew 1966, p. 48). For some religious believers, atheism is not thereby vindicated, for the problem of evil provides the most important context for a tested and mature faith in God.

This chapter focuses on the theistic problem of evil and some of the important ways in which it is addressed in philosophy of religion. Theists who seek to defend the goodness of God notwithstanding the existence of evil often argue that evil is a necessary condition for, or a consequence of, great goods. It is because of the great worth of certain goods that an all-good God may allow evil. The most ambitious theistic project is to argue that we may reasonably see that these justificatory goods either already exist or are likely to exist. This would not amount to securing well-grounded convictions that for *each* evil in the cosmos, theists can name specific goods that justify it, but that an overall reasonable picture of God's cosmos can be outlined in general terms that provides an account of its ills and goods. Such an approach is called a *theodicy* (from the Greek for "God's justice"). A more qualified theistic approach to the problem of evil argues either that atheists have not yet, or that they cannot in principle, reasonably conclude that there is no God on the basis of our estimation of the evils and goods that exist. This line of reasoning is often called a defense rather than a theodicy. According to a theistic defense, the problem of evil is not a problem any human being should expect to be able to solve. On this view, even if we can see no morally sufficient reason as to why God allows evil, this does not itself count as reason to believe there is no such sufficient reason. This position and others are explored in this chapter.

Among the goods that may offset or allow for evil, are goods of a specifically religious kind, the good of divine–human accord both in this life and in what is believed to be an afterlife. This chapter includes an exploration of speculative accounts of the afterlife, as well as of the incarnation.

300

Preliminary Distinctions

To sharpen one's sense of the problem faced by theists it will be useful to cite some of the classifications and examples of evil discussed in the philosophical literature on God. Evils are commonly classified in terms of *moral evils* when they result directly or indirectly from immoral actions (war, murder, rape, genocide, torture, theft, emotional abuse), and *natural evils* when they do not result either directly or indirectly from immoral actions. Natural evils include ills that are inflicted on persons by "nature," as when suffering results from birth defects, disease, floods, volcanoes, and the like. According to some philosophers, natural evils are built into our biological world. For example, our bodies naturally deteriorate and nonhuman animals maim and prey upon each other. The contrast between moral and natural evil is not always clear. Cases may arise where some evil is partly the result of immoral human activity but also partly the result of natural processes.

Here are three descriptions of some of the evils of the world. Roland Puccetti narrates the following cases in the course of addressing the problem of evil for theists:

> The Infant Toddler. A woman takes her eighteen-months old daughter to the club every afternoon, where she lets the child play while chatting with friends. Often enough the little girl wanders towards the swimming-pool, which leads to her mother or some other person dashing to the rescue. But one afternoon it happens no one is looking as the child toddles to the edge of the pool, falls in, and goes straight under. No one is in the pool either; by the time anyone realizes what has happened she is dead.
>
> The Cancer Patient. We have an aged woman down with advanced carcinoma of the stomach and bowels. Exploratory surgery reveals that it is widespread, malignant, inoperable. The doctors put her on morphine sedation but her agony increases without lethal collapse. Everyone hopes she will die quickly, for her sake. But she lingers on during still another week of suffering. Seven days. One hundred and sixty-eight hours. Ten thousand and eighty minutes. Six hundred and four thousand eight hundred seconds.
>
> The Brilliant Pianist. Here we have a man thirty-five years old with a fine musical career behind him and an even more brilliant future predicted by all who know him. One day while practicing at the keyboard he notices a trembling of his fingers. This gets worse in succeeding weeks. In time tiny involuntary muscle spasms occur. In a few months he cannot play any more. During the same period he becomes irritable, slovenly, aggressive. Finally his family and friends insist upon medical attention. The diagnosis is Huntington's Chorea.

He is told he has at the most fifteen years left to live: fifteen years during which he will progressively deteriorate psychically as well as physically. His end will come in a mental institution, a crippled shell of a man, unable to care for himself. And if he had children, half of them may expect exactly the same end. (Puccetti, in Peterson [ed.] 1992, pp. 232, 233)

Marilyn Adams offers this list of what she calls "paradigmatic horrors":

The rape of a woman and axing off of her arms, psycho physical torture whose ultimate goal is the disintegration of personality, betrayal of one's deepest loyalties, cannibalizing one's own offspring, child abuse of the sort described by Ivan Karamazov, child pornography, parental incest, slow death by starvation, participation in the Nazi death camps, the explosion of nuclear bombs over populated areas, having to choose which of one's children shall live and which be executed by terrorists, being the accidental and/or unwitting agent of the disfigurement or death of those one loves best. I regard these as *paradigmatic,* because I believe most people would find in the doing or suffering of them prima-facie reason to doubt the positive meaning of their lives. Christian belief counts the crucifixion of Christ another: on the one hand, death by crucifixion seemed to defeat Jesus' Messianic vocation; for according to Jewish law, death by hanging from a tree made its victim ritually accursed, definitively excluded from the compass of God's people, *a fortiori* disqualified from being the Messiah. On the other hand, it represented the defeat of its perpetrators' leadership vocations, as those who were to prepare the people of God for the Messiah's coming, killed and ritually accursed the true Messiah, according to later theological understanding, God Himself. (Adams, in R. and M. Adams [eds] 1990, pp. 211–12)

Finally, I cite Bruce Russell's description of a particular case of evil that he believes counts against theism:

[Consider] a little girl in Flint, Michigan who was severely beaten, raped and then strangled to death early on New Year's Day of 1986. The girl's mother was living with her boyfriend, another man who was unemployed, her two children, and her 9-month old infant fathered by the boyfriend. On New Year's Eve all three adults were drinking at a bar near the woman's home. The boyfriend had been taking drugs and drinking heavily. He was asked to leave the bar at 8:00 p.m. After several reappearances he finally stayed away for good at about 9:30 p.m. The woman and the unemployed man remained at the bar until 2:00 a.m. at which time the woman went home and the man to a party at a neighbor's home. Perhaps out of jealousy, the boyfriend attacked the woman when she walked into the house. Her brother was there and broke up the fight by hitting the boyfriend who was passed out and slumped over a table when the brother left. Later the boyfriend attacked the woman again, and this time she knocked him unconscious. After checking the children, she went to bed. Later the woman's 5-year old girl went downstairs to go to the bathroom. The unemployed man returned from the party at 3:45 a.m. and found the 5-year old dead. She had been raped, severely beaten over most of her body and strangled to death by the boyfriend. (Russell 1989, p. 123)

Russell concludes that it is improbable that any good end could justify any moral agent in allowing preventable deaths, such as the one he describes. He concludes it is probable that God does not exist. Puccetti reaches a similar conclusion, while Marilyn Adams defends the compatibility of God's goodness and evil.

Theists who subscribe to the goodness of God have various alternatives. Some theists qualify the belief that God is all-powerful. This has been adopted by those known as process theologians and philosophers (including A. N. Whitehead, C. Hartshorne, J. B. Cobb, L. Ford, and D. R. Griffin) and many of those philosophers who are known as "personalists" (e.g. S. Brightman and P. Bertocci). If God cannot prevent the harms that occur, then God should not be expected to do so. One may also argue that, while God is very powerful, God is not omniscient. If God is not aware of evil or of how to prevent evil, and this is not due to negligence or wrongful recklessness on God's part, then, God may not be wrongfully responsible. Theists have also contended that what it means to call God "good" must be profoundly qualified. If God is Being and not an individual, it would be a mistake to think of God's goodness as akin to the goodness of human agency. On this view, God may be good in the sense that God's reality is of supreme value, but this goodness could not be the same as claiming that God is a supremely good agent. A radical commitment to God's unquestionable, indisputable authority may also win some reprieve. That is, if one establishes a divine command theory of ethics to the effect that whatever God wills is, *ipso facto*, good, then God's willing the world to be the way it is constitutes its being good, regardless of how *we* may judge it. God need not "measure up" to human standards. Arguably, there may be something religiously offensive in thinking God should do so.

These alternatives may have considerable promise. But each of them, to some extent, seems to depart from traditional forms of Judaism, Christianity, and Islam. And in this context let us not consider arguments that the cases just cited are not, in fact, evil. Let us assume, for example, that what happened to the girl in Flint, Michigan was evil. In fact, if such cases are not evil, traditional theism would appear to be false as each of these evils is condemned from the point of view of traditional monotheism; if Judaism, Christianity, or Islam are true, then evil exists. Unless there is evil, there would be no purpose in the Hebrew Bible's teaching about God's saving Israel from slavery and the call to live in a just community, Christianity's representation of Christ's teaching about justice and forgiveness, and Islamic beliefs about Allah as all-merciful and just.

Most theistic and anti-theistic treatments of the problem of evil take traditional theism seriously (notions of divine omnipotence, omniscience, goodness, etc., are analyzed) and use evaluative categories of good and evil that are in keeping with such traditions. Drawing on our ordinary use of evaluative terms, James Cornman and Keith Lehrer advance the problem of evil as follows:

> If you were all-good, all-knowing, and all-powerful and you were going to create a universe in which there were sentient beings – beings that are happy and sad; enjoy pleasure, feel pain, express love, anger, pity, hatred – what kind of world would you create? . . . Try to imagine what such a world would be like. Would it be like the one which actually does exist, this world we live in? Would you create a world such as this one if you had the power and know-how to create any logically possible world? If your answer is "no," as it seems to be, then you should begin to understand why the evil of suffering and pain in this world is such a problem for anyone who thinks God created this world. . . . Given this world, then, it seems, we should conclude that it is *improbable* that it was created or sustained by anything we would call God. (Cornman and Lehrer 1970, pp. 340–1)

William Rowe reaches a similar conclusion. He endorses the probabilistic or inductive version of the problem of evil.

> It seems quite unlikely that all the instances of intense human and animal suffering occurring daily in our world lead to greater goods, and even more unlikely that if they all do, an omnipotent, omniscient being could not have achieved at least some of those goods without permitting the instances of suffering that lead to them. In the light of our experience and knowledge of the variety and scale of human and animal suffering in our world, the idea that none of these instances of suffering could have been prevented by an omnipotent being without the loss of a greater good seems an extraordinary, absurd idea, quite beyond our belief. (Rowe 1978, p. 89)

Kai Nielsen, Michael Martin, J. L. Mackie, C. J. Ducasse, and many other philosophers agree that evil shows that traditional theism is either clearly false or at least improbable.

The Great Good Theodicy

What are the conditions in which an all-good, all-powerful, all-knowing God would allow evil? Most theists contend that it is unreasonable to think that no evil at all is permissible in a cosmos created by an all-good God. An evil may be permissible if preventing it would create a worse evil. Alternatively, some evil may be allowable if it is a condition for there being a great good or if it contributes to a great good. As part of a strategy called the *great good theodicy* (sometimes called the *greater good theodicy*), theists appeal to pervasive features of the cosmos which, they argue, are genuinely good. They argue further that either these goods are conditions for there being certain evils, or these goods require (or make probable) certain evils, in order to be realized. God allows evil for the sake of such great goods. Let us consider these proposed goods as part of a composite picture before assessing the merits of this strategy. There is reason to assess the theistic case first as a theodicy. If it fails as a theodicy (that is, if it fails to offer a *plausible* account of the justification of allowing evil) it may still serve as a defense (offering a merely *possible* account of the justification of allowing evil).

A common list of great goods emphasizes the existence of conscious life, including human persons with our moral and spiritual capacities. It is argued by some theodicists that it is good that persons live interdependently whereby the well-being of each is linked to others in important ways, and important, too, that the well-being of the world is significantly linked to the well-being of human life. Richard Swinburne and others have argued that if we are going to be truly responsible for one another's well-being then we must have the power not just of benefiting one another but of harming each other and nature as well. As Swinburne puts it:

> [I]f creatures have only the power to benefit and not the power to hurt each other, they obviously lack any very strong responsibility for each other. To bring out the point by a caricature – a world in which I could choose whether or not to give you sweets, but not whether or not to break your leg or make you unpopular is not a world in which I have a very strong influence on your destiny,

and so not a world in which I have a very full responsibility for you. (Swinburne, in Cahn and Shatz [eds] 1982, p. 8)

While this responsibility has often been abused, it is also the case (so it is argued) that without the possibility of harm there would be very little opportunity for good. Michael Peterson underscores the problems that plague the creation of a world in which there are persons who are responsible for freely caring for one another:

> If God is to bestow upon man a kind of freedom which is not just artificial but really significant, He must allow man a wide scope of choices and actions. Indeed, the kind of freedom which is basic to the accomplishment of great and noble actions is the kind of freedom which also allows the most atrocious deeds. In creating man and giving him free will, God thereby created an astonishing range of possibilities for both the creation and the destruction of value. Although some freely chosen evils sometimes have more disastrous consequences than intended, others seem to be motivated by the very desire to do irreparable damage. Perhaps this second kind of free choice is the true love of evil. (Peterson 1982, p. 103)

According to Peterson, the possibility of such a love of evil has to be allowed if God is truly to create beings who freely elect to love the good. Gratuitous, pointless evil is a cost involved with creating a cosmos of significantly free creatures. God may well elect to intervene to prevent *some* evil, but the prevention of *all* evil is not compatible with a world which constitutes an independent arena in which persons are accountable for their own and others' welfare.

> [I]f the conception of human free will is taken to involve the possibility of bringing about really gratuitous evil (specifically, moral evil), then God cannot completely prevent or eliminate gratuitous evil without severely diminishing free will. That would be logically impossible. At stake here is not merely the ability of humans to choose among options, but the ability to choose among significant kinds of options: between goods and evils, even the highest goods and most terrible evils. Thus, free will is most significant – and most fitting for the special sort of creature man is – if it includes the potential for utterly damnable choices and actions. This is part of the inherent risk in God's program for man. . . . God cannot always meticulously override human choices in order to prevent or eliminate their gratuitous evil effects and still protect a significant free will and [those] who also insist that God must not allow any gratuitous

evil . . . are unwittingly asking for the impossible. (Peterson 1982, p. 104; see also Hasker 1984 and 1992)

Assuming that God cannot do the impossible, Peterson argues that God cannot create free creatures that are substantially responsible for each other's well-being and yet rule out all evil. Bruce Reichenbach concurs:

> If we define pointless or gratuitous evils as evils which are not logically or causally necessary for there being a greater good, it follows that some instances of pointless or gratuitous evils, i.e., those whose possibility is necessary for there being a greater good or preventing a greater evil, are compatible with God's existence and goodness. For example, it might be argued that a world operating with regularity according to natural laws is a necessary condition for the greater good of the realization of moral values. But the former in turn necessitates the possibility of such natural evils as fawns suffering. The suffering of the fawn may be pointless or gratuitous, but the possibility of it is a necessary condition of there being that great good. Thus, the existence of pointless suffering whose possibility is necessary for there being a greater good or preventing a greater evil is compatible with the necessity that God eliminate as much evil as he can without losing a greater good or bringing about a greater evil, and hence with God's existence and goodness. (Reichenbach 1982, p. 39)

Reichenbach, like Peterson and Swinburne, seeks to understand apparent pointless suffering in the broader context of an interdependent cosmos which contains great goods.

A common, very important feature in most theodicies (and defenses as well) is an argument that it is good that the creation exists in some measure independent of God. John Hick and others argue that without some degree of distance between God and the creation there would not be the opportunity for persons to develop rationally and freely. He underscores the need for such independent development in what he calls "the soul-making approach to evil." According to Hick, "Personal life . . . cannot be perfected by divine fiat, but only through the uncompelled responses and willing cooperation of human individuals in their actions and reactions in the world in which God has placed them" (Hick 1967, p. 75). He describes the problem of God creating a cosmos in which God continuously intervenes in human affairs, constantly correcting the harms that people intend to carry out:

> It would mean that no wrong action could ever have bad effects, and that no piece of carelessness or ill judgment in dealing with the world could ever lead

to harmful consequences. If a thief were to steal a million pounds from a bank, instead of anyone being made poorer thereby, another million pounds would appear from nowhere to replenish the robbed safe; and this, moreover, without causing any inflationary consequences. If one man tried to murder another, his bullet would melt innocuously into thin air, or the blade of his knife turn to paper. Fraud, deceit, conspiracy, and treason would somehow always leave the fabric of society undamaged. Anyone driving at breakneck speed along a narrow road and hitting a pedestrian would leave his victim miraculously unharmed; or if one slipped and fell through a fifth-floor window, gravity would be partially suspended and he would float gently to the ground. And so on. We can at least begin to imagine a world custom-made for the avoidance of all suffering. But the daunting fact that emerges is that in such a world moral qualities would no longer have any point or value. There would be nothing wrong with stealing, because no one could ever lose anything by it; there would be no such crime as murder, because no one could ever be killed; and in short none of the terms connoting modes of injury – such as cruelty, treachery, deceit, neglect, assault, injustice, unfaithfulness – would retain its meaning. If to act wrongly means, basically, to harm someone, there would be no way in which anyone could injure anyone else, but there would also be no way in which anyone could benefit anyone else, since there would be no possibility of any lack or danger. It would be a world without need for the virtues of self-sacrifice, care for others, devotion to the public good, courage, perseverance, skill, or honesty. It would indeed be a world in which such qualities, having no function to perform, would never come into existence. Unselfishness would never be evoked in a situation in which no one was ever in real need or danger. Honesty, good faith, commitment to the right would never be evoked in circumstances in which no one could ever suffer any harm, so that there were no bad consequences of dishonesty, bad faith, or moral vacillation. Courage would never be evoked in the absence of any challenges and obstacles. Truthfulness would never be evoked in a world in which to tell a lie never had any ill effects. And so on. Perhaps most important of all, the capacity to love would never be developed, except in a very limited sense of the word, in a world in which there was no such thing as suffering. (Hick 1977, pp. 324–5)

It is partly because of this good of developing a cosmos in which love, courage, faithfulness, and so on, are possible that some distance between Creator and creation must be maintained.

F. R. Tennant, along with Swinburne and others, argues that without the kind of regularity and stability that marks the world as we find it, we would not be able to develop or mature rationally and coherently. Tennant notes that in a world that is not so regulated, and thus free from constant divine adjustments of the kind Hick chronicles above, rationality as well as morality would be compromised:

> It cannot be too strongly insisted that a world which is to be a moral order must be a physical order characterized by law or regularity. The theist is only concerned to invoke the fact that law-abidingness . . . is an essential condition of the world being a theatre of moral life. Without such regularity in physical phenomena there could be no probability to guide us: no prediction, no prudence, no accumulation of ordered experience, no pursuit of premeditated ends, no formation of habit, no possibility of character or of culture. Our intellectual faculties could not have developed. . . . And without rationality, morality is impossible. (Tennant 1928, pp. 199–200)

Some divinely caused interruption of such regularity may be tolerable, but substantial interference to prevent ills would both compromise the responsibility persons have to develop their own characters and identities, as well as undermining our powers to predict and control any of the events around us.

Many contemporary theodicists emphasize that a law-governed cosmos is not good only because of its constituting a forum (or "theatre," to use Tennant's phrase) for the evolution of moral, interdependent, reasoned life. The good of there being nonhuman animals (that are, generally speaking, incapable of acting immorally) and the good of there being a planet with its ecosystems of biota and abiota, also count as great goods notwithstanding animal predation and suffering, and the cycles of organic birth and death.

This approach to evil seems to cohere with the Hebrew and Christian Bibles and the Qur'an. The Hebrew Bible refers to the importance of exercising freedom responsibly. In Deuteronomy 30:19, God is represented as proclaiming, "I [the Lord] have set before you today life and prosperity, death and adversity . . . choose life so that you and your descendants may live" (30:15, 19). And in Ecclesiasticus 15:14–20, there seems to be a straightforward endorsement of the role of freedom in creation:

> It was he [God] who created humankind in the beginning,
> and he left them in the power of their own free choice.
> If you choose, you can keep the commandments,
> and to act faithfully is a matter of your own choice.
> He has placed before you fire and water;
> stretch out your hand for whichever you choose.
> Before each person are life and death,
> and whichever one chooses will be given.

> For great is the wisdom of the Lord;
> he is mighty in power and sees everything;
> his eyes are on those who fear him,
> and he knows every human action.
> He has not commanded anyone to be wicked,
> and he has not given anyone permission to sin.

The Christian New Testament likewise highlights freedom: "For freedom Christ has set us free" (Galations 5:1). The Qur'an contains passages in which God seems all-controlling ("Everything is from God," S.iv 80 (78)f) and freedom eclipsed, but there are also many passages in which persons are presumed to be responsible for their own actions:

> God does not burden a soul except according to its capacity.
> To it belongs what it has earned,
> and against it stands what it has earned . . .
> He who receives guidance receives it for his own self,
> and he who goes astray in error strays to his own loss.
> No bearer of burdens bears the burden of another.
>
> (ii. 286, xvii 16(15)a)

So, those who advance theodicies or defenses that utilize the appeal to freedom and responsibility, work with convictions that have a role in monotheistic religious traditions. These and other scriptural references fill out the thesis that God wills there to be a good world in which persons are to develop and mature, care for one another, and live compassionately during times of trial when the reality of God is not evident.

While theodicists argue that it is reasonable to believe something like the above picture is true (based, in part, on the appeal to religious experience, revelation, arguments for God's existence – to be reviewed in the next chapter), theists who argue for a defense argue more modestly that critics of theism have not shown that these great goods do not exist. Before considering further moves in the debate by way of offering objections and replies, let us consider further what is involved in the theistic claim that God is all-good.

Conditions for Divine Goodness

If God is all-good, omnipotent and omniscient, why would God create less than the best possible world? If theism appears to require that God create only the best possible world, then any reasons for thinking our world is not the best possible count as reasons for thinking theism is false.

A common argument against the thesis that God must create the best possible world is that there cannot be one (Swinburne, Schlesinger, Adams, Reichenbach, and others). Imagine any world with extraordinary pleasure, beauty, and so on. Could there be a better world? Arguably a better world would be one just like that but with more pleasure, beauty, and the like. On this view, the concept of there being a *best possible world* is akin to the concept of *there being a greatest possible number*. The former is as absurd as the latter. If there cannot be a best possible world, then God cannot be expected to create one.

Consider R. M. Adams' approach to the question of whether God was bound to create the best possible world. He contends that even if there could be a best possible world, it is not obvious that God has an obligation to create it:

> Might He [God] have an obligation to the creatures in the best possible world, to create them? Have they been wronged, or even treated unkindly, if God has created a less excellent world, in which they do not exist, instead of creating them? I think not. The difference between actual beings and merely possible beings is of fundamental moral importance here. The moral community consists of actual beings. It is they who have actual rights, and it is to them that there are actual obligations. A merely possible being cannot be (actually) wronged or treated unkindly. A being who never exists is not wronged by not being created, and there is no obligation to any possible being to bring it into existence. I argue, then, that God does not have an obligation to the creatures in the best of all possible worlds to create them. If God has chosen to create a world less excellent than the best possible, He has not thereby wronged any creatures whom He has chosen not to create. He has not even been unkind to them. If any creatures are wronged, or treated unkindly, by such a choice of the creator, they can only be creatures that exist in the world He has created. (Adams, in Peterson [ed.] 1992, p. 277)

Adams' thesis is that God cannot wrong that which does not exist. Assuming that God does not do wrong to those God *does* create, the fact that those whom God creates are not the best possible does not count as a mark against God's goodness:

> A God who is gracious with respect to creating might well choose to create and love less excellent creatures than He could have chosen. This is not to suggest

that grace in creation consists in a preference for imperfection as such. God could have chosen to create the best of all possible creatures, and still have been gracious in choosing them. God's graciousness in creation does not imply that the creatures He has chosen to create must be less excellent than the best possible. It implies, rather, that even if they are the best possible creatures, that is not the ground for His choosing them. And it implies that there is nothing in God's nature or character which would require Him to act on the principle of choosing the best possible creatures to be the object of His creative powers. (Adams, in Peterson [ed.] 1992, p. 281)

Adams and William Hasker understand God's love as focused on this world and bringing good out of the evil that exists.

There are objections to this effort to dismiss the claim that God should create the best possible world. Peter Hare and Edward Madden launch the following twofold reply:

Why cannot a theistic God create a perfect world? A theistic God, after all, is supposed to be all-powerful not only *within* nature but *over* nature as well. Thus God could have created any world he wished, and could have chosen to create a perfect one. The problem centers around what one means by *perfect*. If one means by *perfect world* a world infinitely better than the present one, then God indeed could not create a perfect world. But if one means by *perfect world* a world in which there is no positive evil, then God could certainly create such a perfect world, because the concept is not a self-contradictory one. In any case, even if God could not create a perfect world in the second sense, the problem remains why he should have created any world at all if he could not create one better than the present world. This is the poignant burden of Ivan's question to Alyosha: If you were God, would you have consented to create the present world if its creation depended upon the unexpiated tears of one tortured child crying in its stinking outhouse to "dear, kind God"? The answer to this question, no doubt, is that God is not "man writ large." A terrifying result of this answer is to make one wonder what such a God *would* be like. (Hare and Madden 1968, p. 59)

If this is sound, then the state of the world is evidence that theism is false. Let us consider both of Hare and Madden's arguments.

Hare and Madden's first proposal is that a world with no positive evils would be perfect. But such a world would (if Hick and others are right) be a world that lacks important goods. Would it not be worth enduring *some* harms in order to secure *some* of these goods? Perhaps a world of great good would not be worth "the unexpiated tears of one tortured child," but it is difficult to establish a deductive form of the problem of evil that requires God to rule out *all evil* of any amount. The descriptions of how evil may result from great goods cited earlier, may be enough to offset Hare and Madden's first point that God should not create at all if some evil is in the offing.

The second part of the Hare–Madden thesis returns us to the probabilistic form of the argument against theism. They believe there is so much evil that it is reasonable to conclude there is no good God. There are victims in this life who are tortured, raped, beaten, maligned, and stripped of dignity. Grant that God did not have to create the best possible world. Grant, too, that this world is not the worst possible one (a worse world would be one in which there was even more suffering than there is). What conditions must be met in the creation for God to count as good?

A minimal reply is that an all-good God would create a cosmos that is such that it is better overall that it exists than it does not exist. A more substantial, individualist reply is that an all-good God would create only creatures for whom life is an overall good. Adams describes what he takes to be a suitable, permissible condition of creation by an all-good Creator: "The creature is not, on the whole, so miserable that it would be better for him if he had never existed" (R. Adams, in Petersen [ed.] 1992, p. 283). But this may be too modest. After all, a person would be blameworthy for torturing someone even if the life of the tortured is overall a good. Would God be all-good if God creates beings whose misery is so considerable such that while it is better that the creatures exist than not exist, their lives are racked with unrelieved pain?

The problem faced by theists here is not isolated to theistic philosophy, but also plagues medical ethics, public policy debate, law, environmental ethics, and certainly has a dramatic role in our personal lives. When is someone's life no longer worth living? There is no extant consensus on today's measurements. Some have proposed a kind of self-selecting voluntarism: a person's life is worth living if the person would have chosen to live it again. And, indeed, this may be utilized in debates about the problem of evil (consider suggested question 6 at the end of this chapter). But as it stands, this test alone does not help individuals in deciding whether they would or should make such a choice. Moreover, it appears not explicitly to rule out all kinds of irrational and vicious choices (perhaps a person may have a life worth living but he has an ungrounded self-hatred).

I believe that this debate about the overall good or ill of the cosmos – and the lives of particular individuals – must unfold in the course of a comprehensive look at the resources (and possible weaknesses) of theism. Many theists, for

313

example, believe that the tears shed that are "unexpiated" in this life do not rule out a final expiation or transfiguration in a next life. Moreover, some theists hold that God is intimately present and involved in the life of the cosmos, working to bring about such a transformation from the "stinking outhouses" of the world to something profoundly good and worthy. It will be useful to consider the prospects of theism over and against a series of objections and replies.

Objections and Replies

Let us consider four objections to theism on the grounds of the problem of evil and a series of theistic replies.

(A) OBJECTION: The Great Good Theodicy is based on a number of assumptions, each of which may be questioned: whether indeed the cosmos does have a regular, uniform order; whether we do have free will; and so on. Here is only one worry. Granted that we do have freedom, why think it impossible that God could not so make us that we always freely do the right acts? Mackie puts the question succinctly: "If God has made men such that in their free choices they sometimes prefer what is good and sometimes what is evil, why could he not have made men such that they always freely choose the good?" (Mackie 1982, p. 164).

REPLY TO (A): Some theists argue that without certain persons choosing wrongly there would be no ills that would need defeating through virtue, and no development of the higher goods of character. So, even if God could ensure that no persons commit evil acts, God is not bound to do so. More commonly, however, theists argue that God simply cannot guarantee that free creatures will only choose good. As suggested in chapter three, this is because the free activity of creatures is undetermined and not "up to" God to fix. As Plantinga writes:

> Now God can create free creatures, but He can't *cause* or *determine* them to do only what is right. For if He does so, then they aren't significantly free after all; they do not do what is right *freely*. To create creatures capable of *moral good,* therefore, He must create creatures capable of moral evil; and He can't give these creatures the freedom to perform evil and at the same time prevent them from doing so. As it turned out, sadly enough, some of the free creatures God created went wrong in the exercise of their freedom; this is the source of moral evil. The fact that free creatures sometimes go wrong, however, counts neither against God's omnipotence nor against His goodness for He could have forestalled the

occurrence of moral evil only by removing the possibility of moral good. (Plantinga 1974b, p. 30)

Further debate on such issues is recorded in chapter 5. Theists who are libertarians appear to have a more forceful, direct response to Mackie's charge than do theistic determinists.

(B) OBJECTION: Many, though not all, theists believe in an afterlife in which persons live in the presence of God and never do evil. This state, heaven, is believed to be eminently desirable and yet lacking evil. Why didn't God simply create heaven? Wouldn't heaven represent a world of goods greater than this one?

REPLY TO (B): Let it be granted that heaven represents a realm of great good, even better than this one. So long as God is not bound to create the best possible world, this would not amount to conceding God is not all-good. Should heaven not involve the exercise of certain freedoms it may be an arena in which certain goods are not realized. The creation of both this world and a heaven may together represent a fuller, wider creation insofar as it enables the fulfillment of a wider array of goods than if only heaven existed.

Alternatively, a theist might contend that there is no heaven and could be no such place or if there is a heaven it is most fittingly thought of as a realm of fulfillment for those who have lived this life.

(C) OBJECTION: Theists who adopt the Great Good strategy are in danger either of severing their assessment of God from ordinary, meaningful contexts of evaluation or of promoting a damaging account of human values. If it is good that there are ills in order that virtues flourish, occasions arise in which we ourselves should promote ills. Hare and Madden argue as follows:

> If courage, endurance, charity, sympathy, and the like are so spiritually significant, then the evil conditions which foster them should not be mitigated. Social and political reforms designed to achieve social security, peace, plenty and harmony automatically become pernicious. We do not really believe this, of course, and thereby reflect the fact that we have spiritual values which we place above those negative ones fostered by extremely trying conditions. (Hare and Madden 1968, p. 70)

H. J. McClosky raises a similar point:

> Theists usually hold that we are obliged to reduce the physical evil in the universe; but in maintaining this, the theist is, in terms of his account of physical evil, maintaining that it is his duty to reduce the total amount of real

315

good in the universe, and thereby to make the universe worse. Conversely, if by eliminating the physical evil he is not making the universe worse, then the amount of evil which he eliminates was unnecessary and in need of justification. (McClosky, in Brody [ed.] 1991, p. 179)

The problem faced by theists is as follows: it appears that if they are right about what it is permissible for God to allow, then this implies that it is permissible for us to allow for many ills that we should not. In brief, if we should reduce the amount of ills in the cosmos, why shouldn't God do so?

REPLY TO (C): The theodicy under review contends that God has created and sustains a cosmos in which shared responsibility and collaboration are called for in overcoming evil and which thus is indeed good. If it has the implication that we should ourselves foster environments in which collaboration in overcoming evil is facilitated this may not be an unwelcome conclusion. Given certain theistic models of God, a close-knit paternalism of reducing *all* risks in life may be undesirable. Clearly, though, this need not take the form of arguing that, if such a theodicy is right, we ought to spread disease, harm others, and so on to provide occasions for virtue. Arguably, the existence of significantly free, interdependent creatures will of its own make the creation of a world where there are hardships, and where virtues can flourish, nearly inevitable. In a sense, God's role in our lives might still reflect a certain dimension of appropriate parent–child relationships. While some parents may wish to control their children's lives well after their children mature and are making their own way, parents committed to the development of genuine freedom and responsibility of their children must step back and refrain from trying to control them.

This only partly meets the objection, however. A parent or child would, it seems, have an obligation to prevent train wrecks and floods if doing so was feasible and would save lives. Should not God rightly be thought of as good only insofar as God has, and adheres to, similar obligations?

Here theists may wish to argue that God does indeed have a different moral role than creatures. George Schlesinger offers this response:

A possible answer to this might be that of course the moral rules by which we judge human and Divine conduct are the same, but man and God act under very different circumstances. It may be maintained that A is permitted to cause another person suffering, with the view of providing opportunities for others to respond in a noble way, only if A is absolutely certain that he is capable of compensating the victim fully for his suffering. By fully compensating I mean that the victim will eventually agree that the experience of having to undergo the suffering A subjected him to in the service of his stated goal, together with the subsequent experience of receiving compensation, are no less preferable to the experience of having neither. It is obvious that only God is in the position to be able to guarantee this. (Schlesinger 1988, pp. 51, 52)

According to Schlesinger, it is untenable to assume that God's duties and our own are on the same footing.

If the theistic view of God's ownership of the cosmos is acceptable, then this reply may be bolstered. Recall the discussion of the ownership of God developed in chapter 7. If there is a robust sense in which the cosmos belongs to God, then God's moral standing from the outset is radically unequal to ours. In chapter 7 we considered whether God can steal from you or violate your right to privacy. Arguably our rights are at least hedged if the ownership of God is taken seriously. In the Book of Job, Job declares "The Lord gives. The Lord takes away. Blessed is the name of the Lord" (Job 1:21). Being thus beholden to God would not seem to entitle God to create beings solely to torment them, but if life is indeed a gift from God which no creature deserves (no being had a right to be created), then certain complaints about the created order may be checked.

(D) OBJECTION: Granted (if only for the sake of argument) that the appearance of some gratuitous evil is a justified feature of a good cosmos in which ethical creatures freely develop, is it not reasonable to believe there is an inordinate amount of evil? As William Rowe notes: "Who would say that if only five million had been permitted by omnipotence to perish in the holocaust it would not have been rational to believe that evils occur that omnipotence could have prevented without loss of any greater good?" (Rowe 1991, p. 86). In other words, God could have reduced the amount of evil and still have preserved the reasonable belief that we live in radical independence of God. Hare and Madden advance a point similar to Rowe's:

If it is possible for God to interfere miraculously to avoid a gratuitous evil, then it would seem to be unreasonable and evil for him *not* to do so in some particularly hideous cases. Some theists try to avoid this difficulty by saying God is not able to interfere with his creation once completed. This maneuver, however, abandons traditional theism because it relinquishes the notion that God is unlimited in power. (Hare and Madden 1968, pp. 54, 55)

As to the charge that God's interference in world affairs will invariably compromise human freedom, Hare and Madden argue otherwise:

It is not at all clear that God's intervention would undercut moral fiber. Anthropological studies indicate that belief in the possibility of divine intervention in deserving cases tends not to undercut our moral fiber, but rather to "provide an incentive for moral life . . . [and] also strengthen our wills against adversity." Of course it might be argued that too much intervention would eventually lead to reduction of moral fiber. However, to show that this solution of the problem of physical evil fails we need only show that *occasional* intervention could be expected of an omnipotent and all-good God. And this is not difficult to do. (Hare and Madden 1968, p. 55)

REPLY TO (D):   We have already considered one counter-move, which is simply to insist that the adjustments of world ills would invariably destabilize the goods of freedom and autonomy. Consider Basinger's stance:

> But as many have pointed out, it seems extremely doubtful that God could continually circumvent or modify natural (including psychological) laws in a widespread manner without destroying our belief that anticipated consequences will normally follow given actions – that is, without destroying our belief in predictable regularities. But if we can no longer have the assurance that given consequences will normally follow given actions, we must seriously question whether we can retain a meaningful concept of "free choice." For example, what sense can it make to speak of a hot and thirsty individual meaningfully choosing to take a drink of water if he has no reasonable expectation that this action will have a thirst-quenching effect? Or, more significant, what sense can it make to speak of a terrorist meaningfully choosing to throw a bomb into a crowded room if we assume that such an individual has no reasonable expectation that significant destruction will follow? The answer, it seems to me, is that no sense can be made of the concept of "choice" under such conditions. The concept of "choosing to do X" is inextricably tied to the concept of "willing to bring about one state of affairs rather than another." Accordingly, if an individual has no reasonable expectation that one state of affairs rather than another will result if he performs A, it cannot be said that he has the capacity to exercise a meaningful sense of "choice" in relation to A. (D. Basinger 1992, p. 177)

But the problem remains. Allow that the cases Basinger describes need to be ruled out. God's interfering with terrorist explosives on any routine basis would compromise moral and spiritual development, rationality and the like, and yet are there not cases where it seems the magnitude of evil is inordinate in a God-filled cosmos? Why, to take up Rowe's example, were so many killed in the Holocaust?

Some theists reply that reducing evils in the way Rowe requests would set

318

one on a course with no end. We measure evils in relation to one another. Should one eliminate the greater evils (World War I and II), then other lesser evils would loom and seem to us to be just as horrendous. John Hick objects to the argument that an all-good God should eliminate the worst evils on the grounds that it would not represent a viable alternative to a world of soul-making.

> For evils are exceptional only in relation to other evils which are routine. And therefore unless God eliminated all evils whatsoever there would always be relatively outstanding ones of which it would be said that He should have secretly prevented them. If, for example, divine providence had eliminated Hitler in his infancy we might now point instead to Mussolini as an example of a human monster whom God ought secretly to have excised from the human race; and if there were no Mussolini we should point to someone else. Or again, if God had secretly prevented the bombing of Hiroshima we might complain instead that He could have avoided the razing of Rotterdam. Or again, if He had secretly prevented the Second World War, then what about the First World War, or the American Civil War, or the Napoleonic wars, and so through all the major wars of history to its secondary wars, about which exactly the same questions would then be in order? There would be nowhere to stop, short of a divinely arranged paradise in which human freedom would be narrowly circumscribed, moral responsibility largely eliminated, and in which the drama of man's story would be reduced to the level of a television serial. We always know that the rugged hero who upholds law and order is going to win the climactic gun fight. And if every time a tyrant set out to trample upon human freedom we could be sure in advance that some apparent accident would providentially remove him from the scene it would no longer be true that the price of liberty is eternal vigilance; and indeed vigilance, and the willingness to make sacrifices for human liberty, would no longer be virtues and would no longer be evoked in mankind. If we knew in advance that no really serious threat to them could ever arise, the struggle for righteousness and human dignity would become unreal. Once again, then, we are confronted by the integral character of the existing order of things such that bane and blessing are intimately bound together within it, and such that not even an unfettered imagination can see how to remove the possibility of the one without at the same time forfeiting the possibility of the other. (Hick 1977, pp. 327–8)

Hick's argument challenges the framework of the Cornman–Lehrer thought experiment cited earlier (If you were an all-good, all-powerful, all-knowing being, wouldn't you make a better world?). If Hick is right, then reflections about making a cosmos like ours but with less evil is not as simple an affair as suggested in the Cornman–Lehrer challenge cited earlier.

At this stage, some theists curtail the project of a theodicy, and aim more at a defense. That is, they argue that while it may not be that we possess a plausible account of how the ills of the cosmos are either conditions for or follow from great goods, atheists have not demonstrated that there is no all-good God or that it is probable there is no all-good God. A comprehensive strategy is to argue that because it is reasonable to believe there is an all-good God on other grounds (religious experience for example), it is in general reasonable to believe that the ills of the cosmos are either conditions for or follow from great goods even if we do not know how this comes about.

Alvin Plantinga highlights how judgments of probability are relative to what is already reasonably believed (1974b). Thus, if one is assessing the belief "Miriam can swim," it may be highly probable to believe she cannot if all one knows is:

(1)   Miriam is a Stewart.
(2)   99% of the Stewarts you know cannot swim.

For all that, if you reasonably believe the following, you may reasonably believe Miriam can swim:

(3)   Miriam won an Olympic gold medal for swimming 400 meters.

Similarly, the religious believer may be in a position to reasonably accept both the reality of evil and an all-good God, should the evidence for each be strong and there are no compelling reasons for thinking God cannot be all-good.

To bolster this defense, theists highlight the possibility that events in the cosmos are so profoundly integrated that, *contra* Rowe, Hare, Madden and others, we cannot reasonably adjudicate ways of adjusting the balance of good and ill. As Michael Peterson writes:

When the critic requires "only a small change" in the present set of natural laws in order to avoid their gratuitous evil consequences, we might not realize how great a change is involved. Since almost all natural objects are capable of producing harmful as well as beneficial results, virtually all natural laws would have to be modified, with the correlative modification of virtually all natural objects. Even the slightest modification may produce manifold and intricate differences between this present natural order and the envisioned one. The whole matter becomes so complex that no finite mind can conceive of precisely what modifications the envisioned natural world would have to incorporate in order both to preserve the good natural effects and to avoid the . . . evil ones. And if the desired modifications cannot be detailed, then the further task of conceiving how the proposed natural world is better than this present one seems patently impossible. (Peterson 1982, pp. 115–16)

Theists also suggest possible goods that extend beyond this life in order to address the problem of reconciling the ills of creation and the goodness of God.

Let us consider first whether belief in an afterlife can affect the problem of evil and then consider the implications of what may be called "The Suffering of God Defense."

Evil and the Afterlife

Some theists and proponents of some nontheistic religions highlight the role of the afterlife in reflecting on the problem of evil. Belief in life after death in Judaism, Christianity, and Islam is generally conceived of as continuous with one's present life. The moral and spiritual struggles of this life are met with either future challenge or fulfillment. The point to note here in connection with the problem of evil is that these religions do not conceive of this life as the *only* arena of personal life. Physical death does not involve the absolute cessation of persons.

To contribute to the defense of theism in light of the problem of evil, belief in an afterlife needs to be seen differently than the belief in hedonistic rewards. If one conceives of the afterlife as altogether distinct from the goods and ills of this life, there is a risk of failing to take this life seriously. Grace Jantzen criticizes the traditional belief in the afterlife precisely on such grounds.

One might argue that only if it (the afterlife) is, is God just: the sufferings of this present world can only be justified by the compensation of eternal life. But this, in the first place, is shocking theodicy: it is like saying that I may beat my dog at will provided that I later give him a dish of his favourite liver chowder. What happens after death – no matter how welcome – does not make present evil good. (Jantzen 1984b, p. 40)

Jantzen's point seems well taken: what occurs after death does not (or cannot) make the evil that occurs in this life good. But there are two important points that are often overlooked in this debate.

First, whether or not there is an afterlife and what its character consists of has a bearing upon the extent of evil that exists. Imagine that Sam murders Pat out of deep malice. Imagine, too, that there is no afterlife. Sam is responsible for annihilating a person. Pat has ceased to exist due to Sam's hateful act. Imagine now that there *is* an afterlife. Sam is still profoundly guilty for endeavoring to annihilate Pat. Pat has lost a great good. But Sam did not extinguish Pat's life altogether. Belief in an afterlife need in no way reduce our moral convictions about the moral outrage of murder. Still, if there is no afterlife, the murder seems to have resulted in a greater evil (Pat's perishing altogether) than if there is an afterlife (Pat still exists and some companionship and exchange with Pat is possible after death). Theists may extend this case to the world's greatest evils. Some Jewish thinkers have addressed the Holocaust in the context of belief in an afterlife.

Consider the Holocaust under two conditions: one in which millions were annihilated in an absolute sense, the other in which the millions died but are not annihilated. Under either condition, Nazism remains a moral outrage and horror, but the evil perpetrated by the Nazis is worse if their victims ceased to be altogether and God allowed the millions who suffered to perish absolutely. In an important paper, "Jewish Faith and the Holocaust," Dan Cohn-Sherbok argues for the importance of theistic belief in the afterlife:

> Yet without this belief, it is simply impossible to make sense of the world as the creation of an all-good and all-powerful God. Without the eventual vindication of the righteous in Paradise, there is no way to sustain the belief in a providential God who watches over His chosen people. The essence of the Jewish understanding of God is that He loves His chosen people. If death means extinction, there is no way to make sense of the claim that He loves and cherishes all those who died in the concentration camps – suffering and death would ultimately triumph over each of those who perished. But if there is eternal life in a World to Come, then there is hope that the righteous will share in a divine life. Moreover, the divine attribute of justice demands that the righteous of Israel who met their death as innocent victims of the Nazis will reap an everlasting reward. Here then is an answer to the religious perplexities of the Holocaust. The promise of immortality offers a way of reconciling the belief in a loving and just God with the nightmare of the death camps. As we have seen, this hope sustained the Jewish people through centuries of suffering and martyrdom. Now that Jewry stands on the threshold of the twenty-first century, it must again serve as the fulcrum of religious belief. (Cohn-Sherbok 1990, pp. 292–3)

On this view, the belief in an afterlife does nothing to weaken one's sense of the nightmare of the death camps. It simply provides one way of articulating how the nightmare may end.

Secondly, there are respects in which an evil may give rise to some good in an afterlife. Thus, many ethicists have argued that the act of sorrowing over some past evil one has committed can constitute a good. It would be better if the evil that Sam performed had never occurred; but given that it has occurred, his taking pleasure in his deed enhances or aggravates the evil. In a converse fashion, there is a respect in which a sorrowful regret for a past act can be good. Sam may grow into a right relation to values. To return to Jantzen's example, giving a dog a nice meal after beating him does not make your having beaten him good. But just as the act could give rise to an additional evil (your later relishing the act and pleasure in the memory) it could also give rise to a good (perhaps you will embrace your dog with Franciscan tenderness). And if there is some afterlife for Sam and Pat, perhaps there too is the opportunity for forgiveness and an altered, profoundly good, relationship. A world in which there is no such afterlife is one in which this good is unrealizable after death. (One way to further explore the implications of this issue is to reconsider the cases cited at the outset of this chapter – the infant toddler, the girl in Flint – under conditions where (a) physical death marks the annihilation of persons, and (b) physical death marks a transition to a next life where there is an opportunity for justice and compassion for victims and guilty parties.)

Some theists claim that in the course of an afterlife all persons will eventually come to fulfillment in God. This is John Hick's stance:

> The least that we must say, surely, is that God will never cease to desire and actively to work for the salvation of each created person. He will never abandon any as irredeemably evil. However long an individual may reject his Maker, salvation will remain an open possibility to which God is ever trying to draw him. (Hick 1977, p. 343)

Hick believes God will succeed by bringing about the salvation of all, but some theists believe that God will not succeed in drawing all persons to the good. According to some theists, if God does give creatures genuine freedom to shape their own identity, this freedom must include the power to live in radical distance (moral and spiritual) from God; perhaps, even, as some suggest, annihilation (Wenham, 1993). In traditional terms this amounts to contending that an all-good God would allow free creatures to choose hell. Michael Peterson puts it this way:

> It is reasonable to believe that the terrifying, human potential for evil includes the possibility of some person's willing and loving evil to the extent that hell becomes the emergent, dominant choice of his whole life. Hell is simply the natural culmination of things which he has voluntarily set in motion. Just as God cannot override a person's every evil choice, He cannot contravene the larger, cumulative evil orientation of one's life. If God is going to allow us to exist as significantly free beings, capable of the highest achievements, then he must allow us the most depraved and senseless errors – even if they lead to hell. Hell is the logical extension of the idea that man has the radical power to create gratuitous evil. (Peterson 1982, pp. 124–5)

I list several arguments for and against belief in hell in suggested question 15 at the end of this chapter.

Before exploring a further theistic proposal, "The Suffering of God Defense," consider a basic question about an afterlife. Is it coherent? Is it even possible that there is one? If it is not possible for there to be an afterlife, then it will be of no use in a theistic defense or theodicy. A popular philosophical defense of the afterlife is based on a dualist conception of persons. It is not, however, the only model. Let us look at dualism first.

Dualism was introduced in chapter 4 in the discussion of essential materialism. According to dualism, persons are materially embodied, but not, strictly speaking, the very same thing as their material body. Persons are nonphysical in themselves but materially realized and embodied. Perhaps this dualist picture gains some appeal when we appreciate how we differentiate our identity as persons and as material bodies. In ordinary contexts we identify our personal identity over time in precise terms. Despite radical changes (I hope) in maturity, education, outlook, and so on, I can readily report that *I* was in kindergarten at such and such school. Identifying my bodily continuity is more problematic. In the course of normal growth we constantly lose and gain new cells. In fact, over a period of roughly 7 years, the majority of the cells in our body have been replaced. While there is a continuity of identity between my body when I was in kindergarten and my body now that I am a college professor, it would be paradoxical to claim that my body was in kindergarten. According to dualism, the paradox is partly due to the fact that we rarely consider ourselves as just bodies, but it is also paradoxical because, given the vast changes undergone, it is not strictly speaking true that my present body is numerically the same as the body I had in kindergarten.

There is a range of sophisticated arguments for dualism, some of which build on theories of personal identity, neuroscience, imaginative thought experiments, and the like. In my view, the more plausible versions of dualism insist that in our normal embodied life we constitute an integrated whole. That is, a properly functioning integrated mind–body relationship would not allow us to believe the person is a tenant or prisoner, stuck in a body. Such an integrated holistic embodiment would not, however, rule out disembodiment or body switching. Indeed, if dualism is true, such activities would be deemed possible. I briefly outline this stance and then note some afterlife scenarios that do not require dualism.

According to a principle often called the *indiscernibility of identicals*, identity relations are strict: if A is B, whatever is true of A is true of B. Consider some identity relations: *Cicero is Tully*, and *the Evening Star is the Morning Star*. Both sets are true: the first refers to a Roman Orator and the second to the planet Venus. If the principle of the indiscernibility of identicals is correct, then because Cicero is Tully, whatever is true of Cicero is true of Tully. If Cicero has white hair so does Tully; you cannot shake hands with Cicero without shaking hands with Tully. If dualism is true, then while you enjoy an embodied life now and we may thus regard you as a unified whole, it is possible for you to survive the destruction of your body.

Many texts in various religions and cultures seem to provide evidence that personal survival of death has been widely believed. If so, this can count as *some* evidence to the effect that both dualism and the afterlife represent intelligible possibilities. The case for this may be built on the following principle of evidence: if one carefully considers a state of affairs, examining the properties and relations involved, and it appears that it can obtain, then it is reasonable to believe the state of affairs can obtain (see Taliaferro 1994 for detailed argument, see also Robinson 1982; Swinburne 1986; Hart 1988; Foster 1991).

According to some dualist accounts of the afterlife, death marks one's becoming altogether disembodied, while other accounts construe death as marking one's transition to a different body. Dualists like H. H. Price have used their views about the nature of the mental in defending the coherence of belief in an afterlife that is in a spatial realm, not spatially related to this world. Thus, if you accept the thesis that dreams exist and involve visual imagery not spatially located in this spatio-temporal world (*viz.*, your dream image of a tiger last night was not so many inches from your bed), you would have reason to believe that there can be objects that are not in our spatial world. It is, of course, a considerable leap to go from belief in dreams to belief in an afterlife, but the nature of dreams has been used by dualists to construct afterlife scenarios (see Price 1972; Hick 1976b; Becker 1993).

Other, nondualist scenarios should be noted. Here are several proposals to consider which may be pursued with the help of the references at the end of this chapter, along with suggested essay questions 17 and 18:

(1) Imagine that you are not a nonphysical thing but a material body which is dispersed at death. Perhaps a material afterlife could be brought about by the reassembling of substantial parts of your body (Geach 1969).

(2) Alternatively, perhaps one can secure identity after being recreated in accord with one's psychological identity. There have been accounts of personal life that equate it with something like a software program. Perhaps one can be replicated or reintroduced based on the assembling of objects that match one's present body (Donald Mactray 1980).

(3) Another option involves being literally created again. Imagine that death involves one's ceasing to exist. Why could one not be recreated by God much later? This would involve what some philosophers have called a gap-inclusive life. That is, there would be a gap in one's life when one did not exist, but would exist before and after the gap (Reichenbach 1978).

While dualism has often been used to spell out the nature of an afterlife, many Jewish, Christian and Islamic philosophers do not use it. For a rich survey of positions see *Death and Immortality in the Religions of the World*, edited by Paul and Linda Badham.

The Suffering of God Defense

The belief in an afterlife is not the only speculative dimension to theistic defenses and theodicies. Another avenue explores the prospects of a specific religious good that is made possible in the course of suffering. Marilyn Adams and others have defended the thesis that in suffering one may come to an intimacy with God that is not available otherwise.

Marilyn Adams argues that a great-good defense or theodicy might succeed in meeting the horrors of life, but only if the scope of goods is expanded from those that are commonly recognized. "Standard generic and global solutions [to the problem of evil] have for the most part tried to operate within the territory common to believer and unbeliever, within the confines of religion-neutral value" (Adams, in R. and M. Adams [eds] 1990, p. 218). Departing from this, Adams writes:

326

The worst evils demand to be defeated by the best goods. Horrendous evils can be overcome only by the goodness of God. Relative to human nature, participation in horrendous evils and loving intimacy with God are alike disproportionate: for the former threatens to engulf the good in an individual human life with evil, while the latter guarantees the reverse engulfment of evil by good. Relative to one another, there is also disproportion, because the good that God *is,* and intimate relationship with Him, is incommensurate with created goods and evils alike. Because intimacy with God so outscales relations (good or bad) with any creatures, integration into the human person's relationship with God confers significant meaning and positive value even on horrendous suffering. This result coheres with basic Christian intuition: that the powers of darkness are stronger than humans, but they are no match for God. (M. Adams, in R. and M. Adams [eds] 1990, p. 220)

According to Adams, this invocation of incommensurate goodness is pivotal to defend the plausibility of theism in light of the problem of evil. "In my opinion," writes Adams, "suffering cannot seem a wise, justifiable or loving redemptive strategy except when embedded in the larger context of a Christian world view" (Adams, in Peterson [ed.] 1992, p. 182).

How such a redemption of evil can take place within this relationship with God may not be very clear. It could involve felt religious experience, an awareness of God's proximity and love, the assurance that evil will ultimately be overcome through God's love and healing powers. This redemptive process may involve the *bonum progressum* or the good of development. In part, this appreciation of the good of divine–human accord is why theists like Eleonore Stump believe that natural evils can serve a greater good. Natural disasters may shatter any sense of security that is not built on God:

Natural evil – the pain of disease, the intermittent and unpredictable destruction of natural disasters, the decay of old age, the imminence of death – takes away a person's satisfaction with himself. It tends to humble him, show him his frailty, make him reflect on the transience of temporal goods, and turn his affections towards other-worldly things, away from the things of this world. No amount of moral or natural evil, of course, can guarantee that a man will seek God's help. If it could, the willing it produced would not be free. But evil of this sort is the best hope, I think, and maybe the only effective means, for bringing men to such a state. (Stump 1985, p. 409)

This picture of God bringing creatures into intimate, selfless relation to God is often amplified by the thesis that God shares in the suffering of creation.

Swinburne endorses the following principle:

> A theodicist is in a better position to defend a theodicy such as I have outlined if he is prepared also to make the further additional claim – that God knowing the worthwhileness of the conquest of evil and the perfecting of the universe by men, shared with them this task by subjecting himself as man to the evil in the world. A creator is more justified in creating or permitting evils to be overcome by his creatures if he is prepared to share with them the burden of the suffering and effort. (Swinburne, in Cahn and Shatz [eds] 1982, p. 19)

The belief that God suffers or at least sorrows over the world's ills is sometimes testified to in religious experience and in sacred scriptures. In *The Brothers Karamazov,* which contains what some consider the most powerful literary treatment of the problem of evil, Dostoyevsky points the way to addressing evil in light of God's proximate love for the world. Father Zosima reports:

> Much on earth is hidden from us, but to make up for that we have been given a precious mystic sense of our living bond with the other world, with the higher heavenly world, and the roots of our thoughts are not here but in other worlds. (Dostoevski, trans. 1976, p. 299)

This vision is upheld by many mystics, philosophers, and theologians in the theistic traditions. Alvin Plantinga stresses this affective bond between God and creation:

> As the Christian sees things, God does not stand idly by, coolly observing the suffering of his creatures. He enters into and shares our suffering. He endures the anguish of seeing his son, the second person of the Trinity, consigned to the bitter cruel and shameful death on the cross. Some theologians claim that God cannot suffer. I believe they are wrong. God's capacity for suffering, I believe, is proportional to his greatness; it exceeds our capacity for suffering in the same measure as his capacity for knowledge exceeds ours. Christ was prepared to endure the agonies of hell itself; and God, the Lord of the universe, was prepared to endure the suffering consequent upon his son's humiliation and death. He was prepared to accept this suffering in order to overcome sin, and death, and the evils that afflict our world, and to confer on us a life more glorious than we can imagine. (Plantinga, in Clark [ed.] 1992, p. 167)

The crucial point for the theodicy (or defense) is to conceive of this suffering as part of some overall good (being the cost of free will, for example). Otherwise God would appear to be masochistic to inflict suffering either on others or on God if it was not part of some good.

Theistic approaches to evil may gain assistance from some nontheistic, monist views. In monist tradition, as described in chapter 6, the cosmos may be seen as the differentiation or manifestation of a single reality, Brahman in Hinduism. Vinit Haksar notes how believing that all individuals reveal a singular reality – he refers to as a "cosmic self" – may bear on the problem of evil.

> The problem of evil (i.e. the problem why a just God allows so much suffering in this world) may become easier to solve if there is a cosmic self of which we are all different aspects. On the separate self view, when an innocent separate self suffers a lot in his lifetime, one cannot deny the unfairness of such suffering by pointing out that others are enjoying themselves. But on the cosmic self view one can argue that looked at from the point of view of the cosmic self, the suffering of a particular human being is compensated by the happiness of others. Of course this argument will only get off the ground if there is more happiness than suffering in the world as a whole. If there is more suffering than happiness in the world, then the fact that there is the same cosmic self that keeps suffering on and on, from the beginning of time till the end of time, makes things even worse. For at least on the separate self view the suffering of a particular human being will not go on for an indefinite period (unless perhaps one believes in immortality). (Haksar 1991, p. 206)

If individuals are taken to be manifestations of a deeper reality some of the worries about unfairness and unbalance are overturned. The focus is on the status of the whole, not the particular.

Classical versions of Judaism, Christianity and Islam are largely opposed to construing God as an all-embracing Being of which we are mere parts. Nonetheless, it may be possible for theists to hold a high view of individuals as distinct centers of consciousness and growth, and yet called into a corporate, interconnected relationship with a singular divine consciousness. Stafford Betty has sought to develop such a theodicy which consciously draws on Hinduism but resists its nondualistic tendencies. He summarizes his view over and against some monist strands of Hinduism:

> Most of the Upanishads hold that the goal of us all should be the complete transcendence of our individual identities in an eternal oneness with Brahman. "Where there is consciousness of the Self [Brahman, the Ultimate Reality], individuality is no more," the sage Yajnavalkya tells his wife Maitreyi (*Brihadaranyaka,* II, iv, 12). Elsewhere we read, "As flowing rivers disappear in

the sea, losing their names and forms, so a wise man, freed from name and form, attains the Purusha [Brahman]" (*Mundaka*, III, ii, 8). It should be apparent by now that, from the point of view of this theodicy, the annihilation of individuals is neither desirable nor possible. This theodicy affirms a Brahman, a Father, a Mother, an Allah, as long as there is no final swallowing up of the soul by this Godhead. For such a swallowing up would render meaningless most of human experience. What is gained if the liberated individual *as individual* ceases to exist? What is the meaning and purpose of that individual's experience, and especially his suffering, through many lives? Does such a liberated individual come into possession of some great completeness, some great joy that he did not possess before he was liberated? No, for on an Upanishadic reading he does not even possess the individuality that would give us the right to say he is *able* to possess something; he does not even possess himself. (Betty 1992, p. 77)

So Betty does not accept an uncompromising monism but he still draws on monist notions of interrelatedness and shared identity. This shared identity has been upheld by a range of theists. A. E. Taylor describes the Christian understanding of the afterlife as including "a complete interpenetration of mind by mind" (Taylor 1951, p. 31).

A specific area of the problem of evil where this approach may be important concerns nonhuman animal suffering. In chapter 7 we considered some of the current theistic treatments of nonhuman animals, from an animal rights perspective to deep ecology. Some theists contend that nature is not at all in harmony with God's will, but has fallen. Some hold that nonhuman animal suffering and predation is a result of a radical fall from grace. It has been proposed that this involves a fall by humans or nonphysical spirits (Satan). If this stance is defensible then a theistic defense of natural evil can be subsumed under a defense of moral evil. Alternatively, theists have adopted a holistic view of nature, according to which the good of individuals is considered primarily in terms of the good of the whole. In either case, it seems evident that there is considerable suffering among animals. If God is in some profound sense involved in this evolution in the nonhuman world, one can at least displace the view that God is only a designer and spectator of the evolutionary process. Rather, if Betty is right, evolution involves an ongoing process of differentiation and evolution within the life of God. "We think of God," writes Keith Ward, "as sharing in the pain and sorrow of creation, as well as its joy and happiness, and thus, by his omniscience, as participating in the creative expression of his own reality which is creation" (Ward, in Linzey [ed.] 1988, p. 105). In Ward's view, this identification of God with creation means the ultimate redemption or vanquishing of suffering: "If there is any sentient being which suffers pain, that being – whatever it is and however it is manifested – must find that pain transfigured by a greater joy" (Ward 1988, p. 105). For John Wesley, this transfiguration involves an afterlife for nonhuman animals. For some other theists, nonhuman animal life is worthy of God's creation so long as it is good overall. As Austin Farrer puts it, "The issue we have to consider lies in the simple question, whether animals would be better off, if they had no pains at all" (in Linzey [ed.] 1988, p. 66).

Limits of Inquiry

I conclude this chapter with a consideration of the thesis that if there is an all-good God we should not expect to know why God allows the ills of the cosmos. This argument can be stated succinctly. Imagine you have considered a host of possible solutions to the problem of evil and not found one that is satisfactory. Should the failure to find a solution count as evidence that there is no solution? Only if it is plausible to believe you would find a solution if you looked for it. Richard Swinburne provides the following example:

> Note that the principle is so phrased that how things seem positively to be is evidence of how they are, but how things seem not to be is not such evidence. If it seems to me there is present a table in the room, or a statue in the garden, then probably there is. But if it seems to me that there is no table in the room, then that is only reason for supposing that there is not, if there are good grounds for supposing that I have looked everywhere in the room, and . . . would have seen one if there was one there. (Swinburne 1979, p. 246)

And Stephen Wykstra formulates matters in this way.

> On the basis of cognized situation s. human H is entitled to claim "It appears that p" only if it is reasonable for H to believe that, given her cognitive faculties and the use she has made of them, if p were not the case, s would likely be different than it is in some way discernible by her. (Wykstra, in R. and M. Adams [eds] 1990, p. 152)

This predicament is sometimes cast as a desirable one, for without some degree of autonomy from God, important goods would be lost. John Hick writes:

Our "solution", then, to this baffling problem of excessive and undeserved suffering is a frank appeal to the positive value of mystery. Such suffering remains unjust and inexplicable, haphazard and cruelly excessive. The mystery of dysteleological suffering is a real mystery, impenetrable to the rationalizing human mind. It challenges Christian faith with its utterly baffling, alien, destructive meaninglessness. And yet at the same time, detached theological reflection can note that this very irrationality and this lack of ethical meaning contribute to the character of the world as a place in which true human goodness can occur and in which loving sympathy and compassionate self-sacrifice can take place. (Hick 1977, pp. 335–6)

Is this appeal to mystery acceptable?

William Rowe and J. L. Schellenberg argue that it is not. According to Schellenberg, an all-loving, all-good God would reveal or somehow make evident the overriding goods that constitute the justificatory reason for allowing evil. Schellenberg uses the parent–child relationship to bolster his stance. A loving parent would instruct her or his child on the ills it bears. God should be expected to do likewise (Schellenberg 1993).

Alan Padgett replies that the God–creature relationship in which God is expected to be so exacting represents a cloying, overly paternalistic picture of God.

I find [Schellenberg's] conception of the love of God too narrowly paternal. Schellenberg's understanding of God is controlling, masculine and patronizing. God will ensure belief for his creatures because, after all, he knows best. A more rich and adequate understanding of God avoids the narrow "Father–Child" model for one of two lovers, a model found in Scripture, mystics, and some philosophers (Hegel, Buber, Levinas). God creates the world as Other to himself/herself, to approach the world as a Lover. The love of God, on this model, implies the occurrence of rational non-belief. For the Lover does not wish to impinge upon the freedom of the Beloved to reject the advances of the Lover; the Lover wishes the Beloved to be both fully mature and fully free. Against Schellenberg such love cannot be created into the Beloved, nor begun too soon before the Beloved is fully mature, nor always pressed against her or his long-term choices and character. Thus Schellenberg's argument is unconvincing to those with a more adult-lovers model for Divine–human relationships. (Padgett 1994 , p. 208)

Some theists, then, argue that an appeal to mystery is philosophically acceptable due to our inability to assess the relevant conditions involved (to know whether or not there is an afterlife and so on). But here caution is advisable for theists who want to appeal to mystery in the problem of evil but then appeal to intelligibility in finding the best explanation of the nature of the cosmos. For this reason many theists see the need to argue for more than a defense and continue proposing theodicies.

As noted in the last chapter, theism may be best served by developing a cumulative case involving a host of factors rather than running singular arguments independent of one another. Should a potent argument from religious experience be plausible, then the existence of evil may not count against God's existence, but for it; to a religious believer, the experience of evil may be an experience of that which grieves God. The arguments for theism in the next chapter may also be bolstered by the appeal to religious experience.

Just as theists are served by cumulative arguments, so are naturalist critics. If theism is found wanting in developing an argument from religious experience and the problem of evil counts heavily against theism, then naturalism, or some nontheistic religion or a nonrealist view of religion, appears more plausible.

Appendix on Incarnations

Belief in the incarnation (literally "enfleshment") of God has played a key role in Christian approaches to the problem of evil. It has formed part of "The Suffering of God Defense," noted in this chapter, and the atonement, discussed in chapter 7. It has also been the occasion for considerable recent debate. I review here some initial objections to belief in the incarnation, a current philosophical project designed to meet these objections, and then comment on how the assessment of incarnation claims, whether of God in Christ, or Vishnu as Krishna in Hinduism, needs to take into account how these claims function in relation to one's overall religious and philosophical outlook. What follows is intended to stimulate further inquiry, and not to provide a detailed survey and examination of all relevant, recent philosophical work on this topic.

Initial difficulties. Christian philosophers and theologians have sometimes capitalized on the apparent absurdity of believing that God became incarnate. Even in the Christian New Testament there is some indication that, viewed from a merely human point of view, the incarnation is absurd. The reasons for thinking so are not hard to formulate.

To believe that God became a human being, Jesus Christ, appears to involve believing something that is logically contradictory. Consider these two columns, one lists divine attributes and the other human attributes.

Divine	Human
Omnipotent	Having limited power
Omniscient	Having limited knowledge
Omnipresent	Spatially located
Eternal	Temporal
Necessarily existing	Contingent
Nonphysical	Embodied
Necessarily good	Not necessarily good
Without origin	With origin
Everlasting/Deathless	Mortal

To suppose that a single person has both properties appears to involve a contradiction. The Chalcedonian Creed (451) states that Jesus Christ is fully God and fully human. In what respects is this any more intelligible than believing a geometrical shape could be both a square and a circle?

Philosophies of the incarnation. In lieu of the apparent incoherence of the traditional Chalcedonian claim about Jesus' full humanity and divinity many contemporary Christians reinterpret beliefs in the incarnation along less paradoxical lines.

One popular position, sometimes called *functional Christology*, is to understand the incarnation, not as a metaphysical conjoining of attributes but as Christ functioning as a key reference point in understanding God's nature and will. In the life of Jesus Christ we can discover a human person so united with God in will and consciousness that God becomes manifest in a vivid, penultimate fashion. On this view, the claim that "Jesus Christ is God" would be read as the thesis that Jesus Christ supremely represents God by embodying God's character (compassion, justice) and his life becomes a vehicle or channel by which other persons may come to have fellowship with God.

Another position is more radical, but also seems to avoid holding that a person, Jesus, has incompatible attributes. According to a *kenotic account of the incarnation*, God, in the second member of the Trinity, shed the attributes of omniscience, omnipotence, and so on, in order to become fully human. In the incarnation, God did not thereby retain omniscience and divine, omnipotent power.

One of the challenges facing kenotic theories is whether it makes sense to think that God's attributes are indeed contingent and the sort of thing God can abandon at will (like discarding a name on a piece of clothing). It is also not clear how the kenotic theory can cope with some of the reliant disparities between divine and human properties. How is it that God could abandon the property of being without origin?

Recently there have been two important efforts to meet the initial objections head-on and to restore the Chalcedonian teaching of the incarnation. T. V. Morris and Richard Swinburne have independently proposed what may be called a two-minds theory of the incarnation.

Morris and Swinburne propose that in the incarnation God retains all the divine attributes. According to Morris and Swinburne, the incarnation is made possible in virtue of a division in the divine mind, whereby a "distinctly earthly consciousness" comes into being and assumes all the limitations of human life. The overriding divine mind, which Morris calls "the eternal mind of God," retains omniscience, while the mind within the mind, the distinctly earthly consciousness," does not. Morris describes the two-minds theory as follows:

> There is first what we can call the eternal mind of God the Son with its distinctively divine consciousness, whatever that might be like, encompassing the full scope of omniscience. And in addition there is a distinctly earthly consciousness that came into existence and grew and developed as the boy Jesus grew and developed. It drew its visual imagery from what the eyes of Jesus saw, and its concepts from the languages he learned. The earthly range of consciousness, and self-consciousness, was thoroughly human, Jewish, and first-century Palestinian in nature. (Morris 1986, pp. 102–3)

In the incarnation, Jesus Christ had a human birth and bodily life, fully experiencing the world as an embodied person with limits of knowledge, power, and even goodness. In such a state, for example, Jesus may not have always realized his divine character. Thus, Jesus may not have known that he was necessarily good and thus could not act wrongly. In this way, Jesus could have been truly tempted to do wrong. Swinburne describes the limits of the man Jesus Christ:

> [T]here is a limit to Christ's power *qua* man. If the human actions of God the Son are done only in the light of his human belief-inclinations, then he will feel the limitations that we have. God, in becoming incarnate, will not have limited his powers, but he will have taken on a way of operating which is limited and feels limited. (Swinburne 1994, p. 202)

On this view, God in Christ felt and acted as a finite, circumscribed being, subject to appetites, sensations, vulnerable to pain and suffering. This represented a focusing of consciousness within the broader divine mind. Morris further articulates the relation between the minds of God as follows:

> The divine mind had full and direct access to the earthly, human experience resulting from the Incarnation, but the earthly consciousness did not have such full and direct access to the content of the overarching omniscience proper to the Logos, but only such access, on occasions, as the divine mind allowed it to have. There thus was a metaphysical and personal depth to the man Jesus lacking in the case of every individual who is merely human. (Morris 1986, p. 103)

If Morris is right, this demarcates a genuine incarnation and not a mere pretense to incarnation as with various mythic representations of God, or gods, entering society disguised as a human being (as envisaged by the early heretical movement, docetism).

In support of this division of consciousness, Morris and Swinburne appeal to theories of psychology and intelligence that appear to allow for varying delimitations of consciousness and identity. Thus, Freudian psychoanalysis appears to allow for persons to be understood as in some way composed of distinguishable drives that can function as distinct mindlike intelligent units. Computer programs have been constructed with complex access relationships whereby there are programs within programs. Multiple personality disorders also reveal ways in which (so it seems) a single person might well contain or embody more than one mind. And Morris appeals to contemporary depth psychology and its supposition that human life admits of different strata:

> If modern psychology is even possibly right in this postulation, one person can have different levels or ranges of mentality. In the case of Jesus, there would be a very important extra depth had in virtue of being divine. (Morris 1986, p. 105)

These analogies serve to explicate some of what Morris and Swinburne take to be at the heart of the Christian understanding of the incarnation.

Morris introduces a helpful distinction between being "fully human" and "merely human." The incarnation makes no sense if it is supposed God became "merely human" and by this expression one means "no more than human." But Morris contends we can still talk coherently of Jesus Christ being "fully human" in the sense that Jesus Christ, like us, had bodily life with its mental and physical powers and liabilities.

Consider briefly four objections and replies to this project. Each of these is stated succinctly and invites further analysis and debate.

(A) HUMAN BEINGS ARE MATERIAL ENTITIES. There is nothing nonphysical about being human. God is nonphysical. It is incoherent to suppose something nonphysical can become physical. And it is therefore incoherent to suppose that God could become a human being.

REPLY: Both Morris and Swinburne are dualists and would reply that humans are not exclusively material. Human embodiment is real but our bodily life is not the whole story. The incarnation does not therefore involve something nonphysical becoming something physical. It involves God *qua* nonphysical consciousness being integrally embodied.

(B) THE TWO-MINDS THEORY IMPLICATES GOD IN DECEPTION. Jesus Christ as a human did not know certain things that God *qua* divine consciousness did. This involves God in an elaborate self-deception.

REPLY: The incarnation involved limitations but no essential deception. A deception involves deliberately misleading someone. On the traditional Christian view, the incarnation involved a focused embodiment with all the limitations of human life in order to inform human beings, revealing God in our own terms, not in order to obscure God's will and character. A further reply to the deception objection may well stress that the incarnation involved genuine limitations, e.g. Morris and Swinburne insist that Christ's suffering, pain, hunger, and so on, were all real and not mere appearances.

(C) IF GOD RETAINS THE PROPERTY OF BEING NECESSARILY GOOD, HOW COULD GOD *QUA* JESUS CHRIST HAVE BEEN TEMPTED? The Christian New Testament construes Jesus as struggling with and overcoming temptation. This appears to be at odds with contending that Jesus could not have actually fallen prey to temptations.

REPLY: Several replies may be in order. Morris contends that one can be tempted if one thinks one can sin even if one cannot truly sin:

> It is not necessary that sinning be a broadly logical or metaphysical possibility for Jesus; it is only necessary that it has an epistemic possibility for him . . . On the two-minds view, it can be held that within the beliefs naturally accessible to his earthly consciousness, it was epistemically possible for Christ that he sin. From his earthly point of view, his sinning was not logically ruled out. Thus in his earthly stream of consciousness, it was possible for Jesus to be tempted to sin. The information that he is necessarily good was not contained

in his human range of thought. That allowed for his temptations. (Morris 1986, pp. 148–9)

Alternatively one may reply that Jesus knew he could not sin but felt tempted all the same. Perhaps cases can arise when one knows something cannot be changed and yet one feels no less an urge to change matters. Another option is to concede that while God is supremely good, God's goodness is not necessary but contingent.

(D) OBJECTION. To be fully human surely involves having an origin in time, facing death as a possible annihilation, and certainly failing to have the powers Jesus displays in the New Testament (performing miracles, raising people from the dead, being resurrected).

REPLY: The objection challenges Morris's "merely human"–"fully human" categories. One reply may underscore that Morris and Swinburne give pride of place to genuine limits of Jesus' power and knowledge (e.g. as a child of six months, Jesus did not know he was the incarnation of God). But if this is not successful in overturning the objection, it is difficult to see how it might be met other than by pointing out that the concept of "being human" differs radically between cultures and lacks a stable philosophical meaning. A Buddhist account of being "fully human" differs from Islamic and Marxist accounts. There are some cultures in which it is believed that fully human persons can perform wondrous tasks like raising the dead and in others it is believed that all living beings are reincarnations of the dead (Becker 1993). In lieu of this spread of views, it is less than obvious that objection (D) is decisive.

Incarnations and comprehensive philosophies. The last objection–reply exchange illustrates how one's religious views can reflect one's other commitments. Thus, if one holds certain views of God and humanity, an incarnation is impossible. To further illustrate the integral character of religious beliefs consider the Hindu teaching about Krishna.

In the *Bhagavad Gita* Krishna is represented as a manifestation of Vishnu. Some commentators have noted important parallels between Christian and Hindu teaching. Ovey Mohammed describes Krishna as follows:

> Krishna is God, and God is personal . . . wholly immanent and wholly transcendent . . . God is the origin of all things, and the world depends on God, God does not depend on the world . . . God has another mode of being in the

heavenly home, . . . God is the source and sustainer of all virtues . . . who resides in the heart of all. (Mohammed 1993, p. 11)

Krishna is also described as "No mere teacher of what is right and wrong but God who answers the prayers of God's followers" (Mohammed 1993, p. 11). The parallel is so great that one may well see Krishna and Jesus as proclaiming complementary, if not identical, teachings at certain points:

> The teachings of Krishna and Jesus on salvation are similar in many respects . . . Krishna's offer of salvation is made in terms of grace . . . the efficacy of grace depends on our faith and love. Faith is trust and commitment, self-abandonment to Krishna. When we respond to Krishna's grace in faith, Krishna gives us salvation, forgiveness, and new life . . . In the New Testament Paul also spoke of human salvation in terms of grace . . . grace depends on faith. (Mohammed 1993, pp. 14–15)

This resemblance of teaching prompts many questions, including the question of whether Christians can allow that God may have become incarnated in other times and places. But my focus, in what space remains in this brief appendix, concerns the importance of understanding incarnation claims in their context.

Hindu stories of Krishna are sometimes taken to reflect historical events, but there has not been the fierce commitment and debate about the historical Krishna for Hinduism to match the commitment and debate about the historical Jesus in Christianity. Some Christian theologions have objected to Hindu teaching about Krishna became of its comparative lack of historicity and full embodiment of God (or Vishnu) in Krishna as a human being. Krishna did not suffer by humans putting him to death and so on. I shall dwell on this charge and then propose a modest reply.

In an insightful study of Simone Weil, Diogenes Allen presents Weil's view of Jesus and Krishna as follows:

> Krishna is not an incarnation in the sense that Christ is because Krishna did not suffer. Krishna is a *manifestation* of deity (Vishnu is present) and so he is a revealer or enlightener. His is even a means of salvation. By loving him we can be raised to righteousness. But for justice itself to be incarnate entails suffering, and to be able to suffer requires that the divine become a creature. Among all the instances of alleged incarnations, Christ is the only one who suffered and suffered precisely because of his righteousness. We need not deny that Vishnu is one of the names of God, and that Krishna, as a manifestation of him, inspires, enlightens, and even enables people to reach the presence of righteousness itself

in order to continue to maintain that Christ is the righteousness of God *incarnate* and that through Christ's suffering God suffers the separation of the Word from himself . . . They (Christ and Krishna) function as *metaxu* or mediators between God and human beings. Contact between us and God, which is a "contradiction" since we are on different levels of reality, is made possible by God descending to our level. Thus the Word of God descends as the principle of nature's order and in human form in instances such as Krishna. In addition, incarnations such as Krishna's provide a saving revelation, that is, show and mediate a path to righteousness. The prime incarnation, that of Jesus Christ, however, reveals the *full* depths of God's saving mercy since it is the actual endurance of the suffering which is the cost of God's mercy toward human unrighteousness and which is borne by God himself. (Allen 1989, p. 256)

How should this claim be assessed?

I suggest that any such comparison of views on incarnations take seriously the full context of the relevant religion. From a Christian standpoint, Hindu teaching and narratives of Krishna may seem less "deep" and revelatory. But it is essential to appreciate that Krishna is not an isolated figure; Krishna must be understood within the whole complex setting of Hindu belief and practice. Given alternative (in some respects, nonChristian) views of the person and body, the nature and purpose of suffering, time and liberation, Krishna may well appear the deeper, more illuminating figure. Superficial comparative philosophy of religion is dangerous. A more comprehensive investigation is a different story. And it is a story one must investigate in full, in the further investigation of a religious tradition's view of the problem of evil and the prospect of good, including the good of divine revelation and manifestation.

This fact need not prompt one to abandon the project of philosophically assessing and comparing religions. It should merely prompt one to carry out such an enterprise with respect and careful attention as to how religious beliefs form highly complex subtle patterns with mutually supporting, intricate internal relationships.

Suggested Questions and Topics

(1)   Gottfried Leibniz (1646–1716) held that God could not make a cosmos that is perfect in every respect. If the cosmos was perfect it would be another God.

The imperfections, on the other hand, and the defects in operations spring from the original limitations that the creature could not but receive with the first beginning of its being, through the ideal reasons which restrict it. For God could not give the creature all without making of it a God; therefore there must needs be different degrees in the perfection of things, and limitations also of every kind. (Leibniz, trans. 1951, p. 141)

You may wish to develop an argument defending such a stance and then assess its strengths and weaknesses.

(2)   Hick holds that traditional belief about the fall is unintelligible:

The notion that man was at first spiritually and morally good, oriented in love towards his Maker, and free to express his flawless nature without even the hindrance of contrary temptations, and yet that he preferred to be evil and miserable, cannot be saved from the charge of self-contradiction and absurdity. (Hick 1967, p. 75)

Is this view warranted? How might one defend the thesis that Adam and Eve were created perfect and then committed an evil act?

(3)   Imagine that a basic thesis of the great-good defense is plausible: in order for one to develop virtues and so on, one must at least *believe* that one is surrounded by dangers that people suffer, and so on. Consider the argument that an all-good, all-powerful God had reason to create persons with these *beliefs*, but not create persons with such *true* beliefs. Could not great goods have been brought about with only the *appearance* or *simulation* of great harms? If so, should an all-good God be expected to do so?

(4)   Some have argued that a world with only good would be either impossible or unknowable. It is impossible because good, as a category, requires a contrast. One could not have a world that was all large or thick, for example. Being large or thick requires other objects in contrast to which objects can be small and thin. Similarly with good and evil: it is unknowable because, even if there were a world that was all-good one would have no means to measure it. Hare and Madden object:

Even as far as the problem of pain is concerned the contrast solution breaks down. We need little pain by way of contrast to get the point: One might be allowed to bite his lip occasionally rather than have cancer of the mouth. . . . Moreover, it is doubtful that the underlying principle of this argument is valid. It entails the view that if a person who had never experienced pleasure became infected with tetanus he would not understand and appreciate the pain involved. But this consequence is absurd. "It is true that it might not be distinguished by a special name and called 'pain,' but the state we now describe as a painful state would nonetheless be possible in the total absence of pleasure." In addition, "the converse would seem to apply. Plato brings this out very clearly in Book 9 of the *Republic* in respect of the pleasures of taste and smell. These pleasures seem not to depend for their existence on any prior experience of pain." (Hare and Madden 1968, p. 54)

Assess the relevant arguments, *pro* and *con.*

(5)   Develop a theistic reply to the following charge and assess its adequacy:

> A God unlimited in power and goodness certainly could have created a world with somewhat different laws than the present ones which would have produced the same results in the biological world with the same mechanism of natural selection but without its present fantastic wastefulness. This could be done, e.g., by assuring a larger percentage of favorable mutations. (Hare and Madden 1968, pp. 54–5)

(6)   Hasker develops a defense of theism over and against the problem of evil based on one's being satisfied with one's own life. The crucial initial premise is put this way:

> I ask myself, then, the following question: *Am I glad that I exist?* The question is not whether my life is all that it ought to be or all that it conceivably could be. It is not whether the pleasure–pain balance in my life to date has been, on the whole, favorable or unfavorable. It is not whether my life is, in general, a benefit to those who are affected by it. It is not even the question whether my life, all things considered, contains more good than evil. All of these questions are deeply interesting, and the answers to them, if known, might affect my answer to the question which I am asking. But the question is simply, am I glad that I am alive? Or is my existence, on the whole, something which I regret? Is my life something which I *affirm*, or do I wish, like Job, that I had never been? And what, I go on to ask, of my loved ones, of my wife and sons, and of others whom I know well enough that the question makes sense: Am I glad of their existence? If I could rewrite the script for the tale that we are living, would I leave their parts out? (Hasker, in Peterson [ed.] 1992, p. 154)

He then points out how a condition for our existing includes many evils:

My own father and mother came from widely separated parts of the country and met as a result of a complex series of events, some of which affected many other individuals as well. Not least among these was the First World War, which sent my father to France and brought my mother to Washington to work in the expanded Federal government, leading in each case to life-changing experiences. Quite simply: had there been no war, I should not be here. (Hasker, in Peterson [ed.] 1992, p. 156)

Hasker uses these points to construct the following argument:

(A)   A necessary condition of my coming-into-existence is the coming-into-existence of my body.

(B)   Had major or significant events in the world's past history been different than they were, then in all probability neither I nor the persons whom I love would ever have existed.

(C)   If I am glad that P, I rationally cannot be sorry that P.

(D)   If I am glad that P, and P entails Q, then I rationally must be glad that Q.

(E)   If I am glad on the whole that P, and I know that P entails Q, then I rationally must be glad on the whole that Q.

(F)   If I am glad on the whole that P, and I know that if Q did not obtain neither would P, then I rationally must be glad that Q.

(G)   If I am glad on the whole about my own existence and that of those whom I love, then I must be glad that the history of the world, in its major aspects, has been as it has.

(H)   The world as we know it is morally so objectionable that a God who tolerated it could in no meaningful sense be called good – nevertheless, *I am glad for my own existence and therefore I am also glad that the world exists and that the main events and features of its history have been as they have.*

(I)   Those who would maintain that the world as we know it could be created and governed by a just and loving God "must have led sheltered lives and closed their heart to the voice of their brothers' blood," *nevertheless I am glad on the whole that I have been able to live in this world, and glad also that its history has been such as to give me that opportunity.*

(J)   I cannot reasonably *complain* to someone that P, or *blame* or *reproach* someone for its being the case that P, unless I myself sincerely *regret,* or *am sorry,* that P.

(K)   If I am glad on the whole about my own existence, and that of persons close to me, then I cannot reproach God for the general character or the major events of the world's past history. (Hasker, in Peterson [ed.] 1992, pp. 153–67)

Critically assess Hasker's argument. Can it be plausibly reconfigured into an argument for the conclusion that we should regret existence?

(7)   In this chapter, R. M. Adams' view is presented to the effect that God is not obligated to bring into existence the best possible beings. His condition for creation of a person by a good God seems to be that the person is not, on the whole, miserable. The person need not be the best possible. Assess Adams' description of the case that follows. Did the couple do something wrong?

A certain couple become so interested in retarded children that they develop a strong desire to have a retarded child of their own – to love it, to help it realize its potentialities (such as they are) to the full, to see that it is as happy as it can be. (For some reason it is impossible for them to *adopt* such as child.) They act on their desire. They take a drug which is known to cause damaged genes and abnormal chromosome structure in reproductive cells, resulting in severe mental retardation of children conceived by those who have taken it. A severely retarded child is conceived and born. They lavish affection on the child. They have ample means, so that they are able to provide for special needs, and to insure that others will never be called on to pay for the child's support. They give themselves unstintedly, and do develop the child's capacities as much as possible. The child is, on the whole, happy, though incapable of many of the higher intellectual, aesthetic, and social joys. It suffers some pains and frustrations, of course, but does not feel miserable on the whole. (Adams, in Peterson 1992 [ed.], pp. 282–3)

(8)   How might a theist reply to the problem of nonhuman animal suffering? You may wish to develop a response to the following stance by Hare and Madden.

The by-product solution is perhaps most urgently needed in dealing with animal pain. Since many other arguments obviously will not work with animals (e.g., suffering cannot be punishment to creatures who are not morally responsible) many fall back on the view that the apparently brutal laws of nature make possible the survival of the fittest and consequently the development of species which is in the long run to the betterment of the animal kingdom. If all animals had been herbivorous and healthy, they would mostly starve as a result of their own multiplication.

The chief difficulty with this explanation of animal pain is that it assumes that God could not have chosen another birthrate. To be sure, God could not have chosen another birthrate and still have expected natural selection in its present form to work, but God was not obliged to adopt the present fantastically wasteful mechanism of natural selection. There are many ways in which God could have saved an enormous amount of suffering by altering the mechanism of evolution. For example, he could have seen to it that a larger percent of mutations are favorable. As it is now, advantageous mutations are a minute percentage.

Farrer misunderstands the whole issue of animal pain. "The issue we have to consider" he writes, "lies in the simple question whether animals would be better off, if they had no pains at all." This is precisely what the issue is not. We are not asking whether animals could do nicely without any pain at all but rather whether at least *some* of their pain is not gratuitous in the sense that God could have altered the mechanism of evolution in such a way that its working entailed much *less* suffering. (Hare and Madden 1968, pp. 55–56)

(9) Basinger expresses uncertainty over how to resolve the debate over the problem of evil between atheists and theists. Do you agree or disagree with the following? Why or why not?

But how are we to proceed here? On what common ground are we to build? Both parties may well agree that in a comparison of two possible worlds the one containing the greatest net balance of good over evil is superior. But how are we to assess the quantity of good and evil in each? Let us suppose, for example, that in the mind of a given atheologian (atheist or agnostic) the undeserved suffering of a single individual outweighs any amount of good which might be generated in such a world, while in the mind of a given theist the intrinsic value of "human freedom" outweighs any amount of evil such freedom might entail. How would we determine who is correct? I, for one, have no idea how an objective, non-question-begging determination of this sort could be made. (Basinger, in Peterson [ed.] 1992, p. 150)

(10) Hick emphasizes the importance for theists to ensure a strong, uncompromising view of evil. He writes:

We must not, under the impact of our vision of the demonic, deify evil and dethrone God. . . . It cannot be unforeseen by the Creator or beyond His control. We must not suppose that God intended evil as a small domestic animal, and then was taken aback to find it growing into a great ravening beast! The creator to whom this could happen is not God . . . We have in the end, then, both to recognize the essentially demonic nature of evil, and to maintain the sole ultimate sovereignty and omni-responsibility of God. . . . (Hick 1977 pp. 289–90)

Do you think that classical forms of theism can secure such a negative view of evil or will the belief in an all-good, omnipotent, omniscient God incline persons to diminish the horror of evil? Why or why not?

(11) A. E. Taylor argued for the probability of purgatory as follows:

I cannot conceive that most of us, with our narrow range of understanding and sympathies, our senseless antipathies and indifferences, and our conventional moral outlook, could ever be fitted by the mere fact of escape from the physical limitations of the body to enter at once into the eternal life of the simply loving souls. I should think it more probable – always with deference to wiser judgments – that death leaves us, as it finds us, still far too much takers and too little givers, and that the process of purgation, begun in this life in all who have made any progress in good, needs, for all but the very few, to be continued and intensified, and that, for most of us, this means severe discipline. It may be well to have got rid of the crude imagination of "Purgatory-fire" as a "torment", and still be better to have lost belief that one can purchase remission of the torment by cash payment into an ecclesiastical treasury, but the main thought that the hardest part of the work of putting off temporality may, for most of us, lie on the further side of the physical change called death, seems to me eminently sound. (Taylor 1951, pp. 317–18)

You may wish to assess this stance.

(12) How might Cohn-Sherbok or other defenders of the belief in an afterlife respond to this point by Hare and Madden?

There is, finally, what might be called a wholesale version of the all's-well-that-ends-well doctrine that deserves brief mention. According to this view, immortality sufficiently compensates for whatever evil happens to a person in this life. Eternal bliss is thought capable of making worthwhile any amount of suffering along the route to that goal. However, the afterlife argument is far from convincing because it is very much like a torturer telling his victim on the rack that he need not be concerned for by and by he will be sent to a luxurious spa. To be sure, the victim is delighted to hear that he has such a future ahead of him, but he still cannot understand why he need be tortured before he goes. He cannot understand why the one should be a prerequisite for the other. The torture remains gratuitous for anything the spa argument shows to the contrary. (Hare and Madden 1968, p. 65)

(13) Keith Ward appeals to belief in the afterlife as part of his addressing the problem of evil. How might the following position be either supported or subjected to the objection?

One must remember that the Christian belief is that there is an existence after earthly life which is so glorious that it makes any earthly suffering pale in comparison; and that such eternal life is internally related to the acts and sufferings of worldly life, so that they contribute to, and are essential parts of,

346

the sorts of glory which is to come. The Christian paradigm here is the resurrection body of Jesus, which is glorious beyond description, but which still bears the wounds of the cross. So the sufferings of this life are not just obliterated; they are transfigured by joy, but always remain as contributory factors to make us the sort of individual beings we are eternally. This must be true for the whole of creation, insofar as it has sentience at all. If there is any sentient being which suffers pain, that being – whatever it is and however it is manifested – must find that pain transfigured by a greater joy. I am quite agnostic as to how this is to happen; but that it must be asserted to be true follows from the doctrine that God is love, and would not therefore create any being whose sole destiny was to suffer pain. In the case of persons, the truth of this claim requires the existence of a continuous personal life after death. The Christian will then say that his sufferings, whatever they are, help to make him the unique individual he is. To wish for a better world is to wish for one's non-existence, as the person one is. Often one may indeed wish for that; but the Christian would say that, if one could clearly see the future which is prepared for one, such doubts and fears would disappear; and the resurrection of Jesus is given to confirm this faith. (Ward, in Linzey [ed.] 1988, pp. 104–5)

(14) When might a theistic appeal to mystery be justified? You may wish to assess the following passage from work by Keith Ward:

> We cannot assign a reason why this particular world exists; but we can say that it comes solely from God, whose being contains the possibilities of all the good and evil things alike which we see around us. The appropriate response to this knowledge is, like Job, to bow in acceptance before the unfathomable ground of being. (Ward, in Linzey [ed.] 1988, p. 105)

(15) For recent, illuminating treatments of traditional views of hell, see especially Jonathan Kvanvig's *The Problem of Hell* and Jerry Wall's *Hell: The Logic of Damnation*. You may wish to consider a variety of theories of punishment (retributive, communicative, rehabilitatory, utilitarian) and note how these might or might not be employed in the articulation and defense of believing that an all-good God would permit there being a hell. Among the issues to be explored: (A) Contrasting pictures of hell, e.g. from a place of torment to a place that is not thoroughly bad but marked as hell because of its lack of persons having fellowship with God; (B) Different views of the longevity of hell, e.g. everlasting in time, timeless, or limited; (C) Theories of desert, e.g. can a person ever do an act such that he would then deserve an everlasting punishment?; (D) Arguments against universalism, the thesis that an all-good

God would insure that all persons be saved and, thus, no persons endure everlasting hell.

(16)   Consider the following charge that the appeal to divine incarnation, atonement and redemption is of little or no use in theistic approaches to the problem of evil:

> The first point to notice is that the doctrines of the Incarnation, Atonement, and Redemption, even if true, have no value whatever in solving the problem of evil. Even if true, they would provide only a grateful release from suffering but it would not begin to explain the need for it in the first place. No doubt one should be grateful for being rescued from an intolerable situation, but being rescued does not explain why one was subjected to it in the first place. There is a vast difference between gratitude for precious improvement in one's ghastly lot and an explanation of why it was no better to begin with. (Hare and Madden 1968, p. 71)

(17)   Antony Flew objects to the Christian belief in the resurrection of the body. Assess his criticism that a reconstitution of a person physically would not count as a reconstitution of the person:

> A reconstituted Flew was only an imitation of the Flew that had once been destroyed; and hence that I would not be justified in looking forward to the things that would happen to him, as things that would happen to me. (Flew, in Flew and MacIntyre 1955, p. 270)

(18)   Bruce Reichenbach defends the thesis that personal identity over time does not necessarily involve bodily continuity. Assess the following argument:

> For a half hour each weekday afternoon, a television programme called *As the World Turns* is transmitted in the US, featuring Bob Hughes, Lisa Coleman, and a number of other individuals. During this time these individuals discourse on events occurring at the hospital, who of their acquaintance is having marital problems, and of the various and sundry affairs of their friends. Following the final soap commercial, they disappear until the following afternoon, when they take up living at a point in time and space related in varying degrees to that when and where the previous show ended. Their existence is one of installments encompassing numerous gaps. In this case there is no possibility of tracing their existence between yesterday and today; they did not exist during that time span. (One should be careful here not to confuse the actor – Don Hastings – who plays Bob with Bob; Don Hastings might exist between times, but not Bob Hughes.)

Yet on their next appearance, we recognize and identify them as the same individuals watched yesterday, despite their lack of spatio-temporal continuity. In such cases, bodily continuity does not appear to be a necessary condition for personal identity. (Reichenbach 1978, pp. 29–30)

Further Reading and Considerations

From *A Companion to Philosophy of Religion* see the entries: "Personalism"; "Process Theology"; Goodness"; "Immutability and Impassibility"; "The Problem of Evil"; "Trinity"; "Incarnation"; "Survival of Death"; "Heaven and Hell"; "Providence and Predestination." For a useful treatment of suffering from the standpoint of world religions see John Bowker's *Problems of Suffering in the Religions of the World.* A classic statement of the problem of evil is David Hume's *Dialogues Concerning Natural Religion,* part x. See Douglas Geivett's *Evil and the Evidence for God* for a fine treatment of the problem of evil with special attention to an analysis of John Hick's work. For further work on the problem of evil, see the useful anthologies *The Problem of Evil,* edited by R. M. and M. Adams, and *The Problem of Evil* by Michael Peterson, both of which contain useful bibliographies. Melville Stewart offers a five overview of theistic approaches to evil in *The Greater Good Defense.* For further work on hell, see Eleonore Stump's "Dante's Hell, Aquinas's Moral Theory, and the Love of God," and Marilyn Adams' "Hell and the God of Justice."

For further material on the afterlife see John Hick's *Death and Eternal Life,* T. Penelhum's *Survival and Disembodied Existence,* Penelhum's edited book *Immortality,* Bruce Reichenbach's *Is Man the Phoenix?* and H. D. Lewis's *The Self and Immortality.* Paul Edward's anthology, *Immortality,* is also useful.

For two profoundly personal treatments of the problem of evil from a theistic point of view, see C. S. Lewis's *A Grief Observed* and Nicholas Wolterstorff's *Lament for a Son.*

For material about how one's philosophical outlook contributes to one's understanding of the incarnation in Christianity, see V. A. McCarthy's *Quest for a Philosophical Jesus: Christianity and Philosophy in Rousseau, Kant, Hegel and Schelling.*

10

Theism and Naturalism

This book began with an overview of world religions and a plea for using imagination and thought experiments in the philosophy of religion (chapter 1); realist and nonrealist accounts of religious belief were explored (chapter 2); philosophies of God were first articulated in terms of maximal power and then in terms of perfect power (chapter 3). We went on to consider a materialist and positivist case against religious beliefs about nonphysical reality (chapter 4). Theistic conceptions of divine knowledge and intelligence were considered and the contrast between theism and naturalism highlighted (chapter 5). We next considered religious philosophies that advance radically transcendent portraits of God, focusing first on the belief that God transcends time and then on the belief that God is not an individual at all; a modest defense of monism was developed (chapter 6). Religious values were outlined and the role of religion in a pluralist society explored (chapter 7); we then considered the concept of evidence and arguments about religious experience (chapter 8). The last chapter focused on the problem of evil.

   This chapter begins with brief remarks on a monist religious philosophy and proceeds to consider a range of arguments for theism along with a series of objections and replies. The material of the earlier chapters provides essential background for exploring these arguments. It is certainly *possible* to begin a study of philosophy of religion with a survey of the arguments that follow, but in my view such a study would lack sufficient attention to the philosophical context and orientation of the contemporary issues. An assessment of theism and its chief alternative today, naturalism, calls for considerable groundwork. Once that groundwork is in place, I believe it is easier to assess the arguments and craft one's own independent arguments and positions.

   This chapter displays some recent work on the cosmological, teleological and moral arguments, the argument from miracles, the ontological and wager arguments for God's existence. The name for each of these arguments does not stand for a single line of reasoning but rather for a family of arguments. There are, for example, many versions of the cosmological argument. I present what I take to be the strongest (or, if you prefer, the least weak) form of each. The aim, then, is to advance theistic arguments in a plausible form followed by a series of objections and replies. Suggested essay questions at the end of the chapter include material about additional arguments for and against the credibility of believing there is a God.

In much philosophy of religion, naturalism and theism are often treated as the best, most promising alternative descriptions and explanations of the cosmos. For this reason and because most of the prominent objections to theism in contemporary philosophy of religion stem from naturalism, the chapter is entitled "Theism and Naturalism." Let us begin, however, with reflections on idealist monism.

A Monist Prelude

According to one form of idealist monism, all of what we regard as the material world is a construct of consciousness, sensations, and experiences. It is called monist, in that it posits one singular kind of reality, and "idealist" because that reality is mental ("idea" was once a common term for the mental world as opposed to a mind-independent reality). There are many versions of monism, one of which was considered in chapter 6.

Probably the most common and perhaps the most promising defense of idealist monism begins with the thesis that we have a comparatively clearer, firmer grasp of experience and consciousness than we do of what we commonly describe as material, physical objects and processes. A contemporary defender of idealism, Howard Robinson, argues that our conception of the physical world is itself obscure and opaque. "Belief in a mind independent reality turns out to be too unclear to be refuted" (Robinson 1982, p. 123). Idealists like Robinson construe the positing of a mind-independent reality as a radical supposition that goes beyond both experience and reason. Bishop Berkeley (1685–1753) and David Hume both press this point:

It is a question of fact whether the perceptions of the senses be produced by external objects. . . . [H]ow shall this question be determined? By experience surely; as all other questions of a like nature. But here experience is and must be

351

entirely silent. The mind has never anything present to it but . . . perceptions and cannot possibly reach any experience of their connection with objects. The supposition of such a connection is, therefore, without any foundation in reasoning. (Hume, 1902, section XII, part I)

Our world is, as it were, first and foremost a world of experience, thought and feeling which (probably) most of us assume mediates a physical, mind-independent reality. What Robinson and other idealists call into question is whether we should accept this picture of mediation or, instead, come to see the world as one that is thoroughly shaped and constituted by mind. As H. D. Lewis put it, "I find the idea of some totally independent physical reality almost quite incomprehensible" (Lewis 1974, pp. 210–11).

Theists like Berkeley use this idealism to great effect in explicating an account of creation and God's proximity to the world. Berkeley held that to think of God making a cosmos from nothing is perfectly intelligible, based on analogy with our own intellectual powers. "Why may we not conceive it possible for God to create things out of nothing? Certainly we ourselves create in some wise whenever we imagine" (Berkeley, *Works*, 1, p. 99). John Foster today, along with Robinson, adopts a Berkeleyan account of creation. On this view, the whole material world is itself the unfolding of God's mind. We are not thereby merely states of God's mind (as in *certain* forms of monism) like figments of imagination; we are substantial individuals that are upheld in existence by God's enduring perception and will. In a sense, we exist as minds within a Great Mind.

I mention this monist outlook in order to underscore explicitly that while the main debate in philosophy of religion today is between traditional theism and naturalism, there is a monist alternative to be considered. In a sense traditional theism may be seen as a position mid-way between idealism and naturalism, thus:

Idealist Monism – Traditional Theism – Naturalism

Idealist monists construe the cosmos in thoroughly mentalistic ways. Naturalists range from eliminative materialists to those who preserve the mental, but all naturalists give weight to the material, physical cosmos in contrast to idealism. Theism seeks a high view of both the mental and physical. It may be seen as middle ground between these opposite philosophical systems.

I raise the idealist monist option not simply to sketch a broader philosophical landscape for the theism–naturalism debate. I raise it also because an assessment of theism and naturalism may give some readers reason to explore idealist monism as a promising alternative. Naturalists and theists often appeal to the simplicity and comprehensiveness of their philosophies. Just as the simplicity and comprehensiveness of a scientific theory are often taken to be virtues, so can the simplicity and comprehensiveness of philosophical theories. It may be plausibly argued that idealist monism scores exceptionally highly on this criterion. Most naturalists and traditional theists acknowledge both a mental and nonmental reality. A more simple framework would be to construct a view of the cosmos that is mental through and through. Readers who are eager to explore alternatives to naturalism and theism may find the work by Foster, Robinson, Vesey and other idealists promising. Theists may also find idealism an important theory to defend, at least modestly. If idealism appears to be coherent (even if false), then there is some reason to reject a naturalist objection that the mental cannot form the basis for an explanation of the cosmos.

Cosmological Arguments

In chapter 5 we considered a classic theistic stance whereby God and the cosmos were distinguished on the grounds of necessity and contingency. God exists necessarily, the cosmos contingently. The cosmological arguments to be treated here seek to vindicate such a divide, arguing from the contingency of the cosmos to the reasonability of supposing there is a being that exists independent of the cosmos that is responsible for its existence. If successful, the arguments provide some reason for thinking there is at least one such being of extraordinary power. Taken alone, it may not deliver justification for a full picture of the God of religion (perhaps a First Cause of the cosmos with great power can be vindicated though this falls short of positing an omnipotent, omniscient, all-good God), but it would nonetheless challenge naturalist alternatives and provide some evidential support for theism. After all, if theism is true, there is at least one such being of extraordinary power responsible for the existence of the cosmos.

There are different versions of this cosmological argument from contingency. According to what may be called the *horizontal version*, it is argued that the cosmos had an initial cause in time by something outside of it, a First Cause or Creator. On this view, the history of the cosmos is not infinite; there had to be some generative, initial Godlike cause. According to what may be called the *vertical version* of the argument, the cosmos *at every time that it exists* requires the causal, conserving agency of a Godlike cause. Aquinas states the conclusion to this second argument succinctly: "Nothing can remain in being when the divine activity ceases" (*Summa contra Gentiles* III: LXV).

Both versions of the argument work with principles of explanation. It appears that we can explain the existence and location of certain items in the world in virtue of other items and the laws of nature. A reason why you exist *right now* may have to make recourse to your bodily constitution, the presence of oxygen, gravity, the planet and its location in the solar system and, in turn, its location in the galaxy, and so on. Your existence is, in a sense, dependent upon the presence and stability of such objects and their interrelationships so that if all of them were to cease to be, then (short of some divine miracle, perhaps) you would cease to be. Your dependency may be constitutional, in which you are dependent upon the things that compose you, or external, insofar as the presence of these other factors sustains your existence or at least allows you to remain in existence. All such explanations of your existence concern your current existence. In other words, they do not essentially require reference to past events. In this respect the explanation may be turned vertical. It is one thing to articulate the reasons for one's existence at any time and another to account for how something came to be, if at all. If we then ask why you exist and this includes asking how you came to be, we must invoke additional prior conditions. Thus, we might include data about the history of each of your components – the carbon, hydrogen, oxygen, etc. that make up one's body – and so on, over large tracts of time. Such explanations involving the past may be called horizontal. If we seek both vertical and horizontal explanations of your existence, we seek a complete account of your existence.

In the quest to explain our contingent existence (whether this explanation is restricted to contemporaneous, vertical causes or includes past, horizontal conditions) it appears we do not find any object in the cosmos that necessarily exists, an object that is noncontingent or nondependent. As Richard Taylor writes:

> For we find nothing whatever about the world, any more than in its parts, to suggest that it exists by its own nature. Concerning anything in the world, we have not the slightest difficulty in supposing that it should perish, or even that it should never have existed in the first place. We have almost as little difficulty in supposing this of the world itself. (Taylor 1974, p. 110)

Defenders of the cosmological argument appeal to such thought experiments to secure the thesis that it is reasonable to think the cosmos is contingent. And the search for intelligible, scientific explanations of the world is itself taken by these defenders of the argument as a sign of the reasonability and fruitfulness of recognizing that the cosmos is indeed contingent and that its components can, in part, be intelligibly explained in virtue of the causal dependency of its different items (objects, fields, processes) upon other items.

Some proponents of the argument contend that it is a rational insight, knowable a priori, that if something exists there is a reason for its existence. Taylor believes this principle of explanation "seems to be almost a part of reason itself" (Taylor 1974, 104). Others maintain that it is a pragmatic, reasonable assumption borne out in experience that objects and events have causes. I note six formulations of principles of explanation that have been used in different cosmological arguments:

I.   For everything that exists, there is a reason for its existence, either due to the causal efficacy of other beings or due to the necessity of its own nature.
II.   Nothing is, without sufficient reason why it is, rather than not; and why it is thus, rather than otherwise.
III. For everything that begins to exist, there is a reason why it exists.
IV.   No fact can be real or existent, no statement true, unless there be a sufficient reason why it is and not otherwise (Leibniz, trans. 1951, par. 32).
V.   For every event, there is a sufficient explanation for the event.
VI.   For everything that exists, there is a reason for its existence external to it.

Some theists prefer the first principle because of its generality and because it explicitly builds into it the legitimacy of explaining something by appeal to the necessity of a being's own nature. In what follows, I shall consider cosmological arguments using this principle. Some of the other principles pose problems for theism. If principle "VI" were accepted, it appears that God does not exist, because God is such that there is no external cause of God's existence. (See question 6 at the end of this chapter.)

The thrust of both versions of the cosmological argument is that the contingency of the cosmos gives us reason to look beyond it for the sustaining cause theists call God. For reasons that are outlined below, some theists argue that if we seek for the explanation of something's existence entirely in terms of external causality, where item (object, process, event) A is explained by B, and B by C, etc., then we will never completely explain A's existence. It is argued that complete explanations of any object in the cosmos, and of the cosmos altogether, must take into account the causal efficacy outside the cosmos in a being that exists due to its own essential nature. Richard Taylor highlights the problem of only looking to the cosmos for an account of its existence:

> From the principle of sufficient reason [principle "I" just listed] it follows, of course, that there must be a reason, not only for the existence of everything in the world but for the world itself, meaning by "the world" simply everything that ever does exist, except God, in case there is a God . . . it would certainly be odd to maintain that everything in the world owes its existence to something, that nothing in the world is either purely accidental, or such that it just bestows its own being upon itself, and then to deny this of the world itself. One can indeed *say* that the world is in some sense a pure accident, that there simply is no reason at all why this or any world should exist, and one can equally say that the world exists by its very nature, or is an inherently necessary being. But it is at least very odd and arbitrary to deny of this existing world the need for any sufficient reason, whether independent of itself or not, while presupposing that there is a reason for every other thing that ever exists. (Taylor 1974, p. 105)

In other words, if the parts of the cosmos do not exist necessarily, there is no reason to believe the entire cosmos itself exists necessarily. If we restrict ourselves to the cosmos itself, we seem only to find contingent realities. Theism, on the other hand, provides an explanation of the existence of the cosmos that involves a noncontingent, creative agency.

At this point the two versions of the argument divide. Horizontal arguments for a first cause in time contend that a continuous, contingent, temporal regress cannot account for the existence of the cosmos and they conclude that it is more reasonable to believe there was a first cause than a regress of causes or that the cosmos just popped into being from nothing. On this view, there must be some originative cause, independent of the contingent cosmos, to explain its existence. Perhaps the origin of the cosmos was 20 billion or 20 trillion years ago. The point of this argument is not to date the origin of the cosmos but to argue that it had a beginning, however remote in the past. Vertical arguments to a sustaining cause of the cosmos press the point that explanations of why something exists *now* cannot be adequately given at this present time without assuming a present, contemporaneous, sustaining cause. Each argument may be represented in these diagrams. "A" in figure 10.1 represents one's starting point, one's own existence, for example, or one's environment, the planet or the galaxy. Some deists may adopt the horizontal argument for it does not explicitly require that the first cause in the past

Horizontal Cosmological Argument:

Causal Dependency

A FIRST CAUSE IN THE PAST . . . . . . ←D←C←B←A

Vertical Cosmological Argument:

A SUSTAINING CAUSE AT EVERY TIME

•

•

•

M

↑ Causal Dependency

L

↑

A

Figure 10.1

(or God) be involved with the cosmos at each subsequent moment of its existence.

The horizontal and vertical arguments sometimes run together, for most theists contend both that God created the cosmos at a time and that God upholds the cosmos at each time. David Braine describes how God is thought of in theism as unconditional and not dependent on the cosmos, but responsible for both its origin and perpetuation:

> When I speak of something which causes existence *unconditionally*, I mean a cause which, without causally presupposing anything else, gives existence: that is a cause which does not, in giving existence, rely upon or causally presuppose as already given or established either some system of nature involving regularities over time or the continued existing of any stuff with some persistent nature. Rather this unconditionality is a matter of causing perpetuation without causal presupposition . . . The difference between creation and upholding is precisely this, that in creation what is created comes into existence from nothing, while in upholding, what is upheld is something existing before, which is being given continuance in existence. But that what already exists should be the "object" with respect to which God's action is specified in no way makes it an efficient

causal precondition of this action and in no way compromises the immediacy of His action and presence. (Braine 1988, pp. 178–9)

A successful horizontal and vertical cosmological argument would lend support to this picture of God's all-encompassing creativity.

Both horizontal and vertical arguments have been cast on the basis of the denial of all actual infinities (William Craig). They have also been developed on the grounds that there may be *some* infinities (there is nothing incoherent about supposing there to be infinitely many stars, for example), but there cannot be others, for example, an infinite regress order of explanation when this involves solely contingent states of affairs (Richard Taylor). The latter has been described as a *vicious regress* as opposed to one that is *benign*.

Candidates for what may be vicious infinite regresses – series that would *not* generate satisfactory explanations – include the following. Imagine a mirror with light reflected in it. Would the presence of this light be successfully explained if one claimed that the light was a reflection of light from another mirror A, and the light in that mirror came from B, and so on for infinity? Arguably, if the explanation of the light seen in the mirror went back with indefinitely more mirrors and we never got to the source of light (e.g. the sun), we would never come to explain the light in the mirror. Consider another case: You come across a noun and you do not know its meaning; let it be "ongggt" (a word I have just made up). You ask the meaning for it and are then given an endless regress of single words one at a time that are equally opaque to you. Would you ever know the meaning of the first term even if the list of terms were infinite? Arguably, one would not. The force of these cases is to show how similar they are to the regress of contingent causal explanations.

These are the kinds of cases Richard Purtill advances in his version of the cosmological argument. Consider this cluster of analogies and his application of them to a cosmological argument for God's existence:

Suppose that I want a copy of Kant's *Critique of Pure Reason* and I ask you to loan me one. Let us suppose that you say, "I don't have one but I'll ask my friend Oxmore to lend me one, and I'll lend it to you." But suppose Oxmore says, "I don't have one but I'll ask my friend Home to lend me one and I'll lend it to you to lend to Kirk. And so on into the night. Now in that situation two things are quite certain. If the process goes on to infinity – if everyone says "I don't have one, but I'll ask my friend . . ." then I'll never get the book. And, second, if I do get the book then the process has come to an end somewhere. Someone had the book without having to borrow it. Similarly, if I ask Home to give me my check for travel expenses for this colloquium early, and he says, "I can't give it to you but I'll ask my department chairman," and the chairman says, "I can't authorize it, but I'll ask the Bursar," and so on, then one of two things happens. The process goes on to infinity, in which case I never get my check, or I get my check, in which case someone was able to give permission to issue the check without getting permission. All right, now take any existing thing. It received its existence from some other thing or things, which in turn received its existence or their existences from other things, and so on. Now it seems to me that the same two principles apply. If the process of everything getting its existence from something else went on to infinity, then the thing in question would never come into existence. And if the thing has come into existence then the process hasn't gone on to infinity. There was something that had existence without having to receive it from something else. In other words, a causally independent being. So it seems to me that if anything at all exists, as it obviously does, a causally independent being must exist also. (From Purtill's dialogue, *Philosophically Speaking*, 1975; for background see Aristotle's *Posterior Analytic*, I, 2–3)

This form of reasoning does not require the denial of all actual infinites, only the denial that the recourse to an *infinite series of explanations* will eventually generate a satisfactory explanation.

William Craig takes issue not just with vicious infinite regresses but with actual infinites. By his lights, there can be no extant infinite and thus no infinite past. Craig develops the following illustration (among many others) in an effort to bring to light the difficulty of positing actual infinites. He works with a formal defining feature of infinity, according to which a subset of an infinite set can also be infinite. Take the set of all positive whole numbers. Are there more whole numbers than there are odd numbers, a mere subset of all whole numbers? No. There are no more odd numbers than there are whole, positive numbers, odd and even together. This accurately marks a formal feature of infinity as it is used in mathematics. But it is one thing to posit infinites in mathematical reflection in which the members of an infinite set are no more in number than a part of that set and another to posit actual infinites in the world. Here is one of Craig's illustrations:

> [I]f an actual infinite could exist in reality, then we could have a library with an actually infinite collection of books on its shelves. Remember that we are talking not about a potentially infinite number of books, but about a completed totality of definite and distinct books that actually exist simultaneously in time and space on these library shelves. Suppose further that there were only two colours of books, black and red, and every other book was the same colour. We would probably not balk if we were told that the number of black books and the

number of red books is the same. But would we believe someone who told us that the number of red books in the library is the same as the number of red books *plus* the number of black books? For in the latter collection there are all the red books – just as many as in the former collection, since they are identical – plus an infinite number of black books as well. And if one were to imagine the library to have three different colours of books, or four or five or a hundred different colours of books – can we honestly believe that there are in the total collection of books of all colours no more books than in the collection of a single colour? And if there were an infinite number of colours of books, would we not naturally surmise that there was only one book per colour in the total collection? Would we believe anyone who told us that for each of the infinite colours there is an infinite collection of books and that all these infinites taken together do not increase the total number of books by a single volume over the number contained in the collection of books of one colour? (Craig, in Craig and Smith 1993, p. 12; see also Craig 1979 and 1980)

These and similar thought experiments are designed to bring to light the counter-intuitiveness of positing actual infinites.

Versions of the argument that make a case against all actual infinites whatever, face the difficulty of then considering what is to be made of the first cause. Must the first cause (if there is one) have some features that are actually infinite? In reply, Craig and others contend that their quarrel is not with potential infinites (the fact that the first cause will never cease to be is not a problem for there will never be an actual infinite) and that prior to the creation, the first cause was not in time. It may also be argued that God is outside of time altogether or that if God is temporal, God's temporality should not be understood in quantitative, metric terms. Perhaps God's beginningless existence is not a matter of God enduring over indefinitely many numerical units, whether years or days. (See Padgett 1992).

If successful, would either horizontal or vertical versions of the argument purport to establish the God of Judaism, Christianity and Islam? As noted at the outset: not by themselves. These arguments that the cosmos must have some cause independent of it to account for its existence do not secure that the cause is omniscient, omnipotent, all-good, and so on. Furthermore, these arguments only work to show there is at least one being independent of the cosmos responsible for its being. A form of Ockham's razor may come into play here to assist the theist: Do not posit more entities than required to explain the data. If one only needs to posit one supreme cause to account for the existence of a contingent cosmos, then do not posit more. Still, this use of

360

Ockham's razor only secures the reasonability of assuming there is one being; it does not establish there is only one.

Consider four objections to cosmological arguments and a series of replies.

(A) OBJECTION: The cosmological argument, in either form, is contrary to a central model of scientific explanations. Milton Munitz writes:

> Science is grounded in the use of the Principle of Sufficient Reason and, therefore, always leaves open the possibility of finding the explanation of *any* event. To say there is some unique event marking the beginning of the universe for which no [scientific] explanation *can* be given, is to say something contrary to the method of science. It is for this reason . . . that any conception of the beginning of the universe, when defended under the aegis of some supposedly scientific cosmology, is an indefensible notion. (Munitz 1965, p. 139)

If Munitz is right, then horizontal and vertical cosmological arguments are anti-scientific because they posit some absolute independent reality that cannot be explained in terms of other forces or laws.

REPLY TO (A): An initial reply consists of a defense of the coherence of the concept of a necessarily existing being. One may claim that such a being is not so much without explanation, but self-explaining. Some philosophers assume the legitimacy of self-explanatory notions like the logical law of identity (A = A) and these may provide *some* analogy to positing a first cause, not explained by deeper forces. A defender of a cosmological argument might then press Munitz and other opponents for a demonstration that such a being *cannot* exist. It may be contrary to good science to dismiss the notion of a necessarily existing being out of hand, a priori as it were.

By way of a further reply to Munitz, it may be argued that positing a supreme cause of our contingent cosmos is not at all in conflict, essentially, with science. As noted at the end of chapter 5, theists can construe God's agency as operating at a different level than empirical, physical causation. If either cosmological argument is plausible, the explanation for the existence of the cosmos requires a cosmic cause, but it by no means follows that this cosmic cause can be appealed to in explaining the particular cosmic events (the behavior of certain chemicals, the age of the solar system, etc.) For further objections along the lines of this first objection, see "Arguments from Miracles" and "Ontological Arguments" below.

(B) OBJECTION: The case against actual infinites is not sustainable. Contrary to Craig's principle, we seem committed to believing there actually are infinites. Ernest Nagel writes: "The supposed inconceivability and absurdity of an infinite series of regressive causes will be admitted by no one who has competent familiarity with the modern mathematical analysis of infinity" (Nagel 1976, p. 7).

REPLY TO (B): Craig and others who deny the existence of actual infinities do not deny the legitimacy of mathematical analyses employing the infinite. They only object to positing actual infinities in the world. This might, in principle, be no more odd than allowing for negative integers in mathematics and yet insisting that it would be odd to suppose there are negative events in the world (e.g. there are −1,000 elephants in front of you).

(C) OBJECTION: Why should one conclude that if everything in the cosmos needs to be explained then the cosmos as a whole needs to be explained? If everything in the cosmos can be explained, albeit through infinite forces going back infinitely in time such that there was no first cause, what is left to account for? Arguably, the explanation of everything within the cosmos should count as an explanation of the cosmos as a whole.

REPLY TO (C): In reply, theists may deny that the infinite regresses actually do satisfactorily explain the cosmos. This is Craig's position. But a defender of the argument may also concede that infinites are possible and the cosmos internally explained, and yet it is still reasonable to seek an explanation of the whole cosmos. Arguably, the question "why is there a cosmos?" seems intelligible. If there are accounts for things within the cosmos, why not for the whole? The argument is not built on the fallacy of treating every whole as having the same property as each of its parts (e.g. if every person has a mother, does it follow that there is a big mother for all people?) Rather, the point is, that if everything in the cosmos is contingent, it seems just as reasonable to believe that the whole cosmos is contingent as it does to believe that if everything in the cosmos is made of carbon then the cosmos as a whole must be made of carbon (Reichenbach 1972; Taylor 1974, chapter 10).

The objector may still seek to block this reply on the grounds that it makes no sense to refer to the cosmos as an infinite thing that needs an explanation. J. C. A. Gaskin writes:

> It does not appear to me to make sense to talk about any sort of explanation (internal or external to the universe) of an *infinite* series of states considered "as a whole." No "whole series" of states exists to be explained. If a real infinite series means anything, it means a series incapable of being gathered as a whole – whatever whole you take, there is limitlessly more. It is *impossible* to take such a whole, and yet, every state has a sufficient explanation. (Gaskin 1984, p. 63)

On this view, an infinitely expansive cosmos in space or past time cannot be clustered together philosophically and then be accounted for by something outside it.

Craig would agree up to a point, and, once again, argue that there can be no actual infinite at all. But if one grants actual infinites (in principle), one may still propose that it is reasonable to ask for the explanation of the whole infinite cosmos, taken together. If one posits a contingently existing, beginningless cosmos, one thereby concedes this cosmos does not *necessarily* exist, thus allowing that the cosmos did not *have* to exist. In keeping with this concession, one may have to allow that it is possible that a different, contingently existing, beginningless cosmos could have existed, instead of this one. If one can understand and articulate this contingency, then it appears that Gaskin's thesis is ungrounded; one *can* ask why the present cosmos exists rather than some other contingently existing cosmos.

(D)   OBJECTION: A related objection is that the cosmological argument does not so much explain the contingent cosmos as introduce a vast mysterious entity of which we can make very little philosophical or scientific sense. How can positing at least one first cause provide a more simple, comprehensible account of the cosmos than simply concluding there is not an ultimate account of the cosmos? In the end, is the theist not bound to admit that the explanation of why the first cause created at all is contingent? Or does the theist have to claim that the first cause *had to do what it did* in which case the cosmos is not actually contingent but necessary? In short, theism does not so much simplify matters as compound them, for now one must explain why the first cause created in the first place (horizontal cosmological argument) or sustains the cosmos in existence (vertical cosmological argument).

REPLY TO (D): Some theists come close to concluding that it was indeed an essential feature of God that creation occurred. If God is supremely good, there had to be an overflowing of goodness in the form of a created cosmos (see Stump and Kretzmann's revival of this view of Dionysius the Aereopagite, in MacDonald [ed.] 1991). But theists typically believe in the freedom of God and thus retain the idea that the cosmos is indeed contingent; God's intent to create and sustain the cosmos is not necessitated. Defenders of the cosmological arguments still contend that a theistic account of the cosmos has a comprehensive intelligibility that seems lacking in the alternatives. God's choices may be contingent, but not God's existence. Moreover, the divine choice of creating the cosmos can be understood to be profoundly simple in its supreme, overriding endeavor, namely to create something good. God's goodness may not require creation but it invites creation as a natural, fitting goal of God's intention. Richard Swinburne has argued that accounting for natural laws in terms of God's will provides a simple, overarching framework in terms of which to comprehend the order and purposive character of the cosmos. At this point one can begin to appreciate the desirability (from a theistic point of view) of developing cosmological arguments in tandem with the teleological arguments (from the Latin *telos* for "end" or "purpose"), to be reviewed below.

The importance of linking cosmological arguments with a broader teleological one is that, taken alone, the cosmological argument works with a thin notion of the external, independently existing being. Theistic defenders of cosmological arguments advance what they believe to be a more comprehensive, intelligible view of the cosmos – a theory which is more "intelligible through and through," to use J. L. Mackie's phrase. But without a fuller picture of the cause of the cosmos, many philosophers see little reason why they should not accept the brute, not further explained fact of the cosmos. Mackie reports:

> The principle of sufficient reason expresses a demand that things should be intelligible *through and through*. The simple reply to the argument which relies on it is that there is nothing that justifies this demand, and nothing that supports the belief that it is satisfiable even in principle. As we have seen in considering the other main objection to Leibniz's [version of the cosmological] argument, it is difficult to see how there even could be anything that would satisfy it. If we reject this demand, we are not thereby committed to saying that things are utterly unintelligible. The sort of intelligibility that is achieved by successful causal inquiry and scientific explanation is not undermined by its inability to make things intelligible through and through. Any particular explanation starts with premises which state "brute facts", and although the brutally factual starting-points of one explanation may themselves be further explained by another, the latter in turn will have to start with something that it does not explain, *and so on however far we go.* But there is no need to see this as unsatisfactory. (Mackie 1982, pp. 85–6)

Theists who argue for the reasonability of believing in God's existence based on cosmological argumentation want to provide reasons for thinking Mackie's conclusion is unsatisfactory. On their view, we ought not to settle for recognizing this contingent cosmos as simply a brute fact. More modest theistic philosophers may only aim for their opponents to appreciate that going further than Mackie – and anchoring an account of the existence of the cosmos in light of the powerful activity of God – is itself satisfactory and reasonable. It may not be *required* by reason and reflection but, so it is argued, such a move is justified and *more reasonable* than naturalism. Still, to secure this gain, theists need to provide a fuller account of the nature and role of divine activity. This brings us to the teleological arguments.

Teleological Arguments

These arguments focus on characteristics of the cosmos that seem to reflect the design or intentionality of God or, more modestly, of at least one powerful, intelligent Godlike agent of some kind. Part of the argument may be formulated as providing evidence that the cosmos is the sort of reality that would be produced by an intelligent being, and then another part argues that positing this being is more reasonable than agnosticism or denying it.

Is it more likely that the cosmos is to be accounted for in terms of a powerful, intelligent agency of some kind or in terms of what is surely its closest competitor, namely a naturalistic scheme of natural laws with no overarching, guiding intelligence behind them? Most versions of the teleological argument are built on (or contain sub-arguments for) the intelligibility of purposive explanations. In our own case it appears that intentional, purposive explanations are legitimate and can truly account for the nature and occurrence of events. Theists who employ this argument draw attention to the order and stability of the cosmos, the emergence of vegetative and animal life, the existence of consciousness, morality, rational agents, and the like, in an effort to identify what may plausibly be seen as purposive features of the cosmos. Naturalistic explanations, whether in biology or physics, are then cast as comparatively local when held up against the broader schema of theistic metaphysics. It is due to this appeal to a comprehensive account of the cosmos, that most versions of the teleological argument do not fall prey to arguments from Darwinian biology. Reigning accounts of biological evolution (and their successors) do not address questions about why there are any such evolutionary laws at all, or any organisms to begin with. If Swinburne and some other defenders of teleological arguments are right, then the explanations of life along the lines of contemporary evolutionary biology can themselves be seen as the outcome of purposive design. The *pro* and *contra* moves in the debate will then be like the cosmological ones, with the *con* side contending that there is no need to go beyond a naturalistic account of the cosmos, and the *pro* side aiming to establish that failing to go beyond naturalism is unreasonable.

365

The recent debate over the merits of teleological arguments often begins with disputes about the nature of divine agency. Is it intelligible to posit such a being of extraordinary power? Mackie, Kenny, McPherson and others criticize the coherence of supposing there could be such a being. The popularity of different materialist accounts of human consciousness have led some others to deny the existence of human consciousness altogether (eliminative materialism) or to argue that consciousness, and intentional explanations only make sense when attributed to material beings (essential materialism). These are topics in chapters 3 and 4.

Assuming theistic agency is coherent, which is more reasonable, naturalist or theist accounts of the cosmos? Michael Martin challenges the proposal that, when in doubt, explanations in terms of personal agency should receive a privileged position as being the more reasonable:

> In ordinary life and in science one would be ill-advised to appeal *always* to the choice of a personal agent to explain what happens when two events are equally likely and one occurs. For example, if heads come up in a flip of our unbiased coin, one would try to explain this event by causal factors operating on the coin, none of which might be the result of the choice of a personal agent or agents. It is unclear why the situation should be any different in cosmology. It is unclear also why a mechanical, nonpersonal cause could not have brought about the universe. Perhaps some nonpersonal causes are nontemporal and yet create events in time. Why these events are created at one moment rather than some other by these mechanical causes is surely no more mysterious than how a personal agent operating timelessly creates something at one moment rather than another. (Martin 1990, p. 104)

However when we explain the existence of coins and not just their behavior when flipped, we privilege personal explanations. Presumably we do so not only because we observe persons making coins and other artifacts, but because such things are readily understood as fit objects of intentional, personal activity. Some philosophers contend that just as thoroughly impersonal, mechanistic explanations would leave coins a greater mystery than an explanation involving governments and mints, impersonal explanations also leave the cosmos a greater mystery than if one invokes theism.

Hume drew attention to the flaws in the cosmos as evidence that it did not have a single, all-good, omnipotent and omniscient designer (see Hume 1779, 1980 edition). Chapter 9 focuses on the issues at stake here. Theists seek to recognize and to address the evils of the cosmos and also to highlight its great goods. If the problem of evil is decisive against the God of traditional theism, possibly some highly qualified version of theism may still be vindicated on the basis of a combined cosmological–teleological argument, but God (or gods) will be seen as amoral, or less than completely good, or informed by different values. Alternatively, one may elect to embrace a theism in which the power and knowledge of God are limited.

Hume also sought to undermine the motivation to posit God as a world maker by arguing that the cosmos more closely resembles a vegetable or animal rather than a human artifact. However most contemporary defenders of the teleological argument have not worried about addressing these analogies. Their point is that *the whole cosmos*, with all its animals, vegetables, human and other animal life, is itself something that a purposive, good intelligent being would bring about. In sum, they contend that a theistic explanation of the cosmos is more reasonable than an impersonal, naturalist explanation, and do not pin their whole case on whether the universe is more like a coin, say, than a forest or elephant.

This last point raises a vital, important issue for critics and defenders of the argument alike. The inference to the best explanation of the cosmos seems to be to a unique case. Anthony O'Hear writes:

> Against what standard of probability can we possibly judge in general terms what type of thing is most likely to exist? If experience is anything to go by, and what is *likely* to exist in the abstract is rather like what we do have experience of as existing, then we will have to conclude that what is likely to exist is rather more complex than it need be. (We can easily imagine possible worlds a lot simpler than ours. . . .) If, on the other hand, we do not take our actual experience into account, we might wonder what the probability assessment is being based on. It hardly seems reasonable to say, in the absence of any evidence, that what is most likely to exist is that possible world which the human mind finds more simple. Indeed, in the absence of any way of deciding what is correct here, one doubts whether the question has any meaning at all. In a way, the point being made is the old one made by Peirce, that universes are not as plentiful as blackberries, that, in other words, we have no sample of universes to inspect to infer what is a priori more likely or unlikely in an actual world. (O'Hear 1984, pp. 116–17)

Does this objection dismantle the teleological argument? If O'Hear is right, then teleological as well as cosmological arguments take place at a level of abstraction where we are without any reliable way of confirming our conclusions.

Some theists reply that if we insist that inferences in such unique, abstract cases are out of order, then we would have to rule out otherwise perfectly respectable scientific accounts of the origin of the cosmos. An objection against theism here would seem to work equally well against contemporary cosmology in physics. Besides, while it is not possible to compare the layout of different cosmic histories as if we were examining a series of blackberries, it is, in principle, possible to envisage alternative possible worlds. Some of these may be chaotic, random, or working on the basis of laws that cripple the emergence of life. These worlds may still be worlds we can envisage an intelligent being creating, but in considering their features we may be able to articulate more fully what counts as marks of purposive design that should lead us to conclude that it was designed as opposed to created at random or not created at all.

Some of the debate on the problem of evil may be of use to theists in a further reply to O'Hear. Many of the arguments about God and evil are carried out on the assumption that it makes sense to argue about whether the features of the cosmos should lead us to think its Creator is good, or morally indifferent, or perhaps even wicked. If such debate is intelligible, then it appears we can make sense of comparing different pictures of the cosmos and testing them against various conceptions of God and goodness.

Some critics of the teleological argument (as well as the cosmological critics) appeal to the possibility that the cosmos has an infinite history to bolster and re-introduce the uniqueness objection. Given infinite time and chance, is it not likely something will occur like our world with all its appearance of design? If so, why should we take it to be so shocking that ours has the apparent design or purposive character it does, requiring one or more intelligent designers to explain it?

Replies to this repeat the move, outlined in the last section, of insisting that if this objection were to be decisive, then many seemingly respectful scientific accounts would also have to fall by the wayside. It is often conceded that the teleological argument does not demonstrate that one or more designers are *required* to explain the existence of the cosmos; it seeks to establish that positing such purposive intelligence is reasonable and preferable to naturalism, not that naturalism can be known to be false.

If, as noted earlier, theistic cosmological arguments can gain ground from teleological arguments, the reverse is true as well. Imagine that a cosmological argument provides some reason to think that there is at least one being, independent of the contingent cosmos, responsible (in part, anyway) for its existence. The reasons may not be decisive but they may be sufficient to conclude that believing in such a cause is not unreasonable. Imagine now that the teleological argument gives one some reason to believe there is at least one being, a powerful, intentional agency, behind the ostensibly purposive character of the cosmos. A comprehensive, overall cosmological–teleological argument may help fill out the theistic picture further so that it can count as an intelligent alternative to naturalism.

One feature of the teleological argument receiving increased attention of late, focuses on epistemological grounds (See Plantinga 1993). It has been contended that if we do rely on our cognitive faculties it is reasonable to believe these are not brought about by solely naturalistic forces, forces that are entirely chance-driven or the outcome of laws and processes not directed by an overriding intelligence. An illustration may assist in getting a handle on the argument (taken from Taylor 1974, p. 115). Imagine you come across what appears to be a sign reporting some information about, say, your current location. Some rocks are in a configuration giving you the precise altitude and other information. If you had reason to believe this "sign" was totally the result of chance configurations, would it still be reasonable to trust it? It has been argued by some theists that it would not be, and that trusting our cognitive faculties requires the directing of an overarching, good, creative agent.

Objections to this center on naturalistic explanations, especially those employing evolutionary theory. In evolutionary biology, the reliability of cognitive faculties is accounted for on the basis of trial and error. A rejoinder by theists is that evolutionary survival alone is not necessarily linked to true beliefs. It could, in principle, be false beliefs that enhance survival. In fact, some atheists do think that believing in God has been crucial to people's survival, though it is radically false.

An important point to observe in all extant teleological arguments is the degree to which most of them appeal to particular features of the cosmos only to highlight the overall power of theism as an explanation of the existence and character of the cosmos. Arguments that are less focused on this overriding project are sometimes labeled "God of the gaps" arguments. Such lines of reasoning appeal to the difficulty naturalists face in explaining certain gaps, the development of life from nonlife, the emergence of consciousness from nonconscious forces, the gap between humans and nonhumans. Today teleological arguments typically appeal to the fabric of the cosmos as a whole along with its regularities, organic life, consciousness, human life, and so on. As noted earlier, this is why some theists hold that accounts in evolutionary biology should be seen as serving an overall teleological argument and not as a key challenge.

Moral Arguments

There are a host of moral arguments for theism. Some of these argue that the very existence of objective moral laws requires there to be a supreme law-giver, God, responsible for them. Arguments of this sort are straightforward metaphysical claims, analogous to the earlier arguments from contingency and purposive design. Other versions of a moral argument conclude that moral laws are in some way not intelligible unless theism is true. Given theism, certain moral laws make sense, whereas they seem peculiar or, to use Mackie's term, "queer," if naturalism is true. This latter argument is perhaps best seen as an extension of the teleological argument, for it is constructed on the notion that in a theistic world, the invocation of morality makes sense. The world, as it were, seems constructed in a way that morality makes sense if theism is true, whereas it does not if naturalism is true.

The first version of the argument to be treated here recalls the discussion of divine command theories of chapter 7. There it was noted that appealing to the sheer power of a being backing up the moral laws has difficulties due to the possibility that such a back-up may be arbitrary and cruel. Because of this, it was suggested that the most promising theistic position is to contend that God is necessarily good and thus God necessarily creates or brings into being moral laws. While chapter 7 simply raised this as a possibility, it is time to consider whether such a possibility should be judged to be plausible.

Why should anyone seek to ground objective moral truths in theism? Could the rightness and wrongness of actions not be basic to the cosmos? Perhaps it is simply a fact of the matter that causing pain to the innocent is morally wrong, compassion is good, and so on. Alternatively one may argue that ethics is based on the nature of rationality or on a principle of fairness and the like. I believe the most credible theistic reply is that while one *could do so*, theism offers a comprehensive explanation as to why even these justificatory moves have the force they do. Thus, let it be granted that it is a fact that causing suffering to the innocent is wrong. Might it not still best be seen as further accounted for by divine commands and creativity? It can be argued that theism may enter the picture by providing a richer metaphysical account as to why the cosmos is such that there are objective values. In a theistic cosmos, values lie at the heart of reality, whereas for most naturalists values are emergent, coming into being from evolutionary processes that are themselves neither inherently good or bad.

If theism has some credibility on other grounds, then a theistic moral argument would not be invoking an extraneous hypothesis to account arbitrarily for objective values. Imagine the argument for broad theism based on religious experience and the cosmological argument has some force, as does the teleological argument, and, as a result, one has some reason to believe there is at least one good, purposive force, responsible for the nature and constitution of the cosmos. Theism would then be a rich theory for it could also account for the facts of morality as well. Its fruitfulness lies in its broad-ranging explanatory power. This form of argument, then, would not use morality or objective values as a solitary fact upon which to build a huge metaphysic. It would instead advance something like the following as a description of what theism can explain: The existence of a contingent, ordered cosmos in which life evolves and there is sentience and consciousness, intelligent activity, morality and objective values, and widespread reports of the experience of a divine reality. Does this, as a whole, constitute something that is better accounted for within a theistic or naturalistic framework? If theism is true, one has reason to believe this phenomenon would occur, whereas if naturalism is the case, one does not have an overriding reason to expect such a cosmos – except, as noted earlier, in the sense that given infinite time and opportunity virtually anything might occur. Naturalists sometimes concede that they provide a less comprehensive account as to why the cosmos is the way it is, though they go on to argue that there is no need to adopt such a "deeper" account (see citations on p. 129 and p. 130 to Smart and Hospers). This naturalist strategy has much to commend it if it can be shown that theism is incoherent or in some way conceptually empty. If, on the other hand, theism appears both coherent and partially supported by other arguments, it may be contended that it has some credibility in its comprehensiveness that is missing in naturalism.

Consider the following two objections:

(A) OBJECTION: The idea of God necessarily willing that there be objective values (as outlined here and in chapter 7) is itself absurd. Willing presupposes choices and if there were no alternative to willing these laws then it would not make sense to think of God willing them to be the case. It can then be argued that any project that makes objective values prey to alternation is susceptible to a dangerous exaltation of pure power.

REPLY: Theists may give up on the term "willing" and make recourse to the notion that the moral laws *emanate* or are *brought about* by God without suggesting this involves God's willing them into existence. Alternatively, theists may simply hold the line and contend that it does make sense to claim that a being necessarily wills some things to be the case. Arguably, it is not

371

self-evident that the concept of willing can only be used to describe contingent causes.

(B)   OBJECTION: Theistic moral arguments make objective morality precarious. Theism is not a stable, universally held thesis. By grounding morality on theism, one thereby suggests that a precarious foundation undergirds morality. Michael Moore (1996) argues that theistic moral arguments tend to dethrone or endanger moral objectivism.

REPLY: This need not be so. Theists may take as given that there are objective moral truths and then argue that theism represents the best explanation of this fact. Should it turn out that theism is found to be philosophically suspect, then one may well prefer some competing naturalistic explanation of the cosmos and objective values. Consider an analogy with a cosmological argument. It may be objected that one should not advance a cosmological argument because, if it turns out that theism is false, we shall be in danger of concluding that there is no cosmos. Obviously we may instead conclude that some premise in our argument is unsuccessful or that the cosmos must simply be taken not to be "intelligible through and through" and so on.

Consider a second version of the moral argument. Its format goes back to Kant but may be seen in work today by R. M. Adams, George Mavrodes, Linda Zagzebski, and others. Mavrodes argues that if a naturalist world-view is accepted, our moral obligations will seem queer or odd. If naturalism is true, then it is highly likely that death involves annihilation. In a dramatic, naturalist portrayal of the cosmos, Bertrand Russell paints the following picture:

> That man is the product of causes which had no prevision of the end they were achieving; that his origin, his growth, his hopes and fears, his loves and his beliefs are but the outcome of accidental collocations of atoms; that no fire, no heroism, no intensity of thought and feeling, can preserve an individual life beyond the grave; that all the labors of the ages, all the devotion, all the inspiration, all the noonday brightness of human genius, are destined to extinction in the vast death of the solar system, and that the whole temple of man's achievement must inevitably be buried beneath the debris of a universe in ruins – all these things, if not quite beyond dispute, are yet so nearly certain that no philosophy which rejects them can hope to stand. Only within the scaffolding of these truths, only on the firm foundation of unyielding despair, can the soul's habitation henceforth be safely built. (Russell, cited by Mavrodes 1986, p. 215)

Mavrodes argues that in such a world, values will be odd or they will at least have a less deep hold on us than in a theistic world.

Values and obligations cannot be deep in such a world. They have a grip only upon surface phenomenon, probably only upon a man. What is deep in a Russellian world must be such things as matter and energy, or perhaps natural law, chance, or chaos: . . . [Christian theism] gives morality a deeper place in the world than does a Russellian view and thus permits it to "make sense." (Mavrodes 1986, pp. 225, 226)

In a naturalistic, Russellian universe the call to be ethical and the drive for self-preservation can easily come apart; being ethical and preserving one's existence may be incompatible. Over against the unyielding despair of a Russellian naturalist, the demand to sacrifice oneself for a great good may be very difficult to sustain. In classical theism, however, God acts to sustain human life, even beyond death, and prevents the ultimate extinction of those who act rightly. Kant developed a related argument to the effect that the intelligibility of moral life requires presupposing there will be some ultimate accord between happiness and virtue (*Critique of Practical Reason*). Kant reasons that such a harmony could only be secured by an all-powerful divine being.

One objection to this is to call into question whether we do have moral duties that call upon us to sacrifice ourselves to greater goods. If the metaphysical landscape is as grim as Russell paints it, perhaps we should reconceive the kinds of duties that Mavrodes invokes. This appears to have been Russell's position. He may well have conceded Mavrodes' point linking theism and some duties, but contended that we nonetheless have duties, goods and virtues that still enable us to live satisfactorily:

I admit that the love of God, if there were a God, would make it possible for human beings to be better than is possible in a Godless world. But I think the ethical faith which is warranted yields most of what is necessary to the highest life conceivable, and all that is necessary to the highest life that is possible. (Russell 1969, p. 354)

As a committed atheist, Russell refused to take comfort in philosophies that invoked God's will no matter what the gains in the way of comfort or enhanced ethics.

A second objection may take shape by adopting a quite different tactic: concede that a moral life looks absurd from the standpoint of narrow self-interest but argue that this creates an occasion for courage and heroism. Some theists hold ethical theories that may lend support to this objection. Recall that in chapter 8 it was noted how John Hick and other theists argue that there is some good to be gained by God's existence being less than obvious. Were it to be clearly evident that there is an all-good, omnipotent God, much of our moral activity might be motivated sheerly from self-interest.

Arguments from Miracles

Arguments from miracles are not as popular as they once were. This may be due, in part, to the prevalence of naturalist assumptions that undergird historical research. That is, there may be little temptation to appeal to miracles as evidence for theism because there seems so little in the way of plausible candidates for what may be described as miraculous. It may also be due to the fact that miraculous events have often been interpreted as important events *within a religion* or as *part of religious experience* rather than events that can persuade someone who is not already religious that a religion is true. Let us consider a current treatment of miracles that construes them as internal to religion and then consider a more ambitious external argument.

R. F. Holland advances the following view of the miraculous:

> The significance of some coincidences as opposed to others arises from their relation to human needs and hopes and fears, their effects for good or ill upon our lives. So we speak of our luck (fortune, fate, etc.). And the kind of thing that, outside religion, we call luck is in religious parlance the grace of God or a miracle of God . . . But although a coincidence can be taken religiously as a sign and called a miracle and made the subject of a vow, it cannot without confusion be taken as a sign of divine interference with the natural order. (Holland 1965, p. 44)

In light of such a concept of the miraculous, Holland offers the following illustration of a miracle:

> A child riding his toy motor-car strays on to an ungraded railway crossing near his house and a wheel of his car gets stuck down the side of one of the rails. An express train is due to pass with the signals in its favour and a curve in the track makes it impossible for the driver to stop his train in time to avoid any obstruction he might encounter on the crossing. The mother coming out of the house to look for her child sees him on the crossing and hears the train approaching. She runs forward shouting and waving. The little boy remains seated in his car looking downward, engrossed in the task of pedaling it free. The brakes of the train are applied and it comes to rest a few feet from the child. The mother thanks God for the miracle; which she never ceases to think of as

374

such although, as she in due course learns, there was nothing supernatural about the manner in which the brakes of the train came to be applied. The driver had fainted, for a reason that had nothing to do with the presence of the child on the line, and the brakes were applied automatically as his hand ceased to exert pressure on the control lever. (Holland 1965, p. 43)

Holland's depiction of significant coincidences allows religious believers to recognize miracles without being committed to believing that God intervened in natural processes.

A more ambitious appeal to the miraculous involves reasoning that the best explanation of certain events such as the resurrection of Jesus Christ is that these were brought about by God. I now turn to this more substantial claim, a claim that appears to pit theists against a "scientific view of the cosmos."

David Hume defines a miracle as a violation of the laws of nature brought about by a supernatural agent. This has been used by some theists, but it has also been criticized as failing to capture the religious significance of the miraculous. Consider Richard Swinburne's objection to Hume's definition:

If a god intervened in the natural order to make a feather land here rather than there for no deep ultimate purpose, or to upset a child's box of toys just for spite, these events would not naturally be described as miracles. To be a miracle an event must contribute significantly towards a holy divine purpose for the world . . . Extraordinary events lacking religious significance are more appropriately characterized as magical or psychic phenomena rather than as miracles. (Swinburne 1970, pp. 8–9)

For this reason, contemporary defenders of an argument from miracles usually work toward a concept of the miraculous which does blend into more general considerations of religious experience but also does not become a merely mechanical, quasi-scientific notion.

To this end, a miracle may be defined here as an event brought about by God for a holy or divine purpose, an event that differs from God's general creative activity of sustaining the cosmos and the laws of nature in existence. On this view, God's sustaining the world and its laws regulating organic decomposition and regeneration would not count as a miracle, but God's causing an extraordinary event that differs from this regularity would do so. Grace Jantzen describes how this concept would work:

If a situation arose in which there were compelling evidence for believing that Jesus rose from the dead, a revision of our supposed natural laws would hardly

be the appropriate response . . . Where there is a single exception to a perfectly
well established and well understood law, and one that is inexplicable unless one
appeals to divine intervention (in which case it assumes enormous significance),
what can be gained by making the nomological read, "All men are mortal except
those who have an unknown quality, observed on only one occasion and hitherto
accountable for only by divine intervention." . . . The skeptical response would
be inadequate. (Jantzen 1979, p. 325)

The theistic argument from miracles thereby works with concepts of agency
and evidence that differ from those developed by Holland.

The best known critic of the argument from miracles is David Hume.
Hume's chief objection rests on a concept of intellectual responsibility:

> A wise man, therefore, proportions his belief to the evidence. In such conclu-
> sions as are founded on an infallible experience, he expects the event with the
> last degree of assurance, and regards his past experience as a full *proof* of the
> future existence of that event. In other cases, he proceeds with more caution: He
> weighs the opposite experiments: He considers which side is supported by the
> greater number of experiments: to that side he inclines, with doubt and hesita-
> tion; and when at last he has fixed his judgment, the evidence exceeds not what
> we properly call *probability*. All probability, then, supposes an opposition of
> experiments and observations, where one side is found to overbalance the other,
> and to produce a degree of evidence, proportioned to the superiority. A hundred
> instances or experiments on one side, and fifty on another, afford a doubtful
> expectation of any event; though a hundred uniform experiments, with only one
> that is contradictory, reasonably begets a pretty strong degree of assurance. In
> all cases, we must balance the opposite experiments, where they are opposite,
> and deduct the *smaller number* from the greater, in order to know the exact force
> of the superior evidence. (Hume 1902, section X, part 1)

And Hume therefore concludes that "the proof against a miracle . . .
is as entire as any argument from experience can possibly be imagined."
His objection has been further defended by Antony Flew, J. L. Mackie and
others.

The most widespread theistic response to this objection has been to question whether Hume has simply begged the question. If one assumes at the
outset that there have never been exceptions to the laws of nature, then one has
assumed from the beginning that there have never been any miracles. It is not
clear, however, whether Hume does beg the question in this fashion. Arguably, the strength of Hume's position is that he highlights the great weight of
testimony on behalf of the laws of nature and the comparatively more slender

testimony on behalf of exceptions to these laws. J. L. Mackie articulates this Humean strategy as follows:

> It is . . . not enough for the defender of a miracle to cast doubt (as well he might) on the certainty of our knowledge of the law of nature that seems to have been violated. For he must himself say that this *is* a law of nature: otherwise the reported event will not be miraculous. That is, he must in effect *concede* to Hume that the antecedent improbability of this event is as high as it could be, hence that, apart from the testimony, we have the strongest possible grounds for believing that the alleged event did not occur. This event must, by the miracle advocate's own admission, be contrary to a genuine, not merely a supposed law of nature, and therefore maximally improbable. It is this maximal improbability that the weight of the testimony would have to overcome. (Mackie 1982, p. 25)

If Mackie is right, then an argument for theism based on the appeal to miracles will always be at a disadvantage.

A second theistic reply is to challenge the use of probability employed by Mackie and other Humeans. Stephen Evans points out how Humean arguments presuppose a substantial background of philosophical commitments:

> The defender of miracles may claim that whether miracles occur depends largely on whether God exists, what kind of God he is, and what purposes he has. Given enough knowledge of God and his purposes in relation to human history, occurrence of a miracle might be in some situations highly probable, or at least not nearly so improbable as Hume suggests. . . . In the absence of any firm knowledge about God and his purposes, it would still be rash to claim with Hume that the probability of a miracle is vanishingly small. Rather it would appear more reasonable to conclude that it is hard, if not impossible, to estimate the a priori probability of a miracle; and therefore one should try to look at the evidence for miracles with a somewhat open, though cautiously skeptical, mind. (Evans 1985, p. 113)

Alvin Plantinga similarly notes that Mackie seems to presuppose that it is clear that God does not regularly interact with the cosmos:

> Why should we suppose that a violation of a law of nature (taken Mackie's way) is maximally improbable (prior to testimony) on our evidence? On Mackie's conception, a law of nature describes the way the world works when it is not interfered with (for example, by God); but why should we think it is particularly improbable that it be interfered with? The antecedent probability of a miracle, for me, depends upon what I know and believe about the world; but perhaps I

have no reason to suppose that the world is not regularly interfered with. Why couldn't interferences with nature be the rule rather than the exception? Perhaps God doesn't ordinarily leave nature to herself, but takes a hand in what happens. (Plantinga 1986, p. 112)

Plantinga and Evans thereby place the debate about the miraculous in the context of an overriding debate between theism and naturalism.

Does this latter strategy completely undermine any evidential role for an argument from miracles? Not necessarily, for the argument can be seen as part of a broader, cumulative case for theism. The data advanced on behalf of theism might well be broadened to include not just religious experience, the contingency of the cosmos, and so on, but also certain accounts of what appears to be specific divine activity. The final outcome may resemble the argument for broad theism based on religious experience that was discussed in chapter 8.

Further reflection on the credibility of accounts of miracles is often best carried out in an interdisciplinary fashion where work by historians is conjoined with philosophical work on evidence, testimony, laws of nature, and so on. For additional fruitful work that aims at assessing the case for and against the miraculous, see Evans (1996).

Ontological Arguments

There are a host of arguments under this title; common to all of them is that they are based principally on conceptual, a priori grounds that need not involve a posteriori empirical investigation. If a version of the argument works, then it can be deployed with the use only of the concept of God and some modal principles of inference ("modal" in the sense that they concern matters of possibility and necessity). The argument need not resist all empirical support, however, as I shall indicate. At the center of the argument is the thesis that, if there is a God, then God's existence is necessary. God is neither contingent nor the sort of being that just happens to exist.

One may defend this view of God's necessity by making some appeal to the way God is conceived in Jewish, Christian, and Islamic traditions (McGill and Hick [ed.] 1967). Such an appeal would involve a posteriori, empirical research into the way God is thought of. Alternatively, a defender of the argument may seek to convince others that the idea of God is the idea of a necessarily existing being by beginning with a different thesis, e.g. the belief that God is a maximally excellent being. Anselm begins with the thesis that, if there is a God, God is a being "than which a greater cannot be conceived." This high view of God is not restricted to Jewish, Christian, and Islamic tradition. In Hinduism, God is described as unsurpassably great. "The Lord's pre-eminence is altogether without anything equal to it or excelling it" (Yogabhasya, i. 24). If there were a maximally great being, what would it be like? It has been argued that among the array of great-making qualities (omniscience, omnipotence) would be necessary existence. Once fully articulated, it can be argued that this picture of a maximally excellent being can be called "God" (see Oppy 1995 for review of arguments).

The argument may be seen as rooted in profoundly religious sentiments. Its defenders have appealed to the religious drive to worship a supremely excellent being and to the apparent witness of various scriptural passages of God's noncontingent, necessary reality (exodus 3:14 is a classic reference).

A current version of the argument I shall present here relies heavily on the principle that *if something is possibly necessarily the case, then it is necessarily the case* (or, to put it redundantly, *it is necessarily necessary*). The principle can be illustrated in the case of propositions. $1 + 1 = 2$ does not seem to be the sort of thing that might just happen to be true. Rather, either it is necessarily true or necessarily false. If the latter, it is not possible; if the former, it is possible. If one has good reason to believe it is possible that $1 + 1 = 2$ or that it is not impossible that $1 + 1 = 2$, then one has good reason to believe that 1 plus 1 does, indeed, necessarily equal 2.

Do we have reason to think it is possible God exists necessarily? In support of this, one can appeal to a posteriori matters, noting the extant religious traditions that uphold such a notion. Arguably, there does not appear to be anything obviously amiss in their thinking of God existing; it is at least not obvious that the belief that God exists is incoherent. Indeed, a number of atheists think God might exist, but conclude God does not. If successful in establishing that it is possible God necessarily exists, the conclusion follows that it is necessarily the case that God exists.

There are hundreds of objections and replies to this argument. Perhaps the most radical objection is that, with one minor alteration, the argument can be flipped on its head to conclude that God *cannot* exist. Assume all the above but instead assume that it is possible God does *not* exist. Atheists can point out that many theists who believe there is a God at least allow for the bare possibility that they could be wrong and there is no God. If it is possible there is no God, then it would necessarily follow there is no God.

Replies to this objection emphasize the difficulty of conceiving of the nonexistence of God, especially when God is thought of as being nonphysical (and thus unobservable in "standard ways"). The battle over whether God is necessary or impossible is often fought over the coherence of the various divine attributes discussed in the last section. If you think the theistic attributes as outlined in chapters 1, 3, 5, and 7 are possible, involving no contradictions and violating no known metaphysical truths, then one may well have good grounds for concluding God is possible and thus necessary. Alternatively, if one sees a contradiction with, say, a being who is at once omniscient and omnipotent, one may well have good grounds for concluding God is impossible.

Another objection is that it makes no sense to think of a being existing necessarily; *propositions* may be necessarily true or false but it makes little sense to think of *objects* as necessary or contingent. A standard, if brief, reply is that if it makes sense to think of propositions as being necessarily true, then it seems arbitrary to object in principle to the existence of a being that exists necessarily.

A further objection is that the argument cannot get off the ground to begin with because of the question-begging nature of its premise that, if there is a God, then God exists necessarily. Does admitting this concede that there is some individual thing that has a property like *being such that if it exists, it exists necessarily*? Replies have taken shape to the effect that the argument only requires one to consider what is an ostensible state of affairs, without having to concede initially whether the state of affairs is indeed possible or impossible. It has been argued that considering what is involved with positing the existence of God is no more hazardous than considering what is involved with positing the existence of unicorns. One can securely entertain the latter and its necessary features without believing the state of affairs obtains (e.g. it is necessarily true that if there were unicorns then there would exist beasts that are single-horned).

Finally, consider the objection that if it is successful in providing reasons to believe God exists, the argument could be used to establish the existence of all sorts of paraphernalia like perfect islands. Replies to this sort of objection have typically questioned whether it makes sense to think of an island (presumably a physical thing) existing necessarily or as maximally excellent on a par with God. Does the imagined island have excellences like omniscience, omnipotence (a power which would include the power to make indefinitely many islands), and so on? At this point defenders of the ontological argument typically stress the uniqueness of the concept of God at issue.

Before proceeding to the next section, it is interesting to note a bond between those who advocate the ontological argument (one of the most abstract in philosophy of religion) and those concerned with the religious practical, forms of life that fuel nonrealism. Philip Devine contends that without acquaintance with the religious context of the belief in God, the ontological argument is not liable to be persuasive:

> Although the ontological argument establishes that "God exists" is necessarily true, given the coherence of the concept of "God," to establish that the concept, and hence the statement itself, is coherent requires a context of belief in God which the ontological argument alone is impotent to supply. Without such context the concept of "God" is otiose and for that reason meaningless. (Devine 1975, p. 110)

D. Platt also places the ontological argument in practical religious contexts:

> At the profoundest level, the ontological argument is a rational attempt to explicate and interpret the awe-inspiring impact with the divine dimension in experience. (Platt 1973, p. 461)

In a sense, the ontological argument may be seen as a natural, formal attempt to refine a full-scale concept of excellence or greatness. The intuitions that drive the argument may not be solely intellectual or hyper-theoretical, but located in religious life and practice.

Wager Arguments

These arguments differ from the earlier ones, because wager arguments are not designed to provide evidence that God exists, but rather to provide reasons for why it is good, desirable, wise, or prudent to think, to believe, or at least to act as though God exists. In laying out some wager arguments, let me first comment on their conclusion.

Some wager arguments are formulated to prompt persons to believe there is a God. An immediate worry is whether one can believe on cue, so to speak. Are beliefs so under one's control that one could elect to believe something if it were determined that doing so was wise, prudent, or desirable? Beliefs do not seem to be the sort of thing that are under one's immediate control.

Granted that immediate control over beliefs is not possible, many philosophers concede that we can gradually influence our beliefs. One cannot simply choose to believe, say, that "John and Jane Doe are married," but that is not to say that one could not eventually come to believe such matters. Pascal

(1623–62) contended that acting as though there is a God can cultivate the belief that there is a God. But even if one cannot come to believe that there is a God, it may be that one can come to hope that there is a God. Hoping does not seem to require thinking there actually is a God. Hope may be enough, however, to warrant religious practices such as prayer. As Anthony Kenny notes:

> There is no reason why someone who is in doubt about the existence of God should not pray for help and guidance on this topic as in other matters. Some find something comic in the idea of an agnostic praying to a God whose existence he doubts. It is surely no more unreasonable than the act of a man adrift in the ocean, trapped in a cave, or stranded on a mountainside, who cries for help though he may never be heard or fires a signal which may never be seen. (Kenny 1979, p. 129)

So, wager arguments may be constructed that aim at fully-fledged religious belief or they can be modified in an effort to secure what may be called religious hope.

One version of the argument is as follows. Imagine theism is true and you rightly believe it and act in harmony with God's will. It is likely that there will be great goods, the good of divine–human accord, religious experience, participation in a religious community, a good afterlife, and so on. If theism turns out to be false, you would still be likely to have some goods, such as solidarity with a religious community that strives to promote justice and compassion. Now imagine you do not believe in God and thus do not act in what you take to be God's will. If theism is false, you will have been right and possess whatever goods accrue to you in a cosmos without God. But if theism is true, you will have lost out on great goods. If you wish to maximize the likelihood of bringing about good, it would be better to believe (or cultivate the belief or hope) that God exists and acts in accord with what you take to be God's will than to deny God's existence. The wager argument is pragmatic and will not carry weight for those who have no motives to achieve the kind of flourishing outlined in theistic tradition.

(A) OBJECTION: There are many concepts of God. The wager argument seems to justify too much; it would prompt us to cultivate beliefs in many different divine realities.

REPLY: The wager is best seen as governing a choice between two hypotheses that are judged to be plausible and yet incompatible. For example, the wager may be especially well suited to someone who thinks that either naturalism or traditional theism is true. The fact that the wager argument cannot direct one's choice between a vast array of possibilities, is no reason to think it is worthless once the range is narrowed.

(B)   OBJECTION: The argument appeals to self-interest, which is not a religiously appropriate motive.

REPLY: The argument can make such an appeal, but it need not do so. The motive to wager that God exists can be a motive to bring about great good, a good that will benefit others as well as oneself. The wager, then, may be likened to someone's betting on a friendship, presuming another person is a friend before the evidence is all in. While some friendships may be based on self-interest, prsumably many are constituted by mutual love and selflessness. The wager may thus be cast as a bid for a kind of friendship, rather than a bet to receive some self-centered pleasure.

(C)   OBJECTION: The wager argument promotes intellectual irresponsibility. Surely one should not believe that there is a God unless the evidence justified such a belief.

REPLY: Resolving this objection carries us back to the concerns of chapter 8. If one adopts a stringent account of intellectual virtue like William Clifford does, the wager argument will not carry any weight. If, on the other hand, you hold that our intellectual duties must be understood in a broad context of human welfare and you hold that theism will contribute to such flourishing, matters will differ. Thus, William James held that there are cases in life when decisions would be forced and real goods lost if one were to retain an exacting, purely intellectual approach to belief. By his lights, there are times when believing beyond the evidence can permit one to achieve great goods that one would otherwise lose.

A somewhat more qualified reply concedes that we should not believe something beyond the available evidence, and yet it is far from clear that one should not *hope* for something we do not believe to be evident. It is commonplace to hope for recovery from illness in cases when such a recovery seems highly unlikely. Arguably there is nothing pernicious in such a hope (Muyskens 1979).

(D)   OBJECTION: Consider a third objection that turns the wager argument upside down. A wager argument may be constructed that one ought to bet on hope God does not exist. The gains and losses can be rendered as follows: Imagine you do not believe God exists and you are right; there is no God. One has truth on one's side, a life without illusions and the ills of theistic practice. Imagine you do not believe God exists and you are wrong; there is a God. Why construe this as a great ill? If God is all-good, perhaps God would not wish you to have believed God exists on insufficient evidence. Maybe God has a special fondness for atheists and agnostics. C. S. Lewis suggested this: "I cannot and never could persuade that such defiance [of God] is displeasing to the supreme mind. There is something holier about the atheism of a Shelley than about the theism of a Paley" (Lewis 1967, p. 70). The rest of the naturalist wager argument follows as a matter of course, according to which the belief that God exists does not have nearly the benefits of disbelief.

REPLY: A defender of a theistic wager argument may possess considerable sympathy with the strategy and conclusion. An effective reply would have to take the form of detailed assessments of the perceived (or posited) goods and ills. William James was convinced of the vitality and expansive richness of theistic belief. Based on his survey of religious experience, he argued that theism was more life-enhancing than skepticism (James 1958). If naturalists are able to secure a higher view of the benefits of skepticism, a wager argument may work to their advantage. In the absence of this, a theistic wager argument may still carry weight.

The plausibility (if any) that these theistic arguments will have, and their ultimate evaluation and re-evaluation, will take place over against a large background of assumptions, many of which have been the focus of prior chapters. Someone who holds that the argument from religious experience gives some evidence for theism may find that one or more of the above arguments provides further support. Those who are committed to thinking the notion of God is incoherent will see that the above arguments may, at best, represent a longing for something more, perhaps something "deep about life" that, by their lights, is unfulfillable or should be radically re-conceived.

Another Cumulative Argument

While I have reviewed the arguments of this chapter as part of cumulative arguments for and against theism, my hope is that the survey of positions, arguments, and philosophers in this book over its ten chapters will provide an additional cumulative case, a case for readers who are not already in the field of philosophy of religion, to take it up as an area of sustained and concentrated study.

All the arguments and projects addressed in this book invite further reflection. And there are many fascinating topics it has not been possible to cover. Philosophers of religion have found much value in addressing theories of culture, economics, the ethics of war and peace, literature (autobiography and tragic literature, for example), comparative studies of the soul in different religious traditions, theories of law, art, agriculture, and technology. There are many aspects of religious life that may easily become the focal point of philosophical study, such as the religious use of icons and imagery, sacraments, worship, the religious practice of blessing and cursing, respect for ancestors, religious views of landscape, holy places, and dance. These lists are not intended to be exhaustive. Even "breathing" may be a worthy topic of sustained attention (see suggested question 14). I submit that the topics in the field, taken together, constitute a good reason for further inquiry and engagement.

When I was in my first year of college, I was very disturbed by the final lines of an introduction to philosophy textbook. These are the lines, taken from Shakespeare's *Romeo and Juliet* (III, iii):

> . . . Hang up philosophy!
> Unless philosophy can make a Juliet,
> Displant a town, reverse a prince's doom,
> It helps not, it prevails not: talk no more.

Now, some 25 years later, I offer a less poetic, slightly longer counterpoint on behalf of philosophy of religion.

Philosophy of religion is not some arcane, merely academic exercise. Far from it being an arid terrain, it plays (or at least it *can* play) a crucial role in human flourishing by helping us in our struggle to understand ourselves (what makes Juliet and Romeo who they are) and the limits of our world, political, social, and cosmic (the significance of our towns and the fate of our princes and other leaders). From a religious point of view, philosophy may appear a poor surrogate to religious life, just as from a romantic vantage point, philosophical treatises on love may seem hopelessly boring. But in my view, a deep religious life cannot constitute a sort of philosophical asylum where one circumvents the problems and projects of philosophy, nor can a deep, comprehensive philosophy of life circumvent a sustained investigation into religious beliefs and values. Religious concerns have not played a merely decorative role in world history and it is unlikely that they can be successfully ignored by philosophers any more than they can be ignored by historians or diplomats.

I end this book by returning to an observation in the introduction. I noted how arguments in philosophy of religion need not be wracked by belligerence or competitiveness. Philosophy of religion can be done, indeed I believe it is best done, when affection and camaraderie are at the fore, and philosophical exchanges are framed by respect, by friendship, and, at the risk of sounding sentimental, by love.

Suggested Questions and Topics

(1) In the thirteenth century Thomas Aquinas advanced five reasons for believing there is a God. These have been much debated not only as to their soundness but also as to their role in Aquinas' thought. Some contend these are not so many proofs but ways of thinking of God within a religious tradition; their role is to refine one's concept of God rather than convert atheists and agnostics. Be that as it may, his work has been formalized into arguments. You may wish either to defend, revise, or raise objections to the following interpretation of his work.

I. The argument from *motion*:
   a. Things do move (motion is the most obvious form of change).
   b. Change is a passing from potency to act (i.e., from potentiality to actuality).
   c. Nothing passes from potency to act except by something that is in act (for it is impossible for a potentiality to actualize itself).
   d. There cannot be an infinite regress of actualizers or movers (if there is no first mover, there can be no subsequent motion, since all subsequent motion depends on prior movers for its motion).
   e. Therefore, there must be a first unmoved mover (a pure Act or Actualizer with no potentiality in it that is unactualized).
   f. Everyone understands this to be God.

II. The argument from *efficient causality*:
   a. There are efficient causes in the world (i.e., producing causes).
   b. Nothing can be the efficient cause of itself (for it would have to be prior to itself in order to cause itself).
   c. There cannot be an infinite regress of (essentially related) efficient causes, for unless there is a first cause of the series there would be no causality in the series.
   d. Therefore, there must be a first uncaused efficient Cause of all efficient causality in the world.
   e. Everyone gives to this the name of God.

386

III. The argument from *possibility and necessity*:

    a. There are beings that begin to exist and cease to exist (i.e., possible beings).

    b. But not all beings can be possible beings, because what comes to exist does so only through what already exists (nothing cannot cause something).

    c. Therefore, there must be a Being whose existence is necessary (i.e., one that never came into being and will never cease to be).

    d. There cannot be an infinite regress of necessary beings each of which has its necessity dependent on another because

        (1) An infinite regress of dependent causes is impossible (see argument 2).

        (2) A necessary Being cannot be a dependent being.

    e. Therefore, there must be a first Being that is necessary in itself (and not dependent on another for its existence).

IV. The argument from *gradation* (perfection) in things:

    a. There are different degrees of perfections among beings (some are more nearly perfect than others).

    b. But things cannot be more or less perfect unless there is a wholly perfect being.

    c. Whatever is perfect is the cause of the less-than-perfect (the higher is the cause of the lower).

    d. Therefore, there must be a perfect Being that is causing the perfections of the less-than-perfect beings.

    e. This we call God. (From Geisler and Corduan 1988, pp. 158–60)

V. The argument from *final causation*:

    a. We see that things in the world which lack intelligence act for an end; this is evident from their acting always, or nearly always, to get the best result.

    b. Thus they achieve their ends not fortuitously but designedly.

    c. But what lacks intelligence cannot move towards an end, unless directed thereto by some being with knowledge and intelligence – as an arrow shot to its mark by an archer.

    d. Therefore some intelligent being exists which directs all natural things to their end. (From Meynell 1982, p. 21)

Aquinas sets forth the five ways in *Summa Theologica* 1, 2, 3. This section of the *Summa* is widely represented in standard anthologies in philosophy of religion.

(2)   This is James Ross's version of Scotus' argument as presented in *Opus Oxoniense* and *Reportata Parisiensia* (Ross 1969, p. 176):

1   That there is at least one Uncausable Producer is logically possible.
2   Whatever is logically possible is either actual or potential.
3   Whatever is potential is causable.
4   No Uncausable Producer is causable.
5   Hence, no Uncausable Producer is potential.
6   Therefore, at least one Uncausable Producer is actual, that is exists.

(3)   Here, for review, is a formalized version of Spinoza's ontological argument:

1   There must be a cause for everything, either for its existence or for its nonexistence.
2   A necessary Being (God) necessarily exists, unless there is a cause adequate to explain why he does not exist.
3   There is no cause adequate to explain why a necessary Being does not exist.
    a.   For that cause would have to be either inside God's nature or outside of it.
    b.   But no cause outside of a necessary Existent could possibly annul it.
    c.   And nothing inside a necessary Existent could annul it (there cannot be anything inside a necessary Being denying it is a necessary Being).
    d.   Hence, there is no cause adequate to explain why a necessary Being does not exist.
4   Therefore, a necessary Being necessarily exists. (Geisler and Corduan 1988, pp. 132–3)

This may be given a second formalization as follows:

1   Something necessarily exists (to deny this one would have to affirm that something exists, namely, himself).
2   This necessary Existence is either finite or infinite.
3   It is possible for this necessary Existence to be infinite.
4   There must be a cause as to why this is not an infinite existence.
5   No finite existence can hinder this being an infinite Existence (and to say that an infinite Existence hinders its own infinite existence is contradictory).
6   Therefore, this must be an infinite Existence (God). (Geisler and Corduan 1988, p. 133)

388

(4)   Here is a version of Samuel Clarke's cosmological argument as formalized by Richard Gale (Gale 1991, pp. 244–5). Clarke endorsed the following principle of explanation:

> Every existing thing has a reason for its existence either in the necessity of its own nature or in the causal efficacy of some other being.

Armed with this principle of reason (PSR), Clarke gives the following argument for the existence of a necessary being, an argument you may wish to analyze, critique or defend.

1.   Every being is either a dependent being or an independent being [PSR];
2.   Either there exists an independent being or every being is dependent [by logical equivalence];
3.   It is false that every being is dependent [premise];
3a. If every being is dependent, then the whole of existing things consists of an infinite succession of dependent beings;
3b. If the whole of existing things consists of an infinite succession of dependent beings, the infinite succession itself must have an explanation of its existence;
3c. If the existence of the infinite succession of dependent beings has an explanation, then the explanation must lie either in the causal efficacy of some being outside the succession or it must lie within the infinite succession itself;
3d. The explanation of the existence of the infinite succession of dependent beings cannot lie in the causal efficacy of some being outside of the collection;
3e. The explanation of the existence of the infinite succession of dependent beings cannot lie within the succession itself; therefore,
3.   It is false that every being is dependent [from 3a to 3e].
4.   There exists an independent being [from 2 and 3 by disjunctive syllogism]; and
5.   There exists a necessary being [from 4 by definition of an *independent being* as one for which there is a successful ontological argument].

(5)   Paul Edwards illustrates here what he takes to be the absurdity of seeking an explanation of the cosmos outside of it once everything within the cosmos has been explained. Imagine that you are wondering why five Eskimos are in New York City.

Let us assume that we have now explained in the case of each of the five Eskimos why he or she is in New York. Somebody then asks: "All right, but what about the group as a whole; why is it in New York?" This would plainly be an absurd question. There is no group over and above the five members, and if we have explained why each of the five members is in New York we have *ipso facto* explained why the group is there. It is just as absurd to ask for the cause of the series as a whole as distinct from asking for the causes of individual members. (Edwards, in Brody [ed.] 1991, p. 78)

David Hume raised a similar worry in his *Dialogues Concerning Natural Religion* (part 9):

Did I show you the particular causes of each individual in a collection of twenty particles of matter, I should think it very unreasonable should you afterwards ask me what was the cause of the whole twenty. This is sufficiently explained in explaining the parts.

How might a defender of the cosmological argument mount a reply? Do you find such a reply satisfactory?

(6) Develop an anti-theistic argument by defending principle of explanation "VI" on p. 355. Alternatively, assess this objection to the cosmological argument from Antony Flew:

At every stage explanation is in terms of something else which, at that stage, has to be accepted as a brute fact. In some further stage that fact itself may be explained; but still in terms of something else which, at least temporarily, has simply to be accepted (Hospers). It would therefore seem to be a consequence of the essential nature of explanation that, however much may ultimately be explained in successive stages of inquiry, there must always be some facts which have simply to be accepted with what Samuel Alexander used to call "natural piety" . . . The ultimate facts about God would have to be, for precisely the same reason, equally inexplicable. In each and every case we must necessarily find at the end of every explanatory road some ultimates which have simply to be accepted as the fundamental truths about the way things are. And this itself is a contention, not about the lamentable contingent facts of the human condition, but about what follows necessarily from the nature of explanation. (Flew 1966, p. 83)

(7) Ronald Nash provides the following description of contingency in general, and the apparent contingency of our own existence. According to Nash, we are contingent in the sense both that we do not exist necessarily and that our existence is brought about by external causes. A fruitful essay can be focused on assessing each of these claims:

Contingent beings have their explanation or sufficient reason in something other than themselves. A contingent being is anything that depends on something else for its existence. It is also a being whose nonexistence is possible. If the existence of some being (call it A) depends on some other being (B), the nonexistence of B would entail the nonexistence of A. The nonexistence of a contingent being is logically possible. A contingent being, then, lacks self-sufficiency; it is not the cause or ground of its own existence. Unless one or a number of other beings existed and conditions obtain, A would not exist. Obviously, contingent beings exist. In fact, no one has yet discovered anything but contingent beings in our cosmos. The Ohio River is a contingent being; it did not always exist and its nonexistence in the future is possible. All the automobiles I've owned have proved to be contingent beings. Mount Saint Helens did not always exist, and as recent experience shows, it is within the realm of possibility that it might cease to exist. Even the nonexistence of planet earth is possible, which, of course, implies the contingency of everything that exists on planet earth. Human beings are contingent. We would not have come into existence had it not been for other human beings; we could not continue to exist without favorable conditions in our environment such as food, water, oxygen, the proper temperature, the absence of blood clots in our arteries, and so on. (Nash 1988, p. 127)

(8)   You may wish to consider how any of the arguments represented here may be addressed in different media: poetry, novels, paintings, films, instrumental music, opera, theatre, architecture.

(9)   Would the discovery of intelligent life on other planets have an effect on the credibility of any of the theistic or naturalistic arguments?

(10)   Consider the following critique of cumulative arguments by Antony Flew:

It is occasionally suggested that some candidate proof, although admittedly failing as a proof, may sometimes do useful service as a pointer. This is a false exercise of the generosity so characteristic of examiners. A failed proof cannot serve as a pointer to anything, save perhaps to the weaknesses of those who have accepted it. Nor, for the same reason, can it be put to work along with other throw outs as part of the accumulation of evidences. If one leaky bucket will not hold water that is no reason to think that ten can. (Flew 1966, pp. 62–3)

(11)   In chapter 1 it was argued that thought experiments play a crucial role in philosophy of religion. A fruitful essay could focus on the use (and what you might take to be the misuse) of thought experiments in some of the arguments of this chapter. In reply to an objection to principles of explanation, G. E. M. Anscombe questions whether the apparent ability to imagine some-

thing coming from nothing is truly successful. Consider this criticism of what Anscombe takes to be a cavalier use of thought experiments:

> The trouble about it is that it is very unconvincing. For if I say I can imagine a rabbit coming into being without a parent rabbit, well and good: I can imagine a rabbit coming into being, and our observing that there is no parent rabbit about. But what am I to imagine if I imagine a rabbit coming into being without a cause? Well, I just imagine a rabbit coming into being. That this *is* the imagination of a rabbit coming into being without a cause is nothing but, as it were, the *title* of the picture. Indeed I can form an image and give my picture that title. But from my being about to do *that*, nothing whatever follows about what is possible to suppose "without contradiction or absurdity" as holding in reality. (Anscombe 1974, p. 145)

(12)　In the treatment of teleological arguments it was noted that there is new work on an epistemological argument to the effect that the reliability of our cognitive faculties requires (or is evidence for) some purposive good agency controlling our evolution. Consider the following argument by Richard Taylor:

> It would be irrational for one to say *both* that his sensory and cognitive faculties had natural, nonpurposeful origin and *also* that they reveal some truth with respect to something other than themselves, something that is not merely inferred from them. *If* their origin can be entirely accounted for in terms of chance variations, natural selection, and so on, without supposing that they somehow embody and express the purposes of some creative being, then the most we can say of them is that they exist, that they are complex and wondrous in their construction, and are perhaps in other respects interesting and remarkable. We cannot say that they are, entirely by themselves, reliable guides to any truth whatever, save only what can be inferred from their own structure and arrangement. If, on the other hand, we do assume that they are guides to some truths having nothing to do with themselves, then it is difficult to see how we can, consistently with that supposition, believe them to have arisen by accident, or by the ordinary workings of purposeless forces, even over ages of time. (Taylor 1974, pp. 118–19)

(13)　The chapter ends with a reference to sentimentality. When is a philosophy of religion sentimental? What implications does sentimentality have in this context? Two fine essays on sentimentality may be of use: Anthony Savile's "Sentimentality" and Ira Newman's "The Alleged Unwholesomeness of Sentimentality," both found in *Arguing About Art*, edited by Alex Neill and

Aaron Ridley. Oscar Wilde once characterized the sentimental person as one "who desires to have the luxury of an emotion without paying for it" (cited by Ridley 1995, p. 220).

(14)   Contrast different religious conceptions of breathing. In what prospects do Jewish, Christian, Islamic, Hindu, and Buddhist views of breathing reflect different philosophies of the body? The entry, "Breath and Breathing," in *The Encyclopedia of Religion* contains useful bibliographical material.

Further Reading and Considerations

From *A Companion to Philosophy of Religion*, the following entries are relevant. "Ontological Arguments"; "Cosmological Arguments"; "Teleological and Design Arguments"; "Moral Arguments"; "Pragmatic Arguments"; "Miracles"; "Religious Experience"; "Fideism"; "Reformed Epistemology." Recent work by Alisdair MacIntyre is well worth considering in addressing the role of history and tradition in arguments about God's existence. For additional material on the arguments of this chapter see Charles Hartshorne's *Anselm's Discovery*, James Ross's *Philosophical Theology*, David Hume's *Dialogues Concerning Natural Religion*, W. Craig and Q. Smith's *Theism, Atheism, and Big Bang Cosmology*, and M. A. Corey's *God and the New Cosmology*. Swinburne offers a sympathetic treatment of theistic arguments in *The Existence of God*; Mackie's *The Miracle of Theism*, and Martin's *Atheism* offer a systematic critique. Graham Oppy's critique of the ontological argument contains a nearly exhaustive bibliography of the argument in *Ontological Arguments and Belief in God*. J. Houston has advanced an interesting defense of an argument from miracles in *Reported Miracles: A Critique of Hume*. For a rich treatment of miracles and faith, see Stephen Evans' *The Historical Christ and the Jesus of History*.

For an interesting recent argument for God's existence see "Reference and Refutation in Naturalism" by Peter Forrest in *Our Knowledge of God* by K. J. Clark. Forrest's argument from linguistic meaning is given some support by George Steiner in his *Real Presence*. The groundwork of a wager argument for naturalism is laid out in Annette Baier's paper "Secular Faith." She contends that "the secular equivalent of faith in God, which we need in morality as well as in science or knowledge acquisition, is faith in the human community and its evolving features" (Baier 1985, p. 293).

For a poetic rejoinder to the lines from Romeo and Juliet, I commend John Milton's poem "Comus," L. 475–9.

Bibliography

Anthologies

Abraham, W. and Holtzer, W., eds. (1987) *The Rationality of Religious Belief* (New York: Oxford University Press).

Adams, R. and Adams, M., eds. (1990) *The Problem of Evil* (Oxford: Oxford University Press).

Audi, R. and Wainwright, W., eds. (1986) *Rationality, Religious Belief, and Moral Commitment* (Ithaca: Cornell University Press).

Beaty, M., ed. (1990) *Christian Theism and the Problems of Philosophy* (Notre Dame: University of Notre Dame Press).

Brody, B., ed. (1991) *Readings in the Philosophy of Religion* (Englewood Cliffs: Prentice-Hall).

Cahn, S. and Shatz, D., eds. (1982) *Contemporary Philosophy of Religion* (Oxford: Oxford University Press).

Clark, K. J., ed. (1993) *Philosophers Who Believe* (Downers Grove: InterVarsity).

Clark, K. J., ed. (1992) *Our Knowledge of God: Essays on Natural and Philosophical Theology* (Dordrecht: Kluwer Academic Publishers).

Delaney, C. F., ed. (1974) *Rationality and Religious Belief* (Notre Dame: University of Notre Dame Press).

Diamond, M. L. and Litzenburg, T. V., eds. (1975) *The Logic of God* (Indianapolis: Bobbs-Merrill).

Edwards, P., ed. (1992) *Immortality* (London: Macmillan).

Flew, A. and MacIntyre, A., eds. (1955) *New Essays in Philosophical Theology* (London: SCM Press).

Gaskin, J. C. A., ed. (1989) *Varieties of Unbelief* (London: Macmillan).

Geivett, R. and Sweetman, B., eds. (1992) *Contemporary Perspectives on Religious Epistemology* (Oxford: Oxford University Press).

Helm, P., ed. (1981) *Divine Commands and Morality* (Oxford: Oxford University Press).

Hick, J., ed. (1990, 3rd edition) *Classical and Contemporary Readings in the Philosophy of Religion* (Englewood Cliffs: Prentice-Hall).

Hick, J., ed. (1964) *The Existence of God* (New York: Macmillan).

Hudson, Y., ed. (1991) *The Philosophy of Religion* (London: Mayfield).

Idziak, J., ed. (1980) *Divine Command Morality: Historical and Contemporary Readings* (New York: Edwin and Mellen).

Katz, S. T., ed. (1978) *Mysticism and Philosophical Analysis* (New York: Oxford University Press).

Loades, A. and Rue, L. D., eds. (1991) *Contemporary Classics in Philosophy of Religion* (LaSalle: Open Court).

MacDonald, S., ed. (1991) *Being and Goodness* (Ithaca: Cornell University Press).

Mitchell, B., ed. (1971) *Philosophy of Religion* (Oxford: Oxford University Press).

Morris, T. V., ed. (1987) *The Concept of God* (Oxford: Oxford University Press).

Penelhum, T., ed. (1989) *Faith* (London: Macmillan).

Peterson, M. et al., ed. (1995) *Philosophy of Religion* (Oxford: Oxford University Press).

Plantinga, A., ed. (1965) *The Ontological Argument from St. Anselm to Contemporary Philosophers* (New York: Doubleday).

Pojman, L., ed. (1994, second edition) *Philosophy of Religion: An Anthology* (Belmont: Wadsworth).

Porter, B. S., ed. (1993) *Religion and Reason* (New York: St. Martin's Press).

Quinn, P. and Taliaferro, C., eds. (1997) *A Companion to Philosophy of Religion* (Oxford: Basil Blackwell).

Rowe, W. and Wainwright, W., eds. (1989) *Philosophy of Religion: Selected Readings* (New York: Harcourt Brace Jovanovich).

Sharma, A., ed. (1993) *Our Religions* (San Francisco: Harper Collins).

Stewart, M., ed. (1996) *Philosophy of Religion* (Boston: Jones and Bartlett Publishers).

Tracy, T., ed. (1994) *The God Who Acts* (University Park: Pennsylvania State University Press).

Urban, L. and Walton, D., eds. (1978) *The Power of God: Readings on Omnipotence and Evil* (Oxford: Oxford University Press).

Zagzebski, L., ed. (1993) *Rational Faith* (Notre Dame: University of Notre Dame Press).

Introductions to the Field

Abraham, W. (1985) *An Introduction to the Philosophy of Religion* (Englewood Cliffs: Prentice-Hall).

Clark, K. J. (1990) *Return to Reason* (Grand Rapids: William Eerdmans).

Creel, R. (1991, 2nd edition) *Religion and Doubt* (Englewood Cliffs: Prentice-Hall).

Davies, B. (1993) *An Introduction to the Philosophy of Religion* (Oxford: Oxford University Press).

Evans, S. C. (1985) *Philosophy of Religion* (Downers Grove: InterVarsity).

Gaskin, J. C. A. (1984) *The Quest for Eternity* (Harmondsworth: Penguin Books).

Geisler, N. and Corduan, W. (1988) *Philosophy of Religion* (Grand Rapids: Baker Books).

Hick, J. (1989, 4th edition) *Philosophy of Religion* (Englewood Cliffs: Prentice-Hall).

Hudson, Y. (1991) *The Philosophy of Religion* (London: Mayfield).

Lewis, H. D. (1965) *Philosophy of Religion* (London: The English Universities Press).

Morris, T. V. (1991) *Our Idea of God* (Downers Grove: InterVarsity).

Nash, R. H. (1988) *Faith and Reason* (Grand Rapids: Zondervon).

Nielsen, K. (1982) *An Introduction to the Philosophy of Religion* (New York: St. Martin's Press).

O'Hear, A. (1984) *Experience, Explanation, and Faith: An Introduction to the Philosophy of Religion* (London: Routledge and Kegan Paul).

Peterson, M. et al. (1991) *Reason and Religious Belief: An Introduction to the Philosophy of Religion* (Oxford: Oxford University Press).

Purtill, R. (1978) *Thinking About Religion* (Englewood Cliffs: Prentice-Hall).

Purtill, R. (1974) *Reason to Believe* (Grand Rapids: William Eerdmans).

Ross, J. (1969) *Introduction to Philosophy of Religion* (New York: Macmillan).

Rowe, W. (1993) *Philosophy of Religion* (Belmont: Wadsworth).

Tilghman, B. R. (1993) *An Introduction to Philosophy of Religion* (Oxford: Basil Blackwell).

Wainwright, W. (1988) *Philosophy of Religion* (Belmont: Wadsworth).

Yandell, K. (1984) *Christianity and Philosophy* (Grand Rapids: William Eerdmans).

Other Books and Articles

Abraham, W. J. (1982) *Divine Revelation and the Limits of Historical Criticism* (Oxford: Oxford University Press).

Adams, M. (1991) "Forgiveness: A Christian Model," *Faith and Philosophy* 8.

Adams, R. M. (1993) "Religious Ethics in a Pluralist Society," in *Prospects for a Common Morality* ed. by G. Outka and J. P. Reeder (Princeton: Princeton University Press).

Adams, R. M. (1991) "An Anti-Molinist Argument," *Philosophical Perspectives* 5.

Adams, R. M. (1987) *The Virtue of Faith* (Oxford: Oxford University Press).

Adams, R. M. (1983) "Divine Necessity," *The Journal of Philosophy* 80.

Adams, R. M. (1977) "Middle Knowledge and the Problem of Evil," *American Philosophical Quarterly* 14, pp. 109–17.

Albo, J. (1930) *Sefer Ha-'ikkarim: Book of Principles*, trans. by Isaac Husik (Philadelphia: Jewish Publication Society of America).

Allen, D. (1989) "Incarnation in the Gospels and the Bhagavad Gita," *Faith and Philosophy* 6.

Alston, W. (1994) "Divine Action: Shadows or Substance," in *The God who Acts* (University Park: Pennsylvania State University Press).

Alston, W. (1993) *The Reliability of Sense Perception* (New York: Cornell University Press).

Alston, W. (1991a) "The Inductive Argument from Evil," *Philosophical Perspectives* 5.

Alston, W. (1991b) *Perceiving God* (Ithaca: Cornell University Press).

Alston, W. (1989) *Divine Nature and Human Language* (Ithaca: Cornell University Press).

396

Alston, W. (1988) "The Indwelling of the Holy Spirit," in *Philosophy and the Christian Faith*, ed. by T. Morris (Notre Dame: Notre Dame University Press).

Alston, W. (1987) "Functionalism and Theological Language," in *The Concept of God*, ed. by T. Morris (Oxford: Oxford University Press).

Alston, W. (1986) "Does God Have Beliefs?" *Religious Studies* 22.

Alston, W. (1979) "Yes, Virginia, There is a Real World," *Proceedings of the American Philosophical Association* 52: 6.

Alston, W. (1972) "Ineffability," in *Logical Analysis and Contemporary Theism*, ed. by J. Donnelly (New York: Fordham University Press).

Anscombe, G. E. M. (1974) " 'Whatever has a beginning of existence must have a cause': Hume's Argument Exposed," *Analysis* 34.

Anscombe, G. E. M. (1971) *Causality and Determinism* (Cambridge: Cambridge University Press).

Anselm (1962) *The Basic Writings of St. Anselm* (LaSalle: Open Court).

Anselm (1965) *Proslogion*, trans. by M. J. Charlesworth (Oxford: Clarendon Press).

Aquinas (1963) *Philosophical Texts*, trans. by T. Gilby (Oxford: Oxford University Press).

Aquinas (1947) *Summa Theologica* (New York: Benzinger Brothers).

Aquinas (1945) *Basic Writings of St. Thomas Aquinas*, ed. by A. Pegis (New York: Random House).

Arthur, J. (1993) "Does Morality Depend on Religion?," in *Morality and Moral Controversies*, ed. J. Arthur (Englewood: Prentice-Hall).

Armstrong, D. M., ed. (1968) *A Materialist Theory of Mind* (London: Routledge and Kegan Paul).

Armstrong, S. J. and Botzler, R. G., eds. (1993) *Evironmental Ethics* (New York: McGraw-Hill).

Audi, R. (1989) "The Separation of Church and State and the Obligations of Citizenship," *Philosophy and Public Affairs* 18.

Augustine (1963) *The Trinity*, trans. by S. McKenna (Washington D.C.: Catholic University of America).

Augustine (1948) *Confessions*, trans. by E. B. Pusey (Chicago: Henry Regnery).

Austin, J. L. (1963) *Sense and Sensibilia* (Oxford: Clarendon Press).

Avila, C. (1983) *Ownership: Early Christian Teachings* (London: Sheed and Ward).

Ayer, A. J. (1987) "Reflections on *Language, Truth and Logic*," in *Logical Positivism in Perspective*, ed. by B. Gower (Totowa: Barnes and Noble).

Ayer, A. J. (1963) *The Concept of a Person and Other Essays* (London: Macmillan).

Ayer, A. J. (1956) *The Problem of Knowledge* (London: Macmillan).

Ayer, A. J. (1946, 2nd edition) *Language, Truth and Logic* (New York: Dover Publications).

Ayer, A. J. and Copleston, F. C. (1965, 2nd edition) "Logical Positivism – A Debate," in *A Modern Introduction to Philosophy*, ed. by P. Edwards and A. Pap (New York: The Free Press).

Bacon, F. (1883) *Essays* (New York: H. M. Caldwell).

Badham, P. (1976) *Christian Beliefs About Immortality* (London: Macmillan).

Badham, P. and Badham, L., eds (1987) *Death and Immortality in the Religions of the World* (New York: Paragon House).

Badham, P. and Badham, L. (1982) *Immortality or Extinction?* (Basingstoke: Macmillan).

Baier, A. (1985) "Secular Faith," in *Postures of the Mind* by A. Baier (Minneapolis: University of Minnesota Press).

Baillie, J. (1959) *Our Knowledge of God* (New York: Scribner).

Baillie, J. (1956) *The Idea of the Revelation in Recent Thought* (New York: Columbia University Press).

Baker, L. (1987) *Saving Belief* (Princeton: Princeton University Press).

Barbour, I. (1974) *Myths, Models, and Paradigms* (New York: Harper and Row).

Barbour, J. (1994) *Versions of Deconversion* (Charlottesville: University of Virginia Press).

Barrow, J. (1991) *Theories of Everything* (Oxford: Oxford University Press).

Barth, K. (1948) *Church Dogmatics*, vol. 2 (Edinburgh: T. and T. Clark).

Bartholomew, D. J. (1996) *Uncertain Belief* (Oxford: Clarendon).

Basinger, D. and Basinger, R. (1986) *Philosophy and Miracle* (Lewiston: Edwin Mellen).

Basinger, D. (1992) "Evil as Evidence Against God's Existence," in *The Problem of Evil*, ed. by M. Peterson (1992).

Bayle, P. (1965) *Historical and Critical Dictionary*, ed. by R. H. Popwin (Indianapolis: Bobbs-Merrill).

Beardsmore, T. (1997) *A Sense of Presence* (Oxford: Oxford University Press).

Beaty, M. and Taliaferro, C. (1990) "God and Concept Empiricism," *Southwest Philosophy Review* 6: 2.

Becker, C. B. (1993) *Paranormal Experience and Survival of Death* (Albany: State University of New York Press).

Beckwith, F. J. (1989) *David Hume's Argument Against Miracles* (Lanham: University Press of America).

Beerdyaev, N. (1960) *The Destiny of Man*, trans. by N. Duddington (New York: Harper and Row).

Bell, R. H. (1975) "Theology as Grammar: Is God on Object of Understanding?" *Religious Studies* II.3.

Belliotti, R. (1986) "Honor Thy Father and Thy Mother and to Thine Own Self be True," *Southern Journal of Philosophy* 24: 2.

Beloff, J. (1993) *Parapsychology* (New York: St. Martin's Press).

Beloff, J. (1989) "Dualism: A Parapsychological Perspective," in *The Case for Dualism*, ed. by J. R. Smythies and J. Beloff (Charlottesville: University Press of Virginia).

Berkeley, G. (1948) *Works of George Berkeley,* ed. by Luce and Jessop (London: Nelson).

Benedict, R. (1934) "Anthropology and the Abnormal," *The Journal of General Psychology* 10.

Bertocci, P. (1951) *Introduction to the Philosophy of Religion* (Englewood Cliffs: Prentice-Hall).

Betty, L. S. (1992) "Making Sense of Animal Pain: An Environmental Theodicy," *Faith and Philosophy* 9: 1.

Blackburn, S. (1994) *The Oxford Dictionary of Philosophy* (Oxford: Oxford University Press).

Bloor, D. (1984) "A Sociological Theory of Objectivity," in *Objectivity and Cultural Divergence*, ed. by S. C. Brown (Cambridge: Cambridge University Press).

Blumenfeld, D. (1987) "On the Compossibility of Divine Attributes," in *The Concept of God*, ed. by T. V. Morris (Oxford: Oxford University Press).

Boethius (1918) *The Theological Treatises and the Consolation of Philosophy* (London: William Heinemann).

Bouwsma, O. K. (1982) *Toward a New Sensibility* (Lincoln: University of Nebraska Press).

Bowker, J. (1978) *The Religious Imagination and the Sense of God* (Oxford: Clarendon).

Bowker, J. (1970) *Problems of Suffering in the Religions of the World* (Cambridge: Cambridge University Press).

Boyle, J. et al. (1976) *Free Choice* (Notre Dame: University of Notre Dame).

Braine, D. (1992) *The Human Person* (Notre Dame: University of Notre Dame Press).

Braine, D. (1988) *The Reality of Time and the Existence of God* (Oxford: Clarendon).

Braithwaite, R. (1955) *An Empiricist's View of the Nature of Religious Belief* (Cambridge: Cambridge University Press).

Brann, E. (1991) *The World of the Imagination* (Maryland: Rowman and Littlefield).

Brink, D. (1984) "A Critique of Ethical Skepticism," *Australasian Journal of Philosophy* 62: 2.

Broad, C. D. (1953) *Religion, Philosophy and Psychical Research* (London: Routledge and Kegan Paul).

Brody, B. (1974) "Morality and Religion Reconsidered," in *Readings in the Philosophy of Religion: An Analytical Approach*, ed. by B. Brody (Englewood Cliffs: Prentice-Hall).

Brown, D. (1989) "The Problem of Pain," in *Religion of the Incarnation*, ed. by R. Morgan (Bristol: Bristol Classical Press).

Brown, D. (1987) *Continental Philosophy and Modern Theology* (Oxford: Blackwell).

Brown, F. B. (1989) *Religious Aesthetics* (Princeton: Princeton University Press).

Brunner, E. (1948) *Christianity and Civilization* (London: Nisbet).

Buber, M. (1923) *I and You*, trans. by W. Kaufmann (New York: Scribner).

Burge, T. (1979) "Individualism and the Mental," in *Midwest Studies in Philosophy* 5.

Burke, T. P. (1995) *The Major Religions* (Oxford: Basil Blackwell).

Campbell, C. A. (1967) *In Defense of Free Will* (London: Allen and Unwin).

Camus, A. (1956) *The Rebel*, trans. by Anthony Bower (New York: Vintage Books).

Camus, A. (1955) *The Myth of Sisyphus*, trans. by J. O'Brien (New York: Vintage Books).

Carnap, R. (1959) "The Elimination of Metaphysics," in *Logical Positivism* ed. by A. J. Ayer (Glencoe: The Free Press).

Carter, W. R. (1985) "Impeccability Revisited," *Analysis* 45: 19.

Case-Winters, A. (1990) *God's Power* (Louisville: Westminster Press).

Castaneda, H. N. (1967) "Omniscience and Indexical Reference," *The Journal of Philosophy* 64.

Chance, T. and Taliaferro, C. (1991) "Philosophers, Red Tooth and Claw," *Teaching Philosophy* 14: 1.

Chappell, T. D. J. (1993) "Why God is not a Consequentialist," *Religious Studies* 29.

Chisholm, R. (1986) *Brentanno and Intrinsic Value* (Cambridge: Cambridge University Press).

Chisholm, R. (1981) *The First Person* (Minneapolis: University of Minnesota Press).

Chisholm, R. (1977) *Theory of Knowledge* (Englewood Cliffs: Prentice-Hall).

Chisholm, R. (1976) *Person and Object* (LaSalle: Open Court).

Chisholm, R., ed. (1973) *Empirical Knowledge* (Englewood Cliffs: Prentice-Hall).

Chisholm, R. (1966) "Freedom and Action," in *Freedom and Determinism*, ed. by K. Lehrer (New York: Random House).

Churchland, P. and Hooker, C., eds. (1985) *Images of Science* (Chicago: University of Chicago Press).

Churchland, Patricia (1986) *Neurophilosophy* (Cambridge, Mass.: MIT Press).

Churchland, Paul (1981) "Eliminative Materialism and Propositional Attitudes," *Journal of Philosophy* 78.

Clark, W. N. (1972) "Technology and Man: A Christian Vision," in *Philosophy and Technology*, ed. by C. Mitcham and R. Mackey (New York: The Free Press).

Clifford, W. K. (1879) "The Ethics of Belief," in *Lectures and Essays* (London: Macmillan).

Cobb, J. B. (1965) *A Christian Natural Theology* (Philadelphia: Westminster).

Coburn, R. C. (1963) "Professor Malcolm on God," *Australian Journal of Philosophy* 41.

Code, L. (1991) *What Can She Know?* (Ithaca: Cornell University Press).

Cohn, T. (1983) "Jokes," in *Pleasure Preference and Value: Studies in Philosophical Aesthetics*, ed. by Eva Schaper (Cambridge: Cambridge University Press).

Cohn-Sherbok, D. (1990) "Jewish Faith and the Holocaust," *Religious Studies* 26.

Cohn-Sherbok, D. and Lewis, C., eds. (1995) *Beyond Death* (New York: St. Martin's Press).

Collingwood, R. G. (1946) *The Idea of History* (Oxford: Clarendon Press).

Conee, E. (1985) "Evidentialism," *Philosophical Studies* 48.

Conze, E. (1975) *Buddhism: Its Essence and Development* (New York: Harper Torchbooks).

Cooper, J. (1989) *Body, Soul, and Life Everlasting* (Grand Rapids: William Eerdmans).

Corey, M. A. (1993) *God and the New Cosmology* (Lanham: Rowman and Littlefield).

Cornman, J. and Lehrer, K. (1970) *Philosophical Problems and Arguments* (New York: Macmillan).

400

Corless, R. J. (1989) *The Vision of Buddhism: The Space Under the Tree* (New York: Paragon House).

Coward, H. (1995) "Religious Pluralism and the Future of Religions," in *Religious Pluralism and Truth*, ed. by T. Dean (Albany: State University of New York Press).

Craig, W. (1991) "'Lest Anyone Should Fall': A Middle Knowledge Perspective on Perseverence and Apostolic Warnings," *International Journal for Philosophy of Religion*: 29.

Craig, W. (1990) "God and Real Time," *Religious Studies* 26.

Craig, W. (1985) *The Only Wise God* (Grand Rapids: Baker).

Craig, W. (1984) *Apologetics* (Chicago: Moody Press).

Craig, W. (1980) *The Cosmological Argument from Plato to Leibniz* (London: Macmillan).

Craig, W. (1979) *The Kalam Cosmological Argument* (London: Macmillan).

Craig, W. and Smith, Q. (1993) *Theism, Atheism, and Big Bang Cosmology* (New York: Oxford University Press).

Crawford, D. (1992) "Nature and Art: Some Dialectical Relationships," in *The Philosophy of the Visual Arts*, ed. by P. Alperson (Oxford: Oxford University Press), Originally Published in the *Journal of Aesthetics and Art Criticism* 42, 1983.

Creel, R. (1986) *Divine Impassibility* (Cambridge: Cambridge University Press).

Cupitt, D. (1991) *What is a Story?* (London: SCM Press).

Cupitt, D. (1984) *The Sea of Faith* (Cambridge: Cambridge University Press).

Cupitt, D. (1981) *Taking Leave of God* (New York: Crossroad).

Dancy, J. (1985) *Introduction to Contemporary Epistemology* (Oxford: Basil Blackwell).

Dancy, J., ed. (1992) *A Companion to Epistemology* (Oxford: Basil Blackwell).

Danner, V. (1988) *The Islamic Tradition: An Introduction* (New York: Amity House).

Danto, A. (1983) "Science as an Intentional System," *Behavioral and Brain Sciences* 6.

Darwell, S. L. (1992) "Cambridge Platonists," *Encyclopedia of Ethics* (New York: Garland Press).

Davidson, D. (1970) "Mental Events," in *Experience and Theory*, ed. by L. Foster and J. W. Swanson (Amherst: University of Massachusetts Press).

Davies, B. (Forthcoming) "Aquinas on What God is Not," *Revue Internationale de Philosophie*.

Davies, B. (1987) "Classical Theism and the Doctrine of Divine Simplicity," in *Language, Meaning, and God*, ed. by B. Davies (London: Geoffrey Chapman).

Davies, P. (1983) *God and the New Physics* (New York: Simon and Schuster).

Davis, C. (1989) *The Evidential Force of Religious Experience* (New York: Oxford University Press).

Davis, S. T., ed. (1989) *Death and Afterlife* (Basingstoke: Macmillan).

Davis, S. T. (1983) *Logic and the Nature of God* (Grand Rapids: William Eerdmans).

D'Costa, G., ed. (1990) *Christian Uniqueness Reconsidered* (New York: Maryknoll).

Dennett, D. (1991a) *Consciousness Explained* (Cambridge, Mass.: MIT Press).

Dennett, D. (1991b) "The Nature of Images and the Introspective Trap," in *Readings in Philosophy of Psychology*, ed. by N. Block (Cambridge, Mass.: Harvard University Press).

Dennett, D. (1987) *The Intentional Stance* (Cambridge, Mass.: MIT Press).

Dennett, D. (1984) *Elbow Room* (Cambridge, Mass.: MIT Press).

Dennett, D. (1978) *Brainstorms* (Cambridge, Mass.: MIT Press).

Descartes, R. (1970) *Philosophical Letters*, trans. by A. Kenny (Minneapolis: University of Minnesota Press).

Devine, P. (1986) "On the Definition of Religion," *Faith and Philosophy* 3: 3.

Devine, P. (1975) "The Religious Significance of the Ontological Argument," *Religious Studies* 11.

Donagan, A. (1977) *The Theory of Morality* (Chicago: University of Chicago Press).

Dore, C. (1984) *Theism* (Dordrecht: D. Reidel).

Dostoevski, F. (1976 [1880]) *The Brothers Karamazov*, trans. by R. E. Marlaw (New York: Norton).

Dostoyevsky, F. (1950 [1880]) *The Brothers Karamazov*, trans. by C. Garnet (New York: Random House).

Drabkin, D. (1994) "A Moral Argument for Undertaking Theism," *American Philosophical Quarterly* 31: 2.

Dummett, M. (1992) "The Metaphysics of Verificationism," in *The Philosophy of A. J. Ayer* (LaSalle: Open Court).

Dummett, M. (1973) *Frege* (Cambridge: Harvard University Press).

Edwards, P. (1961) "Some Notes on Anthropomorphic Theology," in *Religious Experience and Truth*, ed. by S. Hook (New York: New York University Press).

Einstein, A. (1973) *Ideas and Opinions*, trans. by S. Bargmann (London: Souvenir Press).

Eliade, M. (1959) *The Sacred and the Profane* (New York: Harcourt, Brace and World).

Evans, S. (1996) *The Historical Christ and the Jesus of History* (Oxford: Oxford University Press).

Ewing, A. C. (1985) *The Fundamental Questions of Philosophy* (London: Routledge and Kegan Paul).

Feenstra, R. and Plantinga, Jr., C., eds. (1989) *Trinity, Incarnation, and Atonement* (Notre Dame: University of Notre Dame Press).

Ferguson, J. (1977) *War and Peace in the World's Religions* (London: Sheldon Press).

Ferre, F. (1993) *Hellfire and Lightning Rods: Liberating Science, Technology and Religion* (Mary Knoll, NY: Orbis Books).

Ferre, F. (1988) *Philosophy of Technology* (Englewood Cliffs: Prentice-Hall).

Feyerabend, P. (1987) *Farewell to Reason* (London: Verso).

Findlay, J. N. (1964) "Can God's Existence be Disproved?" in *The Ontological Argument* ed. by A. Plantinga (New York: Macmillan).

Finnis, J. (1980) *Natural Law* (Oxford: Clarendon Press).

Firth, R. (1952) "Ethical Absolutism and the Ideal Observer," *Philosophy and Phenomenological Research* 12.

402

Fischer, J. (1994) *The Metaphysics of Free Will* (Oxford: Basil Blackwell).

Fischer, J. (1992) "Recent Work on God and Freedom," *American Philosophical Quarterly* 29.

Fishbane, M. (1988) "The Image of the Human and the Rights of the Individual in Jewish Tradition," in *Human Rights and the World's Religions* ed. by L. Rouner (Notre Dame: University of Notre Dame Press).

Flew, A. (1992) "Presumption of Atheism," in *Contemporary Perspectives on Religious Epistemology*, ed. R. Geivett and B. Sweetman, 1992 (Oxford: Oxford University Press).

Flew, A. (1984) *God, Freedom and Immortality* (Buffalo: Prometheus Books).

Flew, A. (1966) *God and Philosophy* (New York: Delta).

Flint, T. (1991) "Middle Knowledge and the Doctrine of Infallibility," *Philosophical Perspectives* 5.

Flint, T. and Fredoso, A. (1983) "Maximal Power," in *The Existence and Nature of God*, ed. by A. Freddoso (Notre Dame: University of Notre Dame Press).

Flood, R. and Lockwood, M., eds. (1989) *The Nature of Time* (Oxford: Basil Blackwell).

Forrest, P. (1996) *God Without the Supernatural: A Defense of Scientific Theism* (Ithaca: Cornell University Press).

Forrest, P. (1989) "An Argument for the Divine Command Theory of Right Action," *Sophia* 28: 1.

Foster, J. (1991) *The Immaterial Self* (London: Routledge).

Foster, J. (1985) *Ayer* (London: Routledge and Kegan Paul).

Frankfurt, H. G. (1988) "On Bullshit," in *The Importance of What We Care About* (Cambridge: Cambridge University Press).

Frankfurt, H. G. (1969) "Alternate Possibilities and Moral Responsibility," *Journal of Philosophy* 66.

Fredoso, A. (1988) "Introduction," in *On Divine Foreknowledge*, by L. Molina (Ithaca: Cornell University Press).

Frege, G. (1956) "The Thought: A Logical Inquiry," *Mind* 65.

Fulmer, G. (1977) "The Concept of the Supernatural," *Analysis* 37.

Gale, R. (1991) *On the Nature and Existence of God* (New York: Cambridge University Press).

Gale, R., ed. (1978) *The Philosophy of Time* (New Jersey: Humanities Press).

Gale, R. (1968) *The Language of Time* (Garden City: Anchor Books, 1967).

Geach, P. (1977) *Providence and Evil* (Cambridge: Cambridge University Press).

Geach, P. (1972) "God's Relation to the World," in *Logic Matters* (Berkeley: University of California Press).

Geach, P. (1969) *God and the Soul* (London: Routledge and Kegan Paul).

Geivett, R. D. (1993) *Evil and the Evidence for God* (Philadelphia: Temple University Press).

Gelner, E. (1979) *Words and Things* (London: Routledge and Kegan Paul).

Goldman, A. (1979) "What is Justified Belief?" in *Justification and Knowledge*, ed. by G. Pappas (Dordrecht: D. Reidel).

Goldstein, R. L. (1983) *International Studies in Philosophy*.

Goodman, L. (1995) "Jewish Philosophy," in *The Oxford Companion to Philosophy*, ed. by T. Honderich (Oxford: Oxford University Press).

Goodman, N. (1978) *Ways of World Making* (Indianapolis: Hackett).

Goulder, M., ed. (1979) *Incarnation and Myth: The Debate Continued* (Grand Rapids: William Eerdmans).

Grensted, L. (1920) *A Short History of the Doctrine of the Atonement* (Manchester: Manchester University Press).

Grice, P. (1989) *Studies in the Way of Words* (Cambridge, Mass.: Harvard University Press).

Griffiths, P. (1994) *On Being Buddha: The Classical Doctrine of Buddhahood* (Albany: State University of New York Press).

Griffiths, P. (1991) *An Apology For Apologetics* (Maryknoll: Orbis Books).

Griffiths, P. (1986) *On Being Mindless* (LaSalle: Open Court).

Gutierrez, G. (1990) "Toward a Theology of Liberation," in *Liberation Theology: A Documentary History*, ed. by A. T. Hennelly (Maryknoll: Orbis Books).

Gutting, G. (1982) *Religious Belief and Religious Skepticism* (Notre Dame: University of Notre Dame Press).

Hamnett, I., ed. *Religious Pluralism and Unbelief* (New York: Routledge).

Hanfling, O., ed. (1988) *Life and Meaning* (Oxford: Basil Blackwell).

Hansen, K. and Forsyth, P. D. (1990) *Understanding Children* (London: Mayfield).

Hanson, N. R. (1971) *What I Do Not Believe*, ed. by S. Toulmin and H. Wolf (Dordrecht: D. Reidel).

Hardy, A. (1979) *The Spiritual Nature of Man: A Study of Contemporary Religious Experience* (Oxford: Clarendon Press).

Hare, J. (1996) *The Moral Gap: Kantian Ethics, Human Limits and God's Assistance* (Oxford: Oxford University Press).

Hare, P. and Madden, E. (1968) *Evil and the Concept of God* (Springfield: Charles C. Thomas).

Harman, G. (1977) *The Nature of Morality* (Oxford: Oxford University Press).

Harris, J. (1992) *Against Relativism* (LaSalle: Open Court).

Hart, W. D. (1988) *The Engine of the Soul* (Cambridge: Cambridge University Press).

Hartshorne, C. (1976). "Theism in Asian and Western Thought," *Philosophy, East and West* 28: 4.

Hartshorne, C. (1970) *Creative Synthesis and Philosophical Method* (LaSalle: Open Court).

Hartshorne, C. (1966) "A New Look at the Problem of Evil," *Current Philosophical Issues* (Springfield: Charles C. Thomas).

Hartshorne, C. (1965) *Anselm's Discovery* (LaSalle: Open Court).

Hartshorne, C. (1953) "The Immortality of the Past," *Review of Metaphysics* 7.

Hartshorne, C. (1941) *Man's Vision of God and the Logic of Theism* (Chicago: Willett, Clark and Co.).

Haskar, V. (1991) *Indivisible Selves and Moral Practice* (Edinburgh: Edinburgh University Press).

Hasker, W. (1994) "A Philosophical Perspective," in *The Openness of God* (Downers Grove: InterVarsity Press).

Hasker, W. (1992) "The Necessity of Gratuitous Evil," *Faith and Philosophy* 9: 1.

Hasker, W. (1989) *God, Time, and Knowledge* (Ithaca: Cornell University Press).

Hasker, W. (1984) "Must God Do His Best?" *International Journal for Philosophy of Religion* 16.

Hebblethwaite, B. (1988) *The Ocean of Truth* (Cambridge: Cambridge University Press).

Helm, P. (1988) *Eternal God* (Oxford: Oxford University Press).

Hepburn, R. W. (1963) "From World to God," *Mind* 72.

Hepburn, R. W. (1958) *Christianity and Paradox* (London: Watts).

Heschel, A. (1976) *God in Search of Man: A Philosophy of Judaism* (New York: Farrar, Straus and Giroux).

Hick, J. (1993a) *The Metaphor of God Incarnate* (Louisville: Westminster/John Knox).

Hick, J. (1993b) *Disputed Questions in Theology and the Philosophy of Religion* (New Haven: Yale University Press).

Hick, J. (1992) "The Universality of the Golden Rule," in *Ethics, Religion, and the Good Society*, ed. by J. Runzo (Louisville: Westminster/John Knox Press).

Hick, J. (1980) *God Has Many Names* (London: Macmillan).

Hick, J. (1977) *Evil and the God of Love* (New York: Harper and Row; revised edn, San Francisco: Harper and Row).

Hick, J. (1976a) "Mystical Experience as Cognition," in *Mystics and Scholars*, ed. by H. Coward and T. Penelhum (The Canadian Corporation for Studies in Religion).

Hick, J. (1976b) *Death and Eternal Life* (San Francisco: Harper and Row).

Hick, J. (1974) "Religious Faith as Experiencing-As," in *Philosophy of Religion*, ed. by N. O. Schedler (New York: Macmillan).

Hick, J. (1973) *God and the Universe of Faiths* (New York: St. Martin's Press).

Hick, J. (1967) "The Problem of Evil," in *Encyclopedia of Philosophy*, ed. by P. Edwards (New York: Macmillan).

Hick, J. (1966a) *Rational Theistic Belief Without Proof* (London and Basingstoke: Macmillan).

Hick, J. (1966b) *Faith and Knowledge* (Ithaca: Cornell University Press).

Hinnells, J. R. (1996, 2nd edition) *A New Handbook of Living Religions* (Cambridge: Blackwell).

Hiriyanna, M. (1951) *The Essentials of Indian Philosophy* (London: Allen and Unwin).

Hirsch, E. (1993) *Dividing Reality* (Oxford: Oxford University Press).

Hobbes, Thomas (1950) *Leviathan* (New York: Dutton).

Hobbes, Thomas (1839) *The English Works of Thomas Hobbes of Malmesbury*, vol. iv (London: John Bohn).

Hoffman, J. and Rosenkrantz, G. (1988), "Omnipotence Redux," *Philosophy and Phenomenological Research* 49.

Hofstadter, D. (1980) "Reductionism and Religion," *Behavioural and Brain Sciences* 3.

Holland, R. F. (1965) "The Miraculous," *American Philosophical Quarterly* 2.

Honderich, T. (1993) *How Free Are You?* (Oxford: Oxford University Press).

Honderich, T. (1988) *A Theory of Determinism* (Oxford: Oxford University Press).

Horowitz, T. and Massey, G. eds. (1991) *Thought Experiments in Science and Philosophy* (Savage, MD: Rowman and Littlefield).

Hospers, J. (1988) *An Introduction to Philosophical Analysis* (Englewood Cliffs: Prentice-Hall).

Hospers, J. (1956) "What is an Explanation?" in *Conceptual Analysis*, ed. by A. Flew (London: Macmillan).

Houston, J. (1994) *Reported Miracles: A Critique of Hume* (Cambridge: Cambridge University Press).

Huby, P. (1991) "Paranormal Phenomena" in *The Purist of Mind*, ed. by R. Tallis and H. Robinson (Manchester: Carcanet Press).

Hudson, W. D. (1977) "What Makes Religious Beliefs Religious?" *Religious Studies* 13.

Hudson, W. D. (1974) *A Philosophical Approach to Religion* (London: Macmillan).

Hughes, C. (1989) *On a Complex Theory of a Simple God* (Ithaca: Cornell University Press).

Humanist Manifestos I and II (1973) (Buffalo: Prometheus Press).

Hume, D. (1988) *A Treatise of Human Nature* (Oxford: Clarendon).

Hume, D. (1980) *Dialogues Concerning Natural Religion* (Indianapolis: Hackett).

Hume, D. (1955) *An Inquiry Concerning Human Understanding* (New York: Liberal Arts Press).

Hume, D. (1902) "Enquiry Concerning Human Understanding," in *Hume Enquiries*, ed. by Selby-Bigge (Oxford: Oxford University Press).

Huxley, A. (1950) *The Perenial Philosophy* (London: Chatto and Windus).

Idziak, J., ed. (1980) *Divine Command Morality: Historical and Contemporary Readings* (New York: Edwin and Mellen).

Ignatius Loyola (1881) *Spiritual Exercises of St. Ignatius* (London: Burns and Oats).

Jackson, F. (1977) *Perception* (Cambridge: Cambridge University Press).

Jacobs, L. (1988) *Principles of the Jewish Faith* (Northvale, NJ: Jason Aronson Inc.).

James, W. (1958) *Varieties of Religious Experience* (New York: Mentor, New American Library).

Jantzen, G. (1994) "Feminists, Philosophers, and Mystics," *Hypatia* 9.

Jantzen, G. (1988) *Julian of Norwich* (New York: Paulist Press).

Jantzen, G. (1987) "Conspicuous Sanctity and Religious Belief," in *The Rationality of Religious Belief*, ed. by A. Holtzer and S. W. Holtzer (Oxford: Clarendon Press).

Jantzen, G. (1984a) *God's World, God's Body* (Philadelphia: Westminster Press).

Jantzen, G. (1984b) "Do We Need Immortality?" *Modern Theology* 1: 1.

Jantzen, G. (1983) "Time and Timelessness," in *A New Dictionary of Christian Theology*, ed. by A. Richardson and J. Bowden (London: SCM).

Jantzen, G. (1979) "Hume on Miracles, History and Politics," *Christian Scholars Review* 8.

Jay, M. (1993) *Downcast Eyes* (Berkeley: University of California Press).

Johnson, E. (1992) "Agent-centered Morality," in *Encyclopedia of Ethics* (New York: Garland Press).

Kant, I. (1965) *Critique of Pure Reason*, trans. by N. K. Smith (New York: St. Martin's Press).

Kant, I. (1956) *Critique of Practical Reason*, trans. by L. W. Beck (Indianapolis: Bobbs-Merrill).

Kearney, R. (1988) *The Wake of Imagination: Toward a Postmodern Culture* (Minneapolis: University of Minnesota Press).

Keller, H. (1904) *The World I Live In* (London: Hodder and Stoughton).

Keller, J. (1995) "A Moral Argument Against Miracles," *Faith and Philosophy* 12.

Kenny, A. (1983) *Faith and Reason* (New York: Columbia University Press).

Kenny, A. (1979) *The God of the Philosophers* (Oxford: Clarendon Press).

Kerr, F. (1988) *Theology After Wittgenstein* (Oxford: Basil Blackwell).

Kierkegaard, S. (1974) *Concluding Unscientific Postscript*, trans. by D. F. Swenson and W. Lowrie (Princeton: Princeton University Press).

King, W. (1957) "Negation as a Religious Category," *Journal of Religion* 37.

Kirk, G. S. et al. (1984) *The Pre-Socratic Philosophers* (Cambridge: Cambridge University Press).

Klostermaier, K. (1989) *A Survey of Hinduism* (Albany: State University of New York Press).

Kneale, W. (1960–61) "Time and Eternity in Theology," *Proceedings of the Aristotelian Society* 61.

Koller, J. (1985) *Oriental Philosophies* (New York: Charles Scribner's Sons).

Kretzmann, N. (1966) "Omniscience and Indexicality," *Journal of Philosophy* 63.

Kuhn, T. S. (1962) *The Structure of Scientific Revolutions* (Chicago: University of Chicago Press).

Kuitert, H. M. (1981) "Is Belief a Condition for Understanding?" *Religious Studies* 17.

Kvanvig, J. (1986) *The Possibility of an All-Knowing God* (London: Macmillan).

Lakoff, G. and Johnson, M. (1980) *Metaphors We Live By* (Chicago: University of Chicago Press).

Langerak, E. et al. (1989) *Christian Faith, Health and Medical Practice* (Grand Rapids: William Eerdmans).

Larmer, R. A. H. (1988) *Water into Wine?* (Montreal: McGill–Queen's University Press).

Larmore, C. (1987) *Patterns of Moral Complexity* (Cambridge: Cambridge University Press).

Leftow, B. (1997) "Eternity," in *A Companion to Philosophy of Religion*, ed. by P. Quinn and C. Taliaferro (Oxford: Basil Blackwell).

Leftow, B. (1991) *Time and Eternity* (Ithaca: Cornell University Press).

Leftow, B. (1990) "God and Abstract Entities," *Faith and Philosophy* 7.

Lehrer, K. (1974) *Knowledge* (Oxford: Clarendon Press).

Leibniz, G. (1951a) "Monadology," in *Leibniz Selections* ed. by Philip P. Wiener (New York: Charles Scribner's and Sons).

Leibniz, G. W. (1951b) *Theodicy*, trans. by E. M. Huggard (London: Routledge and Kegan Paul).

Leuba, J. H. (1912) *A Psychological Study of Religion* (New York: Macmillan).

Levin, M. (1979) *Metaphysics and the Mind–Body Problem* (Oxford: Clarendon Press).

Levinas, E. (1974) *Otherwise Than Being or Beyond Essence*, trans. by A. Lingis (The Hague: Martinus Nijhoff).

Levinas, E. (1961) *Totality and Infinity* trans. by A. Lingis (Pittsburgh: Duquesne University Press).

Leopold, A. (1987) *A Sand County Almanac* (Oxford: Oxford University Press).

Lewis, C. S. (1967) *Christian Reflections*, ed. by Walter Hooper (Grand Rapids: William Eerdmans).

Lewis, C. S. (1961) *An Experiment in Criticism* (Cambridge: Cambridge University Press).

Lewis, C. S. (1952) *Mere Christianity* (London: Collins).

Lewis, C. S. (1940) *The Problem of Pain* (London: Centenary Press).

Lewis, D. (1990) "What Experience Teaches," in *Mind and Cognition,* ed. by W. Lycan (Oxford: Basil Blackwell).

Lewis, D. (1986) *On the Plurality of Worlds* (Oxford: Basil Blackwell).

Lewis, D. (1966) "An Argument for the Identity Theory," *Journal of Philosophy* 63.

Lewis, H. D. (1974) "Realism and Metaphysics," *Idealist Studies* 4: 3.

Lewis, H. D. (1973) *The Self and Immortality* (New York: Seabury Press).

Lewis, H. D. (1962) *Our Experience of God* (London: George Allen and Unwin).

Lindholm, C. (1996) *The Islamic Middle East: An Historical Anthropology* (Cambridge: Blackwell).

Linton, R. (1954) *Method and Perspective in Anthropology* (Minneapolis: University of Minnesota Press).

Linville, M. (1993) "Divine Foreknowledge and the Libertarian Conception of Human Freedom," *Journal of the Philosophy of Religion* 33.

Linzey, A. and Regon, T. (1988) *Animals and Christianity* (New York: Crossroads).

Locke, J. (1983) *A Letter Concerning Toleration* (Indianapolis: Hackett).

Locke, J. (1979) *An Essay Concerning Human Understanding*, ed. by Peter H. Nidditch (Oxford: Clarendon Press).

Lombardi, J. (1984) "Suicide and the Service of God," *Ethics* 95.

Lott, E. (1980) *Vedantic Approaches to God* (London: Macmillan).

Lott, E. (1976) *God and the Universe in the Vedantic Theology of Ramanuja* (Madras: Ramanuja Research Society).

Lovejoy, A. (1970) *The Great Chain of Being* (Cambridge: Harvard University Press).

Lucas, J. R. (1989) *The Future* (Oxford: Basil Blackwell).

Lucas, J. R. (1973) *A Treatise on Time and Space* (London: Methuen).

Lucas, J. R. (1970) *The Freedom of the Will* (Oxford: Clarendon Press).

Lycan, W., ed. (1990) *Mind and Cognition* (Oxford: Basil Blackwell).

Lycan, W., ed. (1988) *Judgement and Justification* (Cambridge: Cambridge University Press).

Lycan, W. (1987) *Consciousness* (Cambridge: MIT Press).

Lyotard, J. (1984) *The Postmodern Condition: A Report on Knowledge* (Minneapolis: The University of Minnesota Press).

Macedo, S. (1993) "Toleration and Fundamentalism," in *A Companion to Contemporary Political Philosophy*, ed. by R. Goodin and P. Pettit (Oxford: Basil Blackwell).

MacKay, D. (1988) *Brains, Machines, and Persons* (Grand Rapids: Eerdmans).

Mackie, J. L. (1982) *The Miracle of Theism* (Oxford: Clarendon Press).

Mackie, J. L. (1977) *Ethics: Inventing Right and Wrong* (Harmondsworth: Penguin Books).

Mackie, J. L. (1955) "Evil and Omnipotence," *Mind* 64.

Madell, G. (1981) *The Identity of the Self* (Edinburgh: University of Edinburgh Press).

Mahathera, N. (1972, 2nd edition) *The Dhammapada* (Columbo: Vajirama).

Maimonides, M. (1956) *The Guide for the Perplexed* (New York: Dover Publications).

Malcolm, N. (1960) "Anselm's Ontological Argument," *The Philosophical Review* 69.

Malcolm, N. (1958) *Ludwig Wittgenstein, A Memoir* (Oxford: Oxford University Press).

Mann, W. E. (1989) "Modality, Morality, and God," *Nous* 23, pp. 83–99.

Margenau, H. and Varghese, R. A. eds. (1993) *Cosmos, Bios, Theos* (LaSalle: Open Court).

Maritain, J. (1938) *The Degrees of Knowledge*, trans. by B. Wall et al. (New York: Scribner).

Martin, M. (1991) *The Case Against Christianity* (Philadelphia: Temple University Press).

Martin, M. (1990) *Atheism* (Philadelphia: Temple University Press).

Matthews, G. B. (1971) "Bodily Motions and Religious Feelings," *Canadian Journal of Philosophy* 1.

Mavrodes, G. (1986) "Religion and the Queerness of Morality," in *Rationality, Religious Belief and Moral Commitment*, ed. by R. Avdi and W. Wainwright (Ithaca: Cornell University Press).

Mavrodes, G. (1983) "Jerusalem and Athens Revisited," in *Faith and Rationality*, ed. by A. Plantinga and N. Wolterstorff (Notre Dame: University of Notre Dame Press).

409

May, L. (1992) "Insensitivity and Moral Responsibility," *The Journal of Value Inquiry* 6: 1.

Mbiti, J. S. (1970) *Concepts of God in Africa* (London: S.P.C.K.).

McCarthy, V. A. (1986) *Quest for a Philosophical Jesus: Christianity and Philosophy in Rousseau, Kant, Hegel and Schelling* (Macon: Mercer University Press).

McClosky (1974) "God and Evil," in *Readings in the Philosophy of Religion*, ed. by B. Brody (Englewood Cliffs: Prentice-Hall).

McGhee, M., ed. (1992) *Philosophy, Religion, and Spiritual Life* (Cambridge: Cambridge University Press).

McGill, A. and Hick, J., eds (1967) *The Many-Faced Argument* (New York: Macmillan).

McGinn, C. (1990) *The Problems of Consciousness* (Oxford: Basil Blackwell).

McGinn, C. (1982) *The Character of Mind* (Oxford: Oxford University Press).

McGrath, A. E. (1996, 2nd edition) *Christian Theology: An Introduction* (Cambridge: Blackwell).

McTaggart, J. M. E. (1906) *Some Dogmas of Religion* (London: Edward Arnold).

Messer, R. (1993) *Does God's Existence Need Proof?* (Oxford: Clarendon Press).

Meynell, H. (1982) *The Intelligible Universe* (Totowa: Barnes and Noble).

Midgley, M. (1984) *Wickedness* (London: Routledge and Kegan Paul).

Midgley, M. (1981) *Heart and Mind* (New York: St. Martin's Press).

Miles, T. R. (1966) "On Excluding the Supernatural," *Religious Studies* 1: 2.

Mitchell, B. (1994) *Faith and Criticism* (Oxford: Clarendon).

Mitchell, B. (1973) *The Justification of Religious Belief* (London: Macmillan).

Mohammed, O. N. (1993) "Jesus and Krishna," *Asian Faces of Jesus,* ed. by R. S. Sugirtharajah (Maryknoll: Orbis Books).

Mortimore, G., ed. (1971) *Weakness of Will* (New York: St. Martin's Press).

Molina, L. (1988) *On Divine Foreknowledge*, trans. by A. Fredoso (Ithaca: Cornell University Press).

Moody, R. (1989) *The Light Beyond* (New York: Bantam Books).

Moore, M. (1996) "Good Without God," in *Natural Law, Liberalism, and Morality*, ed. by R. George (Oxford: Oxford University Press).

Morris, P. (1990) "Judaism and Pluralism," in *Religious Pluralism and Unbelief*, ed. by Ian Hamnett (London: Routledge).

Morris, T. V., ed. (1988) *Divine and Human Action* (Ithaca: Cornell University Press).

Morris, T. V. (1987) *Anselmian Explorations* (Notre Dame: University of Notre Dame Press).

Morris, T. V. (1986) *The Logic of God Incarnate* (Ithaca: Cornell University Press).

Morris, T. V. and Menzel, C. (1986) "Absolute Creation," *American Philosophical Quarterly* 23.

Munitz, M. K. (1965) *The Mystery of Existence* (New York: Appleton-Century-Crofts).

Murray, G. (1943) *Five Stages of Greek Religion* (London: Watts).

Muyskens, J. L. (1979) *The Sufficiency of Hope: The Conceptual Foundations of Religion* (Philadelphia: Temple University Press).

Nagel, E. (1976) "Philosophical Concepts of Atheism," in *Critiques of God*, ed. by P. Angeles (Buffalo: Prometheus Books).

Nagel, T. (1987) *What Does it all Mean?* (New York: Oxford University Press).

Nagel, T. (1974) "What is it like to be a bat," *Philosophical Review* 83.

Nagel, T. (1965) "Physicalism," *Philosophical Review* 74.

Neurath, O. (1983) "Protocol Statements," in *Philosophical Papers*, trans. by R. S. Cohen and M. Neurath (Dordrecht).

Neusner, J. (1995) *Judaism in Modern Times* (Cambridge: Blackwell).

Neusner, J. (1991) *Studying Classical Judaism: A Primer* (Louisville: Westminster and John Knox Press).

Neusner, J. (1986) *Judaism and Scripture* (Chicago: University of Chicago Press).

Newton-Smith, W. H. (1980) *The Structure of Time* (London: Routledge and Kegan Paul).

Nicholas of Cusa (1928) *The Vision of God*, trans. by E. G. Salter (New York: Frederick V. Publishing Co.).

Nielsen, K. (1997) "Naturalistic Explanations of Theistic Belief," in *A Companion to Philosophy of Religion*, ed. by P. Quinn and C. Talliaferro (Oxford: Basil Blackwell).

Nielsen, K. (1996) *Naturalism Without Foundations* (Buffalo: Prometheus Press).

Nielsen, K. (1973) *Scepticism* (Edinburgh: St. Martin's Press).

Nielsen, K. (1971) *Contemporary Critiques of Religion* (New York: Herder and Herder).

Nielsen, K. (1967) "Wittgensteinian Fideism," *Philosophy* 42.

Nietzsche, F. (1966) *Beyond Good and Evil* (New York: Vintage Books).

Oakes, R. (1990) "The Wrath of God," *International Journal for the Philosophy of Religion* 27: 3.

Ogden, S. M. (1966) *The Reality of God* (New York: Harper and Row).

Oppy, G. (1995) *Ontological Arguments and Belief in God* (Cambridge: Cambridge University Press).

O'Shaughnessy, B. (1980) *The Will*, vol. 1 (Cambridge: Cambridge University Press).

Otto, R. (1936) *The Idea of the Holy: An Inquiry into the Non-rational Factor in the Idea of the Divine and Its Relations to the Rational* (Oxford: Oxford University Press).

Owen, H. P. (1965) *The Moral Argument for Christian Theism* (London: George Allen and Unwin).

Padgett, A. (1992) *God, Eternity, and the Nature of Time* (New York: St. Martin's Press).

Padgett, A. (1994) Review of *Divine Hiddenness and Human Reason* by J. S. Schellenberg. Philosophical Books 35: 3.

Panikkar, R. (1981) *The Unknown Christ of Hinduism* (London: Anchor Press).

Pap, A. (1958) *Semantics and Necessary Truth* (New Haven: Yale University Press).

Parfit, D. (1984) *Reasons and Persons* (Oxford: Clarendon Press).

Peirce, C. S. (1931–68) *Collected Papers*, ed. by C. Hartshorne and P. Weiss (Cambridge: Harvard University Press).

Peirce, C. S. (1958) *Collected Papers,* vol. vii (Cambridge, Mass.: Harvard University Press).

411

Pelikan, J. (1995) *Jesus Through the Centuries: His Place in the History of Culture* (New Haven: Yale University Press).

Penelhum, T. (1997) "Fideism," in *A Companion to Philosophy of Religion*, ed. by P. Quinn and C. Taliaferro (Oxford: Basil Blackwell).

Penelhum, T. (1983) *God and Skepticism* (Dordrecht: Reidel).

Pepper, S. (1957) *World Hypotheses* (Berkeley: University of California Press).

Perrett, R. W., ed. (1989) *Indian Philosophy of Religion* (Dordrecht: Kluwer Academic Publishers).

Peterson, M., ed. (1992) *The Problem of Evil* (Notre Dame: University of Notre Dame Press).

Peterson, M. (1982) *Evil and the Christian God* (Grand Rapids: Baker).

Phillips, D. Z. (1993) *Wittgenstein and Religion* (New York: Macmillan).

Phillips, D. Z. (1991) *From Fantasy to Faith* (London: Macmillan).

Phillips, D. Z. (1988) *Faith and Foundationalism* (London: Routledge and Kegan Paul).

Phillips, D. Z. (1981a) *The Concept of Prayer* (Oxford: Basil Blackwell).

Phillips, D. Z. (1981b) "Belief, Change, and Forms of Life," in *The Autonomy of Religious Belief*, ed. by F. J. Crosson (Notre Dame: University of Notre Dame Press).

Phillips, D. Z. (1976) *Religion Without Explanation* (Oxford: Basil Blackwell).

Phillips, D. Z. (1971) *Faith and Philosophical Inquiry* (New York: Schocken Books).

Phillips, D. Z. (1970) *Death and Immortality* (New York: St. Martin's Press).

Piaget, J. (1955) *Play, Dreams and Imitation* (New York: Norton).

Piaget, J. (1952) *The Origins of Intelligence in Children* (New York: International Universities Press).

Pike, N. (1992) *Mystic Union* (Ithaca: Cornell University Press).

Pike, N. (1970) *God and Timelessness* (New York: Schocken Books).

Pinnock, C. et al. (1994) *The Openness of God* (Downers Grove: InterVarsity Press).

Plantinga, A. (1993) *Warrant*, 2 vols (Oxford: Oxford University Press).

Plantinga, A. (1986) "On Ockham's Way Out," *Faith and Philosophy* 3.

Plantinga, A. (1983) "Reason and Belief in God," in *Faith and Rationality*, ed. by Plantinga and Wolterstorff (Notre Dame: University of Notre Dame Press).

Plantinga, A. (1982) "How to be an Anti-Realist," *Proceedings and Addresses of the American Philosophical Association* 56: 1.

Plantinga, A. (1981) "A Contemporary Response," in *Introduction to Philosophy*, ed. by J. B. Rogers and F. Baird (San Francisco: Harper and Row).

Plantinga, A. (1980) *Does God Have a Nature?* (Milwaukee: Marquette University Press).

Plantinga, A. (1974a) *The Nature of Necessity* (Oxford: Oxford University Press).

Plantinga, A. (1974b) *God, Freedom and Evil* (Grand Rapids: William Eerdmans).

Plantinga, A. (1967) *God and Other Minds* (Ithaca: Cornell University Press).

Platt, D. (1973) "What the Ontological Argument Can and Cannot Do," *New Scholasticism* 47.

Pojman, L. (1995) "Relativism" in *The Cambridge Dictionary of Philosophy*, ed. by R. Avdi (Cambridge: Cambridge University Press).

Pole, D. (1983) *Aesthetics, Form and Emotion* (London: Gerald Duckworth).

Pollock, J. (1986) *Theory of Knowledge* (Totowa: Rowman and Littlefield).

Pope John Paul II (1995) Evangelium Vitae, *Origins* 24.

Price, H. H. (1972) *Essays in the Philosophy of Religion* (Oxford: Clarendon Press).

Price, H. H. (1969) *Belief* (London: George Allen).

Purtill, R. (1975) *Philosophically Speaking* (Englewood Cliffs: Prentice-Hall).

Putnam, H. (1990) *Realism With a Human Face* (Cambridge: Harvard University Press).

Putnam, H. (1988) *Representation and Reality* (Cambridge: MIT Press).

Putnam, H. (1975) *Mind, Language, and Reality* (New York: Cambridge University Press).

Quine, W. V. (1992) "Structure and Nature," *Journal of Philosophy* 89.

Quinn, P. (1978) *Divine Commands and Moral Requirements* (Oxford: Clarendon Press).

Rachels, J. (1986) *The Elements of Moral Philosophy* (New York: Random House).

Radhakrishnan, S. (1960) *The Brahma Sutra* (New York: Harper).

Radhakrishnan, S. (1959) *Eastern Religions and Western Thought* (New York: Oxford University Press).

Rhadhakrishnan, S. (1958a) *An Idealist View of Life* (London: George Allen and Unwin).

Radhakrishnan, S. (1958b) "Spirit in Man," *Contemporary Indian Philosophy* trans. by J. J. Muirhead (London: George Allen and Unwin).

Rawls, J. (1993) *Political Liberalism* (New York: Columbia University Press).

Reichenbach, B. (1990) *The Law of Karma* (Honolulu: University of Hawaii Press).

Reichenbach, B. (1984) "Omniscience and Deliberation," *International Journal for Philosophy of Religion* 16.

Reichenbach, B. (1982a) *Evil and a Good God* (New York: Fordham University Press).

Reichenbach, B. (1978b) *Is Man the Phoenix? A Study of Immortality* (Grand Rapids: William Eerdmans).

Reichenbach, B. (1978c) "Monism and the Possibility of Life After Death," *Religious Studies* 14: 1.

Reichenbach, B. (1972) *The Cosmological Argument: A Reassessment* (Springfield: Charles Thomas).

Reid, T. (1941) *Essays on the Intellectual Power of Man* (London: Macmillan).

Rescher, N. (1985) *Pascal's Wager* (Notre Dame: University of Notre Dame Press).

Rhees, R. (1969) *Without Answers* (New York: Schocken Books).

Richard, Y. (1995) *Shi'ite Islam: Polity, Ideology and Creed* (Oxford: Blackwell).

Ridley, A., ed. (1995) *Arguing About Art* (New York: McGraw-Hill).

Robinson, H., ed. (1993) *Objections to Physicalism* (Oxford: Clarendon Press).

Robinson, H. (1982) *Matter and Sense* (Cambridge: Cambridge University Press).

Robinson, J. A. T. (1967) *Exploration into God* (London: SCM).

413

Rorty, A. (1988) "Characters, Persons, Selves, Individuals," in *Mind in Action* (Boston: Beacon Press).

Rorty, R. (1989) *Philosophy and the Mirror of Nature* (Princeton: Princeton University Press).

Rorty, R. (1965) "Mind–Body Identity, Privacy, and Categories," *Review of Metaphysics* 19: 1.

Ross, J. (1982) Review of *The God of the Philosophers, Journal of Philosophy* 79.

Ross, J. (1969) *Philosophical Theology* (Indianapolis: Bobbs-Merrill).

Rouner, L. S., ed. (1988) *Human Rights and the World's Religions* (Notre Dame: University of Notre Dame Press).

Rowe, W. (1991) "Ruminations About Evil," *Philosophical Perspectives* 5.

Rowe, W. (1982) "Religious Experience and the Principle of Credulity," *International Journal for the Philosophy of Religion* 13.

Rowe, W. (1978) *Philosophy of Religion* (Encino: Dickenson).

Runzo, J. (1992) "Ethics and the Challenge of Theological Nonrealism," in *Ethics, Religion, and the Good of Society* (Westminster: John Knox).

Russell, B. (1984) *The Collected Papers of Bertrand Russell* (London).

Russell, B. (1969) *The Autobiography of Bertrand Russell: The Early Years* (London: Bantam Books).

Russell, B. (1960) "The Harm That Good Men Do," in *Sceptical Essays* (London: George Allen and Unwin).

Russell, B. (1945) *History of Western Philosophy* (New York: Simon and Schuster).

Russell, B. (1938) *Power: A New Social Analysis* (New York: W. W. Norton).

Russell, Bruce (1989) "The Persistent Problem of Evil," *Faith and Philosophy* 6: 2.

Ryle, G. (1949) *The Concept of Mind* (New York: Barnes and Noble).

Sanders, J. T. (1966) "Of God and Freedom," *Philosophical Review* 75.

Sartre, J. P. (1948) *Existentialism and Humanism*, trans. by P. Mairet (London: Methuen).

Savile, A. (1982) *The Test of Time: An Esssay in Philosophical Aesthetics* (Oxford: Claredon Press).

Schellenberg, J. S. (1993) *Divine Hiddenness and Human Reason* (Ithaca: Cornell University Press).

Schiller, J. C. F. (1962) *Letters on the Aesthetic Education of Mankind*, trans. by E. M. Wilkinson and L. A. Willoughby (Oxford: Oxford University Press).

Schlesinger, G. (1988) *New Perspectives on Old-Time Religion* (Oxford: Oxford University Press).

Schlesinger, G. (1987) "On the Compatibility of the Divine Attributes," *Religious Studies* 23.

Schlesinger, G. (1980) *Aspects of Time* (Indianapolis: Hackett).

Schoen, E. (1985) *Religious Explanations* (Durham: Duke University Press).

Scriven, M. (1966) *Primary Philosophy* (New York: McGraw-Hill).

Searle, J. (1992) *The Rediscovery of Mind* (Cambridge: MIT Press).

414

Senor, T. (1993) "Divine Temporality and Creation Ex Nihilo," *Faith and Philosophy* 10: 1.

Sessions, L. (1994) *The Concept of Faith* (Ithaca: Cornell University Press).

Shalkowski, S. (1992) "Atheological Apologetics," *Contemporary Perspectives in Religious Epistemology*, ed. by R. Geivett and B. Sweetman (Oxford: Oxford University Press).

Shankara (1970) *Shankara's Crest Jewel of Discrimination* trans. by Swaimi Prabhavanada and C. Isherwood (New York: Mentor Books; Hollywood: Vedanta Press).

Shankara (1962) *Vedanta Sutras of Badarayana with Commentary*, trans. by G. Thibaut (New York: Dover).

Sharma, A. (1995) *The Philosophy of Religion and Advaita Vedanta* (University Park: The Pennsylvania State University Press).

Sharma, A. (1990) *A Hindu Perspective on the Philosophy of Religion* (New York: St. Martin's Press).

Shideler, M. M. (1962) *The Theology of Romantic Love: A Study in the Writings of Charles Williams* (New York: Harper and Brothers).

Siegel, H. (1987) *Relativism Refuted* (Boston: D. Reidl).

Simon, C. J. (1995) "Evil, Tragedy and Hope: Reflections on Tolstoy's 'Father Sergius'," *Christian Scholar's Review* 24: 3.

Singer, P., ed. (1991) *A Companion to Ethics* (Oxford: Basil Blackwell).

Singer, P. (1972) "Moral Experts," *Analysis* 32.

Slote, M. (1983) *Goods and Virtues* (Oxford: Clarendon Press).

Smart, J. J. C., ed. (1964) *Problems of Space and Time* (New York: Macmillan).

Smart, J. J. C. (1963) "Materialism," *Journal of Philosophy* 661.

Smart, N. (1972) *The Concept of Worship* (London: Macmillan).

Smart, N. (1966) "Mythical Transcendence," *Monist* 50.

Smith, Q. and Craig, W. (1993) *Theism, Atheism and Big Bang Cosmology* (Oxford: Clarendon Press).

Smith, W. C. (1963) *The Meaning and End of Religion* (New York: Macmillan).

Smythies, J. R. and Beloff, J., eds. (1989) *The Case for Dualism* (Charlottesville: University Press of Virginia).

Soelle, D. (1984) *The Strength of the Weak: Toward a Christian Feminist Identity*, trans. by R. Kimber and R. Kimber (Philadelphia: Westminster Press).

Sorabji, R. (1983) *Time, Creation, and the Continuum* (London: Duckworth).

Sorabji, R. (1980) *Necessity, Cause, and Blame: Perspectives on Aristotle's Theory* (Ithaca: Cornell University Press).

Sorensen, R. A. (1992) *Thought Experiments* (Oxford: Oxford University Press).

Sosa, E. (1988) "An Internalist Externalism," *Synthese* 74: 3.

Soskice, J. M. (1985) *Metaphor and Religious Language* (Oxford: Oxford University Press).

Sprigge, T. (1983) *The Vindication of Absolute Idealism* (Edinburgh: Edinburgh University Press).

Stace, W. T. (1960) *Mysticism and Philosophy* (London: Macmillan).

415

Stace, W. T. (1952) *Time and Eternity* (Princeton: Princeton University Press).

Stace, W. T. (1937) *Ethical Relativism: A Critique* (New York: Macmillan).

Stewart, M. (1993) *The Greater Good Defense* (New York: St. Martin's Press).

Stich, S. (1996) *Deconstructing the Mind* (New York: Oxford University Press).

Stich, S. (1983) *From Folk Psychology to Cognitive Science* (Cambridge: MIT Press).

Stoeber, M. (1992) *Evil and the Mystics' God: Towards a Mystical Theodicy* (Toronto: University of Toronto Press).

Strawson, G. (1995) *Mental Reality* (Cambridge, Mass.: MIT Press).

Strawson, G. (1992) "The Self as Software," *Times Literary Supplement*, 21 August.

Strawson, G. (1991) *Freedom and Belief* (Oxford: Clarendon Press).

Strawson, P. (1952) *Introduction to Logical Theory* (London: Methuen).

Stump, E. (1985) "The Problem of Evil," *Faith and Philosophy* 4.

Stump, E. and Kretzmann, N. (1981) "Eternity," *Journal of Philosophy* 78, pp. 429–58.

Sturgeon, S. (1995) "Epistemology," *Philosophy: A Guide Through the Subject*, ed. by A. C. Grayling (Oxford: Oxford University Press).

Sullivan, H. S. (1953) *The Interpersonal Theory of Psychiatry* (New York: Norton).

Sutherland, S. (1984) *God, Jesus and Belief* (Oxford: Basil Blackwell).

Suzuki, D. T. (1933) *Essays in Zen Buddhism* (London: Luzac).

Swinburne, R. (1996) *Is There A God?* (Oxford: Oxford University Press).

Swinburne, R. (1994) *The Christian God* (Oxford: Oxford University Press).

Swinburne, R., ed. (1989a) *Miracles* (New York: Macmillan).

Swinburne, R. (1989b) *Responsibility and Atonement* (Oxford: Clarendon Press).

Swinburne, R. (1986) *The Evolution of the Soul* (Oxford: Oxford University Press).

Swinburne, R. (1981) *Faith and Reason* (Oxford: Clarendon Press).

Swinburne, R. (1979) *The Existence of God* (Oxford: Clarendon Press).

Swinburne, R. (1977) *The Coherence of Theism* (Oxford: Clarendon Press).

Swinburne, R. (1970) *The Concept of Miracle* (London: Macmillan).

Swinburne, R. (1968) "The Argument from Design," *Philosophy* 43.

Taliaferro, C. (1994) *Consciousness and the Mind of God* (Cambridge: Cambridge University Press).

Taliaferro, C. (1992) "The Intensity of Theism." *Sophia* 31: 3.

Taliaferro, C. (1990a) "The Limits of Power," *Philosophy and Theology* 5: 2.

Taliaferro, C. (1990b) "The Ideal Aesthetic Observer," *British Journal of Aesthetics* 30: 1.

Taliaferro, C. (1989) "The View from Above and Below," *The Heythrop Journal* 30.

Taliaferro, C. (1988a) "The Environmental Ethics of an Ideal Observer," *Environmental Ethics* 19.

Taliaferro, C. (1988b) "Relativizing the Ideal Observer Theory," *Philosophy and Phenomenological Research* 49.

Tanner, K. E. (1994) "Human Freedom, Human Sin, and God the Creator," in *The God Who Acts*, ed. by T. Tracy (University Park: Pennsylvania State University Press).

Taylor, A. E. (1951) *The Faith of a Moralist* (London: Macmillan).

416

Taylor, R. (1974, 3rd edition) *Metaphysics* (Englewood Cliffs: Prentice-Hall).

Taylor, R. (1970) *Good and Evil* (Buffalo: Prometheus Press).

Taylor, R. (1966) *Action and Purpose* (Englewood Cliffs: Prentice-Hall).

Tennant, F. R. (1928) *Philosophical Theology* (Cambridge: Cambridge University Press).

Teresa of Avila (1946) *Life* trans. by E. A. Peers (London: Sheed and Ward).

Thatcher, A. (1985) "The Personal God and a God who is a Person," *Religious Studies* 21.

Tiles, M. (1984) *Gaston Bachelard: Science and Objectivity* (Cambridge: Cambridge University Press).

Tillich, P. (1951) *Systematic Theology* vol. 1 (Chicago: University of Chicago Press).

Tinder, G. ([1898] 1976) *Tolerance: Toward a New Civility* (Amherst: University of Massachusetts Press).

Tolstoy, L. (1967) "Father Sergius," in *Great Short Works of Leo Tolstoy*, trans. by L. Maude and A. Maude (New York: Harper and Row).

Tracy, D. (1981) *The Analogical Imagination* (New York: Crossroads).

Trigg, R. (1993) *Rationality and Science* (Oxford: Basil Blackwell).

Trigg, R. (1989) *Reality at Risk* (New York: Harvester Wheatsheaf).

Trigg, R. (1973) *Reason and Commitment* (Cambridge: Cambridge University Press).

Underhill, E. (1975) *The Mystics of the Church* (Southampton: James Clarke).

Underhill, E. (1955) *Mysticism* (Cleveland: Meridian Books).

Unger, Peter (1975) *Ignorance* (Oxford: Oxford University Press).

Upanishado (1957) trans. by S. Prabhavanda and F. Manchester (New York: Mentor Book).

Updike, J. (1986) *Roger's Version* (New York: Alfred A. Knopf).

Van Fraassen, B. C. (1983) *An Essay on Free Will* (Oxford: Clarendon Press).

Van Fraassen, B. C. (1980) *The Scientific Image* (Oxford: Clarendon Press).

Van Fraassen, B. C. (1970) *An Introduction to the Philosophy of Time and Space* (New York: Random House).

Van Hildebrand, D. (1953) *Ethics* (Chicago: Franciscan Herald Press).

Van Inwagen (1993) *Metaphysics* (Boulder: Westriew Press).

Van Inwagen, P. (1995) *God, Knowledge, and Mystery* (Ithaca: Cornell University Press).

Van Inwagen, P. (1983) *An Essay on Free Will* (Oxford: Clarendon Press).

Veatch, H. (1962) *Rational Man* (Bloomington: Indiana Press).

Vesey, G., ed. (1982) *Idealism Past and Present* (Cambridge: Cambridge University Press).

Wainwright, W. (1995) *Reason and Heart* (Ithaca: Cornell University Press).

Wainwright, W. (1981) *Mysticism: A Study of its Nature, Cognitive Value, and Moral Implications* (Madison: University of Wisconsin Press).

Wainwright, W. (1978) *Philosophy of Religion: An Annotated Bibliography of 20th Century Writings in English* (New York: Garland).

Waismann, F. (1959) *Introduction to Mathematical Thinking* (New York: Harper and Row).

Waismann, F. (1952) "Verifiability," *Logic and Language* ed. by A. Flew (Oxford).

Waithe, M. E. (1987–95) *A History of Women Philosophers* 4 vols (Dordrecht: Martinus Nijhoff).

Waldron, J. (1987) "Theoretical Foundations of Liberalism," *Philosophical Quarterly* 37.

Walsh, W. H. (1958) *Philosophy of History: An Introduction* (New York: Harper and Row).

Ward, K. (1982) *Rational Theology and the Creativity of God* (Oxford: Basil Blackwell).

Warren, K. (1990) "The Power and the Promise of Ecological Feminism," *Environmental Ethics* 12: 2.

Watson, G., ed. (1982) *Free Will* (Oxford: Oxford University Press).

Weil, S. *The Notebooks of Simone Weil* (London: Routledge and Kegan Paul).

Weil, S. (1951) *Waiting for God*, trans. by E. Craufurd (New York: Harper and Row).

Wenham, J. W. (1993) "The Case for Conditional Immortality," in *Universalism and the Doctrine of Hell*, ed. by N. Cameron (Ada: Baker Books).

Westermarck, E. O. (1932) *Ethical Relativity* (London: Routledge and Kegan Paul).

Westphal, M. (1993) *Suspicion and Faith: The Religious Uses of Modern Atheism* (Grand Rapids: William Eerdmans).

Whitehead, A. N. (1931) *Science and the Modern World* (New York: Macmillan).

Wierenga, E. (1989) *The Nature of God* (Ithaca: Cornell University Press).

Wierenga, E. (1979) "Intrinsic Maxima and Omnibenevolence," *International Journal for Philosophy of Religion* 10: 1.

Wilkes, K. (1988) *Real People* (Oxford: Clarendon Press).

Winch, P. (1964) "Understanding a Primitive Society," *American Philosophical Quarterly* 1.

Wiredu, K. (1997) "African Religions from a Philosophical Point of View," in *A Companion to Philosophy of Religion*, ed. by P. Quinn and C. Taliaferro (Oxford: Basil Blackwell).

Wisdom, J. (1944–45) "Gods," *Proceedings of the Aristotelian Society* 45.

Wisdom, J. (1970) *Paradox and Discovery* (Berkeley: University of California Press).

Wittgenstein, L. (1972) *On Certainty*, ed. by G. E. M. Anscombe and G. H. van Wright (New York: Harper Torchbooks).

Wittgenstein, L. (1969) *Zettell*, ed. by G. E. M. Anscombe (Oxford: Basil Blackwell).

Wittgenstein, L. (1967) *Lectures and Conversations on Aesthetics, Psychology and Religious Belief*, ed. by Cyril Barrett (Berkeley: University of California Press).

Wittgenstein, L. (1961) *Tractatus Logico-Philosophicus*, trans. by D. F. Pears and B. F. McGuinness (London: Routledge and Kegan Paul).

Wittgenstein, L. (1953) *Philosophical Investigations*, trans. by G. E. M. Anscombe (Oxford: Basil Blackwell).

Wolterstorff, N. (1995) *Divine Discourse* (Cambridge: Cambridge University Press).

Wolterstorff, N. (1988) "Suffering Love," in *God, the Good, and Christian Life*, ed. by T. V. Morris (Notre Dame: University of Notre Dame Press).

Wolterstorff, N. (1982) "God Everlasting," *Contemporary Philosophy of Religion*, ed. by S. Cahn and D. Shatz (Oxford: Oxford University Press).

Wood, J. (1994) Book Review of Phillips' *Faith After Foundationalism, International Journal for Philosophy of Religion* 36.

Wood, T. (1991) *Mind-Only* (Honolulu: University of Hawaii Press).

Wood, T. (1990) *The Mandukya Upanishad and the Agama Sastra* (Honolulu: University of Hawaii Press).

Yandell, K. (1993) *The Epistemology of Religious Experience* (Cambridge: Cambridge University Press).

Young, R. (1977) "Theism and Morality," *Canadian Journal of Philosophy* 7.

Zaehner, R. (1957) *Mysticism: Sacred and Profane* (Oxford: Clarendon Press).

Zagzebski, L. (1997) "Foreknowledge and Human Freedom," in *A Companion to Philosophy of Religion*, ed. by P. Quinn and C. Taliaferro (Oxford: Basil Blackwell).

Zagzebski, L. (1996) *Virtues of the Mind* (Cambridge: Cambridge University Press).

Zagzebski, L. (1991) *The Dilemma of Freedom and Foreknowledge* (New York: Oxford University Press).

Index

421

Brink, D., 198
Broad, C. D., 141, 264–5, 268, 283–4
broad theism, 268–9, 293, 371, 378
  arguments for/against, 270–287
Brody, Baruch, 215, 216
Brothers Karamazov (Dostoyevsky), 1–2, 192, 328
Brown, David, 12, 136
Brown, F. B., 245
Brunner, Emil, 244
Buber, Martin, 185, 245, 332
Buddha, 20, 107, 181, 195, 280, 285
Buddhism, 18, 20–1, 22, 26, 299
  karma doctrine, 180–1, 182, 236
  and pluralism, 229, 231, 232, 233, 236
  and the self, 179–80, 181–2, 188, 280
  and theism, 279–81
burden of proof arguments, 255
  against naturalism, 259–64
  against theism, 255–9

Callicott, J. B., 226–7
Calvin, John, 138, 244, 262
Campbell, C. A., 113, 117
Camus, Albert, 2, 12
Carnap, R., 105
Carson, Thomas, 207
Carter, W. R., 76
Cartesianism *see* Descartes, René
causa sui (self-causation), 70–1, 82, 204
causality, causation, 64, 69, 72, 94, 113, 127, 131–2, 150, 160–2, 202, 307, 314, 353–87 *passim*
Chalcedonian Creed, 334, 335
Chance, Thomas, 13
Chappell, J. D. J., 242–3
Chisholm, Roderick, 108, 113, 115, 139–40, 177, 252
Christianity, 4, 6, 14, 15, 16, 17–18, 25, 53, 56
  and afterlief, 321, 326, 330, 346–8
  and divine excellence, 278, 279
  and divine impartiality, 210
  and divine ineffability, 170–1

and divine knowledge, 106, 120–1
and divine ownership, 216
and divine passibility, 183–4, 328
and divine power, 61–2, 65, 71–2, 73, 77
and divine transcendence, 143, 144, 145, 163
and environment, 223, 224
and evil, 303, 304, 327
and Hinduism, 20, 234, 338, 339–40
and monism, 174, 329
and philosophy, 2, 7
and pluralism, 229, 232–3, 233–6
and religious practice, 281–2, 293
Churchland, Patricia, 87
Churchland, Paul, 88, 104
Clark, Kelly, 12, 211
Clarke, Samuel, 388–9
Clifford, William, 257, 258, 263, 290, 382
Cobb, J. B., 303
Coburn, Robert, 140
coherentism, 252, 253, 254, 256, 260
Cohn-Sherbok, Dan, 322
Collingwood, R. G., 27, 28, 33, 36
communitarianism, 58, 222, 228
compatibilism, 111–12, 113, 116–18, 138
comprehensive philosophies, 5–6, 8–9, 287–90
Conee, Earl, 252
consequentialism, 221, 228, 231, 242–3
contextual moral realism, 191
"Continental thought", 12
contingency (chance), 13, 33, 72, 79, 90, 120–30 *passim*, 141, 333, 334, 338, 353–90 *passim*
Contribution to Self Principle, 242
Conze, Edward, 279–80
Copleston, F. C., 84, 99
Corduan, W., 388
Corey, M. A., 393
Corless, Roger, 35
Cornman, James, 304, 319–20
cosmological arguments, 351, 353–65, 367, 368–9, 371, 372, 388–90